CONTENTS

P = POEM ALSO PRESCRIBED FOR ORDINARY LEVEL 2010 EXAM

P = POEM ALSO PRESCRIBED FOR ORDINARY LEVEL 2010 EXAM

NEW EXPLORATIONS

Critical Notes

ON PRESCRIBED POETRY FOR THE 2010 EXAMINATION
(HIGHER AND ORDINARY LEVEL)

UNIVERSITY *of* LIMERICK

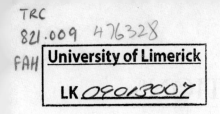

Gill & Macmillan Ltd
Hume Avenue
Park West
Dublin 12
with associated companies throughout the world
www.gillmacmillan.ie

© Carole Scully, Bernard Connolly, John G. Fahy, Sean Scully,
John McCarthy, David Keogh 2008
978 07171 4059 6

Design and print origination in Ireland by O'K Graphic Design, Dublin

The paper used in this book is made from the wood pulp of managed forests. For every tree felled, at least one tree is planted, thereby renewing natural resources.

Acknowledgments

For permission to reproduce copyright material in this book the publishers are grateful to the following:

Michael Longley and Lucas Alexander Whitley for extracts from *Tipperary Stung*: Autobiographical Chapters by Michael Longley; Penguin Putnam Inc. for an extract from *The Iliad* by Homer, translated by Robert Eagles, translation copyright © 1990 by Robert Eagles, introduction and notes copyright © 1990 by Bernard Knox. Used by permission of Viking Penguin, a division of Penguin Putnam Inc.

Carcanet Press for complete poems and extracts from other poems by Eavan Boland from her *Collected Poems*, and also for extracts from her autobiography *Object Lessons: The Life of the Woman and the Poet in our Time* (1995).

P = POEM ALSO PRESCRIBED FOR ORDINARY LEVEL 2010 EXAM

P = POEM ALSO PRESCRIBED FOR ORDINARY LEVEL 2010 EXAM

1   *John* KEATS

John G. Fahy

A brief view of a brief life

John Keats was born in Finsbury, near London, on 31 October 1795, the eldest child of Thomas Keats, a livery stable keeper (at the Swan and Hoop Inn) and Frances Jennings Keats.

Two brothers, George and Thomas, were born in 1797 and 1799, respectively, and a sister, Frances (Fanny), in 1803. A fifth child, Edward, was born in 1801 but died in 1802.

From 1803 to 1811 John and his brothers attended Revd John Clarke's school in an old country house at Enfield, London. John Keats was a small boy (he was only five feet tall when he was fully grown), but he was athletic and liked sports, and although he had a quick temper he was generally popular.

Clarke's was a liberal and progressive boarding-school that did not allow the 'fagging' or flogging popular at the time. The pupils, who were mostly of middle-class background and destined for the professions, received a well-rounded education. They had their own garden plots to cultivate; interest in music and the visual arts was encouraged, as well as the normal study of history, geography, arithmetic, grammar, French and Latin. Keats received a particularly good classical Latin education. For instance, he was able to compose a prose version of Virgil's long epic poem, the *Aeneid*. Classical mythology is used in Keats's own poetry, particularly in the long narrative poems 'Endymion', 'Hyperion', and 'The Fall of Hyperion', and also in 'Ode on a Grecian Urn'.

Keats was both helped and befriended by the headmaster's son and assistant master, Charles Cowden Clarke, who lent him books such as Spenser's *Faerie Queene*. He also introduced him to the *Examiner*, a weekly paper that advocated reform both in politics and poetry. It was edited by Leigh Hunt, later to become an influence on Keats's poetic career.

In 1804 Keats's father died in a riding accident. Frances Keats married again, to William Rawlings, but the marriage was unhappy. The Keats children went to live with their grandparents, John and Alice Jennings, at Enfield. In 1805 John Jennings died, leaving about £8,000 to the Keats children. This was a substantial sum: £50 was a typical annual wage for a worker at that time. But the will was complicated and led to legal disputes.

In 1810 Frances Keats, who had left William Rawlings some years earlier and had begun to drink heavily, returned to look after the children, but she died from tuberculosis in March of that year. Two guardians were appointed for the children, one of whom was Richard Abbey, a tea merchant and respected public figure. Both George and Tom later worked for a time as clerks in his office, and, apart from four years at school, Fanny Keats lived with the Abbeys until she was 21. It was a strict household, and she was discouraged from visiting her brothers. Abbey proved notoriously mean about money, and John Keats had great difficulty getting funds from his inheritance.

In 1811 Keats left school to begin an apprenticeship as a surgeon with Thomas Hammond. Surgery was at that time the manual side of the medical profession, involving bone-setting, teeth-pulling and amputations, and was considered socially inferior to becoming a physician, which would have entailed expensive university education.

Keats's Grandmother Jennings died in 1814, and after some years as an apprentice he registered as a student at Guy's Hospital, London in 1815, attending lectures in anatomy, physiology and chemistry.

In May 1816 the sonnet 'O Solitude' was the first of Keats's poems to be published – by Hunt, in the *Examiner*. In June Keats wrote 'To One Long in City Pent'. In July of the same year he qualified and was licensed to practise as a surgeon and apothecary; but by now he had developed an aversion to surgery, which was performed without anaesthetic and in primitive conditions. He devoted more of his time to writing poetry. His early poems reflected liberal attitudes and a rebellious outlook on life. For instance, he celebrated in verse Hunt's release from prison (Hunt had called the Prince Regent 'a fat Adonis of forty', among other things). Some of his poems show a romantic idealisation of women. He also formed a strong aversion to Christianity, as a poem of December 1816 demonstrates: 'Written in Disgust of Vulgar Superstition'.

In October 1816 he composed 'On First Looking into Chapman's Homer'. He made a number of important acquaintances and friendships, including Hunt, the editor of the *Examiner* and a supporter of Romantic poets, especially of Shelley, Byron and Keats; Benjamin Haydon, an unsuccessful painter; John Reynolds, a fellow-poet, with whom he exchanged many letters; and Joseph Severn, a poet and painter, who became a supporter and friend.

In December 1816 'Sleep and Poetry' was written. Keats told Abbey, who was not best pleased, that he was going to be a poet, not a surgeon.

In March 1817 Haydon took Keats to see the Parthenon Marbles (called the 'Elgin Marbles' in England) at the British Museum. These were huge classical sculpture fragments taken by Thomas Bruce, Earl of Elgin, from the ruins of the Parthenon, with the permission of the Turks after they had conquered Athens. (The return of the Marbles is now being demanded by Greece.) Keats was fascinated by the imagery. Perhaps the 'heifer lowing at the skies' in 'Ode on a Grecian Urn' may have been suggested by a procession in one of the marbles.

Keats's first book, *Poems*, was published in 1817, and though it was favourably received it did not sell well. In April of that year he left London for six months to work on 'Endymion'. He also met Charles Armitage Brown, a wealthy educated gentleman who became a friend and patron. The 4,000-line poem was completed by the autumn. It tells the story of Endymion, a typical romantic hero, who achieves perfect love and immortality through loving and being loved by the goddess of the moon, Cynthia. There are two main themes, concerning the search for love and the quest for poetic achievement. The opening lines of the poem are famous:

> A thing of beauty is a joy for ever:
> Its loveliness increases; it will never
> Pass into nothingness . . .

Keats now began to express his ideas on poetry. From his letter to Benjamin Bailey of 22 November 1817 we get some idea of the value he placed on the imagination, the importance of feelings, and the central place of beauty in poetry:

> I am certain of nothing but of the holiness of the Heart's affections and the truth of Imagination – What the imagination seizes as Beauty must be truth – whether it existed before or not – for I have the same Idea of all our Passions as of Love, they are all in their sublime, creative of essential Beauty . . . the Imagination may be compared to Adam's dream – he awoke and found it truth . . . O for a Life of Sensations rather than of Thoughts!

In a letter to George and Tom Keats in the following month he talked about the essential attitude or operational mode necessary to be a great poet, which he called 'negative capability', 'that is when man is capable of being in uncertainties, Mysteries, doubts, without any irritable reaching after fact and reason.' He began to denigrate the current classical tradition of correctness.

In December he met William Wordsworth and Charles Lamb at a dinner given by Haydon. He much admired Wordsworth, though the feeling was not reciprocated.

The sonnet 'When I Have Fears that I May Cease to Be' was written some time in January or February 1818. It deals with three important concerns in his life: love, death and his poetry. In April 'Endymion' was published, to very hostile reviews, in particular from the very influential *Blackwood's Magazine* and the *Quarterly Review*.

In May, Keats's brother Tom became ill with tuberculosis. George lost his job and was forced to emigrate to America.

In the spring of 1818 Keats wrote 'Isabella', a poetic translation of a story from Boccaccio's *Decameron*. It is a gruesome story of love and death with an unhappy ending, in which Isabella's brothers murder her lover, Lorenzo. He appears to her in a dream and tells her where he is buried. She digs up his head, hides it in a pot of basil, and weeps over it every day; eventually her brothers find it and take it away, and she dies of a broken heart.

From June to August 1818 Keats toured the Lake District and Scotland with Brown. He returned to nurse Tom, who died of his tuberculosis on 1 December. During this winter of nursing Keats worked on 'Hyperion', an epic story from classical mythology featuring the overthrow of the old gods by the young Olympians. Its themes are change, progress, and the victory of youth and beauty. But he abandoned it after Tom's death, and it was published unfinished in 1820 as 'Hyperion: A Fragment'. It was much praised by his contemporaries Byron and Shelley.

In September Keats met Fanny Brawne. She and her mother rented part of Wentworth Place, Hampstead, where Keats's friends Charles and Maria Dilke lived. She was the great love of his life, and they became engaged in the autumn of 1819. When Keats was dying he wrote to Brown: 'I can bear to die – I cannot bear to leave her.'

The year 1819 was an extraordinary one and the most productive of Keats's career. He was writing mature poems, sometimes dashing them off at great speed. In January he composed 'The Eve of St Agnes', a long narrative about the carrying off of a young woman by her lover. This incorporated the legend of St Agnes, the patron saint of young virgins, which stated that girls would dream of their future husband on 20 January, the Eve of St Agnes, provided certain ritual ceremonies were carried out. In February he worked on 'The Eve of St Mark', an unfinished poem set in the Middle Ages. In April 'La Belle Dame Sans Merci' was written.

Between April and May 1819 the five great odes were written, also known as the Spring Odes: 'Ode to Psyche', 'Ode to a Nightingale', 'Ode on a Grecian Urn', 'Ode on Melancholy', and 'Ode to Indolence'. Keats's poetic reputation today rests chiefly on these, though their power was scarcely noticed when they were written, even by critics like Lamb and Shelley, as the long poem was then in fashion.

Keats was deeply in love with Fanny Brawne, as we can see from his letters; but, paradoxically, he tried to stay away from her, perhaps fearing the conflict between the real and the ideal that he deals with in his great poetry. In June he wrote to her:

If I were to see you today it would destroy the half comfortable sullenness I enjoy at present into downright perplexities. I love you too much to venture to Hampstead, I feel it is not paying a visit, but venturing into a fire . . . Knowing well that my life must be passed in fatigue and trouble, I have been endeavouring to wean myself from you . . .

Nevertheless, they became engaged in the autumn.

Between June and September he worked on 'Lamia', a long narrative poem, his third attempt at the theme of the sexual encounter between mortal man and immortal woman. This union symbolises the human being's desire to perpetuate eternally the moment of passion, the experience of love. Here, as in 'La Belle Dame Sans Merci', the human hero ends up alone and abandoned; Lamia, the enchantress, is forced to return to her original state of being – a serpent – and Lycius, the lover, pines and dies. Of the three such poems, only 'Endymion' has a happy ending.

Keats then returned to the theme of Hyperion, composing 'The Fall of Hyperion', which he had to abandon unfinished. He worked on two plays, *Otho the Great* and *King Stephen*, which were undertaken because of financial need: Keats could not get his hands on enough of his inheritance to enable him to marry Fanny. He talked of going to sea as a ship's doctor in order to make money. With the famous actor Edmund Kean in mind for the principal role, Brown and Keats collaborated on *Otho the Great*, a gothic story of deception, unhappy love, and death, involving the family of the tenth-century ruler who became Holy Roman Emperor. Drury Lane Theatre had accepted it, but when Kean left to perform in America they refused to go ahead with it. In the meantime Keats had begun work on *King Stephen*, another mediaeval play dealing with courage and chivalry; but he abandoned it after the disappointment of *Otho*.

'Bright Star', the sonnet to Fanny Brawne, dates from this time, as does the ode 'To Autumn', considered by some critics to be the best of the year's work.

In 1820 Keats's brother George returned briefly from America, as he had had a financial setback and needed to raise some money. It is suspected that John Keats put himself further into debt on George's account.

In February Keats suffered a severe lung haemorrhage, the significance of which was apparent to him, as he wrote to Brown:

I know the colour of that blood; – it is arterial blood; – I cannot be deceived in that colour; – that drop of blood is my death-warrant . . .

Indeed it was the beginning of the end. That summer he spent being cared for by, and falling out with, various friends, including Brown and the Hunts, and eventually he ended up in the care of Mrs Brawne and Fanny, who nursed him in their home at Wentworth Place.

In July a volume of his poetry, *Poems, 1820*, was published, which included 'Lamia', 'Isabella', and 'The Eve of St Agnes'. The Shelleys invited him to Pisa, and, as the doctors were urging him to avoid the English winter, he agreed to go to Italy. But Abbey refused him funds, and he was forced to sell the copyright of his poems. In September he set sail, accompanied by his friend Thomas Severn as companion and nurse. After a violent stormy passage and quarantine at Naples they finally reached Rome in November and took rooms at 26 Piazza di Spagna. Though ably nursed by Severn, Keats deteriorated throughout the winter, and he died on 23 February 1821, aged 25. He is buried in the Protestant Cemetery in Rome, having requested as an inscription for his tombstone, 'Here lies one whose name was writ in water'.

To One Long in City Pent

Text of poem: New Explorations Anthology page 24

BACKGROUND

By June 1816 lectures had finished, and, as Keats was not on duty in the hospital as a dresser (a surgeon's assistant, a post he held while still a student), there was some time to study for his Society of Apothecaries licentiate examination at the end of July. Keats and his room-mate would take their books into the fields and often swam in the river. But Keats was reading poetry rather than pharmacy, and the sonnet was, according to George Keats, 'written in the fields.' It was the first of three linked Miltonic sonnets that Keats wrote during June 1816.

IDEAS IN THE POEM
* The happiness brought to human beings by nature; the therapeutic power of nature for humankind
* Urbanisation – the unnatural state of people as city dwellers, pent up, fatigued
* Nature's power to rejuvenate the city dweller
* The healing force of literature – tales of love and languishment
* The transience of beauty and happiness ('he mourns that day so soon has glided by').

FORM AND STRUCTURE

A Miltonic sonnet, the poem follows the Petrarchan division into octave and sestet, with a strict rhyming scheme *abba abba cdcdcd*. The main thought is stated in the octave, with a *volta* or turn to the second idea (or a development or refinement of the first) in the sestet. Here the octave deals with the happiness experienced by the poet while enjoying a summer's day in the fields, and the sestet mourns the passing of that day. So it has a very simple, straightforward structure as the speaker moves from an awareness of the beauty of nature to thoughts of love, to a realisation that beauty is transient. The mood too follows this pattern, moving from feelings of happiness to tenderness, to a quiet sadness.

IMAGERY

The images are all linked to an extended metaphor of face, which is just discernible through the whole sonnet: 'fair and open face of heaven', 'the smile of the blue firmament', 'an ear catching the notes of Philomel', 'an eye watching the smiling cloudlet's bright career', 'an angel's tear'. The imagery reflects the joy and sadness of the theme: smiles, music and a tear. As one would expect, images of nature are prominent.

MUSIC OF THE LANGUAGE

There is a musical quality to the sonnet, over and above the reference to the nightingale. The repeated strands of long vowel sounds give it its languidness: the long **a** of 'lair', 'air' etc., the long **e** of 'ear', 'evening', 'career', 'tear', 'clear', 'ether' etc., and the long **o** of 'notes' and 'mourns'. The enjambment of some lines (splitting a phrase over two lines) – for example 'fair | and open face of heaven', 'lair | of wavy grass' – gives the poem a momentum and a rhythm that add to this flowing, relaxed atmosphere.

On First Looking into Chapman's Homer

Text of poem: New Explorations Anthology page 26

[*Note: This poem is also prescribed for Ordinary Level 2010 exam*]

BACKGROUND

In October 1816 Keats visited Charles Cowden Clarke, the son of the headmaster of his old school, with whom he had frequently conversed about poetry. Clarke had been lent a rare 1616 folio edition of Chapman's translation of Homer. They had previously read Homer only in Pope's neo-classical translation, where the long hexameters of the Greek line had been tailored into elegant couplets. Chapman's verse was freer and more energetic. Utterly fascinated, they read all night.

At dawn Keats walked the two miles home, wrote the sonnet (which needed only slight amendments later), and sent it off to Clarke, who had received it by ten o'clock! It was published by Leigh Hunt in the *Examiner* on 1 December 1816.

THEME

The poem is really about the aesthetic thrill of reading poetry, about new worlds opened up and horizons revealed to the reader, and about the excitement of discovery in general. This is never stated explicitly, but it is communicated through the use of metaphor. Perhaps the young poet also has some awareness, or at least expectation, of the limitless possibilities of his own future stretching out before him.

LANGUAGE OF METAPHOR

The metaphorical language of journey is used to describe the narrator's encounter with various poets ('travell'd in the realms of gold', 'states and kingdoms', 'western islands'). Images of actual travel and discovery are used to convey the rapture of aesthetic discovery.

> Then felt I like some watcher of the skies
> When a new planet swims into his ken.

It is ironic that Chapman's speaking out 'loud and bold' is compared to an experience that induced profound silence! There is also a suggestion in the imagery that the poet too sees his life's journey as a search and exploration. This imagery gives the poet a particular romantic appeal: the dreamy, bookish speaker identifies with men of action, with people who push out the frontiers of knowledge and geography.

SENSOUS LANGUAGE

The poem abounds in sound echoes and patterns of repeated letters, which give it a rich, sensuous musical quality. Notice, for example, the internal echoes of 'travell'd – realms' and 'breathe – serene', and also the s sounds in 'states and kingdoms seen'. In the sestet, n echoes everywhere: then, when, planet, ken, men, silent, upon, Darien. The sensuous s sounds also abound: skies, swims, stout, stored, pacific, surmise, silent. Altogether we find a rich pattern of verbal echoes.

WHAT IT REVEALS OF THE YOUNG KEATS

Keats may not have had much time for the neo-classical style of poetry, which he was helping to bring to an end. Ironically, his outlook was backwards rather than forward. As the critical commentator Brian Stone points out, the sonnet demonstrates his profound preference for Renaissance language and thought over those of the eighteenth century. It also indicates his growing fascination with the world of classical Greek mythology. However, it also shows him fired with excitement for exploration, innovation, risk-taking, and living life to the full.

When I Have Fears that I May Cease to Be
Text of poem: New Explorations Anthology page 28

THE POET'S CONCERNS

The poem deals with three of Keats's constant concerns: love, death and poetry. The predominant fear is of untimely death. This is expressed in a euphemism ('I may cease to be') that conveys the absolute finality of death, though in a tranquil tone. Death for Keats would mean the end of what he hopes to achieve. His fear is of not fulfilling his poetic destiny, not employing his 'teeming brain', and poetry is about expressing beauty, whether of nature ('the night's starr'd face') or of women. This beauty is a rare and transient visitor ('fair creature of an hour'), like an apparition granted to the poet but outside his control. The poetic process too is somewhat outside the poet's control, a mysterious process, a fortuitous gift ('the magic hand of chance'). There is a typical romantic view of the poet as solitary soul, pensive and operating at the frontiers of experience.

> then on the Shore
> Of the wide world I stand alone and think

Love here is more an idealisation of female beauty than a real human encounter. The love object is a transient, unattainable beauty, to be worshipped from a distance, without hope of reciprocation ('fair creature of an hour', 'never look upon thee more', 'the faery power of unreflecting love'). Is this not an adolescent perspective on love as unrequited adoration?

His fear, then, is that untimely death may interfere with his poetic destiny and his worship of beauty.

FORM

Keats's study of the Shakespearean form evidently influenced this sonnet. Notice:

- the three distinct quatrains
- the rhyming scheme
- the end-stopped lines (for the most part)
- the syntactic structure ('when . . . when . . . then' was a favourite Shakespearean structure: see Sonnet 12).

The couplet really begins in line 12 ('then on the Shore . . .') and so softens the epigrammatical nature of the couplet that Keats faulted.

La Belle Dame Sans Merci

Text of poem: New Explorations Anthology page 30

[*Note: This poem is also prescribed for Ordinary Level 2010 exam*]

LOVE, CORRUPTION AND DEATH

This is one of three poems by Keats dealing with love between a human male and a superhuman female (see also 'Endymion' and 'Lamia'), and only in 'Endymion' is there a happy outcome. Here, as in 'Lamia', we are dealing with a female enchantress, this time a murderous one. La Belle Dame is the fatal woman-figure often found in romantic literature who seduces the knight and fatally weakens him in the act of love. She is viewed as a 'demon muse' by the critic Katherine Wilson. But whether or not she is inspirational she is certainly fatal. Love is here associated with death. Some commentators have wondered if this is an expression of Keats's feelings of guilt about love. Robert Graves (in *The White Goddess*) took a more complex view and felt that 'the Belle Dame represented love, death by consumption . . . and poetry all at once.'

But the knight here did not succeed in resisting: he has been fatally corrupted and is languishing ('palely loitering'). So we presume that he was to some degree responsible, to some extent a compliant partner in the seduction. Corruption follows seduction in the world of this poem.

This is another of Keats's poems to feature the human being in a strange transitional state. It is as if the knight has been transported beyond the reality of this life and has visited the underworld, where he encountered others seduced like himself. He managed to return, but was fatally weakened.

BACKGROUND

Establishing a biographical rationale for a poem is risky at the best of times. Here it is doubly so, because the evidence is definitely circumstantial. But Aileen Ward makes a number of fascinating comments concerning the background circumstances. Earlier in that month of April 1819 Keats had come across a bundle of love letters to his late brother Tom from Amena, a mysterious French acquaintance of Tom's school friend Charles Wells. There had been a long, sentimental correspondence between the two, with Wells as intermediary. Tom had even gone to France in a vain effort to meet her. Now Keats discovered that it had all been a hoax by Wells and was furious at the strain that had been inflicted on his already dying brother. This may not have been the conscious inspiration for the poem, but it lends a certain poignancy to the figure of the pale knight and the theme of love, delusion and betrayal.

Ward also makes the point that Keats himself exhibited a fear of involvement in his own love affair with Fanny Brawne about this time, writing, 'Ask yourself my love whether you are not very cruel to have so entrammelled me, so destroyed my freedom.' Though he was enormously drawn to her, writing poetry had a superior claim on him, and he seemed to see the two in opposition. Though the experience of love was the life blood of his poetry, he seemed to shy away from the actual. 'Knowing well that my life must be passed in fatigue and trouble, I have been endeavouring to wean myself from you,' he wrote to her in September of that year. Whether this refers to his personal and financial circumstances or to his notion of the life of a poet is not clear; but the point is that his ambiguity about love and his fear of involvement at that time may be reflected in 'La Belle Dame Sans Merci'.

MEDIAEVAL RESONANCES IN THE POEM

Keats had a particular fascination with the mediaeval, and this is one of the last of the poems in which he used the literature and folklore of the Middle Ages.

- Consider the origin of the title. The phrase 'la belle dame sans merci' comes from the terminology of courtly love and refers to the withholding of the lady's favours.
- A characteristic of the mediaeval supernatural ballad was the seduction of a human being by one of the fairies, who took power from men by luring them into making love.
- Spenser's *Faerie Queene*, which was a model for some of Keats's work, also features an enchantress from the mediaeval world.
- The mediaeval ballad sometimes featured a wasteland that could be made green again through the intervention of a virtuous knight.

THE BALLAD

The poem exhibits many of the classic characteristics of the ballad form. The most common features of ballads are:

- themes of love, war or death, often exhibited as a supernatural encounter
- a narrative poem – narration through dialogue
- archaic language and phrasing
- simplicity of vocabulary
- repetition of phrases
- dramatic qualities of action and conflict
- ballad metre, usually four-line stanzas of 4, 3, 4, 3 stresses. This moved the story along at a fairly swift pace. Keats has altered this to produce a slower and more haunting rhythm. He lengthened the second line by a foot and shortened the last line by two feet, with a weighty last foot using a spondee ($^-\,^-$):

˘ ‾ ˘ ‾ ‾ ‾ ˘ ‾

O what | can ail | thee knight | at arms

˘ ‾ ˘ ‾ ˘ ˘ ˘ ˘

Alone | and pale | ly loit | ering?

‾ ˘ ‾ ˘ ˘ ˘ ˘ ‾

The sedge | has with | ered from | the Lake

˘ ‾ ‾ ‾ ‾

And no | birds sing!

In the last line we are slowed by the concentration of stressed syllables unrelieved by any unstressed ones and also by the placing of the two s sounds in 'birds sing', where we have to pause to enunciate the second s. An atmosphere of doom is created both by the weight of the syllables and by the sibilance.

Ode to a Nightingale

Text of poem: New Explorations Anthology page 33

THE NIGHTINGALE AS SYMBOL

Since classical times the nightingale has been associated with poetry and with love. In the Middle Ages it was associated with passionate courtly love. But it also carries connotations of suffering and sadness, through the classical myth of Philomela. Philomela was seduced by her brother-in-law, but she and her sister took a terrible revenge, and she was punished by being turned into a nightingale; hence the notion that suffering produces song and poetry. Renaissance English poets used the myth, as did T. S. Eliot later in 'The Waste Land'.

Keats uses the nightingale as the central symbol, and one of the main dramatic developments in this poem is the gradual transformation of the real bird into a symbol of visionary art. David Perkins (in *Keats: Twentieth-Century Views*) feels that the poem can be regarded as 'the exploration or testing out of a symbol'. He argues that the nightingale as symbol has the advantage of being a living thing, appealing to the senses, and so it is possible to identify with it. The disadvantage is that, unlike the urn, it does not easily lend itself to being thought of as eternal. But Keats, through a certain 'bendy' logic, attempts to give the song a sort of immortality, at least a continuity through history, in stanza 7. So the nightingale becomes a symbol of beauty and the immortality of art, which the poet explores and with which he wishes to identify.

Perkins also draws attention to the fatality of this symbol. Keats came to associate death with visionary journeys, fantasies and dreams. The fainting or swooning that precedes the vision he viewed as a kind of death. Perkins noted the development of this ode from the 'drowsy numbness', a swoon, as it gathers momentum towards darkness and death, and temporarily accepts it in stanza 6. And he asks whether the nightingale – the immortal bird – is somewhat similar in role to the Belle Dame, 'luring men to fantasy and death'.

The poem traces the twists and turns, rises and falls of the poet's creative mood as he explores this symbol and embarks on his imaginative journey with the nightingale. So we could read the poem as an exploration of the process of creativity, centred on this symbol.

A READING OF THE POEM

The ode begins with the poet in a drowsy state, as though sedated. The long vowel sounds ('aches', 'drowsy', 'numbness', 'pains') lull us into sharing that semi-conscious state. This suspension of consciousness seems to release the imagination, and the poet begins to see the nightingale not just as a bird but as a dryad of the trees. He is able to participate imaginatively in the creativity of the bird, and this brings him great happiness. He expresses his feelings in paradoxical terms (aching with pleasure): 'being too happy in thine happiness, – that thou . . . singest of summer in full-throated ease.' The repeated s sounds in that last line, along with the long vowels of the last three words, evoke the sensuousness of the melody and allow the reader to share in the experience of the bird.

To prolong this drowsy, sensuous enjoyment the poet appeals to wine in the second stanza ('O, for a draught of vintage!'). Wine catches the mood of his excited imagination as he recalls the rich, sensuous pleasures of its Mediterranean origins ('the warm South'). In an impressionistic confusion of senses the tastes, touch, smells, sights and sounds of its Mediterranean background are conjured up ('cool'd a long age', 'tasting of Flora', 'Provençal song', 'beaded bubbles winking', 'purple-stained mouth'). The nightingale is going to fade away, and he wants to fade with it. This is not a fading into drunken stupor but a journey of the imagination, as intimated by the reference to the Hippocrene (the fountain of poetic inspiration). Wine here is the medium of inspiration, the vehicle of imaginative flight, enabling the poet to continue sharing in the aesthetic life of the bird. This impulse to fade away leads in the third stanza to a recollection of the real world he is leaving, with its suffering, disease, and despair ('Here, where men sit and hear each other groan'). This is probably the lowest point of the poem, when he recalls the transience even of beauty and love:

Where Beauty cannot keep her lustrous eyes,
Or new Love pine at them beyond tomorrow.

This is not a world to inspire poetry ('where but to think is to be full of sorrow'), where he is thinking, or fully conscious, rather than in the drowsy state conducive to visions and poetry. So he attempts to escape with even greater urgency in the fourth stanza ('Away! away!'). Wine has failed to lift him from the horrors of life. Here he realises that the only way of escape and of sharing in the happiness of the bird is 'on the viewless wings of Poesy'. This can be taken in two senses: through (a) an imaginative poetic sharing in the life of the bird; or (b) the poetry he is actually writing. His poetic imagination conjures up the natural world of the nightingale, and so he shares in the 'verdurous glooms and winding mossy ways.'

The fifth stanza recreates the sensuous perfection of this natural world through the mingling of the senses of smell, taste, touch and hearing. This use of synaesthetic imagery (the production of a mental sense impression of one kind by stimulation of a different sense, as in 'soft incense' and 'embalmed darkness') evokes the richness of the imagined environment. The sensuousness of the experience is also conveyed through the repeated sound patterns in the language used:

> And mid-May's eldest child,
> The coming musk-rose, full of dewy wine,
> The murmurous haunt of flies on summer eves.

and also through the repeated **m** alliteration (mid-May, coming, musk, murmurous, summer), the **f** repetition (full, flies), the assonance (child, wine, flies), and the repetition of the related **m** and **f** sounds. This stanza also demonstrates what David Perkins described as 'a vivid assertion of the power of the imagination to see more than the sensory eye'. These two stanzas, 4 and 5, represent the zenith of imaginative power, a successful escape on the 'viewless wings of Poesy'.

The poet feels that the only way to prolong the ecstasy is to die at the moment of greatest sensual happiness, in stanza 6 ('now more than ever seems it rich to die'). This desire for death is not a negative wish for extinction but an attempt to make the happiness he knows to be transient last for ever (see also 'Bright Star'). Death is desirable as a fulfilment of experience and a continuation of it. This has been prepared for through the emphasis on darkness in the previous stanza and by the sensuous adjective 'embalmed', which means fragrant but also carries connotations of death. But even as the poet suggests it the rational side of his consciousness qualifies it. He has merely been 'half' in love with easeful death and it only 'seems' rich to die. So it is decisively rejected as a solution at the end of the stanza.

Still wouldst thou sing, and I have ears in vain –
To thy high requiem become a sod.

The onomatopoeia of the Germanic word 'sod' brings us back to earth with a realistic bump. Death would not have meant a prolongation of his union with the nightingale.

But he does find a type of permanence in art. In the seventh stanza the nightingale's song as symbol of art is shown to have been present throughout history. Its manifestations are traced back through the Middle Ages, through biblical times, to the archetypal world of myth and story, which is also Keats's own romantic world, with its 'charm'd magic casements', 'perilous seas', and 'faery lands'. The song was present both at moments of consequence and of comedy ('was heard . . . by emperor and clown'), at moments of human suffering and alienation ('the sad heart of Ruth'), and throughout romantic literature. The stanza asserts one of Keats's main philosophical beliefs: the immortality of art. Yet the stanza also traces the further fading of the nightingale's song, back through time to the insubstantial world of legend, myth and magic.

With this dying of the song the inspirational creative mood fades. 'Forlorn', with its onomatopoeic and semantic connotations of desolation and wretchedness, maintains the link with Keats's magical world of stanza 7 and also expresses the poet's feelings at the fading of inspiration. Together with the allusion to a tolling funeral bell, it recalls the Keats of stanza 3, who is bowed down with the suffering of the world ('where but to think is to be full of sorrow'). So we are returned to reality in stanza 8. Poetry cannot achieve a permanent transformation of life ('Adieu! the fancy cannot cheat so well . . . deceiving elf'). Yet this is a reality somewhat transformed by the poetic experience: nature has been imbued with the nightingale's song ('now 'tis buried deep In the next valley-glades'). The experience was of great power, yet the poet is in some uncertainty about its nature ('Was it a vision, or a waking dream?'). Was it a truly visionary experience, an aesthetic experience with the power to transform the everyday, or merely a dream, an illusion? (See the association of dream with death in 'La Belle Dame Sans Merci'.)

The final stanza leaves Keats with this uncertainty, this niggling doubt about the value of the poetic experience to real life. And he leaves us with this uncertainty, an intellectual attitude he regarded as a prerequisite for the creation of good literature and which he termed 'negative capability' – 'when a man is capable of being in uncertainties, mysteries, doubts, without irritable reaching after fact and reason.' Whatever the theory, the effect is that Keats's poetry remains anchored to reality. Whatever mental flight his mind makes on the viewless wings of poesy, his feet remain on the ground; he maintains a healthy scepticism.

POETIC THEMES

- An examination of the power of the imagination ('the viewless wings of Poesy') and its limitations ('deceiving elf'). This was an issue that absorbed all Romantic poets. Does the imagination open a door to truth and higher reality – vision – or is it an escape from reality, a waking dream (see 'La Belle Dame Sans Merci')? This ode charts the poet's various attempts to maintain the imaginative inspirational mood engendered by the nightingale's song.

- The ephemeral and transient nature of human happiness in contrast to the ever-present reality of suffering. Beauty and love are transient ('Where Beauty cannot keep her lustrous eyes, Or new Love pine at them beyond tomorrow').

- A view of life that is deeply pessimistic. Life is a struggle ('The weariness, the fever, and the fret'), full of disease ('Where palsy shakes') and suffering ('where men sit and hear each other groan'), and it features the tragic death of the young ('Where youth grows pale'). Beauty and love are transient, and despair is the inevitable reaction ('Where but to think is to be full of sorrow And leaden-eyed despairs').

- The desire for an ideal state beyond the misery of the world, a state of beauty and happiness.

- The search for permanence in a world of constant change. It is suggested in stanza 7 that art, as symbolised in the song of the nightingale, might provide that immortality and that permanent beauty.

- Death seen almost as a desirable fulfilment. Keats momentarily toys with the idea of using death to prolong the moment of ecstasy.

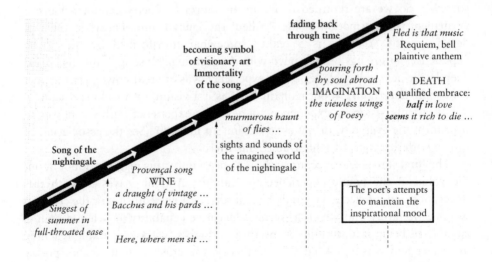

Ode on a Grecian Urn

Text of poem: New Explorations Anthology page 38

A READING OF THE POEM

The relationship between art and reality is examined in some detail in this poem. Keats takes up the thought of the seventh stanza of 'Ode to a Nightingale'. Aware of the brevity of mortal beauty and of human love, he searches for some kind of permanence and finds it in the beauty of art. The advantages and the shortcomings of this immortality conferred by art are discussed in detail in the ode.

In the first stanza the static artefact is brought to life in a most spectacular way. In a swift and successful transition the urn, at first associated with quietness and silence, at the end of the stanza is communicating 'mad pursuit', 'struggle', and 'wild ecstasy'. The transition is all the more spectacular because of the slow tempo of the opening lines, with the meandering enjambment in lines 3 and 4 and again in lines 5, 6 and 7. The slow pace gives way to the frantic six questions in the final three lines of the stanza.

The inherent contradiction in the notion of inanimate art having a living energy or life of its own is carried in the many paradoxes of the stanza. The urn, itself an 'unravish'd bride', portrays a typical classical Grecian erotic ceremony, at first featuring 'maidens loth' but quickly turning to 'mad pursuit' and 'wild ecstasy'. The 'foster-child of silence' proceeds to convey the music of 'pipes and timbrels'. This paradox of silent utterance is continued as the silent sylvan historian tells a story that is superior to poetry or rhyme. This ambiguity sometimes extends to individual words (for instance 'still' in line 1 can mean 'stationary' or 'yet'). This proliferation of ambiguity and paradox underlines one of the essential conflicts of the poem: that of art versus life, permanence versus impermanence.

In the first quatrain of the second stanza the poet is confident that art is superior to reality, again expressed in a paradox ('heard melodies are sweet, but those unheard Are sweeter'). One can imagine far sweeter music than anything one has heard. The critic Cedric Watts has suggested that behind this section is the Platonic notion of an ideal world of eternal abstract forms of which we find only perishable imitations in this world. Only the noblest side of humankind has access to the ideal world, and so it is the spirit, not the sensual ear, that hears the music of art. At any rate art, the creation of the imagination, is superior to real experience, because of its eternity ('nor ever can those trees be bare', 'She cannot fade', 'For ever wilt thou love, and she be fair'). But even here Keats is not without misgivings. Art is not life, nor even a viable alternative. Art can give immortality, certainly, but also immobility and coldness. (Does this prefigure the coldness and death of 'Cold Pastoral'?)

> Bold Lover, never, never canst thou kiss . . .
> She cannot fade, though thou hast not thy bliss.

And so is conveyed the central flaw of the urn: that the beauty shown and the happiness conveyed are frozen in time and can never achieve fulfilment. This contradiction is also conveyed through the antithesis in the syntax (not–but, never–though, yet–though).

Yet in the third stanza Keats seems to express unreserved enthusiasm as he imaginatively enters the life of the urn ('Ah, happy, happy boughs!'). The urn here has both the warm, panting life of flesh and blood and also the eternity of art, and so is superior to real life ('For ever panting, and for ever young'). The portrayal of passion in art is superior to sexual passion in real life ('All breathing human passion far above'), because it is not followed by disappointment and sorrow ('That leaves a heart high-sorrowful and cloy'd') or by the illness and suffering inevitable in the changing process of time ('A burning forehead, and a parching tongue').

Many commentators feel that Keats protests too much here ('happy' six times, 'for ever' five times). Is he trying to hypnotise himself into belief in the urn, desperately trying to convince himself of the superiority of art? Brian Stone notes that he always celebrates the dream of a harmonious love relationship rather than the reality of love.

Stanza 4 provides a dramatic contrast, both in content and tone. It is as if the poet turned the urn around to examine another panel, a complete contrast, a religious procession and sacrifice. The tone is much more detached, the rhythm stately. There is a formal dignity to the stanza, as befitting a sacrificial process ('To what green altar, O mysterious priest'). There is a sense of emptiness in the scene. The absence of life in the town emphasises the absence of real life in the urn and further prepares us for a return to the coldness and reality of the next stanza.

The fifth stanza retains some slight allusions to the orgiastic excitement of earlier verses ('forest branches and the trodden weed') and perhaps also in the ambiguous 'overwrought', which could refer either to the nature of the design on the urn or to the excited state of the maidens. But much stronger is the return to an awareness of the urn as mere artefact, an inanimate if beautiful object ('marble men and maidens', 'silent form', 'Cold Pastoral'). It is an artefact that 'dost tease us out of thought'. The ambiguity of this phrase and of the last two lines has given rise to a great deal of critical disagreement. 'Tease us out of thought' could refer to the capacity of a work of art to entice us to leave aside logical thought and enter the world of the imagination, progressing to a visionary state of creativity. Or it may mean merely that it puzzles and baffles us. This latter interpretation would fit in with Cedric Watts's reading of the two final lines:

> The ending of the ode is a statement in character by the riddling, paradox-loving urn; and one which appropriately concludes this teasing poem . . . The urn is a consolatory 'friend to man'; but also a mocking, tantalising one.

Is it the poet's conclusion that the relationship between art and reality is mysterious and baffling?

Most critical discussion has centred on the final two lines of stanza 5. There are two main aspects of this debate.

1. How should the lines be punctuated, and who speaks them? The present version is punctuated as it was in the collection *Poems, 1820*, which Keats saw through the press, though the quotation marks are not present in any surviving transcript of the poem. It is generally agreed now that the urn is the speaker both of the aphorism and of the recommendation to humankind.

2. Does the aphorism 'Beauty is truth, truth beauty' make sense? Some critics have described it as an over-simplification, a pseudo-statement. T. S. Eliot felt that it was meaningless. But many of these critics also admitted that it brought together the paradoxes and oppositions of the poem and is therefore dramatically appropriate at least. But what does it really mean? Does it mean that 'aesthetic perfection [i.e. beauty] and conceptual truth are identical' (Watts)? Keats's letters would lend credence to this. He wrote:

> I am certain of nothing but the holiness of the Heart's affections and the truth of the Imagination. What the imagination seizes as Beauty must be truth . . . The excellence of every Art is its intensity, capable of making all disagreeables evaporate, from their being in close relationship with Beauty and Truth . . .

But we know from experience that some truths are not beautiful: human cruelty, for example. So what does Keats mean by 'truth'? Examine Graham Hough's interpretation: 'In this context, where transience and permanence are the two poles of the argument, truth means that which has lasting value . . . Keats is saying that beauty is truer than love, pleasure and other forms of value, because they pass away while beauty can be embodied in a lasting quasi-permanent form.'

Perhaps Keats intended this ambiguity. He relished the immortality of beauty found in art, but its cold stasis was unsatisfying. He was too much an advocate of passionate, sensuous living to accept that. So he is left with this somewhat unsatisfactory symbol of immortality. Yet the urn, emblem of beauty, conveys some lasting value or truth to humankind. It is a sign of eternity in the midst of impermanence ('when old age shall this generation waste'), an embodiment of beauty in the midst of human woe. The poet is asserting the importance of art to humankind.

THEMES

- An examination of the relationship between art and life. Art, because it is timeless, is superior to life. Art catches the perfection of beauty, love and passion and preserves them out of time. Yet art is cold and lifeless and does not answer humanity's need to feel, to experience, to achieve fulfilment.
- Natural beauty and love are transient, yet art is there as a sign of beauty and loveliness, which is timeless.
- Art is a consolation, a friend to humankind, displaying an ideal and demonstrating the continuity of human affairs.
- Keats seems to champion the visual arts over poetry.

> Sylvan historian, who canst thus express
> A flowery tale more sweetly than our rhyme.

SOME LINKED THOUGHTS ON 'ODE TO A NIGHTINGALE' AND 'ODE ON A GRECIAN URN'

Both the nightingale's song and the urn are manifestations of eternal beauty, and both are found to be unsatisfactory in some way. The imagination fails to allow the poet to escape permanently into the world of the nightingale, and the immortalisation of beauty in the Grecian urn is not entirely satisfactory, because of its frozen immobility.

Yet the creative experiences are very different. The nightingale can only be experienced through the imagination and needs to be sustained by the creative mood. It is less substantial than the solid urn, which stands there available for viewing at any time.

The prevailing atmosphere in 'Ode to a Nightingale' is one of sensuous darkness, a sort of creative twilight zone. The figures on the Grecian urn are always in full view, the atmosphere either of frenzied sensuous excitement or of sombre dignity illuminated by the light of the 'pious morn'.

As a symbol of immortal art, the urn is more satisfying. Consider:
- the duration of its existence: it has already survived down through history
- it is a record of a much-valued and idealised culture, which it has outlasted
- it is a circular object, suggesting endlessness
- it is a three-dimensional, solid, substantial object, readily available for

viewing
- there is a balanced realism about the symbol; while it may be a sign of eternity, it also carries reminders of mortality (as a funeral urn for the ashes of the dead).

'Ode to a Nightingale' is a very personal experience, told in the first person. 'Ode on a Grecian Urn' is a more objective poem. We are very much aware that it is an object out there, not just a product of the poet's imagination. There is no first-person voice of the poet.

Keats expresses doubts in both poems but seems more confident and assured at the end of 'Ode on a Grecian Urn'.

To Autumn
Text of poem: New Explorations Anthology page 42

THEME
The poem celebrates the natural abundance of autumn. Certain aspects of the season are celebrated in each stanza: the rich fruiting of the vegetable world (stanza 1), the varied and thrilling musical sounds of the animals, birds and insects (stanza 3), and the calm, lethargic mood of the season, with which human activities and moods are completely in tune (stanza 2).

Furthermore, Keats celebrates the beauty of the season in the full knowledge that it is transient, part of the changing cycle of life:

> Where are the songs of Spring? Ay, where are they?
> Think not of them, thou hast thy music too, –
> While barred clouds bloom the soft-dying day.

STRUCTURE
Outwardly at least the poem has a very clear, even symmetrical structure. Each stanza examines an element of the season: stanza 1, the vegetable world; stanza 2, human activities; stanza 3, animals, birds and insects. The critic Walter Jackson Bate has explored the complexity and tension beneath the surface. Each stanza concentrates on a dominant aspect of autumn but at the same time preserves an element of its opposite. For example, the theme of the first stanza is ripeness, the maturity of autumn fruit, yet growth is still going on ('to set budding more, And still more'). 'So process is continuing within a context of attained fulfilment' (Bate).

We find a similar but opposite pattern in the second stanza. The activities of harvesting are mainly represented through images of stillness and inactivity. In

the third stanza the birds, animals and insects are portrayed in active, concrete imagery full of energy and life, yet there are hints of transience and death also ('the small gnats mourn' and 'gathering swallows twitter in the skies'). So beneath the simple structure we find something of Keats's paradoxical complexity.

Other critics have noted the logical progress of the poem as it moves slowly through the season: pre-harvest ripeness in the first stanza, followed by the harvesting of the second stanza and the post-harvest 'stubble-plains' of the third stanza.

The day provides a further symmetry for the structure of the ode: morning ('the maturing sun') in the first stanza, through the activities of the day in the second, to evening ('the soft-dying day') in the third stanza.

PERSONIFICATION OF AUTUMN

Personified autumn is addressed throughout all three stanzas ('Close bosom-friend of the maturing sun' in stanza 1, 'thou hast thy music too' in stanza 3). The autumn of stanzas 1 and 3 is very real, the images concrete, depicting the actual sights of the season ('the moss'd cottage-trees', 'the stubble-plains with rosy hue', 'The red-breast whistles from a garden-croft').

But the second stanza features an elaborate and varied personification of the season as a person engaged in the various activities of harvesting – or not engaged, because three of the four poses depict postures of casual inactivity, 'a kind of beautiful lethargy,' as Brian Stone describes it: 'sitting careless on a granary floor', sound asleep or drugged on a furrow, or just calmly watching the oozings of the cider press. The only activity is performed in the picture of the gleaner balancing a load on her head as she crosses a brook. Even that activity is stately and unhurried, the balancing tension conveyed by the line bisection of the phrase 'keep | Steady'. Most critics are agreed that these figures show the human at one with the natural world, interacting with calm empathy.

Less readily agreed is whether this is a masculine or a feminine personification. Stone feels that the first figure is feminine, influenced perhaps by the languid delicacy of the 'hair soft-lifted by the winnowing wind.' The third figure, of the gleaner, he also takes as feminine, as this work was traditionally performed by women and children. The sleeping reaper he takes as male, while the watcher of the cider press could be of either sex, though he sees him as male. His conception is coloured by social history.

Cedric Watts sees the entire personification as of indeterminate sex, though traditionally it has been regarded as masculine. Helen Vendler views the stanza as a totally feminine personification of autumn:

Keats's goddess of autumn, nearer to us than pagan goddesses because, unlike them, she labours in the fields and is herself thrashed by the winnowing wind, varies in her manifestation from careless girl to burdened gleaner to patient watcher, erotic in her abandon to the fume of poppies, intimate of light in her bosom friendship with the maturing sun, worn by her vigil over the last oozings.

Leon Waldoff agrees, seeing autumn as a goddess of fruition and plenty, taking her place with the imaginative figures of the other odes: a feminine soul (Psyche), a bird whose mournful song was heard by Ruth, a mysterious urn, and a goddess of melancholy.

How do you see it?

A POEM OF KEATS'S MATURE PHILOSOPHY

Though the great odes have many elements in common, strictly speaking they are not a sequence. Yet we are justified in finding in this ode a development of thought and tone that indicates a more mature, integrated outlook on life. In this respect 'To Autumn' is a fitting culmination to the odes.

Gone is the restless searching after beauty in nightingale and Grecian urn; gone the quest for permanence (nightingale and Grecian urn); no more headlong flight and attempts to escape the horrors and suffering of life (nightingale). Past too is the conflict between beauty and transience, joy and sorrow, which was partially resolved in 'Ode on Melancholy', with the realisation that melancholy is in everything, an intrinsic part of the search for beauty and joy. Here the restlessness has eased, replaced by the fulfilled and lethargic spirit of autumn.

The human spirit is at ease with the world rather than in flight from it. There is a hint that the eternal search for perfection might still haunt the poet's soul ('Where are the songs of Spring? Ay, where are they?'), but it no longer presents itself with the same desperate need as in 'Ode on a Grecian Urn' ('Ah, happy, happy, boughs! that cannot shed your leaves'). Here thoughts of spring are pushed aside ('Think not of them, thou hast thy music too'). And it is this acceptance of life as it is, in all its transient beauty, that we find in the third stanza, that exemplifies Keats's mature philosophy. He is accepting here that maturity, death and regeneration are interconnected. The faint hints of death in the 'soft-dying day', 'the small gnats mourn' and the 'light wind' that 'dies' are an integral part of the season that includes 'the stubble-plains with rosy hue', the 'full-grown lambs', and the 'gathering swallows'. He is accepting the transient nature of existence, but this no longer takes from his enjoyment. As Leon Waldoff says, 'Keats gives expression to a keen sense of transience and loss, but it is integrated into an acceptance of a natural process that includes growth as well as decay.'

This is not to suggest that Keats has suddenly become harshly realistic. This ode paints an idealised picture of the English countryside, a green land of plenty, with the pace of life unhurried and humankind in tranquil empathy with nature. The poem exhibits a mixture of realism and what Cedric Watts calls 'consolatory fantasy'. It is as if all this richness just appeared spontaneously. He has chosen to hide the toil, the sweaty labour, the peasant squalor. Would a Marxist critic say this was a dishonest poem? At any rate, in choosing the representative features of autumn Keats has exercised an 'optimistic selectivity' (Watts).

TONE

Readers are generally agreed on the calm tone of this poem. There are no introspective passages, no dramatic debate, and hardly any qualifications such as we find in the other odes. Instead we find a calm assurance, both in the fruitfulness of the season (stanza 1) and in its value (stanza 3: 'thou hast thy music too'). The tranquillity and serenity of stanza 2 are obvious.

But it is a valediction, a farewell to the season, and the awareness of coming winter is felt particularly in the third stanza, as we have seen. Yet it is not sentimental, saved perhaps by the wealth of apt detail and precise description, which give a balanced context for the hints of mourning and the sense of impending loss ('in a wailful choir the small gnats mourn | Among the river sallows').

IMAGERY

As usual, the images assail the whole range of our senses, often simultaneously in the synaesthetic imagery characteristic of Keats (synaesthesia is the fusion of two or more senses in the one image, as in the tactile-visual 'touch the stubble-plains with rosy hue'). This allows us to experience what is being described in a real, three-dimensional way. Keats also makes a dominant appeal to one particular sense in each of the three stanzas: tactile in stanza 1, visual in stanza 2, and auditory in stanza 3. For example, in stanza 1 the abundance, the sumptuousness, the ripe plenty of autumn is communicated in tactile imagery, in particular through the full weighty verbs ('load', 'bend', 'fill', 'swell the gourd', 'plump the hazel shells', 'set budding'). The images of the second stanza are visual in the main, personifying autumn in human poses that are relaxed yet alert (in three of the four), communicating, according to Bate, 'energy caught in repose' ('sitting careless on a granary floor, | Thy hair soft-lifted by the winnowing wind', 'by a cyder-press, with patient look'). The critic Ian Jack suggested that the pictorial details are probably inspired by paintings, but Keats concentrates on realistic detail of actual harvest operations (the granary, winnowing, a gleaner, a cyder-press). This weight of concrete detailed imagery, combined with apt observation, gives this poem a sense of actuality. This saves it from becoming mere bucolic fancy, even though the details are selective and avoid unpleasant reality, as we saw earlier.

The densely packed nature of the imagery also fosters the sense of actuality. This density often results from the poet's habit of packing a number of elements, often hyphenated, into a single image ('close bosom-friend', 'moss'd cottage-trees', 'a half-reap'd furrow', 'the soft-dying day').

THE MUSIC OF THE LANGUAGE

Qualities of the season are carried not just by the imagery but also by the very sounds of the words, in dense patterns of alliteration, assonance, onomatopoeia and musical echoes that reverberate throughout the poem. For example, in the first stanza the sensuousness of the season is conveyed through the soft alliterative m sounds of 'mists', 'mellow', 'maturing' and the tacky 'clammy cells'. The sense of calm fullness comes through the long vowels of 'trees', 'bees', 'cease'. And 'swell', 'hazel', 'shells' and 'kernel' might suggest bells echoing across the autumn stillness. The onomatopoeic 'winnowing wind' gives a lift to the otherwise lethargic second stanza, a calmness perfectly rendered by the sibilant s sounds and the lazy long vowels of 'watchest the last oozings hours by hours.'

The third stanza plays the music of autumn in its auditory imagery but also through the actual sounds of the words. For example, the inherent tinge of sadness is carried in the long vowels of 'mourn', 'borne', 'bourn'.

Bright Star

Text of poem: New Explorations Anthology page 45

GENESIS OF THE POEM

For many years this was considered to be Keats's last poem, as he wrote this version of it aboard ship on his final journey to Italy in the autumn of 1820. But earlier and somewhat different versions have turned up, and biographers and scholars can now, with some confidence, trace the composition to late July 1819.

The sonnet is a love poem to Fanny Brawne. Aileen Ward links its composition to this letter of 25 July 1819 from the poet to his beloved:

> Sunday Night
> My sweet Girl,
> I hope you did not blame me much for not obeying your request of a Letter on Saturday: we have had four in our small room playing at cards night and morning leaving me no undisturb'd opportunity to write. Now Rice and Martin are gone, I am at liberty. Brown to my sorrow

confirms the account you give of your ill health. You cannot conceive how I ache to be with you: how I would die for one hour – for what is in the world? I say you cannot conceive; it is impossible you should look with such eyes upon me as I have upon you: it cannot be. Forgive me if I wander a little this evening, for I have been all day employ'd in a very abstract Poem and I am in deep love with you – two things which must excuse me. I have, believe me, not been an age in letting you take possession of me; the very first week I knew you I wrote myself your vassal; but burnt the Letter as the very next time I saw you I thought you manifested some dislike to me. If you should ever feel for Man at the first sight what I did for you, I am lost. Yet I should not quarrel with you, but hate myself if such a thing were to happen – only I should burst if the thing were not as fine as a Man as you are as a Woman. Perhaps I am too vehement, then fancy me on my knees, especially when I mention a part of your Letter which hurt me; you say speaking of Mr. Severn 'but you must be satisfied in knowing that I admired you much more than your friend.' My dear love, I cannot believe there ever was or ever could be any thing to admire in me especially as far as sight goes – I cannot be admired, I am not a thing to be admired. You are, I love you; all I can bring you is a swooning admiration of your Beauty. I hold that place among Men which snubnos'd brunettes with meeting eyebrows do among women – they are trash to me – unless I should find one among them with a fire in her heart like the one that burns in mine. You absorb me in spite of myself – you alone: for I look not forward with any pleasure to what is call'd being settled in the world; I tremble at domestic cares – yet for you I would meet them, though if it would leave you the happier I would rather die than do so. I have two luxuries to brood over in my walks, your Loveliness and the hour of my death. O that I could have possession of them both in the same minute. I hate the world: it batters too much the wings of my self-will, and would I could take a sweet poison from your lips to send me out of it. From no other would I take it. I am indeed astonish'd to find myself so careless of all charms but yours – remembring as I do the time when even a bit of ribband was a matter of interest with me. What softer words can I find for you after this – what it is I will not read. Nor will I say more here, but in a Postscript answer any thing else you may have mentioned in your Letter in so many words – for I am distracted with a thousand thoughts. I will imagine you Venus to night and pray, pray, pray to your star like a Hethen.
Your's ever, fair Star,
John Keats

My seal is mark'd like a family table cloth with my mother's initial F for Fanny: put between my Father's initials. You will soon hear from me again. My respectful Compts to your Mother. Tell Margaret I'll send her a reef of best rocks and tell Sam I will give him my light bay hunter if he will tie the Bishop hand and foot and pack him in a hamper and send him down for me to bathe him for his health with a Necklace of good snubby stones about his Neck.

Ward feels that all the conflicts expressed in this letter – the passion that absorbs him in spite of himself, his fear of 'domestic cares' and 'being settled in the world' yet his willingness to face them for her – are resolved temporarily in the imagery of the sonnet.

The image of the ever-wakeful North Star unblinkingly contemplating the world can be traced back further to a letter Keats wrote to his brother Tom, describing a visit to Lake Windermere in June 1818:

> . . . the two views we have had of it are of the most noble tenderness – they can never fade away – they make one forget the divisions of life; age, youth, poverty and riches; and refine one's sensual vision into a sort of north star which can never cease to be open lidded and stedfast over the wonders of the great Power . . .

He seems to see the attitude of the North Star as the appropriate one for poetry: one of calm, detached contemplation.

A READING OF THE POEM

If we take an autobiographical approach to the sonnet we see it to be about the conflicting claims of poetry and love in the life of the poet.

The octave deals primarily with his poetic preoccupations – the nature of the ideal attitude for a poet. The star symbolises a perfect state of awareness – a calm, contemplating consciousness gazing on the changes wrought by nature ('the moving waters') and on the quiet, unheralded beauties of nature that had always fascinated him ('the new soft-fallen masque | Of snow upon the mountains and the moors'). But the 'creative loneliness', which is a characteristic mode of all Romantic poets, he rejects categorically ('Not in lone splendor hung aloft the night'). Human company is preferred above this poetic isolation, and the beauty he prefers to contemplate is not that of nature but the physical body of his love.

And it is to the sensuous aspect of love that the sestet is devoted, painting a picture of romantic intimacy that involves sensuous physical closeness ('pillow'd upon my fair love's ripening breast') and an awareness of his beloved so intense that he seems almost to share her life breath ('still to hear her tender-taken breath'). Just as the star stands for permanence, Keats wishes to preserve permanently this experience of love ('To feel forever its soft swell and fall').

This paradoxical attempt to hold the moment, to preserve unchanged real, breathing, sensuous love, is illogical and vain but emotionally defensible. It ends in the already invalidated endeavour to preserve the moment through dying at the pinnacle of happiness ('Ode on a Grecian Urn'). Also, the star symbolises the steadfastness he longed for in his relationship with Fanny Brawne. He too wishes to be 'still stedfast, still unchangeable'. So once again we have the timeless but ultimately unsatisfying perfection of art contrasted with the transient but sensuous enjoyment of real experience. Keats is attempting to have the best of both sides, the permanence and the experience. The excited tone of the sestet, with its enthusiastic verbal repetitions ('Still, still', 'for ever'), suggests that human love is preferable to poetry or art.

Keats always admired the purity of nature, and here we find the tides performing a cleansing religious ritual for the world ('priestlike task | Of pure ablution round earth's human shores'). The 'religious' aspect of nature is emphasised ('sleepless Eremite', 'priestlike task', 'pure ablution'). The benevolent relationship of nature to humankind is stressed. Nature purifies. In previous poems the skies were searched for signs of value, of truth ('huge cloudy symbols of a high romance'). Now the perspective has changed. The stars are no longer watched, they have become the watchers. Is this a more benevolent guardianship role for nature? But nature too is found to be less important than love.

IDEAS EXPLORED

- The importance of the sensuous experience of love, even above poetry or the contemplation of nature
- A great need to make this experience permanent
- Steadfastness and unchangeability as the marks of true love
- The purity and permanence of nature and its beneficial relationship with humankind
- An understanding of the poet as disinterested viewer and lonely creator.

An overview

ROMANTIC POETRY IN CONTEXT

The 'Revolution' of 1688, which put the Protestant William of Orange and Mary on the throne of England, put an end to the religious and political conflict of the seventeenth century and ushered in a century of relative peace and order that became known as the Augustan Age (because of a perceived parallel with the golden age of Augustus Caesar). It was also referred to as the Age of Enlightenment (roughly 1690–1790).

While it is always false to generalise, we can say that the following notions were characteristic of the period.

- Order – in life, in society, and in literature – was considered of vital importance. The human being was seen as part of the great chain of life, an established hierarchy that stretched from primitive vegetable life all the way up to God. It was an era of deep social conservatism.
- Reason rather than passion was the supreme virtue. The emotions were suspect. John Dryden wrote: 'A man is to be cheated into Passion, but to be reasoned into Truth.'
- It was an era of profound scepticism: doubt about people's ability to reform, change or develop; scepticism about the possibility of human progress. This was reflected in the satires of Dryden and Pope and in the satirical fables of Jonathan Swift, all emphasising human failings and corruption and attempting to show humankind the error of its ways.

The foremost poets of this period were:
- John Dryden (1631–1700)
- Alexander Pope (1688–1744)
- Jonathan Swift (1667–1745).

NEW TRENDS IN THE ROMANTIC PERIOD

Cult of feeling

If Augustan poetry was known for its reason (the poet using his rational and argumentative faculties to guide humankind by the light of reason) and its intellectual style of composition (the use of wit, paradox, irony, bathos, and classical and other learned allusions), then Romantic poetry was distinguished by the cult of feeling. For Wordsworth, poetry was 'the spontaneous overflow of powerful feelings'; yet it was not uncontrolled, it was 'emotion recollected in tranquillity'. Wordsworth also felt that the feelings were restrained, of necessity, by the observation of the outer world. The English Romantics were, for the most part, more objective than the French. But Shelley said: 'Poetry is not subject to the control of the active powers of the mind, and its birth and recurrence have no necessary connection with consciousness or will' (*Defence of Poetry*).

Keats wished for 'a Life of Sensations rather than of Thoughts'. For Keats, the necessary frame of mind for writing was the accepting of things as they are without trying to rationalise them. This is behind his notion of 'negative capability' ('when a man is capable of being in uncertainties, mysteries, doubts, without any irritable reaching after fact and reason'). There was a definite downgrading of reason. Sincerity, sensitivity and self-expression were the key qualities.

New subject matter

The poets of the eighteenth century generally turned to the social environment and to the nature of human beings for their subjects and themes. 'The proper study of mankind is man', wrote Alexander Pope. The poets of the rationalist age found their inspiration in the world of matter (Dryden and Pope in politics, for example). The Romantic poets looked for inspiration to the more mysterious aspects of human experience and to the world of dreams (see 'La Belle Dame Sans Merci'). The poet looked inside his own mind rather than to society as a subject of study. The imaginative and the spiritual were fostered, instead of the rational.

New understanding of the imagination

Dryden feared the ungoverned imagination: 'for imagination in a poet is a faculty so wild and lawless, that, like a high ranking spaniel it must have dogs tied to it, lest it outrun the judgment.' He felt that the imagination should be restrained by the need for rhyme and by the regular discipline of the heroic couplet.

But the Romantics transformed the concept of the imagination, seeing it as a creative force central to the process of poetry. Shelley went so far as to define poetry as 'the expression of the imagination'. Wordsworth spoke of poetry as 'works of imagination and sentiment'. Keats said: 'I am certain of nothing but of the holiness of the Heart's affections and the truth of Imagination – what the imagination seizes as Beauty must be truth . . .'

Whereas the Augustan poets were content to convey in poetry the outer manifestation of their subjects, the Romantics were trying to convey the inner essence of things. The sheer power of imagination allows the poet to share in the life of the subject, as in 'Ode to a Nightingale', 'To Autumn', and 'Ode on a Grecian Urn'. Keats was constantly experiencing the tension between these visionary moments and the real world.

New poetics

Because the Romantics were dealing with abstract themes and trying to express the inward essence in concrete terms, the significance of imagery changed. The image was no longer merely decorative, as in Augustan poetry, but became a more complex carrier of meaning, often having symbolic weight, such as the Grecian urn and the nightingale.

The regularity and self-control of the rhyming couplet was regarded by the new poets as a straitjacket, producing facile and insincere poetry. Keats belittled the rhyming couplet:

With a puling infant's force
They swayed upon a rocking horse
and thought it Pegasus.

Reacting against the stylised dictum of the Augustans, Wordsworth in particular felt that the language of poetry should be ordinary and simple: poetry should be written 'as far as was possible in a selection of language really used by men'. He also felt that the poet should write about 'incidents and situations from common life'. So we get the conversational blank verse of 'Tintern Abbey'. Keats's views on poetic diction were different, often favouring the archaic, even the mediaeval expression, such as that used in 'La Belle Dame Sans Merci'.

For the Romantics the role of the poet in society was different also. Poets were no longer sarcastic social commentators but were often withdrawn completely from society, more concerned with their own inner vision. But because of their belief in the power of the imagination to discover truth, the poet was a very powerful creative force in society. Paradoxically, although the poet was less concerned with social issues, a great claim was made for the importance of poetry in society. While Keats hardly ever dealt with social themes, he made substantial claims for art as a mediator of eternal truth for society:

Beauty is truth, truth Beauty! that is all
Ye know on earth, and all ye need to know.

The importance of nature
For many of the Romantics the varied and overpowering moods of nature provided the occasion for moments of personal revelation or of intense private experience, which replaced the experience of orthodox religion. For example, Wordsworth felt nature to be a moral guide, a teacher, a comforter to humankind. Keats did not dwell very much on the significance and power of nature, but he enjoyed its sensuous aspects, particularly evident in 'Ode to a Nightingale' and 'To Autumn'.

The foremost poets of the Romantic period were:
• William Blake (1757–1827)
• William Wordsworth (1770–1850)
• Samuel Taylor Coleridge (1772–1834)
• Lord Byron (1788–1824)
• Percy Bysshe Shelley (1792–1822)
• John Keats (1795–1821)

Though elements of Romanticism are found both before and after, the high point of the period is generally dated between 1789 (the year Blake's *Songs of Innocence* was published) and 1824, when Byron died.

THE SENSUOUS VERSE OF KEATS

Keats's basic apprehension of the world is through the senses. Joy and sorrow are to be tasted ('strenuous tongue can burst Joy's grape against his palate fine', 'glut thy sorrow', 'feed deep, deep upon her peerless eyes'). Misery is audible ('here, where men sit and hear each other groan'). Death is visible ('youth grows pale'); despair and beauty are visible ('leaden-eyed despairs', 'Beauty cannot keep her lustrous eyes'). Seduction is through taste ('she found me roots of relish sweet | And honey wild and manna dew'). Literature is to be breathed in ('yet did I never breathe its pure serene'). Poetry is born of touch ('the magic hand of chance'). The spiritual is accessed through sound ('pipe to the spirit ditties of no tone'). Passion is apprehended in all its wild sensuousness ('for ever warm . . . for ever panting').

Keats delighted particularly in nature, not for its mystical power or moral influence, as with Wordsworth, but for the sheer enjoyment of its luxurious life and growth. A sensuous appreciation of nature and of all life is one of his main themes. He recreates for us the seductive fascination of the nightingale's song; the sensuous world of the trees inhabited by the bird; the visual beauty of the Grecian urn; the tactile awareness as well as the sounds of autumn.

Keats is not entirely naive about the negative side of sensual delight. He is aware that excess physical delight can satiate, glut the feeling, and so lessen the sensitivity.

> That leaves a heart high-sorrowful and cloy'd,
> A burning forehead, and a parching tongue.

He is aware that all delight is transitory. Even the physical appetite wanes. He is aware, too, of the inherent decay in all things:

> aching Pleasure nigh,
> Turning to poison while the bee-mouth sips.

Keats's sensuous imagery, which he uses liberally, is his way of communicating half-glimpsed truths, making the eternal present, trying to express the abstract in terms of the concrete, the intangible in terms of the very tangible. So beauty is encapsulated in the visible urn or in the tangible fruits of autumn ('thou shalt remain . . . a friend to man', 'swell the gourd'). Hints of immortality float to us on the notes of the nightingale ('the voice I hear this passing night was heard | In ancient days by emperor and clown'). The awareness of transience is mediated in the music of autumn ('and gathering swallows twitter').

Sometimes the senses fuse and mingle in an image. Keats uses this synaesthetic imagery to create the most complete and rounded sensuous effect possible. We get some fine examples of the working of this technique in 'Ode to a Nightingale', where the bird sings in 'some melodious plot | Of beechen green'. The fusion of the senses of sound and sight emphasises that the bird is at one with the location, as the song merges with the undergrowth.

Synaesthetic imagery allows the location to be presented with a realism that might rival 3-D in modern cinematic terms. Consider:

> But here there is no light,
> Save what from heaven is with the breezes blown.

Light is blown, aptly describing the flickering light intermittently penetrating through the wind-blown leaves. The use of such imagery to evoke the natural habitat of the nightingale in stanza 5 is much commented on (see page 14). Stanza 2 is also worth examining to see how the images link, providing a chain of sensual effects that achieve a forward momentum, spiriting the poet 'away into the forest dim'. The 'draught of vintage' leads to 'tasting of Flora'. Taste calls up a series of pictures: goddess of flowers, fertility ('country green'); country green refers perhaps to country dance, to song, to outdoor celebration. 'Provençal song' recalls the warm south, and so back to the taste of wine and the possibilities for escape into oblivion. The synaesthetic imagery aptly evokes the full richness of the pleasures of wine but also the poet's confused reeling between sensuous pleasure and the need to escape. It is as if he is quite overcome by the variety of the world.

In general, the synaesthetic use of imagery allows the poet to evoke a richness and an immediacy of experience that might not otherwise be possible. Other critics have felt that it indicates a 'unified' vision of the world on the part of the poet. 'His synaesthetic imagery is an outward manifestation of his intuitive sense of the oneness of things, of the relationship between widely separate and dissimilar phenomena, of the intimate kinship of man and nature' (Richard Fogle, in *Keats: Twentieth-Century Views*, edited by Walter Jackson Bate).

Keats also uses the sensuous aspects of language: rhyme, alliteration, assonance, onomatopoeia, and repeated and echoing sound effects; for a detailed study of this examine 'To One Long in City Pent', 'On First Looking into Chapman's Homer', and 'To Autumn', together with their critical commentaries.

The critic Brian Stone feels that there is evidence that Keats began to control his exuberance as he developed, refining his vocabulary by reducing the number of adjectives and adverbs, strengthening the verse by a greater use of verbs, and reducing the reliance on melodic words of Latin origin. Would you agree with this assessment?

KEATS AND VARIETY OF FORMS

Keats was amazingly versatile and constantly experimental in his approach to poetry. We have seen something of the range of poetic genres he used: long narratives, lyric poems and ballads. During his short career he experimented with all the chief forms of English poetry, such as heroic couplets, octosyllabic couplets, ottava rima, the Spenserian stanza, blank verse, and both the Petrarchan and Shakespearean sonnet forms.

As we have seen, he was not greatly enamoured of the eighteenth-century use of the heroic couplet, finding it too constricting in thought and rhyme. So he altered it – sometimes using run-on lines instead of end-stopped ones, using irregular stresses, and sometimes 'feminine rhymes' (with an additional unstressed final syllable). The desired effect was to allow the verse to flow more easily and so carry more complex and deeper ideas without the necessity of boxing them securely in couplets. He used this form of verse in 'Endymion'.

The sonnet form was little used in the eighteenth century, but Keats was greatly drawn to it. Over a third of his completed poems are sonnets. Most of the early sonnets are autobiographical in theme and almost exclusively Petrarchan in form, with an octave, *abba abba*, and a sestet, *cdcdcd* or *cdecde*. Keats observed the formal thought structure: main thought or problem stated in the octave, with a *volta*, or turn, to a new thought or a resolution of the problem in the sestet. 'On First Looking into Chapman's Homer' is structured in this form. But he also used the Shakespearean form, as in 'When I Have Fears that I May Cease to Be'. This follows the Shakespearean rhyming scheme (*abab cdcd efef gg*), is structured into three separate but linked quatrains and a rhyming couplet, and uses end-stopped couplet lines for the most part. But even here Keats is straining at the regularity of the form, and he has the final couplet actually beginning in the middle of the twelfth line, 'deliberately frustrating the epigrammatic tendency inherent in the regular form,' as Brian Stone says.

He returned to the sonnet form again in 1819, prepared to experiment even further. 'Bright Star' follows the normal Shakespearean rhyming scheme but has the Petrarchan division of octave and sestet, albeit with a distinct rhyming couplet to finish. He wrote to his brother George and George's wife, Georgiana, in May 1819:

> I have been endeavouring to discover a better sonnet stanza than we have. The legitimate [i.e. Petrarchan] does not suit the language over-well from the pouncing rhyme – the other kind [i.e. Shakespearean] appears too elegiac – the couplet at the end of it has seldom a pleasing effect – I do not pretend to have succeeded.

Experiment was not confined to sonnets. He adapted the mediaeval ballad for

'La Belle Dame Sans Merci'. He used three four-stress iambic lines and a shorter final three-stress or two-stress line in each stanza. The last line is rendered particularly slow and heavy because of the lack of unstressed syllables. The effect is to build up the unreal, forlorn atmosphere of the poem: 'And no birds sing.'

The ode is a very formal, dignified and heavyweight form of lyric poetry, usually of some length. It is derived from an ancient Greek form that was often sung or accompanied by music. Odes were relatively new on the scene in English poetry, Wordsworth's ode 'Intimations of Immortality', written in 1815, being one of the more well-known contemporary ones. Keats maintains the lofty tradition of the ode in the serious tone he employs and in the serious subject matter: the nature of the immortality of art, the transience of beauty, the pain and suffering of life, and the ideal of love.

In the odes, to carry his deep and abstract themes, he turned to the sonnet form as the basis for his experimental stanzas. 'Ode to a Nightingale' has a Shakespearean quatrain, *abab*, followed by a Petrarchan sestet, *cdecde*, for each stanza. The lines are predominantly iambic pentameter, except for the typical experimental gesture – a trimeter for every eighth line. 'Ode on a Grecian Urn' had regular ten-line stanzas of iambic pentameters. The large, weighty stanzas of these odes function like paragraphs, with a main idea that is developed and rounded off at the end of each. Yet, as in good prose composition, the end of each also points forward and is linked to the next. For example, in 'Ode to a Nightingale' the 'full-throated ease' at the end of the first stanza prefigures the 'draught of vintage' at the start of the second.

There is an even more obvious linkage between stanzas 2 and 3:

> And with thee fade away into the forest dim:
> Fade far away, dissolve, and quite forget

This weighty stanza form is increased even further in 'To Autumn', with its eleven-line stanzas, where a couplet has been inserted at lines 9 and 10. They are regular lines of iambic pentameters, rhyming *abab cdedcce*. When taken together with the simplicity of diction, these full, heavy stanzas are perfect for conveying the richness, melody and serenity of the season.

Examples of the Spenserian stanza – ottava rima, octosyllabic couplets, and blank verse – are to be found in Keats's other verse. His achievement is summed up by Brian Stone: 'He had decisively broken with the style of the eighteenth century, both metrically and in vocabulary, to achieve a new sort of fresh sensuousness and perception.'

THE EXPLORATION OF THRESHOLD STATES IN THE POETRY OF KEATS

In reading Keats we are aware of a certain restlessness, a continuing search for the ideal, a perpetual attempt to reconcile opposites, such as the eternal and transient, ideal love and human passion, the perfection of art and the misery of real life. This tension results in the poet occupying an in-between, transitional or threshold state for many of the key moments in his poems.

These threshold states have been described by Cedric Watts as 'moments or phrases of transition from one mode of being to another'. Watts also notices 'the ambiguous status of the modes of being on each side of this threshold'. There are numerous examples of threshold states in this selection. We find the knight of 'La Belle Dame Sans Merci' in this limbo state between dream and waking, between fantasy and reality. We find the poet experiencing a similar state in 'Ode to a Nightingale'. Having inhabited, however briefly, the world of the song, the fantasy world of magic casements and 'faery lands forlorn', he is tolled 'back from there to my sole self'. In this poem Keats finds himself straddling both the ideal world of beauty (symbolised in the song) and the real world of pain and suffering ('with thee fade away into the forest dim . . . and quite forget . . . The weariness, the fever, and the fret').

In 'Ode on a Grecian Urn' he inhabits the world of ideal, timeless, perfect love but simultaneously holds the opposing concept of real live passion ('She cannot fade, though thou hast not thy bliss').

In this poem we find the focus shifting between animate and inanimate, mortal and eternal, warmth and coldness, as Keats makes constant transitions in and out of the urn. Perhaps the most perfect embodiment of a transitional state is to be found in 'To Autumn'. The whole season is in transition: matured and yet continuing to grow (stanza 1); harvest activities personified as static and immobile (stanza 2); the end of a process already prefiguring another move ('the gathering swallows' of stanza 3).

But the most significant threshold state, and one often fancied by Keats, is that between life and death. Death as the doorway to eternity, to a flawless world of perfect beauty and ideal love, is an ever-present allure to the poet, particularly in 'Ode to a Nightingale' and 'Bright Star'. It is present too in 'When I Have Fears that I May Cease to Be', 'Ode on a Grecian Urn', and 'La Belle Dame Sans Merci'.

We notice that Keats often uses the rhetorical question as a bridge between fantasy and reality ('O what can ail thee knight at arms?', 'Was it a vision, or a waking dream? . . . Do I wake or sleep?', 'Who are these coming to the sacrifice?'). These unanswered questions further blur the boundaries between states, smoothing the transition.

This ability to have a foot in contrasting worlds, to experience different states, to hold opposites in the mind simultaneously – also implicit in the notion of 'negative capability' – is a key feature of the poetry of Keats. It might be interpreted as confusion or indecisiveness by some, but by many it is seen as a mark of greatness: 'His house was, most of the time, divided against itself, but his consciousness of the fissure, his unceasing endeavour to solve the problem of sense and knowledge, art and humanity, are in themselves an index of his stature' (Douglas Bush, in *Keats: Twentieth-Century Views*).

A PSYCHOANALYTICAL LOOK AT KEATS

Literary critics of the Freudian school have examined the poetry to demonstrate how Keats's works are affected by unconscious fears, desires and conflicts. We certainly find some conscious fears – fear of mortality, for instance. But then, Keats was surrounded by death in his own family. We notice conscious desires, such as the quest for beauty and permanence; and the numerous conflicts the poet consciously presented have been well discussed.

But what of unconscious desires and fears? 'La Belle Dame Sans Merci' has been interpreted as exhibiting a fear of sex, which is linked to death in that poem, a poem that also presents woman as fatal temptress. Is this reading substantiated by the relationship between Keats and Fanny Brawne, in which he yearned for her yet often kept her at a distance?

Freudian critics find a pervasive melancholia at the centre of Keats's work, which they say was influenced by the early death of his father and separation from his mother. In Freudian terms, 'melancholia' is a kind of mourning, except that in mourning the loss is known, whereas with melancholia the loss is unknown. We do find a sense of loss in many of his poems: mourning for the day in 'To One Long in City Pent'; for lost time and lost love in 'When I Have Fears that I May Cease to Be'; for lost virtue in 'La Belle Dame Sans Merci'; mourning for loss of the poetic vision that leaves him forlorn in 'Ode to a Nightingale'; and loss of timeless, perfect love in 'Ode on a Grecian Urn'. Leon Waldoff (in *Romanticism: A Critical Reader*, edited by W. Duncan) feels that the tone of melancholy in the odes arises from this sense of loss, which is really a longing for a fading immortal and vanished pastoral world. Ironically, the quest for permanence through a union with a symbolic presence (nightingale, urn, etc.) actually led to a deeper awareness of transience.

Freudian critics draw attention to the female presence that features in all Keats's major works, arousing powerful but ambiguous feelings in the poet, and it is suggested that Keats wants to reclaim her but has doubts about her fidelity ('La Belle Dame Sans Merci'?). Waldoff identifies the symbols at the centre of each ode as feminine: the personification of autumn has many female qualities, as we have seen (page 22); the urn is an 'unravish'd bride'; even the nightingale is a 'light-winged Dryad of the trees' (a female spirit of the woods). Each symbol is immortal in some way, and a sympathetic relationship exists between poet and symbol. Waldoff says the odes represent an ancient longing for restoration and reunion as Keats tries to restore the symbolic female presence. The strategy fails with the nightingale and the urn; but at least the nightingale is preserved in the historical and literary imagination ('emperor and clown', 'the sad heart of Ruth', 'charm'd magic casements'), while the urn survives as part of the wisdom of humankind.

The many scenes of embracing lovers in Keats's poems are seen by Freudian critics to represent 'a persistent longing for merger with a feminine figure or symbol of beauty' (Waldoff), and this longing is heightened by an internal awareness of separation that the poet has carried with him since childhood. They feel that this was the motivation for the romantic quest on which much of his poetry is based.

A BRIEF OVERVIEW OF POETIC PREOCCUPATIONS AND THEMES

Consider the statements, then return to the individual poems for corroborative references and quotations.

The quest for perfection

- The quest for beauty in art ('Ode to a Nightingale', 'Ode on a Grecian Urn') and in nature ('To Autumn')
- The quest for permanence and immortality ('Ode to a Nightingale', 'Ode on a Grecian Urn', 'Bright Star')
- The ideal of love, timeless and unchanging ('Ode on a Grecian Urn'); rejected as cold, lifeless; still striving for it ('Bright Star')
- The quest for joy and happiness, the need to escape the misery of the world ('Ode to a Nightingale')
- The quest for perfection in literature ('On First Looking into Chapman's Homer')
- The quest for the perfect poetic attitude, disinterested contemplation (octave of 'Bright Star')
- All these quests are found to be in vain
- Transience (of beauty, happiness, etc.)
- The battle with mutability, one of the poet's chief preoccupations
- Awareness of personal mutability and impermanence ('When I Have Fears that I May Cease to Be')
- The transience of the beauty of nature is mourned ('To One Long in City Pent') but develops into an acceptance of transience in the scheme of things: he can still enjoy the beauty of nature in spite of its short life ('To Autumn')
- The transience of beauty and love:

  Where Beauty cannot keep her lustrous eyes,

Or new love pine at them beyond tomorrow
['Ode to a Nightingale']

- Also the transience of love: 'fair creature of an hour' ('When I Have Fears that I May Cease to Be')
- The fading of artistic beauty (song of 'Ode to a Nightingale')
- Art stops this mutability, but at a price ('Ode on a Grecian Urn'); coldness of artistic immortality
- Attempts to resolve this dilemma of having to choose either transient passion or cold immortality ('Bright Star').

Nature

- Nature is ever-present in Keats's poetry: as a backdrop ('When I Have Fears that I May Cease to Be', 'Ode to a Nightingale', 'Ode on a Grecian Urn', etc.); in visions ('La Belle Dame Sans Merci'); as metaphor ('On First Looking into Chapman's Homer'); as an image for his own poetry ('granaries' in 'When I Have Fears that I May Cease to Be'); and once as the central theme ('To Autumn')
- The therapeutic power of nature refreshes the city dweller ('To One Long in City Pent')
- The sensuous qualities of nature are to be enjoyed ('Ode to a Nightingale', 'To Autumn')
- Awareness of the essence of the season, the moods of nature ('To Autumn')
- Nature as inspiration, carrying signs of truth: 'huge cloudy symbols of a high romance' ('When I Have Fears that I May Cease to Be')
- Nature also provides inspiration for the proper approach to poetry ('Bright Star')
- Nature is the proper subject of poetry ('Bright Star')
- The poet is seen as a contemplator of nature ('Bright Star')
- Keats idealises the countryside ('To Autumn', 'To One Long in City Pent').

Literature, art, creativity

- The healing power of literature ('To One Long in City Pent')
- The excitement of poetry (as discovery, as exploration); poetry opens out the world; the effect on the reader ('On First Looking into Chapman's Homer')
- The mysterious process of creativity, writing, inspiration: 'the magic hand of chance' ('When I Have Fears that I May Cease to Be')
- The exciting, frantic pace of writing ('When I Have Fears that I May Cease to Be')
- The power of imagination, to achieve union with the eternity of art, to preserve the moment, to arrest beauty in time – but only temporarily ('Ode

to a Nightingale')

- All the odes are concerned with poetry as art – its materials, images, moods of the poet, claims to immortality etc. ('Ode to a Nightingale', 'Ode on a Grecian Urn', 'To Autumn')
- The permanence and immortality conferred by art ('Ode to a Nightingale', 'Ode on a Grecian Urn')
- The permanence of art versus the transient but fulfilled experience of life ('Ode on a Grecian Urn')
- The contrast between the imaginary world of poetic joy and the real world of pain and misery ('Ode to a Nightingale')
- How art communicates the ideal, the perfect, Platonic: 'pipe to the spirit' ('Ode on a Grecian Urn')
- The portrayal of sexual passion in art is superior to real passion ('Ode on a Grecian Urn')
- The shortcomings of art: it lacks the fulfilment of experience, immortal but cold ('Ode on a Grecian Urn')
- The visual arts as superior to poetry ('Ode on a Grecian Urn')
- Beauty and truth: art as a sign of eternity, an embodiment of beauty; art conveys truth ('Ode on a Grecian Urn').

Death
- Death as the end of creativity ('When I Have Fears that I May Cease to Be')
- The allure of death – soft, rich, a luxury, a pleasant sensation, an old longing: 'call'd him soft names' ('Ode to a Nightingale')
- Death as a means of preserving the moment of ecstasy, capturing for ever moments of supreme happiness; rejected as an unsatisfactory solution ('Ode to a Nightingale'), but tried again ('Bright Star')
- The linking of love and death ('Bright Star'); as fatal seduction ('La Belle Dame Sans Merci').

Love
- The aspect of love generally presented is the sensuous, the passionate ('Ode on a Grecian Urn', 'Bright Star'); the emotional aspect also ('When I Have Fears that I May Cease to Be')
- The overwhelming desire or need is to immortalise the moment ('Ode on a Grecian Urn', 'Bright Star')
- What important aspects of love are not dealt with?
- Is the view of love in the poems somewhat immature?

View of the human being, view of life
- As exhausted city-dweller ('To One Long in City Pent')

- Yearning for love ('La Belle Dame Sans Merci', 'Ode on a Grecian Urn', 'Bright Star')
- A tragic dupe of love ('La Belle Dame Sans Merci')
- Life is sickness and misery ('Ode to a Nightingale')
- The need of the human being to escape from this grim reality: he tries wine, poetry (the imagination), death – all are inadequate in some way ('Ode to a Nightingale')
- The essential condition of humankind is to be in conflict – yearning for perfection, eternity etc. – but the reality is different ('Ode to a Nightingale', 'Ode on a Grecian Urn').

Importance of feelings
- Joy, sorrow, depression etc. ('Ode to a Nightingale', 'Bright Star' etc.)
- The importance of real experience rather than poetic observation ('Bright Star')
- The importance of sensuous fulfilment, of living life to the full ('Ode on a Grecian Urn', 'Ode to a Nightingale')

Perception of the poet
- As solitary soul, lonely thinker ('When I Have Fears that I May Cease to Be')
- This creative loneliness is rejected (in 'Bright Star')
- The poet's dilemma: disinterested vision or closer view and experience of real life ('Bright Star')
- The poet as pursuer of beauty ('Ode to a Nightingale')
- The artist-poet as philosopher, mediator of truth for humankind ('Ode on a Grecian Urn')
- The poet as escapist ('Ode to a Nightingale')
- Melancholic mode of the poet: unavoidable, since melancholy results inevitably from the pursuit of beauty
- Keats's own excitement at encountering poetry ('On First Looking into Chapman's Homer')
- The excitement and frenzy of writing, the sense of a personal race against time ('When I Have Fears that I May Cease to Be')
- The power of the poet's imagination.

Forging a personal reaction to the poetry of Keats

1. What has reading this poet meant for you? What did it add to your understanding of life, of love, of poetry, of the human mind, of human needs, of human limits?
2. Do you share any of his preoccupations?

3. Consider the ideas and attitudes found in the poetry. What ideas made you reflect hardest? What attitudes provoked you into thinking?
4. Consider his expression and use of language. What did you find exciting, or unusual, or pleasing, or beautiful? Refer to individual poems, lines, or phrases.
5. What did you find unappealing about his poetry? What did you dislike, and why?
6. Which form of poetry practised by Keats do you like best? Explain.
7. If you could choose only two poems of his to include in an anthology, which ones would you select? Justify your choice.
8. Do you think Keats should be studied in schools today? Make a case for or against.
9. From reading his poems, what kind of person do you think Keats was? Consider such things as his preoccupations, his attitudes to significant matters such as love and death, his prevailing moods.
10. What questions relating to his poetry and life would you like to ask him?

Questions

1. 'The relation of art to human life was one of the main questions that consistently preoccupied Keats.' Discuss.
2. 'The odes taken together can be seen as an investigation of the imagination's ability to cope with time and change.' Discuss.
3. 'The quintessentially Keatsian world is one in which the flawed imaginary world of dream and the hard truth of waking reality interact.' Discuss.
4. 'Keats's poetry could be summed up as merely sensuous subject matter in sensuous diction.' Discuss.
5. 'Sheer versatility with poetic form is an impressive characteristic of Keats's poetry.' Discuss.
6. 'There is a sadness at the heart of all Keats's poetry.' Discuss this statement, with reference to three or four of the poems you have read.
7. 'Tranquillity and serenity lie at the heart of the most profound artistic response to life' (Brian Stone). Do you find any sense of tranquillity or serenity in the poetry of Keats?
8. 'Keats's imagery shows a quality of delicate and particular observation.' Discuss.
9. Gerard Manley Hopkins said of Keats: 'It is impossible not to feel with weariness how his verse is at every turn abandoning itself to unmanly and enervating luxury.' Would you agree?
10. W. B. Yeats said of Keats:
    I see a schoolboy when I think of him,

With face and nose pressed to a sweet-shop window,
For certainly he sank into his grave
His senses and his heart unsatisfied.

How do you think the first two lines might apply to Keats? From the evidence of the poems you have read, do you think the remark of the last line is justified? Explain your reasoning.

11. 'His sensuous nature, his concern to define the individuating essence of things (the haecceitas, "thisness", or what Hopkins was to call "inscape"), his preoccupation with the kinds of immortality attainable through art, his Platonic yearnings and his down-to-earth scepticism, his death-wish and his sense of humour: all these coalesced in three of the supreme poems of the language – "Ode on a Grecian Urn", "Ode to a Nightingale" and "To Autumn"' (Cedric Watts). Examine the three poems mentioned to discover the truth of any two of the qualities listed.

Bibliography

Bate, Walter Jackson (editor), *Keats: Twentieth-Century Views*, Englewood Cliffs (NJ): Prentice-Hall 1964.

Coote, Stephen, *John Keats: A Life*, London: Hodder and Stoughton 1995.

Duncan, W. (editor), *Romanticism: A Critical Reader*, Oxford: Blackwell 1995.

Gittings, Robert, *John Keats*, London: Pelican 1968.

Hough, Graham, *The Romantic Poets*, London: Hutchinson 1953.

Motion, Andrew, *Keats*, London: Faber and Faber 1997.

Ridley, M., *Keats's Craftsmanship*, London: Methuen 1964.

Stone, Brian, *The Poetry of Keats*, London: Penguin 1992.

Ward, Aileen, *John Keats: The Making of a Poet*, New York: Farrar Straus Giroux 1986.

Watts, Cedric, *A Preface to Keats*, London: Longman 1985.

Wilson, Katherine, *The Nightingale and the Hawk: A Psychological Study of Keats's Ode*, 1964.

2 *William Butler* YEATS

John G. Fahy

A *literary life*

William Butler Yeats was born on 13 June 1865 at number 1 Sandymount Avenue, Dublin, a son of John Butler Yeats and Susan Pollexfen. John Butler Yeats originated from Co. Down, where his father was Church of Ireland rector and whose father before him had been rector at Drumcliff, Co. Sligo. The Butler part of the family name came from an eighteenth-century marriage to a relative of the Butlers of Ormonde, one of the oldest Anglo-Irish families. That marriage brought with it the more tangible asset of a few hundred acres of land in Co. Kildare, the rents from which continued to provide a measure of financial support for the family until the land had to be sold in 1886.

John Butler Yeats had trained as a barrister before his marriage but decided to become an artist instead, and in 1867 the family moved to London so that he could study painting. This was the first move of a peripatetic childhood and youth for the young William, as the family moved from one house to another in London or between London and Dublin in pursuit of the father's artistic career, which never really became financially viable.

William was the eldest surviving child, followed by Susan Mary (called Lily), Elizabeth Corbet (called Lollie), and John Butler (Jack) – all born within six years of each other. Their mother, Susan Pollexfen, was the daughter of a wealthy merchant and shipping family from Co. Sligo; and when John Butler Yeats got into financial difficulties the family spent a good deal of time there, which the poet remembered with great affection. So a good deal of Yeats's childhood and youth was spent in an atmosphere of genteel poverty, supported by better-off relatives.

He was educated at the Godolphin School, London, 1875–80; the High School, Dublin, 1880–83; and the Metropolitan School of Art, Dublin, 1884–86. At first the young Yeats found it difficult to learn to read, and when by the age of seven or eight he still could not distinguish all the letters of the alphabet, his father is reputed to have thrown the reading book at him in a rage. In later life Yeats's spelling continued to be idiosyncratic, supporting the later conclusion that he suffered from dyslexia. As it was unlikely that he would pass the entrance examination for Trinity College, his father's old university, he was tutored to some extent by his father, who regarded himself as the young man's chief mentor, and was therefore largely self-educated. Consequently his acquaintances and readings assumed a very significant role in his development.

Among the people introduced to him by his father was the old Fenian John O'Leary, and this sparked off an interest in nationalism, particularly as a subject for poetry. He was influenced also by the writings of Douglas Hyde, Katherine Tynan and Samuel Ferguson, as well as James Clarence Mangan's versions of Irish poems. But it was probably the histories and the fiction of Standish O'Grady that most impelled Yeats to investigate Irish mythology. At this time he was fascinated by the folk tales, fairy tales and supernatural beliefs found in Co. Sligo and Co. Galway, which resulted in the collection *Fairy and Folk Tales of the Irish Peasantry* (1888). He also wanted to reformulate in English the old Irish legends and so re-create Ireland's lost intellectual and cultural heritage. This found expression in his collection of poetry *The Wanderings of Oisín* (1889).

At this time also Yeats began to search for alternative philosophies to Christianity, such as Buddhism, magic, spiritualism and astrology. Influenced to some degree no doubt by his discussions with his friend George Russell, the poet, he began to explore mysticism and the occult, often through the practices of esoteric groups and cults. Among these were the theosophists (through whom he encountered the notorious Elena Blavatsky), who believed that knowledge of God could be achieved through spiritual ecstasy and direct intuition. He became involved also with the 'Hermetic Order of the Golden Dawn', a Rosicrucian order that practised ritual demonstrations of psychic power, which he joined in 1890. The Golden Dawn was based on the desire for alchemical change – the transformation of people into gods, the possibility of transforming the world. Yeats became quite dedicated to the practice of magic, believed in the evocation of spirits, and indeed was convinced that he himself was a magician.

Among the principal beliefs that he subscribed to were:
- that the borders of our minds are ever shifting and that minds can melt and flow into each other, creating a single entity or 'Great Mind';
- that there is a 'World Soul' or shared memory in nature;
- that the Great Mind can be evoked by symbols, which Yeats introduced into poetry in order to access truths.

He learnt a great deal about symbolism from Shelley and Blake. Symbols reveal themselves in a state of trance. He felt that the purpose of rhythm in poetry is to create meditative rhythms in which the mind is lulled into a state of trance. So, when poetry is working well it operates like a mantra or chant, helping us to see past the ordinary. Yeats believed that 'simple' people (those who were considered fools), ascetics and women can see beyond modern culture into the world of magical truths.

Yeats also believed that Celticism was the remnant of a former world religion, that the occult is really the remnant of this old religion or magic, and that Ireland is the place where it can best be contacted. So Celticism and the occult are important and connected twin pillars of his poetic philosophy.

During the 1890s Yeats's poetry developed from simple pastoral poetry and verses about fairy tales to the use of cycles of mythology of Ulster and the Fianna. He introduced heroes from these tales into his poetry: Cú Chulainn, Méabh, Deirdre and others. He began to use the Celtic material in a visionary way to create mystical poetry, which culminated in the volume *The Wind Among the Reeds* (1899).

Women were important in Yeats's life, and he had a number of troublesome and tempestuous love affairs. Of all the women he encountered two were to be most influential: Maud Gonne and Lady Augusta Gregory. The former, whom he met in the late 1880s, was the source of passionate romantic involvement and disappointment for him over the succeeding three decades; but she was also the inspiration for some of his work, such as the play *The Countess Kathleen,* was a frequent reference point in his poetry, and was the focus for some of his ideas on nationalism, women in politics, the aesthetic, ageing and others.

He first met Lady Gregory in 1894, and from 1897 onwards her home, Coole Park, near Gort, Co. Galway, was a summer refuge from his somewhat nomadic life. As well as helping him collect folk tales she provided both psychological and financial support and the opportunity to meet other writers, such as George Russell, George Bernard Shaw, George Moore and Edward Martyn.

Lady Gregory, Yeats and Martyn were the principal co-founders of the Irish Literary Theatre. Their manifesto clearly outlines the driving philosophy and ambition of the movement.

> We propose to have performed in Dublin in the spring of every year certain Celtic and Irish plays, which whatever be their degree of excellence will be written with a high ambition, and so to build up a Celtic and Irish school of dramatic literature. We hope to find in Ireland an uncorrupted and imaginative audience trained to listen by its passion for oratory, and believe that our desire to bring upon the stage the deeper thoughts and emotions of Ireland will ensure for us a tolerant welcome, and that freedom to experiment which is not found in the theatres of England, and without which no new movement in art or literature can succeed. We will show that Ireland is not the home of buffoonery and of easy sentiment, as it has been represented, but the home of an ancient idealism. We are confident of the support of all Irish people, who are weary of misrepresentation, in carrying out a work that is outside all the political questions that divide us.

Eventually this movement led to the founding of the Abbey Theatre, Dublin, in 1904, where Yeats was manager from 1904 to 1910. But the public did not always appreciate the movement's artistic vision. There was adverse reaction to Yeats's play *The Countess Kathleen*; and in 1907 John Millington Synge's play *The Playboy of the Western World* sparked off riots in the theatre. Yeats was deeply disillusioned by this lack of understanding and aesthetic appreciation, a feeling that was deepened by the controversy over the Hugh Lane proposal. This disillusionment is reflected in his poetry *The Green Helmet* (1910), *Responsibilities* (1914) and *The Wild Swans at Coole* (1917). In contrast, his visit to Italy in 1907 with Lady Gregory and her son, Robert, pointed up the difference between the mob in Ireland and what it had been possible to create through aristocratic patronage in Florence and Ravenna.

The Easter Rising of 1916 forced Yeats to rethink his view of Irish society, as we see in the poem 'Easter 1916'. These years ushered in other decisive changes for Yeats. After a final round of marriage proposals to Maud Gonne and then to her adopted daughter, Iseult, he settled into marriage with Georgina Hyde-Lees on 20 October 1917. The marriage produced two children and much-needed domestic stability for Yeats. And, whether by chance or design, it also produced the 'automatic writing' created by his wife, who, while in a sort of trance, transcribed the words of certain spirit guides or instructors. This seemed to offer a new system of thought to Yeats, incorporating themes of change within a new view of history, which he developed in his book *A Vision* (1925).

The central idea of his philosophy was that civilisation was about to reverse itself and a new era of anti-civilisation was about to be ushered in. The signs of this were everywhere: in mass movements in Europe, in the rise of communism, fascism, etc. Yeats examined change against the backdrop of world history. In his review of history he noticed that certain eras favoured the development of human excellence in art and learning and also produced social harmony: Athens of the fifth century BC, Byzantium, the Italian Renaissance – all of which developed political culture and artistic culture and in general fostered human achievement, creating what Yeats termed 'unity of being'. These eras were separated by a thousand years, each reaching its peak about five hundred years after it replaced the previous 'millennium'. There were two main forces at work: what Yeats called 'anti-thetical' energies, which created this unity of being, and the opposite force, which he termed 'primary' energy. These two energies grew or waned in their turn over the course of each millennium.

Yeats represented this theory of change by the symbolism of the 'gyres', two interpenetrating cones (see page 65), one primary and the other anti-thetical, each growing or decreasing in strength as the centuries pass. He felt that his own time was now reaching the end of the primary gyre and that the growing violence on the Continent and in Ireland was an indicator of its imminent collapse, to be replaced by a new anti-thetical gyre. This is the philosophical background to the bleak view he took of the current fractious age in the volumes *Michael Robartes and the Dancer* (1921) and, in particular, *The Tower* (1928). See in particular his poems 'The Second Coming', 'Sailing to Byzantium' and 'Meditations in Time of Civil War'.

This philosophy, which had as its central belief the notion that the times were out of joint and that cataclysmic changes were about to happen, may help to explain Yeats's flirtation with extreme political philosophies and movements: for example, his consideration of fascism, his exploration of the place of violence in politics, his scepticism about democracy and his preference for the political model of Renaissance prince–ruler (a model that cast the Anglo-Irish gentry in a similar role), and his engagement with theories of eugenics.

This search for solutions, for paradigms of thought and models for living, continued into the poet's old age, but it took more conventional forms in his volume *The Winding Stair and Other Poems* (1933). Here we find many elegies – to dead friends, to past times and to other more unified eras, such as the eighteenth century, from which Yeats took his chief model, Jonathan Swift, whom he wished to emulate as poet–statesman.

Indeed, he was pursuing that ideal in his role as a senator in the new Irish Free State. He devoted much energy to his work in the new senate, which first sat on 11 December 1922 and of which he was a member until 1928. During 1923, for instance, he spoke nineteen times on such subjects as law enforcement, manuscripts, the Lane pictures, film censorship and Irish, and he continued over the years to contribute on issues such as partition, divorce and the new coinage. In 1922 the University of Dublin conferred an honorary doctorate on him, and he was similarly honoured by the Universities of Oxford and Cambridge in 1931 and 1933, respectively. But the crowning international recognition was the award of the Nobel Prize for Literature in 1923.

In the late 1920s and early 1930s Yeats experienced a number of health problems, and the family began to spend more time in the sunnier regions of southern Europe. The house at 82 Merrion Square, Dublin, was sold and exchanged for a flat in Fitzwilliam Square. In 1933 Yeats took himself out of the city altogether when the family took a long lease on a house, 'Riversdale', in Rathfarnham, 'just too far from Dublin to go there without good reason and too far, I hope, for most interviewers and the less determined travelling bores'. (See 'An Acre of Grass'.) But he continued to write, indeed with renewed vigour, and *New Poems* was published in 1938. His last public appearance was at the Abbey Theatre in August 1938. He died on 28 January 1939 at Roquebrune in the south of France; in 1948 his body was re-interred, as he had wished, in Drumcliff churchyard.

PRINCIPAL VOLUMES OF POETRY	Poems in this selection
The Wanderings of Oisín (1889)	
Crossways (1889)	
The Rose (1893)	– 'The Lake Isle of Innisfree'
The Wind Among the Reeds (1899)	
The Green Helmet and Other Poems (1910)	
Responsibilities (1914)	– 'September 1913'
The Wild Swans at Coole (1917; second edition 1919)	– 'The Wild Swans at Coole'
	– 'An Irish Airman Foresees His Death'
Michael Robartes and the Dancer (1921)	– 'Easter 1916'
	– 'The Second Coming'
The Tower (1928)	– 'Sailing to Byzantium'
	– 'Meditations in Time of Civil War'
The Winding Stair and Other Poems (1933)	– 'In Memory of Eva Gore-Booth and Con Markiewicz'
	– 'Swift's Epitaph'
A Full Moon in March (1935)	
New Poems (1938)	– 'An Acre of Grass'
Last Poems (1939)	– 'Under Ben Bulben'
	– 'Politics'

The Lake Isle of Innisfree

Text of poem: New Explorations Anthology page 49

[*Note: This poem is also prescribed for Ordinary Level 2010 exam*]

This poem was written in 1888, when Yeats was living in London, where he was unhappy and homesick for Ireland. A somewhat altered version was first published in the *National Observer* in December 1890, to much acclaim; this really was the poem that first made Yeats's name. It is included in the collection *The Rose* (1893).

Yeats had been greatly influenced by the vision of self-sufficiency in nature found in Henry David Thoreau's book *Walden* (1854), which his father had read to him. And he too dreamed of living alone in nature in a quest for wisdom. This was a theme he explored not just in verse but in his prose writings also, an indication of the pervasive autobiographical nature of the quest. For instance, there are close similarities between this poem and the scenario in *John Sherman*, a novel Yeats had written in 1887–88, in which a young Sligo man who had left home in search of a fortune and was now homesick in London recalls an island on a lake where he used to pick blackberries. He dreams of returning there, building a wooden hut, and listening to the ripple of the water.

YEATS'S VISION AND QUEST

The vision of self-sufficiency in nature obviously pervades this whole poem. However unlikely a scene, it shows the poet as rustic woodsman and gardener, writing in the first person, actually planning to build a simple, crude dwelling and attempting agricultural self-sufficiency. 'Clay and wattles' were the traditional rural building materials for centuries past. The hive and the bees suggest the simple sweetness and richness of life, as well as providing a natural musical ambience. Altogether the vision is one of idyllic rural primitiveness, with a hint of the hermit's ascetic: a life 'alone in the bee-loud glade'.

This is a romantic view of the human being in perfect harmony with nature, at one with its sights and sounds. It is an alluring picture, sensual even, where the feminised morning is draped in veils. But there is also a strange, slightly unreal quality about it. The light is different: noon is a 'purple glow'. The archaic language in the expression of 'midnight's all a glimmer' reinforces the strange, even magical nature of the atmosphere. For representative sounds Yeats chooses the simple, rhythmic, calming sound of lake water lapping and also the repetitive rustic sounds of the cricket on the hearth, a common feature of rural stories and tales. Co. Sligo is one of the few places in the country that provides an all-year-round habitat for the linnet, a small unspectacular bird that likes rough hillsides and uncultivated lands near the sea. With accurate recall, Yeats is celebrating the indigenous wildlife of the area. His vision of happiness is a romantic one – a simple, unsophisticated lifestyle in an unspoilt habitat, surrounded by the sights and music of nature. It is a picture full of the rich textures of colour, sound and movement, in total contrast to his present environment, that of the cold, colourless and lifeless 'pavements grey'. So in one sense the poem can be read as an expression of Yeats's romanticised and nostalgic yearning for his native countryside.

But it is also more than this. For it is no frivolous weekend in the woods that he is planning: it is rather a quest for wisdom, for deep, eternal truths – an attempt to see into the heart of things. This is the sentiment that comes across in the first line. The sound of water, one of the essential elements and a life force, haunts him and seems to suggest that only in nature will he find the truths of the heart. The ambiguity about whose heart is in question here further strengthens the connection between the poet's heart and the heart of the earth. This is a move he feels compelled to make, a compulsion. We can sense the strength of his resolve in the verbs 'I will arise' and 'I shall have'. But the biblical allusions underlying this expose even more complex layers of compulsion. The repeated 'I will arise' echoes the words of the Prodigal Son, who has wasted his inheritance, led a profligate few years in exile, and finally resolves to go home: 'I will arise and go to my father.' So the words of the poem carry great unhappiness, a sense of failure and loss, the loneliness of exile and separation and perhaps even a feeling of guilt or remorse. The phrase 'always night and day' could also be a Biblical allusion. St Mark's gospel (5:5) refers to a man possessed by an evil spirit who was freed from his torment by Christ: 'Night and day among the tombs and on the mountains he was always crying out and bruising himself with stones.' This allusion, if intended, hints at a somewhat manic compulsion and mental and spiritual turmoil, or at the very least a great discontent.

THE MUSIC OF THE VERSE

The poet's feelings of unease and discontent and of being driven to take this course of action are hidden by the musical quality of the verse. Apart from the obvious repetitions of the end rhymes in alternate lines, there are subtle musical vowel repetitions throughout the poem. For example, there is a profusion of long 'i' sounds in the first stanza ('I', 'arise', 'Nine', 'I', 'hive') and a repetition of long 'o' and 'a' sounds in the final stanza ('go', 'low', 'shore', 'roadway', 'core' and 'day', 'lake', 'pavements', 'grey'). The repetition, particularly of long broad vowels, gives this a languidness and soporific calmness that belies the tension at the heart of it.

ISSUES

Among the issues that preoccupy the poet here we might emphasise:

- the yearning for self-sufficiency in natural surroundings
- the search for truth, wisdom and peace
- the poet's discontent, which impels him on this quest.

September 1913

Text of poem: New Explorations Anthology page 51

This poem was written in September 1913 and was first published on 8 September in the *Irish Times,* where it was entitled 'Romance in Ireland (on reading much of the correspondence against the Art Gallery)'. It was included in the volume *Responsibilities* (1914) under its present title.

YEATS AND POLITICS: SOME OF HIS VIEWS ON SOCIETY

At one level of reading this is just a political poem – an angry poetical response to a particular event in which Yeats was passionately involved. Sir Hugh Lane, a wealthy art collector (and Lady Gregory's nephew), had presented to the city of Dublin a unique collection of modern paintings, with the proviso that the city build a suitable gallery to house them. There were various suggestions for building a gallery, such as one on a bridge over the River Liffey; but the entire project became entangled in increasingly bitter public disputes about the location, the architecture, and particularly the cost. Yeats was furious about what seemed a mean-spirited, penny-pinching and anti-cultural response to Lane's generous offer. The opponents of the project drew attention to the poverty and slum living conditions that many Dubliners endured at the time and accused the proponents of the gallery of putting art before bread and also of an elitist arrogance typical of the Ascendancy class. The controversy developed strong overtones of class conflict and set Yeats thinking about the recent changes in Irish society.

The make-up of society, the need for particular kinds of people in a cultured society, and the responsibilities of particular classes – these were issues that had long preoccupied Yeats. In 1907, on the death of the old Fenian John O'Leary, Yeats wrote an essay entitled 'Poetry and tradition', in which he talks about the ideals that he and O'Leary had discussed and shared. Though the primary emphasis in the essay is on poetry and culture, the views reflect Yeats's notions of the ideal society.

> Three types of men have made all beautiful things. Aristocracies have made beautiful manners, because their place in the world puts them above the fear of life, and the countrymen have made beautiful stories and beliefs, because they have nothing to lose and so do not fear, and

the artists have made all the rest, because Providence has filled them with recklessness. All these look backward to a long tradition, for, being without fear, they have held to whatever pleases them.

So for Yeats, the really important constituents of society were the aristocracy, country people and artists. It should not surprise us that Yeats was bitterly disillusioned with the changes in society that were proceeding apace from the end of the nineteenth century and into the twentieth: changes in land ownership hastened the demise of the aristocracy; a new upper and lower middle class emerged. Yeats saw only a new Ireland of small shopkeepers, clerks and traders; and it is at this section of the new society that he directs his wrath in the poem.

In the main he makes two accusations. Firstly, their only preoccupations are making money and practising religion, as he ironically says:

> For men were born to pray and save.

They are a money-grubbing and fearful people, tyrannised by their religion. And Yeats is revolted by this combination of materialism and religious serfdom; it is the antithesis of his Renaissance model of a cultured society, where art and literature are valued. Secondly, these small-minded, self-regarding, blinkered people are incapable of understanding the generosity of spirit and the self-sacrifice that motivated the patriots of old. Lines 25–30 can be read in this way. The selfless patriotism of the heroes of past time would now be misinterpreted by this unenlightened generation as love-crazed emotion merely to impress a woman.

> You'd cry, 'Some woman's yellow hair
> Has maddened every mother's son'

So the present generation and society are contrasted, most unfavourably, with previous generations.

It is worth exploring Yeats's notion of the heroic past and his view of the influential figures of romantic Ireland. They all were political rebels, risk takers who tried and failed gloriously to free Ireland. They all were men of action, soldiers who willingly gave liberty or life for the cause: 'They weighed so lightly what they gave.' They were hugely energetic, forceful characters:

> They have gone about the world like wind,
> But little time had they to pray.

In particular, Yeats seems to admire their extraordinary selflessness and courage, their almost manic bravery: 'All that delirium of the brave'.

Yeats's thinking accommodated two sometimes conflicting notions of the heroic: the hero as representative leader of a people, and the hero as a solitary figure, often even in opposition to the people. There are elements of both notions here. There are some hints of their popular influence ('the names that stilled your childish play') and perhaps also in their willing sacrifice ('all that blood was shed'). But the overwhelming impression is that of the solitary figure, apart, different: 'they were of a different kind'; 'the wild geese spread | The grey wing upon every tide'; 'those exiles as they were | In all their loneliness and pain.' And it is this difference that gives them status in the poem. And, by implication, the present generation lack their qualities of nobility, courage, selflessness, and self-sacrifice for an ideal.

Tone

This poem is built on contrast – an extreme, somewhat simplistic contrast between a present and a past generation, or what Yeats sees as representative figures from these generations. The heroic past he idolises in tones of reverence and awe. There is a suggestion of their strange power in 'the names that stilled your childish play' and in the reference to their going 'about the world like wind'. He empathises with their loneliness and pain and inevitable fate:

> But little time had they to pray
> For whom the hangman's rope was spun,
> And what, God help us, could they save?

His undoubted admiration for their selfless courage is carried in 'They weighed so lightly what they gave' and in that 'delirium of the brave'.

In contrast, the new middle class is lampooned in the caricature of the shopkeeper as a kind of sub-human creature, fumbling, shivering, and certainly not capable of understanding more noble motives. The tone of savage mockery is often achieved by the use of irony – for example the perverse irony of 'What need you, being come to sense' – or the ironic statement of philosophy, 'For men were born to pray and save.' The bitter contempt is hammered home through the repetition of 'For this . . . for this . . . for this.' The sneer of disdain rings through these lines.

Altogether this is a poem exhibiting passionate but contrasting emotions.

Some themes and issues
- Bitter disillusion with recent social changes
- Contempt for the perceived materialism and religious serfdom of the new middle class of business people

- Concerns for the well-being of a cultured society; concern for its lack of altruistic principles and generosity of spirit
- A particular view of Irish history as a history of courageous failure in the struggle for independence
- A nostalgic, romanticised view of Irish history
- Thoughts on patriotism and the notion of the heroic.

The Wild Swans at Coole

Text of poem: New Explorations Anthology page 54
[*Note: This poem is also prescribed for Ordinary Level 2010 exam*]

The poem was written in 1916 and first published in the *Little Review* in 1917, and it is the title poem of the volume *The Wild Swans at Coole* (1917).

This poem is structured as a retrospection by Yeats as he records how his life has changed since he first stayed at Coole Park during the summer and autumn of 1897 ('the nineteenth autumn'). It is important to be aware that this is an artistic construction, because in reality his state of mind had changed very little. Though he chooses to say that he was more carefree ('trod with a lighter tread') at that earlier period, probably for aesthetic purposes and to set up a contrast, in fact he had been in a state of mental and nervous exhaustion during that visit in 1897. His love affair with Diana Vernon had just ended. He was 'tortured with sexual desire and disappointed love', and, as his diaries reveal, 'It would have been a relief to have screamed aloud.'

In the summer of 1916, the year the poem was written, Yeats went to France to Maud Gonne, the great, omnipresent, passionate love of his life for the previous quarter of a century. Her husband, Major John MacBride, had been shot for his part in the Easter Rising. She was working as a volunteer nurse with the war wounded, and Yeats once again proposed marriage to her. On her refusing for the last time he contemplated the possibility of marriage with her adopted daughter, Iseult. Possibly it was this turmoil and the disparity in their ages that set him thinking of time, age and immortality, the death of love or the possibility of its being eternal. But this is one instance where a biographical approach does not help very much, as the poet orders and alters events and ideals to suit an artistic construction rather than any actual reality.

When Iseult finally refused him in 1917 he married Georgina Hyde-Lees and bought a tower-house, Thoor Ballylee, not far from Coole in Co. Galway.

THEMES AND ISSUES

This poem, as Yeats's literary biographer Terence Brown says, 'sets a mood of autumnal introspection'. In a certain sense it is quite a personal poem, in which Yeats, at fifty-one, unmarried and alone despite many passionate love affairs, takes stock of his emotional situation. Primarily he laments the loss of youth, passion and love. He regrets the loss of his carefree youth, 'trod with a lighter tread', however inaccurate this nostalgia is. Now his 'heart is sore'; he is a man broken-hearted, discontented, emotionally unsatisfied. He no longer has what the swans appear to have – youthful passion.

> Unwearied still, lover by lover . . .
> Passion or conquest . . .
> Attend upon them still.

And he has not got unchanging or constant love, while 'their hearts have not grown old'. Above all else, the poet seems to resent the loss of passionate love in his life; we cannot mistake this yearning in the many references to hearts, lovers, passion and conquests.

The loss of love is just one aspect of Yeats's general sense of regret here, which concerns ageing and the passage of time. Indeed he seems to have been ambushed by time – the nineteenth autumn 'has come upon me' – and is forced to accept that 'all's changed'. His awareness of this and his resentment are accentuated by the seeming immortality of the swans: 'Their hearts have not grown old'. By implication we sense the poet's yearning for changelessness, for immortality.

Yet another kind of loss is hinted at here: the possible loss or diminution of the poetic gift, insight or vision. Perhaps that is what he fears at the end of the poem, in that final plaintive image: that the poetic sight or vision will have deserted him and passed to others. For him, the swans are in some way a manifestation of his poetic vision. So we can see that he explores

- the personal loss of youth, passion, and love
- the consequences of ageing
- the passage of time and the yearning for changelessness and immortality
- the loss of poetic power and vision – the sense of failure.

IMAGERY AND SYMBOLISM

The entire poem is structured around the swans, real and symbolic, which have particular significance because they appear to have defied time for the past nineteen years. They give the illusion of immortality: 'Unwearied still . . . Passion or conquest . . . attend upon them still.' Our rational mind tells us that of course they may not be exactly the same swans; but the poet glosses over and even builds further on this poetic illusion. He concentrates our attention on the patterns they establish, patterns that will survive even though they may die. These 'great broken rings', the spiral imagery they create, are similar to the 'gyres' or cones of time (see pages 65–6) that Yeats saw as the cyclical pattern behind all things, time and eternity. So there is a hint of the eternal about the spiral imagery the swans establish. Also, they link the water to the sky, link earth and heaven; and so in a way they are both mortal and immortal. The swans provide an exciting, vibrant, multi-layered symbolism, but they are also hauntingly and accurately described as real creatures. The real power and energy of the movement is evoked by the breathless enjambment of the lines and by the use of sinuous and muscular verbs and adverbs:

> All suddenly mount
> And scatter wheeling in great broken rings
> Upon their clamorous wings.

The swan imagery carries great resonances and symbolic value in the poem; but there are other images also that add to the richness of texture. The 'woodland paths' can be either the straight paths of the intellect or the winding paths of intuition. Whatever symbolic weight they carry they are dry here, in keeping with the themes – lack of passion and creativity. The trees, a great symbol of permanence for Yeats, are in the ageing cycle of their lives, as is the poet.

Three of the four symbolic elements are used in the poem: earth, air and water. Only fire is not used, indeed is conspicuously absent. The suggestion is that this is more than just a poem, that it carries elements of magical divination. Even the musical image 'The bell-beat of their wings above my head' reinforces this sense of the magical. And of course Yeats believed in and practised magic. Our sense of this is strengthened further by an exploration of the degree of patterning in the poem. Notice how the swans on the lake take to the air and finish by drifting on the still water again – creating a perfect round or circular pattern. Consider the pattern of antitheses in the poem – between the swans and the speaker and between the poet now and the poet nineteen years ago. And, as the critic Donald Stauffer points out, the essential pattern is a contrast of moods, something experienced only by humans. The essential contrast in the poem is that between transient humanity and eternity.

All in all, there is a richness of imagery and symbolism here that can be enjoyed and appreciated at many levels.

STRUCTURE

There is a gradual opening out of both the voice and the vista as this poem progresses. Stanza 1 just paints the picture, unemotionally and accurately, as any ornithologist or naturalist might do. From this very anchored and particular opening we go to the poet's personal reminiscences in the second and third stanzas, before moving on to more generalised speculative philosophising in the fourth stanza. The final stanza opens up unanswerable questions, speculating on the future, leaving us with the possibility of a completely empty final scene, a blank canvas. The future is as unclear and ungraspable as that final question – incidentally the only question in the poem.

The poem goes from the particular to the general and then to the entirely speculative. Beneath the tranquillity of the imagery, the languidness of language and the sounds of the words, the ideas of the poem are tightly linked and structured. Notice how images or ideas are picked up from one stanza to the next, and so the stanzas are chain-linked.

The first stanza ends with the enumeration of 'nine-and-fifty swans', and the second stanza takes up the count.

> The nineteenth autumn has come upon me
> Since I first made my count;

Stanzas 2 and 3 are linked by the poet's looking: 'I saw . . . I have looked'. At the end of stanza 3 he remembers or fancies his carefree 'lighter treat' of nineteen years earlier. Stanza 4 opens with the still 'unwearied' creatures.

The fifth stanza picks up phonetically on the word 'still', and, though semantically different, it provides a phonic linkage. There is of course the imagery link also, where swans 'paddling in the cold | Companionable streams' of the fourth stanza are picked up in the fifth stanza as they 'drift on the still water'.

An Irish Airman Foresees his Death

Text of poem: New Explorations Anthology page 57

[Note: *This poem is also prescribed for Ordinary Level 2010 exam*]

This poem was one of a number written by the poet for Robert Gregory, Lady Gregory's son, including 'Shepherd and Goatherd' and 'In Memory of Major Robert Gregory'. Yeats saw Gregory as an educated aristocrat and all-round Renaissance man ('Soldier, scholar, horseman, he'). He was also an energetic boxer and hunter and a painter who designed sets for Yeats's own plays. The poem was written in 1918 and first published in the second edition of *The Wild Swans at Coole* (1919).

CRITICAL COMMENTARY

At one obvious level of reading, this is a type of elegy in memory of the dead man. But it is a variation on the form, in that it is structured as a monologue by the dead man rather than the more usual direct lament by a poet, praising the person's good qualities and showing how he is much missed, and so on.

It makes an interesting contribution to war poetry in its attempt to chart the motivation and psychological state of the volunteer. What strikes one immediately is not just the fatalism – he knows his death is imminent – but the bleakness of his outlook on life, his disenchantment with living, despite his privileged background.

> The years to come seemed waste of breath,
> A waste of breath the years behind . . .

In contrast, the war seemed an adventure, an 'impulse of delight', a 'tumult in the clouds'. The poem captures well the excitement and exhilaration felt by many a volunteer. As Ulick O'Connor put it (in *The Yeats Companion*, 1990), 'There can seldom have been a better summing up of the sense of elation which the freedom to roam the uncharted skies brought to the young men of Gregory's pre-1914 generation.'

Yet the decision to volunteer was not a heady, emotional one. The poem stresses the thought and calculation brought to the decision. The concept of balance is repeatedly stressed:

> I balanced all, brought all to mind . . .
> In balance with this life, this death.

He was not carried away by the emotion of enlistment meetings ('Nor public men, nor cheering crowds'). He was not moved by any sense of 'duty' or 'patriotism'; neither was there conscription in Ireland ('Nor law, nor duty bade me fight'). These 'nor – nor' negatives of the rejected motives are balanced against the excitement of action. The general picture is of a young man who has chosen, after careful consideration, this path of action, almost indeed chosen his death.

This heavy sense of fatalism is most obvious in the opening lines. But there is never a sense in which this fatalism is merely weak surrender or opting out. He accepts his fate, he goes consenting to his death, but more like one of Homer's heroes. Yeats gives Gregory Homeric stature by allowing him to choose a heroic death; and this gives meaning to an otherwise meaningless conflict. The airman feels none of the great passions of war, neither patriotic love nor hatred of the foe:

> Those that I fight I do not hate,
> Those that I guard I do not love;

Further, he does not think the war will make a whit of difference to his own countrymen:

> No likely end could bring them loss
> Or leave them happier than before.

But it is the self-sacrificing death, 'this death' freely chosen, that raises the young man above the events of his time and confers particular significance on him. The awareness of impending death also brings this moment of insight, this clearness of vision that allowed him to evaluate his past life and contemplate a possible future as a country landowner – all of which he rejects for the 'tumult' of action.

So, as a war poem, this is an interesting, personal, even intimate approach, charting the thoughts and motivation of this young man. But it has a more general aspect also. Gregory may be seen as representative of all those young men of talent who were cheated of their promise by the slaughter of the First World War.

We have already mentioned that Yeats saw Gregory as the all-round Renaissance man – in other words, an educated man and person of culture as well as a man of action. Yeats had felt that the 'lonely impulse of delight' was what differentiated the artist from others, that the artistic impulse was essentially lonely and solitary. Here we see this artistic impulse motivating a man of action, who is essentially instinctive rather than intellectual. Yeats felt that the impulse was sometimes hampered in the artist, who often thought too much. So the later Yeats began to champion the non-intellectual hero and the instinctive man; the sportsman and the adventurer are given the status of mythic figures. The airman Gregory is essentially a solitary figure, like other mythic figures created by Yeats, such as the 'Fisherman'.

Some critics read this poem as a classic statement of Anglo-Irishness as Yeats saw it. In later life Yeats used to talk about the 'Anglo-Irish solitude'. Is there a sense here of not quite fully belonging to either side, of being neither fully committed English nor unreservedly Irish? There is certainly a sense of emotional distance on the part of the subject, both from those he guards and those he fights. Though he has an affinity with Kiltartan's poor ('my countrymen'), he is aware that the war and his involvement in it will have no impact on their lives. In general, the feeling one gets is of some detachment from the events in which he participates, and this could be read as a metaphor for 'Anglo-Irish solitude'.

Easter 1916

Text of poem: New Explorations Anthology page 60

On Monday 24 April 1916 a force of about seven hundred members of the Irish Volunteers and the Irish Citizen Army took over the centre of Dublin in a military revolution and held out for six days against the British army.

At first the rising did not receive widespread support; but the British military authorities regarded it as high treason in time of war, and the subsequent systematic executions of fifteen of the leaders between 3 and 12 May brought a wave of public sympathy and created heroes and martyrs for the republican cause.

Though Yeats's poem was finished by September 1916 and a number of copies had been printed privately, it was not published until October 1920, when it appeared in the *New Statesman*. It is included in the volume *Michael Robartes and the Dancer* (1921).

THE NATIONAL QUESTION: YEATS'S POLITICAL VIEWS

Yeats spent a good deal of his time in England during his early life, but he felt that the English understanding of the Irish was stereotypical and condescending. One of his main ambitions was to help change Ireland's view of itself through a revival of its unique cultural identity. He had denounced the English government of Ireland, and his refusal of a knighthood in 1915 is a statement of his political stance. Yet his view did not prevent him living there, and indeed he was in England when the Easter Rising took place.

This ambiguity was further complicated by Yeats's arrogant and scathing dismissal of the current generation of Irish people as ignoble, self-focused, materialistic and priest-controlled, who were totally incapable of the idealism or courage necessary for heroic leadership and personal sacrifice. These views he had expressed very trenchantly in 'September 1913'.

The Rising took Yeats by surprise and blew some serious holes in his thinking. Firstly, he now had to rethink his public stance and views on the new Irish middle class. These people had been prepared to give their lives for an ideal. Yeats had been quite wrong. Secondly, though he was disgusted, like most people, at the savagery of the executions, he began to realise that the establishment's brutality had created martyrs, had transformed ordinary men into patriots with a strange new unchallengeable power. Perhaps Pearse's idea of a blood sacrifice was correct. Yeats had to rethink the place and value of revolutionary determination. So Yeats had to work out how this cataclysmic change had occurred in Irish society – 'all changed, changed utterly'.

A READING OF THE POEM

Though it may not appear on the surface to be a questioning poem, this work is really an attempt to answer or clarify a great number of questions that the 1916 Rising stirred up in Yeats's mind, an attempt to come to terms with:

- how everything had changed
- how wrong he had been
- how ordinary people had been changed into heroes
- the deep structure of change in society, the mysterious process, a kind of fate that directed and powered change (Terence Brown puts it eloquently: 'It seeks to penetrate beneath the appearance of history to comprehend the mysteries

of destiny.')
- the place and functioning of revolutionary violence in the process
- the change in his own position: how to resolve his own complex and contradictory feelings towards this violent process.

The diplomatic difficulty of having to recant his views on Irish society Yeats faced honestly and generously in the first section of this poem. Technically he achieved this by structuring the poem as a *palinode* or recantation of his opinions in the earlier 'September 1913'. Re-creating the drab, unexciting milieu of pre-revolution evenings, the poet acknowledges his own blindness and failure to engage with these people in any depth:

> I have passed with a nod of the head
> Or polite meaningless words,
> Or have lingered a while and said
> Polite meaningless words,

He confesses to his own unpleasant, condescending mockery ('a mocking tale or a gibe . . .') and his belief that all the pre-1916 organising was mere comical posturing:

> Being certain that they and I
> But lived where motley is worn . . .

He includes himself ('they and I') in this attempt at identification.

He spends the second section looking again at these people that he knew, as he needs to understand how they have changed. They are still the flawed characters he remembers: Constance Markievicz wasted her time in misplaced volunteer work ('ignorant good-will') and became a shrill fanatic ('nights in argument . . . voice grew shrill'); MacBride he thought 'a drunken vainglorious lout' who 'had done most bitter wrong' to Maud Gonne and Iseult. These are very ordinary, fallible, flawed and unlikely heroes.

Furthermore, the impression Yeats perceives is not one of energetically active heroes, but rather the passive recipients of this mysterious change. MacDonagh 'might have won fame in the end'. MacBride 'has resigned his part | In the casual comedy'. This smacks of an unknown actor giving up his part in an inconsequential work. The impression given is of relatively insignificant lives, out of which MacBride 'has been changed in his turn'. Note the passive voice: the change was effected on him, rather than by something he did, and it happened 'in his turn'. He waited his turn – perhaps a reference to the executions. Is Yeats saying that it was the executions that effected this change, transformed everyone utterly, and gave birth to this terrible beauty? That it was not due to the nature or any action of heroes?

Another aspect of these patriots that Yeats refers to is their feminine qualities. 'What voice more sweet' than Constance Gore-Booth's (in younger days)? MacDonagh's thought is 'daring and sweet'. Even MacBride has his passive side. So there is a sensitivity about these people that balances their more aggressive and masculine qualities, also referred to.

It is this softer, feminine quality in man and woman that is destroyed by fanaticism, something Yeats explores in the third and fourth sections. But first it is worth noticing the feminine aspect of the new order. This utter transformation of the social and historical reality is imagined as a new birth; but Yeats is so disturbed and confused by it that he can only describe it in paradoxical terms as a 'terrible beauty' – something that is partly feminine, aesthetically pleasing, sexually alluring even, but also carries suggestions of terror and of destructive power. This magnificent image carries all Yeats's confusions and contradictory feelings about the dramatic change.

In the third section he explores how change is effected. Only a stone, usually taken as a metaphor for the fanatical heart, can change or trouble the course of a stream, and it can achieve this only at a price. The heart will lose its humanness:

> Too long a sacrifice
> Can make a stone of the heart.

In the 1909 *Journals* Yeats had already written about the effects of political fanaticism on Maud Gonne, in metaphors akin to those used here:

> Women, because the main event of their lives has been a giving of themselves, give themselves to an opinion as if it were some terrible stone doll . . . They grow cruel, as if in defence of lover or child and all this is done for something other than human life. At last the opinion becomes so much a part of them that it is as though a part of their flesh becomes, as it were, stone, and much of their being passes out of life.

In this third section Yeats is exploring the dangers of fanatical devotion to a cause or ideal, and he represents this metaphorically as the conflicting forces between a stone and a stream.

The living stream is marvellously evoked. It is a picture of constant change, the flux of natural life and bursting with energy. The seasons are changing 'through summer and winter'; the skies change 'from cloud to tumbling cloud'; all is life and regeneration, as 'hens to moor-cocks call'. It is full of transient animal and human appearances, as they slide or plash or dive. And all this activity happens 'minute by minute'. Against this stream of ever-changing energy and life is set the unmoving stone, the fanatical heart. It is not difficult to conclude that the weight of the poet's sentiment is with the living stream rather than the unmoving stone. And yet out of this confrontation is born the 'terrible beauty'.

There is no easy answer to the conflicts posed by the poet. And indeed he seems to weary of the dialogue and of this dialectic in the fourth section. Having concluded that prolonged devotion to an ideal is dehumanising –

> Too long a sacrifice
> Can make a stone of the heart.

– he seems to accept the necessity of it and at the same time wishes for an end, in that sighing plea: 'O when may it suffice?'

The first seventeen lines of this fourth section are structured in questions – rhetorical questions, or questions that cannot be answered – thereby revealing the poet's uncertainties about the validity of the entire process of revolution and change. There is a kind of shocked vulnerability about the poetic voice here, a realisation of helplessness as all the doubts flood in with the questions: Are they really dead? Was it necessary if England intended to grant home rule after the war? What if they were just confused and bewildered by an excess of patriotism? There is an awareness that some things cannot be answered, that some of this mysterious dynamic of change cannot be understood – 'That is Heaven's part.' And the poet adopts a soothing mother's voice and persona, murmuring 'As a mother names her child'.

But then he seems to shake off the uncertain and shocked voice and finds a new assurance for that very definite, confident ending. Why is this? Terence Brown believes it has to do with the magical significance of the poem, deliberately created by Yeats. He suggests that the poem is a 'numerological artefact', based on the date when the rising began: 24 April 1916. There are four movements or sections, with the following numbers of lines in each: 16, 24, 16, 24. It is suggested also that Yeats intended this to be a verse of power, a magical recitation, seen in for example 'I number him in the song'; 'I write it out in a verse'. Certainly there is a surge of powerful assurance in those final lines, whether we read them as a litany of respectful remembrance or an occult incantation.

> I write it out in a verse –
> MacDonagh and MacBride
> And Connolly and Pearse
> Now and in time to be,

Wherever green is worn,
Are changed, changed utterly:
A terrible beauty is born.

The Second Coming

Text of poem: New Explorations Anthology page 66

This poem was finished in January 1919, to a background of great political upheaval in Europe: the disintegration of the Austro-Hungarian, German and Russian empires, and uprisings and revolution in Germany and Russia. The events in Europe are most likely to have prompted the speculation that 'mere anarchy is loosed upon the world'; but as the poem was not published for twenty-two months, in the *Dial* of November 1920, it came to be read as a reaction to the atrocities of the War of Independence in Ireland. It is included in the volume *Michael Robartes and the Dancer* (1921).

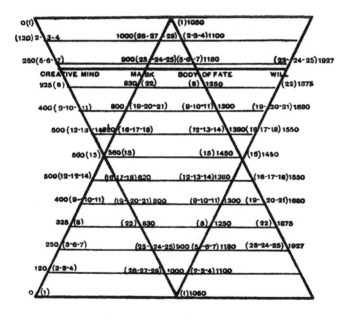

YEATS'S OCCULT PHILOSOPHY AND THEORIES OF HISTORY

Yeats was deeply interested in the patterns of history. He was also engaged in the study and practice of the occult and maintained regular contact with the spirits. These 'spirit communicators' helped him develop a cyclical theory of change in history, which is outlined in *A Vision* (1925). He used geometrical forms to express abstract ideas; and the concept of 'gyres' or cones representing time zones is one of these. In this poem the reference is to a single gyre or inverted cone. But the full representation of the gyres consists of two interpenetrating cones, expanding and contracting on a single axis. These represent the contrary forces, always changing, that determine the character of a person or the culture of a particular phase in history. There are particularly significant moments both for individuals and in historical time when the dominant influence passes from one gyre to its contrary. In history, he believed, this can happen every two thousand years. Hence the reference to 'twenty centuries of stony sleep' that preceded the Christian era, which is now waning and giving way to a new and antithetical era.

In its Christian interpretation, the 'Second Coming' refers to the prediction of the second coming of Christ; in Yeats's occult and magical philosophy it might also refer to the second birth of the Avatar or great antithetical spirit, which Yeats and his wife felt certain would be reincarnated as their baby son, whose birth was imminent. In fact the child turned out to be a girl, dashing that theory.

In this poem the hideous 'rough beast' that 'slouches towards Bethlehem to be born' is suggestive of the Anti-Christ, that legendary personal opponent of Christ and his kingdom expected to appear before the end of the world. See, for example, the Book of Revelations (chapter 13) on the portents for the end of the world:

> And I saw a beast rising out of the sea, with ten horns and seven heads, with ten diadems upon its horns and a blasphemous name upon its heads. And the beast that I saw was like a leopard, its feet were like a bear's, and its mouth was like a lion's mouth. And to it the dragon gave his power and his throne and great authority. One of its heads seemed to have a mortal wound, but its mortal wound was healed, and the whole earth followed the beast with wonder. Men worshipped the dragon, for he had given his authority to the beast, and they worshipped the beast, saying, 'Who is like the beast and who can fight against it?'

A READING OF THE POEM

This poem reflects Yeats's interest in historical change and his real fear that civilisation would break down and be replaced by an anti-civilisation or an era of anarchy. This was sparked off in part by his disgust and revulsion at what was happening in European politics and history around this time (1919). But, as we have seen, he was also preoccupied with patterns in history and immersed himself in the occult, with signs, portents, astrological charts and spirit communicators, and had developed a cyclical theory of change in history, which was represented graphically by the 'gyre' symbol.

So this poem deals with the turbulence of historical change; but what is particularly exciting is the enormous perspective that the poet takes. Time is not counted in years or decades but in millennia; and it is this vast perspective that is both exhilarating and terrifying.

First section

Essentially what is happening here is that Yeats is exploring the breakup of civilisation in metaphorical language. The falcon, that trained bird of prey, cannot hear the falconer and is reverting to its wild state. The falconer has also been interpreted as a representation of Christ, and so the image has been read as representing the movement of civilisation away from Christ. This dissipation is happening within the framework of its allotted time span, at a point within the gyre, representing the present. Yeats is bringing a critical philosophical viewpoint to bear on the social and political structures. He suggests that there is failure at the very heart of society, presumably in human beings themselves: 'Things fall apart; the centre cannot hold'. Instead of clear-sighted vision and forward progress there is this confusing circular movement, an out-of-control centrifugal force that threatens to send everything spinning away in disorder. In this chaos human beings are changing, becoming ignoble and destroying innocence: 'The ceremony of innocence is drowned.' People either have no convictions at all or are irrationally and passionately committed to causes; they have become either cynics or fanatics.

> The best lack all conviction, while the worst
> Are full of passionate intensity.

This first section embodies this very tension in its structure. Consider how the ideas are set up as opposites: centre – fall apart; falcon – falconer; indifference – intensity; innocence – anarchy. This polar oppositional tension is seen in the terrifying image of 'the blood-dimmed tide . . . loosed . . . innocence is drowned.' This sinister image has connotations of the great flood and its destruction of the world, but might also suggest a ruthless cleansing or purging. The repetition of 'loosed upon' and 'loosed' might suggest a savage wild animal, at the very least the 'dogs of war'. The circular imagery creates a sense of continuous swirling movement. Look at the repetition of -*ing*: 'turning, turning, widening'. There is a sense of a world out of control, of inevitable disaster.

Really it is the force of the imagery that carries the ideas in this section. Consider the falconry image. This was the pastime of kings and lords, so the image carries associations of an aristocratic life, civilised living, affluence. We know how much Yeats valued civilised living. Falconry was a 'noble' pastime, requiring skill and patience. Now this trained bird of prey is reverting to its wild state – a metaphor for the destruction of civilised living. It would also carry religious overtones and signal the breakdown of ordered religious systems. The falcon has also been interpreted as symbolic of the active or intellectual mind, so the breakdown of intellectual order might be signalled as well. Either way the image suggests dissolution in a number of different spheres and levels.

The second graphic image, of the 'blood-dimmed tide', has already been explored for its layers of suggestiveness. Its general impact is powerful, both visually and intellectually: innocence is drowned in a sea of blood. This is the ultimate nihilism, a world without justice, reason or order. Note Yeats's emphasis on the 'ceremony' of innocence. The rituals of civilised living will also be destroyed, of course.

The final image of the section, though somewhat ill defined, is a political one, suggesting that fanatical people have now got all the influence and are in power. The general impact of the imagery is one of frightening and irrational disorder and breakup in life and society.

Second section

Yeats begins by casting around for a reason for the breakdown of civilisation, and the possibility of a second coming together with the end of the world suggests itself as the only one great enough to cause this. 'Surely the Second Coming is at hand.' But it turns out not to be the Second Coming of Christ as foretold in the Gospels but rather the emergence of the Anti-Christ that Yeats imagines, an Anti-Christ who embodies the absolute reverse of the Christian era, which is now drawing to its end in the gyre of time. This rough beast, a nightmare symbol of the coming times, signals the end of this era, with its values and order.

Again, the image of this rough beast carries all the ideas about the new era. It is a 'vast image', overwhelming and troubling. It is a horrific hybrid of human and animal – suggesting unnatural times, such as foretold in the Book of Revelations. Its blank gaze suggests no intelligent sight or understanding; indeed it is as 'pitiless as the sun', incapable of empathy or feeling. The qualities it conjures up are gracelessness and brutishness: 'moving its slow thighs . . . Slouches towards Bethlehem to be born'. The final paradox is explained by the fact that its era has already begun, overlapping with the demise of the Christian era, so it is moving into position to initiate the new age or be born. The paradox further emphasises the antithetical nature of the coming age: how totally contradictory or opposite it is. There is something blasphemously shocking in the idea of the beast being born at Bethlehem. The nugget of insight gained by the poet out of this horrific vision concerns the nature of time and changing eras. He realises that eras have come and gone before, and that the advent of the Christian era must have been as troubling to the previous age.

Now I know
That twenty centuries of stony sleep
Were vexed to nightmare by a rocking cradle.

Sailing to Byzantium

Text of poem: New Explorations Anthology page 68

This poem was written sometime in the autumn of 1926 and is the opening poem in the collection *The Tower* (1928).

A READING OF THE POEM

Writing for a radio programme in 1931, Yeats outlined some of the preoccupations of his poetry at that time, in particular the spiritual quest of 'Sailing to Byzantium':

> Now I am trying to write about the state of my soul, for it is right for an old man to make his soul [an expression meaning to prepare for death], and some of my thoughts upon that subject I have put into a poem called 'Sailing to Byzantium'. When Irishmen were illuminating the Book of Kells and making the jewelled crosiers of the National Museum, Byzantium was the centre of European civilisation and the source of its spiritual philosophy, so I symbolise the search for the spiritual life by a journey to that city.

So this poem is structured, as he says, in the shape of a journey – more of a quest, really – with a tightly argued personal commentary by the poet. The main theme surfaces immediately in the first stanza. With that strong, declamatory opening he renounces the world of the senses for that of the spirit and the intellect, the timeless.

> That is no country for old men. The young
> In one another's arms . . .

Notice the perspective ('that'): he has already departed and is looking back, not without a little nostalgic yearning for the sensuality of youth. The sensual imagery of lovers and the teeming rich life of trees and seas, the athletic vigour of the hyphenated words ('the salmon-falls, the mackerel-crowded seas') and the sensual '*f*' and '*s*' sounds of 'fish, flesh or fowl' – all used to describe the cycle of life in the flesh – would strongly suggest that he does not renounce it easily. Indeed this ambiguity is carried in the paradox of 'those dying generations', with its linking of death and regeneration.

The importance of the spirit is re-emphasised in the second stanza as the poet asserts that it is the soul that gives meaning to a person: 'An aged man is but a paltry thing . . . unless I Soul clap its hands and sing.' And art enriches the soul, teaches it to sing: 'studying I Monuments of its own magnificence,' i.e. works of art inspired by the spirit. Byzantium, as a centre of religion, philosophy and learning and also of a highly formalised art, is the ideal destination for the intellectual and spiritual person. In 'A Vision' (1925) Yeats wrote about the harmoniousness of life in fifth-century Byzantium: 'I think that in early Byzantium, maybe never before or since in recorded history, religious, aesthetic and practical life were one.' He had visited Ravenna in 1907 and when he composed the third stanza probably had in mind a mosaic on the wall of S. Apollinore Nuova showing martyrs being burnt in a fire.

Addressing these sages or martyrs directly in the third stanza, he entreats them to traverse history in the gyre of time, come to him and teach his soul to sing. He wants them to 'make' his soul, as he said, to purify it, separate it from emotions and desires and help it transcend the ageing physical body:

> Consume my heart away; sick with desire
> And fastened to a dying animal
> It knows not what it is . . .

These lines betray a seriously troubled state of mind. Central to the conflict is a dualist view of the human being as composed of two radically different and warring elements: body, and soul or spirit. Yeats values one element – the soul – imaged as singer and bird but is filled with self-disgust and loathing for his ageing body, imaged as a dying animal, not even dignified as human, that has entrapped the soul.

This confusion is evident even in the ambiguity of language here, in for example 'sick with desire'. Is he sick because of the desires of the flesh he cannot shake off, or does the desire refer to his spiritual aspiration, which continues to elude him? This acute existential conflict has led to a loss of spiritual identity: 'It knows not what it is'; hence his emotional entreaty to the sages to 'gather me I Into the artifice of eternity'.

It is worth exploring the richness of this ordinary language here. By using 'gather me' the poet is acknowledging how fragmented and scattered his condition is and how he needs both direction and comfort; it is as if he needs to be embraced, gathered in arms. Ironically, he wants to be gathered into the coherence and timelessness of art – 'the artifice of eternity'. It is through this transition that he will find immortality. But the language carries hints of ambiguity, even about this much-desired goal. 'Artifice' refers primarily to a work of art, but it can also mean 'artificiality'. Is this the first hint that this great quest might be flawed?

Still he begins the fourth stanza with great confidence that art holds the answer to the problem of mortality. 'Once out of nature' he will be transformed into the perfect work of art and so live on. The golden bird is ageless and incorruptible and will sing the song of the soul. The final irony, though, is that the song it sings is about the flux of time, 'what is past, or passing, or to come'. There is no perfect solution after all.

THEMES AND ISSUES

Discuss these and see if you can justify each from the evidence of the poem.

- Yeats in old age is attempting to develop his spiritual side. It is a poem about the values of the soul as against the world of the senses.
- It is an attempt to escape the harsh reality of old age and death through the immortality of spiritual things and of art.
- The view of the human being portrayed is that of a fractured, divided entity in an uncomfortable state of war between the spiritual and the physical.
- It is a meditation on the nature of art and its importance to humanity.
- It delivers fine insights into the nature of Byzantine imagination and culture.

STRUCTURE

As befits the theme of conflict, the ideas and images in this poem are developed in a series of *antinomies* or contrasts. In the very first line youth and age are set opposite each other: 'That is no country for old men . . .' While youth is imaged in those wonderful scenes of sensuous life in the first stanza, age is realised in the scarecrow image – 'a tattered coat upon a stick' – with all its suggestions of fake outward show, a grotesque parody of the human being and the sense of powerlessness and indignity. The body is imaged as a dying animal, while the soul is imaged as a priceless golden bird, singing.

The mortality of life is contrasted with the timelessness of art. The teeming sensuality of Ireland is set against the culture of Byzantium, with its religious ethos ('holy city'; 'God's holy fire'), its reputation for learning and philosophical thought ('O sages'), and its artistic achievement ('artifice'; 'a form as Grecian goldsmiths make | Of hammered gold and gold enamelling', etc.). These conflicts reflect the internal struggle, the yearnings and the reality within the poetic persona here.

Yet the struggle is smoothed over by the grace and elegance of the language used. There is a regular pattern of end-rhymes or sometimes half-rhymes, which gives the verses a musical ease. Yeats also uses a rhythmic phrasing, often grouping in lists of three, which has magical significance as well as producing a rhythmic rise and fall: 'fish, flesh, or fowl'; 'Whatever is begotten, born, and dies'; 'unless | Soul clap its hands and sing, and louder sing'; 'Of what is past, or passing, or to come'. We might also notice other rhetorical qualities, such as the strong, declamatory opening, the rhetorical plea to the sages, indeed the strong, confident, first-person voice of the poet all through. These sometimes belie the conflicts and uncertainties at the heart of the work.

The Stare's Nest By My Window
Text of poem: New Explorations Anthology page 72

FROM 'MEDITATIONS IN TIME OF CIVIL WAR'

'Meditations in Time of Civil War' is quite a lengthy poem, structured in seven sections. Apart from the first, composed in England in 1921, it was written in Ireland during the Civil War of 1922–23 and was first published in the *Dell* in January 1923. It is included in the volume *The Tower* (1928).

In the poem as a whole, Yeats explores aspects of the Anglo-Irish ascendancy tradition: its origins and heritage and his own sense of sharing in the values of that tradition, particularly those of continuity, culture and family line. Conflict too was a necessary element of that planter culture, and now he is brought face to face with the violence of the Civil War and must re-evaluate his own role in the continuing tradition of history.

Images of houses and building provide one of the unifying metaphors and themes throughout this poem. Yeats acknowledges the violence out of which the great Anglo-Irish culture was built:

> Some violent bitter man, some powerful man
> Called architect and artist in, that they,
> Bitter and violent men, might rear in stone
> The sweetness that all longed for night and day.

His own house in Co. Galway, Thoor Ballylee, was originally a defensive fifteenth-century tower. He acknowledges proudly that conflict is part of his tradition; he wishes that his descendants too will find 'befitting emblems of adversity'. So in section V, when a band of Irregulars calls to his door, he experiences a certain envy of the men of action. Perhaps it is the graphic details of that war in section VI that led to a reappraisal. The terrifying vision of the nightmarish destruction of civilisation in section VII throws him back to thinking on his own role as poet in his isolated tower.

Yeats wrote the following description of the genesis and context of section VI:

> I was in my Galway house during the first months of civil war, the
> railway bridges blown up and the roads blocked with stones and trees.

For the first week there were no newspapers, no reliable news, we did not know who had won nor who had lost, and even after newspapers came, one never knew what was happening on the other side of the hill or of the line of trees. Ford cars passed the house from time to time with coffins standing upon end between the seats, and sometimes at night we heard an explosion, and once by day saw the smoke made by the burning of a great neighbouring house. Men must have lived so through many tumultuous centuries. One felt an overmastering desire not to grow unhappy or embittered, not to lose all sense of the beauty of nature. A stare (our West of Ireland name for a starling) had built in a hole beside my window and I made these verses out of the feeling of the moment . . . [here he quoted from 'The bees build in the crevices' to 'Yet no clear fact to be discerned: come build in the empty house of the stare.'] . . . That is only the beginning but it runs on in the same mood. Presently a strange thing happened. I began to smell honey in places where honey could not be, at the end of a stone passage or at some windy turn of the road, and it came always with certain thoughts. When I got back to Dublin I was with angry people who argued over everything or were eager to know the exact facts: in the midst of the mood that makes realistic drama. (From *The Bounty of Sweden*)

A READING OF THE POEM

At one level, this poem is an attempt to balance the horrors of war with the healing sweetness and regenerative power of nature. As Yeats himself saw it, 'Men must have lived so through many tumultuous centuries. One felt an overmastering desire not to grow unhappy or embittered, not to lose all sense of the beauty of nature.' The brutality of war is graphically represented here:

> Last night they trundled down the road
> That dead young soldier in his blood . . .

The onomatopoeic sound of 'trundled' carries suggestions of some primitive war machine or evokes the tumbrels and savage excess of the French Revolution. There is none of the traditional respect for a dead enemy here, but rather the ferocity of civil war enmity in the indignity with which the dead solder was treated – 'trundled . . . in his blood'. The bees are evoked as an antidote to this savagery. They may symbolise patience and creative force, as opposed to the destructive forces round about. They bring sweetness, healing and the richness of life. These may also be a classical allusion to Pomphyry's bees, who visited the world to perform tasks for the gods. So the bees could be seen as a manifestation of the divine in the world. Whether they evoked for Yeats the simple beauty of nature or carried more complex connotations, his plea to them is a desperate, plaintive cry. That cry for healing and for natural regeneration of life echoes through that repeated refrain at the end of each stanza, culminating in the final direct personal address, 'O honey-bees'. There is honest emotion here.

But this is more than simply a reaction to a specific event. Taken in the context of the poem as a whole, we could read this section as a metaphor for Yeats's own life situation and that of his traditional class, the Anglo-Irish ascendancy. The tower-house, once a fortified planter house, used as a place of both safety and dominance, is now a place of 'loosening masonry'; the structures of that colonial past are crumbling. The Yeats' isolation in the tower during that particular fortnight is symptomatic of the isolation and uncertain future of the entire minority but once-powerful class.

> We are closed in, and the key is turned
> On our uncertainty.

This is not just physical imprisonment but a mental segregation, a way of viewing themselves as different, distinct and separate – a cultivated isolation. The key has been turned from the inside. The physical barriers of stone or wood accord with the mental barriers created by class and outlook, so that we are acutely aware of how introverted and cut off the poet is. Yet there is a hint in the first stanza that some sweetness can come with the ending of his self-isolation:

> My wall is loosening; honey-bees,
> Come build in the empty house of the stare,

Or is this just a vain hope?

In the final stanza he faces up to the illusions on which his philosophy is based and which are explored in the rest of the poem: that sweetness and beauty might grow out of bitter and violent conquest, that conflict and a life of adversity could be a glorious thing. These are the fantasies that sustain his class outlook and for which he now indicts himself. The consequence has not been beauty but self-brutalisation.

> The heart's grown brutal from the fare.

He strips away any delusions of superiority or righteousness as he admits that negative emotions are strongest.

> More substance in our enmities
> Than in our love.

It is as if the violence outside has forced him to confront the past violence of his own class, in an honest moment of shared guilt. This is a critical moment of bleak insight, yet one that he attempts to balance with the final plea: 'O honey-bees' – a plea for sweetness and healing at a time of pain, for order in a time of chaos.

IMAGERY

Images of houses and buildings dominate this poem; but they are either abandoned, like the house of stone, or destroyed by violence ('a house burned'), or are gradually crumbling away in time ('loosening masonry'; 'My wall is crumbling'). They are symbols of a way of life being destroyed; or else they are isolating and self-imprisoning:

> We are closed in, the key is turned
> On our uncertainty.

Any building done is for destructive and disorderly purpose: 'A barricade of stone or wood'. So the poet's plea, while romantic and positive in outlook, is rather pathetic in the context. Only the bees and birds may build where the once-powerful colonising class raised great edifices.

In Memory of Eva Gore-Booth and Con Markiewicz

Text of poem: New Explorations Anthology page 74

This poem was written in the autumn of 1927, was first published in 1929, and is included in *The Winding Stair and Other Poems* (1933). Constance Markievicz had died in August 1927, her sister Eva the previous year.

A READING OF THE POEM

This is one of Yeats's poems of age, the reverie of an old man addressing the now-dead companions of his youth: 'Dear shadows . . .' It is very much a retrospective piece, viewing life from the perspective of the end. Yeats avoids sentimentality, opting instead for retrospective judgments, assessing the significance of their lives. He felt that they had wasted their lives. Constance Markievicz's years of political agitation for socialist and republican ideals he dismisses as dragging out lonely years – 'Conspiring among the ignorant' – while Eva's social and women's suffrage work is merely 'some vague Utopia'.

To understand this harsh condemnation of what to us seem idealistic and committed lives we need to take the poet's value system into account. His view was that the Anglo-Irish ascendancy class, with its wealth and great houses, had a duty to set an example of gracious and cultured living; this was its value for society. As the critic Alasdair MacRae says, 'The graciousness of accustomed affluence, the unostentatiousness of inherited furnishings and family traditions, what he saw culminating in courtesy, appealed to Yeats and he considered Eva and Con along with Maud Gonne as betraying something precious and feminine.' Yeats's idea of beauty is linked to the feminine. The image of feminine beauty he creates here is exotic. The silk kimonos give a hint of eastern mysteriousness, while the comparison with a gazelle suggests both a natural elegance and a certain wild, unknowable quality. And the two sisters are a decorative part of the big-house scene, a house that is elegant, imposing, a symbol of Anglo-Irish achievement and cultured way of life. It is primarily this image and what it symbolised that Yeats is nostalgic for: it is not the people he missed in the first instance, but the house and the cultured dinner-table conversation!

> Many a time I think to seek
> One or the other out and speak
> Of that old Georgian mansion, mix
> Pictures of the mind, recall
> That table and the talk of youth . . .

Yeats's negative retrospective judgments are not so much the bitter rantings of an old man, but rather what he saw as a failure to fulfil an inherited role in society.

But this has some of the more usual features of an 'age' poem – the contrast of youth and age. The 'two girls in silk kimonos . . . one a gazelle' become 'withered old and skeleton-gaunt'. It is interesting that old bodies are rarely beautiful for Yeats: he is repelled and disgusted by physical ageing. We are made aware of the ravages of time very early on in the poem, right after the first four lines of that beautiful limpid opening, and it comes as quite a shocking contrast:

> But a raving autumn shears
> Blossom from the summer's wreath.

Autumn is 'raving', mad, hysterical, out of control, and the sharp-edged onomatopoeic sound of 'shears' conveys its deadly potential. Even summer carries the seeds of death in its 'wreath'.

Out of this retrospection Yeats attempts to distil a certain wisdom about life. This philosophy he sets down in the second section. In a more kindly address to the 'dear shadows' he presumes they now agree with him about the vanity of all causes and all zeal, irrespective of rightness:

All the folly of a fight
With a common wrong or right.

And, secondly, he knows that the great quarrel is with time, destroyer of innocence and beauty. He reflects on the vanity of it all, as it will end in a great apocalyptic conflagration, which will consume not just all they've built – great houses or mere gazebos – but all the anguished decisions of their lives. All is vanity before the end.

TONE

At times he manages to be gently nostalgic, such as at the beginning and end of the first section. But he can be very censorious about lives wasted in political agitation. And he seems quite excited by the possibility of the great final conflagration. This is communicated by the energy and repetition of strong verbs (strike, strike, climb, run) and by the repetition of phrases ('strike a match').

THEMES AND ISSUES

- What is a worthwhile way to live life?
- The vagaries of life, the imperfections
- Is it all vanity? What is the point of it all?
- The real enemy is time.
- Contrasting youth and age.

RHYMES AND RHYTHMS

Though Yeats imposes a quatrain rhyming scheme, *abba,* on the poem, he does not structure the thought in quatrains, apart from the first four lines. The first section, for instance, is structured periodically in groups of 4, 5, 4, 7. So the thought structure provides a sort of counter-rhythm to the rhyming structure and gives it a conversational naturalness.

This naturalness is emphasised by the use of off-rhymes rather than full rhymes, for example south – both, wreath – death, ignorant – gaunt, recall – gazelle. Some could argue that the imperfect rhyme befits the theme – the imperfections of life. The rhythmic quality of the language is achieved partly through repetitions: repetitions of phrases such as 'And bid me strike a match', but more obviously with the repetition of the well-known refrain 'Two girls . . .' However, the tone of the second repetition differs markedly from the first, because of the context, where it now carries all the bleak irony and the disappointment of hindsight.

STRUCTURE

The structure of this poem is almost unnoticed, so deftly is it done. It opens with

'The light of evening', proceeds to the darkness of 'Dear Shadows', and erupts again into the final apocalyptic inferno of the end of time. It begins with youth and ends with death; it opens with the great house of Lissadell and ends with a fragile gazebo.

Swift's Epitaph
Text of poem: New Explorations Anthology page 78

Begun in 1929 and finished in September 1930, this was first published in the *Dublin Magazine* in the winter of 1931. It is included in the volume *The Winding Stair and Other Poems* (1933). The poem is essentially a translation, with some alterations, of the Latin epitaph on Jonathan Swift's memorial in St Patrick's Cathedral, Dublin.

Hic depositum est Corpus
JONATHAN SWIFT S.T.D.
Hujus Ecclesiae Cathedralis
Decani,
Ubi saeva Indignatio
Ulterius
Cor lacerare nequit.
Abi Viator
Et imitare, si poteris,
Strenuum pro virili
Libertatis vindicatorem.
Obiit 19º Die Mensis Octobris
A.D. 1745. Anno Aetatis 78º.

Here is laid the body of
JONATHAN SWIFT, doctor of sacred theology,
dean of this cathedral church,
where savage indignation
can no longer
rend his heart.
Go, traveller,
and imitate, if you can,
an earnest and dedicated
champion of liberty.
He died on the nineteenth day of October
AD 1745, in the year of his age 78.

Jonathan Swift (1667–1745) was dean of St Patrick's Cathedral, Dublin. Poet, political pamphleteer and satirist, he was the author of such famous works as *The Drapier's Letters, A Modest Proposal, A Tale of a Tub* and *Gulliver's Travels*. Politically conservative, Swift voiced the concerns and values of Protestant Ireland with an independence of spirit and a courage that Yeats admired greatly. Swift's writing made him enemies on all sides, but this isolation endeared him even further to Yeats, who often spoke admiringly of 'Anglo-Irish solitude'. Yeats thought of Swift as a heroic figure, an artist–philosopher who, despite the conflicts of his personal life, served liberty by speaking out in his writings and freeing the artist from the tyranny of the mob. He ranked Swift together with Berkeley, Goldsmith and Burke as one of the intellectual founders of the Anglo-Irish tradition.

Yeats's play *The Words upon the Window Pane* (1930) explores some of the conflicts of Swift's life.

A FREE TRANSLATION

Among the chief interests of the Yeats poem are the significance of the changes he made. For instance, 'Swift has sailed into his rest' is much more confident, energetic and vigorous than the original. It sounds more like a victorious progress, while being at the same time a gentle and graceful journey. There are also clearer overtones of a spiritual afterlife – 'his rest' – where the original merely notes the depositing of the body!

He retains the famous reference to *'saeva indignatio'* (savage indignation), which was the driving force of Swift's satirical work, and the reference to his capacity for empathy and for being affected by the injustices and miseries he encountered ('cannot lacerate his breast'). The challenge to the observer is stronger than in the original – to imitate him 'if you dare' rather than 'if you can'. And the traveller is described as 'world-besotted', worldly, lacking in spiritual values and outlook. The implication may be to enhance, by contrast, the unworldly qualities of Swift (which would be somewhat at variance with the facts). Yeats also retains the epithet noting Swift's defence of liberty, a philosophy they shared.

In general it might be said that Yeats has nudged the epitaph more in the direction of a eulogy. And there is more transparent emotion and admiration in the Yeats version.

An Acre of Grass

Text of poem: New Explorations Anthology page 80

This poem was written in November 1936 and first published in *New Poems* (1938).

A READING OF THE POEM

This poem is quite a remarkable response to old age and thoughts of death. The first stanza captures the shrinkage of an old person's physical world in the twilight years. With the ebbing of physical strength his world is reduced to the gardens of his house, 'an acre of green grass | For air and exercise'. The final two lines of the stanza are a marvellous evocation of the stillness, isolation and sense of emptiness that can be experienced at night by the wakeful elderly, a feeling carried in part by the broad vowel rhymes 'house – mouse':

> Midnight, an old house
> Where nothing stirs but a mouse.

He could easily resign himself to restfulness and silence. 'My temptation is quiet.'

But this old man, this poet, needs to write, to continue to find new truths, and he knows that neither a 'loose imagination' – an imagination that is not disciplined by the structure of writing – nor any ordinary observation of everyday occurrences will deliver up any significant truths.

> Nor the mill of the mind
> Consuming its rag and bone,
> Can make truth known.

Real creativity needs something more, like mystical insight; and that comes only through really passionate endeavour or frenzy. Hence his prayer, 'Grant me an old man's frenzy.' That frenzy or madness produced insight and truth for King Lear at the end of his life; and mystical visions, which some interpret as madness, produced the beautiful wisdom of William Blake's poetry. Even at the end of his life, Yeats knows the huge transforming energy necessary to forge new insights and truths, and he faces up to it.

> Myself I must remake

What courage for a person in his seventies!

Yeats had been reading Nietzsche's *The Dawn of Day,* about people of genius who can distance themselves from character and temperament and rise above the weight of personality like a winged creature. Yeats had used Nietzsche's ideas to develop his theory of the Mask: he felt the need to continually transform himself. And this is the ideology driving this poem – the need for transformation in order to achieve new insights and truths. So the poet must discard the persona of dignified old man and remake himself as a wild, mad prophet-like figure, such as Timon or Lear or Blake, and that will bring the searing vision, the 'eagle mind' 'that can pierce the clouds'. This is a poet's fighting response to old age and approaching death. It may remind us of Dylan Thomas's later 'Rage, rage against the dying of the light.'

THEMES AND ISSUES

Explore the following ideas, and expand on each with reference to what you find in the poem.

- A response to ageing: refusing to accept a quiet retirement; summoning reserves of energy to continue working; aware of the huge demands, yet praying for the chance.
- The process of creativity: the ordinary imagination processing or milling everyday events is not sufficient; a frenzy or madness is necessary in order to see things differently or see into things; the after-truths or insights are all-consuming; the power of that insight can 'pierce the clouds' and 'shake the dead'.
- The poet's need for continued transformation. Is it comfortable being a poet? Is it worth it?

Politics

Text of poem: New Explorations Anthology page 82

A READING OF THE POEM

We know that Yeats had intended that the volume *Last Poems* should end with 'Politics'. It is suggested that it was written as an answer to an article that had praised Yeats for his public language but suggested that he should use it more on political subjects. If so, then this is written as a mocking, ironic, tongue-in-cheek response. The speaker affects the pose of a distracted lover who is too preoccupied with the woman to give any attention to the political chaos of European politics of the mid-1930s: Franco, Mussolini, etc. He is little concerned for these earth-shattering events, dismissing them casually in a throw-away comment:

> And maybe what they say is true
> Of war and war's alarms . . .

We can almost see the shrug of indifference.

But the mask of the dispassionate observer slips in the final two lines as his passionate yearning breaks through and we realise that the 'she' is probably 'Caitlín Ní Uallacháin' – Ireland. So we understand Yeats's mocking response to those who have not understood one of his major poetical preoccupations.

The regularity of the four-stress lines alternating with three-stress lines and the simplicity of alternative end-line rhymes, together with the simplicity of the language, give the impression that this is lightweight verse. But, as with all good satire, we are lulled into a false sense of security until the final punch is thrown.

From 'Under Ben Bulben'
Text of poem: New Explorations Anthology page 84

SECTIONS V AND VI
The final draft of this poem is dated 4 September 1938, about five months before the poet's death. Parts of it were published in 1939.

BACKGROUND AND CONTEXT
Some acquaintance with the poem as a whole is necessary for an understanding of the context of sections V and VI. It is recommended that you read through all six sections.

'Under Ben Bulben' can be seen as Yeats's poetic testimony, an elegy for himself, defining his convictions and the poetical and social philosophies that motivated his life's work.

Section I incorporates the two main belief systems that informed his poetry: the occult philosophy, and folk beliefs and traditions.

Section II features another aspect of his belief system: reincarnation.

Section III suggests that poetic insight is born out of moments of violence; that violence and conflict can be invigorating.

Section IV outlines what he considers to be the great tradition in art, from Pythagoras through Egyptian and Greek sculpture to Michelangelo's Renaissance.

In Sections IV and V Yeats urges all artists, poets, painters and sculptors to do their work in this great tradition of art, to promote the necessary heroic images that nourish civilisation. Specifically, he had in mind the forms of the perfected human body as the necessary poetic inspiration, a concept linked to his ideas on eugenics (the pseudo-science of improving the human race through selective breeding). Yeats had joined the Eugenics Society in London in 1936 and became interested in research on intelligence testing. During 1938 he worked on a verse tract on this topic, published as *On the Boiler* (1939). Convinced that eugenics was crucial to the future of civilisation, he wrote: 'Sooner or later we must limit the families of the unintelligent classes and if our government cannot send them doctor and clinic it must, till it gets tired of it, send monk and confession box.'

Section VI of 'Under Ben Bulben' rounds his life to its close and moves from the mythologies associated with the top of Benbulbin to the real earth at its foot, in Drumcliff churchyard.

Section V
This is Yeats's advice to Irish poets concerning the model or tradition they should follow. And the model he recommends is a new, composite one, attempting to fuse together two cultural traditions, those of peasant and aristocratic cultures.

> Sing the peasantry and then
> Hard-riding country gentlemen . . .

The former is the Irish tradition of folk and fairy tales and fantastical mythology; the latter is the Anglo-Irish cultural tradition, which Yeats traced back to the 'other days' referred to, the eighteenth century and the intellectual contribution of Swift, Berkeley, Goldsmith and Burke. He valued this tradition for its spirit of free enquiry, its sense of order and the example of gracious living it produced in Georgian mansions and fine estates. To this fusion he adds the religious tradition as worthy of celebration ('The holiness of monks'), followed immediately by 'Porter-drinkers' randy laughter', which rather devalues the former. Perhaps it's meant to be ironic. The Irish nobility are worthy of celebration, even though they 'were beaten into the clay | Through seven heroic centuries'. So heroic defeat is a fitting subject.

But once again Yeats scorns the present generation. Physically they do not conform to the traditional model of aesthetic beauty ('All out of shape from top to toe'). With an arrogance derived from the reprehensible theories of eugenics, he scorns their low intelligence and inferior lineage:

> Their unremembering hearts and heads
> Base-born products of base beds.

That arrogant tone continues, to end in that triumphant note – 'Still the indomitable Irishry.' The trouble with this poem is that it is so 'well made' – the rhythms of the language, the regular metre, the alliterative repetitions, the graphically grotesque imagery, etc. – that it can distract us from the seriously questionable class and racist attitudes.

Section VI
This section is beautifully structured, like a film shot. Opening with a long shot of the mountain, the camera draws back and focuses on the churchyard, panning by the church and the ancient cross until it finishes with a close-up of

the epitaph cut in limestone. The effect is of a closing down of Yeats's life, a narrowing in to death. Many of the important elements of Yeats's life are here: the mythology and folklore associated with Benbulbin; the sense of ancestry, family and continuity provided by the rector; and the continuity of cultural tradition in the 'ancient cross'. No ostentatious marble tomb or conventional, tired phrases are permitted, but rather a piece of indigenous material, local stone, to carry his epitaph.

This is a curiously impersonal epitaph, neither celebrating the person's virtues nor asking remembrance or recommending the soul to God: rather it is a stark piece of advice that the challenges of life and death should not be taken too seriously but should be regarded with a certain detachment. It is his final summation, that all the great issues merely come to this.

Developing a personal understanding

1. Select the poem by Yeats that made the greatest impact on you, and write about your reaction to it.
2. What issues raised by the poet did you think significant?
3. On reading this selection, what did you find surprising or interesting?
4. What impressions of Yeats as a person did you form?
5. What questions would you like to ask him?
6. Do you think it important for Irish pupils to study Yeats?
7. What do you find difficult about the poetry of Yeats?
8. What do you like about his poetry?

Overview of themes and issues

On each point, return to the poem for reference and further exploration.

YEATS AND THE NATIONAL QUESTION

Among the issues explored by the poet under this heading are the following:
- the heroic past; patriots are risk-takers, rebels, self-sacrificing idealists who are capable of all that 'delirium of the brave' (see 'September 1913')
- how heroes are created, how ordinary people are changed ('Easter 1916')
- the place of violence in the process of political change; the paradox of the 'terrible beauty' (see 'September 1913', 'Easter 1916', and 'Meditations in Time of Civil War')
- the place of 'fanaticism' and the human effects of it – the 'stone of the heart' (see 'Easter 1916', 'September 1913', 'In Memory of Eva Gore-Booth and Con Markiewicz')
- the force of political passion (see 'Easter 1916', 'Politics').

Yeats's notions of the ideal society

- The vital contribution that both the aristocracy and artists make to society; the importance of the Anglo-Irish tradition in Irish society (see 'September 1913', 'In Memory of Eva Gore-Booth and Con Markiewicz', 'Meditations in Time of Civil War', 'Swift's Epitaph', 'Under Ben Bulben')
- His contempt for the new middle class and the new materialism (see 'September 1913')
- Aesthetic values and the place of art in society (see 'Sailing to Byzantium', 'Under Ben Bulben')
- The yearnings for order and the fear of anarchy (see 'Meditations in Time of Civil War', 'The Second Coming')
- His views on the proper contribution of women to society (see 'In Memory of Eva Gore-Booth and Con Markiewicz', 'Easter 1916').

Theories of history, time and change

- His notion of thousand-year eras, 'gyres', etc. (see 'The Second Coming')
- The world and people in constant change and flux (see 'The Second Coming', 'Easter 1916')
- Personal ageing, the transience of humanity (see 'The Wild Swans at Coole', 'An Acre of Grass')
- The yearning for changelessness and immortality (see 'The Wild Swans at Coole', 'Sailing to Byzantium')
- The timelessness of art, or the possibility of it (see 'Sailing to Byzantium').

Conflicts at the centre of the human being

- The conflict between physical desires and spiritual aspirations (see 'Sailing to Byzantium')
- The quest for aesthetic satisfaction (see 'Sailing to Byzantium')
- The search for wisdom and peace, which is not satisfied here (see 'The Lake Isle of Innisfree')
- A persistent sense of loss or failure; loss of youth and passion (see 'The Wild Swans at Coole'); the loss of poetic vision and insight (see 'An Acre of Grass').

General questions

1. Select any major theme explored by Yeats and outline his treatment of it.
2. Review critically any poem by Yeats that you considered interesting.
3. 'Yeats displayed great reverence for the past but little respect for his own time.' Consider the truth of this statement in the light of the poems you have examined.
4. 'W.B. Yeats explored complex issues of national identity with great honesty.' Discuss.

5. Having read his poetry, what do you think Yeats chiefly valued in life?
6. 'Yeats's poetry is fuelled by conflict – conflict between past and present, youth and age, mind and body.' Explore this view of his poetry.

Bibliography

Brown, Terence, *The Life of W.B. Yeats,* Dublin: Gill and Macmillan 1999.

Cullingford, Elizabeth Butler, *Yeats: Poems, 1919–1935* (Casebook Series), Basingstoke: Macmillan 1984.

Cullingford, Elizabeth Butler, *Gender and History in Yeats's Love Poetry,* Cambridge: Cambridge University Press 1993.

Donoghue, Denis (editor), *W.B. Yeats: Memoirs,* London: Macmillan 1972.

Ellman, Richard, *The Identity of Yeats,* London: Faber and Faber 1968.

Ellman, Richard, *Yeats: The Man and the Masks,* Oxford: Oxford University Press 1979.

Foster, R.F., *W.B. Yeats: A Life, vol. 1: The Apprentice Mage,* Oxford: Oxford University Press 1997.

Harwood, John, *Olivia Shakespear and W.B. Yeats,* Basingstoke: Macmillan 1989.

Hone, Joseph, *W.B. Yeats,* Harmondsworth (Middx): Pelican Books 1971.

Jeffares, A.Norman, *W.B. Yeats: Man and Poet,* London: Routledge and Kegan Paul 1966.

Jeffares, A. Norman, *W.B. Yeats: The Poems,* London: Edward Arnold 1979.

Jeffares, A. Norman, *W.B. Yeats: A New Biography,* London: Hutchinson 1988.

Jeffares, A. Norman (editor), *Yeats's Poems,* Basingstoke: Macmillan 1989.

Jeffares, A. Norman, and MacBride White, Anna (editors), *The Gonne–Yeats Letters, 1893–1938,* London: Hutchinson 1992.

Kelly, John (editor), *The Collected Letters of W.B. Yeats* (three vols), Oxford: Clarendon Press 1986, 1997, 1994.

Kinahan, Frank, *Yeats, Folklore and Occultism,* Boston: Unwin Hyman 1988.

MacRae, Alasdair, *W.B. Yeats: A Literary Life,* Dublin: Gill and Macmillan 1995.

Martin, Augustine, *W.B. Yeats,* Gerrards Cross (Bucks): Colin Smythe 1983.

Smith, Stan, *W.B. Yeats: A Critical Introduction,* Dublin: Gill and Macmillan 1990.

Tuohy, Frank, *Yeats,* London: Macmillan 1976.

Yeats, W.B., *A Vision* [1925], London: Macmillan 1937.

Yeats, W.B., *Autobiographies: Memoirs and Reflections,* London: Macmillan 1955.

Yeats, W.B., *Mythologies,* London: Macmillan 1959.

Yeats, W.B., *Essays and Introductions,* New York: Macmillan 1961.

3 *Thomas Stearns* ELIOT

Sean Scully

Timeline

September 26, 1888	Thomas Stearns Eliot is born in St Louis, Missouri.
1906–1909	Undergraduate at Harvard. Becomes interested in the symbolists and Laforgue.
1909–1910	Graduate student at Harvard. Studies in France and Germany. 'Prufrock' is completed but not published.
1911–1914	Graduate student at Harvard. Begins work on the philosophy of Francis Herbert Bradley.
1914–1915	Study in Germany stopped by war. Moves to Oxford. Short satiric poems. 'Prufrock' is published in Chicago, June 1915. Marriage to Vivienne Haigh-Wood, July 1915.
1915	Eliot moves to London.
1915–1916	Teaching and doing book reviews in London. Bradley thesis is finished.
1915–1919	Eliot has many different jobs, including teaching, bank clerk and assistant editor of the literary magazine *Egoist*.
June 1917	*Prufrock and Other Observations* is published.
1917–1920	Works in Lloyd's Bank. Many editorials and reviews. Writing of French poems, quatrain poems.
1921–1922	London correspondent for *The Dial*.
1922–1939	Founder and editor of *The Criterion*.
1922	'The Waste Land'. Eliot wins Dial Award for *The Waste Land*. London correspondent for *Revue Française*.
1925	Senior position with publisher Faber & Faber.
1927	Eliot is confirmed in the Church of England and becomes a British citizen.
1927–1930	*Ariel Poems*.
1940–1942	'East Coker', 'The Dry Salvages' and 'Little

	Gidding'.
1943	'The Four Quartets'.
1947	Death of Eliot's first wife, Vivienne Haigh-Wood, after long illness.
1948	King George VI awards the Order of Merit to T.S. Eliot. Eliot is awarded the Nobel Prize in Literature.
1957	Marries Valerie Fletcher.
1958	*The Elder Statesman*.
January 4, 1965	T.S. Eliot dies.

The Love Song of J. Alfred Prufrock (1917)

Text of poem: New Explorations Anthology page 116

THEMES/ISSUES AND IMAGERY

Title

This is, perhaps, one of Eliot's most striking titles. Yet the poem is neither a song nor a traditional, conventional expression of love. Neither is J. Alfred Prufrock a conventional name for a love poet. It is more evocative of a respectable small-town businessman. (In fact, there was a furniture dealer named Prufrock in St Louis when Eliot lived there.)

The name can be seen as mock-heroic, if not comically ridiculous, in the circumstances of the poem. Indeed 'Prufrockian' has entered the language as an adjective indicative of a kind of archaic idealism which is paralysed by self-consciousness. The rather self-conscious 'J.' before Alfred recalls Mark Twain's distrust of men who 'part their names in the middle'.

Overall the incongruity of associations between the two halves of the title prepares us for the tension developed in the poem.

Epigraph

A literal translation of the epigraph reads:

> *'If I thought that my answer were to one who might ever return to the world, this flame should shake no more; but since no-one ever did return from this depth alive, if what I hear is true, without fear of infamy I answer you.'*

The passage is from Dante's *Inferno*, XXVII, lines 61–66, in which Guido de Montefeltro, tortured in hell for the sin of fraud, is willing to expose himself to Dante because he believes that the poet can never return from the pit of hell to the world. In Eliot's poem, too, the speaker tells of himself, because he feels his audience is also trapped in a hell of its own making. This is so since he is speaking to himself.

The use of the extract from Dante's *Inferno* also suggests that the lovesong is not sung in the real world, but in a 'hell' which is the consequence of being divided between passion and timidity.

Lines 1–12

Most critics agree that the 'you and I' of the first line are two sides of the same personality, the ego and alter ego, as it were. Thus the poem is an interior monologue, an exposure of the self to the self. However, the reader is, of course, free to think that it is he who is being addressed, as the self he addresses may be in all of us.

At any rate, the character Prufrock is struggling with the idea of asking the 'overwhelming question' of line 10.

The poem opens with a command to accompany him, presumably to the room of line 13. However the air of decisiveness collapses immediately with the simile of describing the evening (line 3). This image may be quite striking but it does not give us an immediate visual image. Rather, it reveals a great deal about Prufrock's psychological state. He is helpless – 'etherised'.

The setting of these opening lines is evening or twilight – a sort of halfway period, neither night nor day. This enhances the theme of indecision.

The description of what appears to be the seedy side of the city in the next four lines is presented in a series of quite sordid images. They may indicate the pointlessness of Prufrock's search. His emotional numbness would appear to have led him to unsatisfactory, sordid sexual relations in the past, in 'one-night cheap hotels'. The image of the 'sawdust restaurants with oyster-shells' suggests the vulgarity of these encounters, while also introducing sea imagery, which is a feature of the poem.

These seedy retreats show the tiresome, weary nature of city life. So the streets are compared to 'a tedious argument | Of insidious intent'. Thus Prufrock's encounters and perhaps life itself are seen as mechanical and repetitive and characteristic of an inner sickness. Such an area and such a lifestyle naturally lead to 'an overwhelming question'.

Prufrock is unwilling to face this question. It remains isolated and hidden within, and the 'you' is told not to ask. Thus we are beginning to see the depiction of a melancholic character who cannot satisfy his desires.

Lines 13–14

This room would appear to be Prufrock's destination. The women are satirised and seen as quite pretentious. Their 'talking of Michelangelo' as they 'come and go' is made to seem quite trivial and empty-headed. This is suggested by the jingling rhythm and rhyme.

The subject of their conversation, Michelangelo, is the great sculptor of heroic figures. This is a figure to whose magnanimity and greatness Prufrock could not possibly aspire. So how could the women find him (Prufrock) interesting, even if their knowledge is limited and their talk pretentious? Prufrock is a most unheroic figure.

Lines 15–22

There is a fusion of imagery here. The fog which surrounds the house (presumably the house which contains the room) is described in terms of a cat. This essentially metaphysical concept suggests the theme of unfulfilled promise. This is seen in particular by the fact that the action leads to sleep.

Cats, it must be noted, have been traditionally associated with sexuality and so much of the imagery here may also suggest unsatisfied desire.

The image of the fog serves another purpose. It may convey blurred consciousness or vision, a constant theme in Eliot's poetry. Thus on a wider note, through the imagery of the poem and the character of Prufrock, Eliot is speaking of the degenerated vision and soul of humanity in the twentieth century.

Lines 23–34

Time is one of the important themes, not only of this poem, but also of Eliot's poetry generally. Prufrock takes great comfort in time, repeating rather hypnotically, 'there will be time'.

There will be time to 'prepare a face' against the exposure of the true self, or 'To prepare a face' to make small talk over 'a toast and tea', and to 'murder and create' reputations or characters in a gossipy fashion, perhaps.

This unexciting prospect, with its mundane 'works and days of hands' merely leads him back to the question, which he puts off because of his timidity and hesitancy. The sarcasm of lines 32–33 emphasises the avoidance of decision. The play on the words 'vision' and 'revision' adds further emphasis to this.

And all this anxiety and procrastination doesn't lead to some momentous event, but merely to taking 'toast and tea'. The element of mock-heroic is clear.

Lines 35–36

The repetition of lines 13–14 here underscores the tediousness of the women's talk. It further emphasises Prufrock's limitations and how he is inhibited and perhaps intimidated by so-called social discourse. It, together with the reference to Hamlet later, represents the greatness of the past in contrast to the modern world.

Lines 37–48

Here Prufrock speculates on the women's view of his physical self. The 'prepared face' is no protection against the pitiless gaze of the women. The time for decisive action may be at hand, yet he wonders if he dares. He fears a rebuff and even if he retreats – 'turn back and descend the stair' – he may still seem absurd. He is aware of his unheroic appearance. He is growing bald and 'his arms and legs are thin!' He dresses well – albeit in a very conventional manner – possibly to compensate for these physical shortcomings, and indeed his attractive clothes may be part of his mask – his need to make an appearance.

His doubts are expressed in obvious hyperbole – 'Do I dare | Disturb the universe?' How could *he* possibly disturb the universe? The possibility may lie in the immediate sense of the 'universe' of his own world or in his realisation that even trivial human actions may have immeasurable consequences. This self-conscious awareness precludes his taking any decisive action. Emotionally, at least, Prufrock is impotent.

Lines 49–54

Here Prufrock puts forward the first of three arguments against deciding the overwhelming question. Again, Prufrock is hesitant to act due to the limitations of his inner self. He lacks self-confidence due to the sterility and meaninglessness of his life – which is merely an endless round of 'evenings, mornings, afternoons'. The line 'I have measured out my life with coffee spoons' not only epitomises the repetitive tedium of his everyday existence, but may also suggest a desire to escape the pain of living via the use of a stimulant.

How could he, Prufrock, challenge the meaninglessness of such a life? Such a challenge would be presumptuous.

Lines 55–61

His second argument is presented here. He is afraid of being classified and stereotyped 'in a formulated phrase' by the perhaps contemptuous looks of the women. He recoils from the absolute horror of being pinned down and dissected like an insect in some biological experiment. He has a phobia of being restricted, linked perhaps to a fear of emasculation. So how could a man with such fears risk, or presume, to expose himself to further ridicule? The image of the 'butt-end' of a cigarette to which he compares his life suggests further self-disgust.

Lines 62–69

His third argument against deciding the overwhelming question is presented here. He cannot ask the question because he is simultaneously attracted and revolted by the physicality of women.

The ideal perfection of 'Arms that are braceleted and white and bare' develops into the physicality of '(But in the lamplight, downed with light brown hair!).' The sense of the ideal becoming real reflects his being overwhelmed at the prospect of turning desire into action.

The altered but effectively repeated question of 'And should I then presume?', reflecting his insecurity, suggests an apparent increase in tension towards a sense of impending climax. Yet he cannot conceive any formula for his proposal – 'And how should I begin?'

Lines 70–74
Prufrock offers a possible preface or preamble to his question. He wonders if he should mention that he is aware of a different type of world from that known by the women in the room – the seedy world of lines 4–9 recalled in the imagery here. This awareness may be his justification for asking the question. He knows more, but the fact that he poses the preamble in the form of a question suggests uncertainty as to its relevance.

Again the imagery suggests he is a passive observer, not an active participant. Failure to address the overwhelming question leads, as in line 10, to a trailing off into silence indicated by the three dots.

This section ends with his wish to be something like a crab. This sea imagery in fact is reduced to 'claws'. Thus Prufrock seems to wish to dehumanise himself completely, to become a thing of pure action without self-awareness – living, yet mentally inanimate; to be in a place where he can survive in the depths and yet avoid the pain of living. Obviously this is the very opposite of Prufrock's true situation.

Lines 75–88
This section must be seen as a form of reverie. It is also the turning point of the poem.

Having previously seen the fog as a cat (lines 15–22), Prufrock now sees the afternoon as such. All the tensions up to now are resolved, not in action but in images of inaction and weakness. The afternoon/evening/cat 'sleeps', 'malingers', 'Stretched on the floor'. The sense of being etherised (line 3) is recalled.

The triviality of Prufrock's existence is seen in the mock-heroic rhyming of 'ices' and 'crisis'. This prepares us for Prufrock's efforts to put himself in a heroic perspective. However, his greater sense of personal inadequacy won't permit him to sustain the comparison with St John the Baptist. The ironic discrepancy between John the Baptist and Prufrock is heightened by the self-mockery of '(grown slightly bald)'. Prufrock's head would simply look absurd. He is aware of this and immediately denies the possibility of heroic status for himself – 'I am no prophet' (line 84). The continuation of this line can be read as 'it doesn't really matter' or 'I'm not important.' Either way it is an acknowledgement of his own inadequacy.

The final image in this section is of the eternal Footman. This is Death personified. Even death is laughing at him, but the image also suggests that the servants of the polite society hosts whom he visits do not take him seriously. He feels he is the butt of their jokes. To both death and the ridicule of servants, the profound and the trivial, Prufrock admits his fear. It is too late for him to act. Fear is his reality.

Lines 89–115

Prufrock's speculation on whether forcing the crisis, asking the overwhelming question, would have been worthwhile reads like an excuse for inaction. He is rationalising his failure.

He names again the trivial aspects of his polite environment, recalling earlier lines (49–51, 79). However, now the 'you and I' of line 1 are very much part of the trivia of this environment. They are 'Among the porcelain, among some talk of you and me'. Perhaps he cannot accept that any significant action can take place in this type of environment. He is afraid of being misunderstood. What would he do if his 'overwhelming question' should meet with an offhand rejection like:

'That is not what I meant at all.
That is not it, at all.'

The fact that these lines are repeated shows the extent of his fear.

Two references in this section suggest that Prufrock continues to compare himself to those of heroic status.

Line 94 is a reference to Andrew Marvell's poem 'To His Coy Mistress' in which the poet urges his beloved to enjoy immediate sexual union with him as a sort of victory over time. Prufrock's inaction is the antithesis of this.

Both men by the name of Lazarus in the Gospels were figures of triumph over death: one, the brother of Martha and Mary, by being recalled to life by Jesus; the other, a poor man, by gaining Heaven – unlike the rich man, Dives.

Prufrock fears that even the most profound knowledge may be decorously, but casually, rejected.

Essentially Prufrock's fear here is of never being able to connect emotionally with another person. The gulf between human beings' inner selves cannot be bridged. This has him cry out in frustration:

It is impossible to say just what I mean!
(line 108)

The possibility of the insensitive comprehension of the other exposes his own sensitivity. It is 'as if a magic lantern threw the nerves in patterns on a screen' (lines 109–110). Thus throughout this section women again appear as catalysts to Prufrock's inadequacy and inferiority.

Lines 116–124
Here Prufrock settles for a less than heroic version of himself. He recognises that any further heroic action would be absurd. He may have something in common with Shakespeare's Prince Hamlet, for he too was indecisive, but any direct identification would be ridiculous.

Rather, he sees himself as a Polonius figure – an advisor to kings – or even a lesser person. The theatrical imagery of lines 117–119 suggests a bit player. Prufrock has become consciously unheroic. In lines 119–124 he is quite self-deprecating, reducing himself eventually to the level of a wise Fool. A passage that begins with 'Hamlet' ends with 'the Fool'.

However, there is the possibility, with the capitalisation of 'the Fool', that Prufrock does not see himself as any old fool, but perhaps akin to the Fool in Shakespeare's *King Lear* – a wise fool who utters uncomfortable truths, which powerful people would prefer not to hear. Maybe this is Prufrock's final fantasy.

Lines 125–136
A world-weariness introduces this section. This in effect becomes a process of dying, until 'we drown' in the last line.

He does, however, make a decision in line 126 – to 'wear the bottoms of my trousers rolled'. The triviality of the decision, in contrast to the 'overwhelming question', suggests his resignation to a trivial existence. This decision is followed by two further trivial questions, which underscore the point. Parting his hair may hide his bald spot. Eating a peach may be the riskiest behaviour he will ever again indulge in.

This hopeless, empty existence has him resort to the beach. Sea imagery throughout the poem (lines 7, 73–74) has suggested some alternative lifestyle – some hope of avoiding the pain of consciousness.

The mermaids of line 129 symbolise a sort of idealised erotic beauty similar to the arms in line 63. But Prufrock realises that this is only a fantasy, a dream. He has been deluding himself. His realisation of this is expressed in the simple bathos of line 130: 'I do not think that they will sing to me.'

Yet delusions are hard to let go and he asserts the existence of the mermaids, of the erotic ideal, in a defiant final cry (lines 131–133).

But he has 'lingered in the chambers' of his world of ideal relationships and heroic actions for too long, perhaps. The dream is unattainable. The use of 'we' here is not just the 'you and I' of line 1, but also the universal plural. All of us can get lost in our reveries, until we are called to reality by other human voices – a reality where 'we drown'. All struggle is ended and we accept the death of our inner selves.

The irony inherent in the title has already been described. It is the self-irony of Laforgue, adapted to a dreadful seriousness. The poem is a tragic comedy, the epitaph sets the mood.

The lyricism of the opening is appropriate to a love-song, but it collapses almost immediately in the simile of Line 3. The simile is quite comically inappropriate for a love-song but is tragically appropriate for the hapless Prufrock and his situation.

The repetition of 'Let us go' suggests that he is already faltering.

The sibilant sounds which dominate the opening sequence underscore the seedy imagery and the sense of being 'etherised'. This is continued into the simile of 'like a tedious argument'. These sounds combined with the rhyming couplets do give a lyrical or musical effect, but also enhance the sense of ennui.

The dramatic pause indicated by the three dots in line 10 emphasises Prufrock's tragic flow and reinforces the bathos.

This bathos is further felt in the jingling rhythm and rhyme of lines 13–14: 'In the room the women come and go | Talking of Michelangelo.'

The fog/cat passage (lines 15–22) is also dominated by sibilant sounds which enhance the tone. These sounds are in contrast with the more cacophonous lines 23–34 which follow.

The fog/cat metaphor is in effect a metaphysical conceit. It is a flight of fancy, a sort of *jeu d'esprit*. Adding to the sensual sibilant sounds is the use of the letter 'L', often seen as the liquid letter, enhancing the sinuous movement of the fog.

The solemn incantatory tone of lines 23–34, echoing the Old Testament speaker in Ecclesiastes, contributes to the mock-heroic element of the poem, which is further added to by the pun on 'revisions' (lines 34 and 48).

Unlike the contrasts in the Book of Ecclesiastes, the opposing forces here do not show a sense of balance or equilibrium, but add to the confusion. The repetition of lines 13–14, which are in danger of becoming a refrain, emphasises the sterility and shallowness of the modern human condition, as mentioned above.

The constant repetition of rhetorical questions is a feature of the next several sections:

> 'Do I dare?'
> So how should I presume?
> And how should I begin?

These suggest a tone of uncertainty and underscore the sense of inaction.

The dominant verbs of lines 58–61 – 'formulated', 'sprawling', 'pinned', 'wriggling' – suggest not only the fear of individual inadequacy, but also a sense of being a victim.

His self-contempt, and possibly anger, are seen in the mixture of sibilants and cacophonous consonants in lines 73–74:

> I should have been a pair of ragged claws
> Scuttling across the floors of silent seas.

The ridiculous rhyming of 'ices' and 'crisis' (lines 79–80) has already been alluded to for its mock-heroic, satiric effect. The same effect is achieved with the rhyming of 'flicker' and 'snicker' in lines 85 and 87. The pathetic admission of:

> I am no prophet – and here's no great matter;
> I have seen the moment of my greatness flicker,

is reduced to a snort of mockery with the word 'snicker'.

The note of tragic satire is also in the bathetic joke on his 'head (grown slightly bald)' and the prophetic Biblical echoes of:

> 'I am Lazarus, come from the dead,
> Come back to tell you all, I shall tell you all' –
> (lines 96–97)

The broad vowels here remind us of one crying in the wilderness and being ignored.

The tone changes in the last section. Now that he acknowledges that 'It is impossible to say just what I mean!', and the 'overwhelming question' is gone, the poem settles down to a lyricism which merely flickered earlier. The use of alliteration, assonance and onomatopoeia in lines 131–136 both intensifies the description and underscores the tone and mood:

> I have seen them riding seaward on the waves
> Combing the white hair of the waves blown back
> When the wind blows the water white and black.
>
> We have lingered in the chambers of the sea
> By sea-girls wreathed with seaweed red and brown
> Till human voices wake us, and we drown.

The reference to Prince Hamlet does not seem pedantic, given the tone of this section. The rather comic bewilderment of:

> Shall I part my hair behind? Do I dare to eat a peach?

helps to raise our sympathy for him. Thus both the 'serious' references and the mocking tone serve to emphasise the comic-tragedy of Prufrock's situation.

Overall, the poem is quite fragmented, full of quickly changing images – aural, visual and tactile – presented in a cinematic, stream-of-consciousness style, reflecting both his character and situation.

THE CHARACTER OF PRUFROCK

- He is consciously unheroic.
- Melancholic and contemplative
- Feels inferior, inadequate and inhibited
- Fears rejection
- Both attracted to and threatened by women
- Women fall short of his idealised vision.
- Cannot find a language in which to express himself
- Indulges in escapist fantasies to avoid despair
- Indecisive, self-contemptuous and sees himself as a victim
- In a 'hell' – the consequence of being divided between passion and timidity – his tragic flaw
- A sensitive man in a psychological impasse
- An ageing romantic, incapable of action
- Tormented by unsatisfied desire
- A comic figure made tragic by his acute self-awareness
- The poem gives us not only the thoughts and feelings of Prufrock, but also the actual experience of his feeling and thinking.

PRUFROCK'S PROBLEMS WITH LANGUAGE

- Much of the meaning of the poem arises from its form: the digressions, hesitations, references, all suggest Prufrock's inability to express himself.
- Language regularly fails him. The first section never arrives at the question.
- Prufrock struggles with his own inarticulateness – 'Shall I say?' 'It is impossible to say just what I mean!'
- The failure of his love-song is also a failure to find a language in which to express himself.
- The fragments that make up the poem are essentially a collection of potential poems, which collapse because Prufrock cannot express his 'overwhelming question'.
- He is not included in the mermaids' song.
- Human voices suffocate and drown him.

MAIN THEMES

- Indecision
- Confronting the difficulty of action
- Time
- Emotional impotence
- The obduracy of language
- Superficiality and emptiness

- The hidden and isolated inner self
- The limitations of the real world
- Dying – spiritually, mentally, physically – death in life
- The movement in the mind.

MAIN IMAGES

- Sordid, seedy city life
- Fog/cat
- The room of pseudo-gentility
- Sea imagery – shells, crab, mermaids
- Cultural imagery – Michelangelo, John the Baptist, Lazarus, Hamlet
- Hair, clothes
- Coffee, tea, cakes and ices.

Preludes (1917)

Text of poem: New Explorations Anthology page 124

[*Note: This poem is also prescribed for Ordinary Level 2010 exam*]

INTRODUCTION

The 'Preludes' present us with urban scenes where what is seen reflects a particular state of mind. For the deeply disillusioned young poet they illustrate the ugliness, decline, emptiness and boredom of modern life.

The city here is effectively the same as that described by Prufrock in the 'Love Song of J. Alfred Prufrock'. It is a sordid world of deadening monotony and empty routine. The time-sets of the poem – evening, morning, night and day – reinforce the feeling of tedious monotony.

The title 'Preludes' can be seen as a reference to this sequence of evening, morning, night and day. They, as it were, are a 'prelude' to more sameness in the purposeless cycle of life.

'Preludes' could also point to the musical or lyrical effects in the poems.

As is usual with Eliot the poetry here is fragmented, full of quickly changing images – visual, aural, tactile and olfactory – in what is often described as a cinematic style. In what is essentially also a stream-of-consciousness style, Eliot takes us on a journey through the senses and the minds of his observers.

A READING OF THE POEM

Section I

Here the 'winter evening' is personified as it 'settles down' in a way reminiscent of the fog/cat in 'The Love Song of J. Alfred Prufrock'.

Olfactory images and tactile images abound – 'smell of steaks', 'burnt-out', .

'smoky', 'grimy', 'withered leaves about your feet', the showers 'wrap' and 'beat' – leaving a sense of staleness and decay. This is compounded by the image of cramped apartments in 'passageways'.

'The burnt-out ends of smoky days' is a visual image that reminds us of Prufrock's 'butt-ends of my days and ways' and also evokes a sense of weariness and disgust.

Adjectives such as 'withered', 'broken', 'lonely' and 'vacant' suggest the decay and isolation of city life, while the insistent beating of the rain adds to the misery. The visual image of the uncomfortable and impatient cab-horse completes the picture of dreariness.

The isolated last line of this section: 'And then the lighting of the lamps', suggests that something dramatic might be about to happen. But nothing does. The opening words 'And then' are not a prelude to drama, but rather a closing in of the night.

Thus the imagery of the section evokes the speaker's mood. The reader can imagine him trudging home through the wet misery of a winter's evening, surrounded by withered leaves and discarded newspapers and inhaling the burnt and musty smells of his living quarters. What else could he be but depressed by it all? The feeling of a numb, aimless, struggle in an ugly, sterile environment suggests a mood of spiritual and mental decay.

Section II

Like 'evening' in the first section, 'morning' is here personified. It is as if the monotonous time-sets were living an independent life from the actors in this tedious drama of life.

Olfactory and tactile images – 'smells of beer', 'sawdust-trampled street', 'muddy feet that press', 'coffee-stands' – again suggest a sense of staleness and decay. Words such as 'trampled' and 'press' add to the mood of oppressiveness.

Individual life is submerged in the city and by the onward march of time and what emerges is a mass conformity and uniformity:

> One thinks of all the hands
> That are raising dingy shades
> In a thousand furnished rooms.

This sense of sameness and monotony is also suggested by:

> all its muddy feet that press
> To early coffee-stands.

Eliot regularly depersonalises the character of individuals to show the mechanical nature of their lives. Here people are reduced to 'hands' and 'feet', invoking something living yet spiritually inanimate. Life has become an enslavement to pressure – the pressure of time, crowds and gulped-down coffee.

For Eliot this morning rush to work is a masquerade. It is an act put on by all the 'feet' and 'hands' to give their lives some meaning. The poet is suggesting that behind all the mad masquerade of activity there is a paralysis of the metaphysical, as people's lives are constituted solely by their mundane masquerades.

Section III
The third section illustrates physical inaction as a woman (the 'you' of the poem) struggles to wake and sluggishly prepares to get out of bed, where during the night she fitfully dozed.

Her uncomfortable, sleepless night is caught in the verbs of the first three lines – 'tossed', 'lay', 'waited', 'dozed', 'watched'. She is trapped between sleep and wakefulness which allows her imagination to wander randomly:

> . . . revealing
> The thousand sordid images
> Of which your soul was constituted;

Thus her paralysis, just like the city's, is also a paralysis of the metaphysical. She is quite inert, apart from throwing the blanket from her bed.

As is typical of Eliot, we are again presented with a character's state of mind. The woman cannot sleep and when she dozes her semi-conscious mind projects, like a film on a screen, her interior self which 'flickered against the ceiling'. These 'sordid' images reflect not only her degradation, but are symbolic of the degenerated consciousness and spirit of mankind in the twentieth century. As a projection of the twentieth century she is more passive and vulgar than the woman in 'A Game of Chess'.

When morning arrived, its light 'crept up between the shutters', almost as if it were an unwelcome intruder, while the sparrows are stripped of all beauty by being heard 'in the gutters'. Her vision of the street is not clarified. It is again blurred – a vision that is hardly understood. Both woman and street appear earthbound – she is supine in bed, while the personified street is 'trampled' in both Sections II and IV.

The feeling of degradation and disgust is continued in the last four lines of this section. Eliot again depersonalises the character of the woman to portray this. She is dehumanised into bodily parts – 'hair', 'feet', 'hands' – to evoke the image of a living person who is spiritually inanimate, just as in Section II.

The sense of disgust is more intense here, however. Her hair is artificially curled with paper, her feet are unhealthily 'yellow' and her hands are 'soiled'. This is quite unlike the meticulous image of Prufrock in the 'Love Song of J. Alfred Prufrock'. He may be ridiculous. She is repulsive. The capacity for spiritual growth is non-existent.

Section IV

This final section in this poetic sequence reveals the speaker more fully. Like the woman in Section III whose soul's images are 'flickered against the ceiling', his soul is also mirrored upwards. But the skies on which it is stretched are not attractive. They 'fade behind a city block'. Indeed, the image is rather tortured – 'His soul [is] stretched tight', reflecting the tension and strain of urban life. The passing of the hours – 'At four and five and six o'clock' – merely reflects the tense tedium and emptiness of his existence.

Eliot again dehumanises and depersonalises individuals to show the mechanical nature of city life – 'trampled . . . feet', 'short square fingers', 'and eyes'. Their daily routine consists of 'newspapers' and 'pipes' and being 'Assured of certain certainties'. Thus the human reality of the street reveals itself as neither conscious nor aware of its own insecurities and sordid dilapidation. The poet sees these people as living lives of drudgery, whose 'conscience' has been 'blackened'. This is a valueless, dreary society, which is now menacingly seen as being 'Impatient to assume the world.'

In one of those abrupt shifts for which he is famous, Eliot suddenly reveals himself in a moving, pathos-filled quatrain:

> I am moved by fancies that are curled
> Around these images, and cling:
> The notion of some infinitely gentle
> Infinitely suffering thing.

What saves the poet from being swamped by his disgust for modern life is his clinging to a belief in 'some infinitely gentle | Infinitely suffering thing.' This is, perhaps, indicating his move towards Christianity as a source of order and veneration.

However, in an equally abrupt shift he returns to cynicism and encourages us to laugh at, and not sympathise with, the human condition:

> Wipe your hand across your mouth, and laugh

The emptiness in life and the struggle for survival are suggested in a simile which underscores the horrific drudgery of deprivation:

> The worlds revolve like ancient women
> Gathering fuel in vacant lots.

The process of dying, which is prevalent among most, if not all, of the characters in Eliot's poetry, is dramatically evident here also.

LANGUAGE AND MOOD

Lyrical devices are common throughout.

The monotonous metre of the first section emphasises the drudgery and oppression of these mean streets. Most lines have four iambic stresses, while the others have two. This is in keeping with the image of trampling feet in Sections II and III and, matched by the inexorable flow of time, emphasises the general weariness of moods.

The emphatic rhymes equally convey the sense of oppression. This is particularly the case with the rhyming couplets – 'wraps – scraps' and 'stamps – lamps'.

The insistent beating of the rain is further emphasised by the use of alliteration:

> The showers beat
> On broken blinds . . .

while the impatience of the horse is intensified by alliteration and the strong iambic rhythm:

> And at the corner of the street
> A lonely cab-horse steams and stamps.

Earlier in this section the use of alliteration and consonance furthers the sense of decay and staleness. The use of sibilant 's' sounds is particularly effective in this:

> The winter evening settles down
> With smell of steaks in passageways.

Thus, in keeping with the musical note of its title, the poet uses lyrical devices to emphasise his themes and underscore imagery and mood.

While Section I is generally composed of end-stopped lines, Section II is composed of lines which run on. This use of enjambment serves to convey a sense of movement – the movement of 'muddy feet' on a 'trampled street'. It also emphasises the pressure of time.

The use of synecdoche, in which a part is substituted for the whole, has been alluded to earlier for the way in which it depersonalises individuals and emphasises monotonous conformity:

> One thinks of all the hands
> That are raising dingy shades
> In a thousand furnished rooms.

While Eliot favoured 'vers libre', he does use rhyme to draw attention to or satirise a situation, as we saw in Section I. The rhyming of 'consciousness' with 'press' and 'masquerades' with 'shades' here underscores the theme of pretence; the desire to put on an act to give life some meaning. It also intensifies the mood of oppression.

Overall in this section there is a strong sense of contrast between the descriptions of movement and the sense of spiritual paralysis.

The essentially passive nature of the verbs used at the beginning of Section III reflects her supine state and degenerated consciousness.

The repetition of 'And', which introduces three lines, intensifies the experience of dull monotony, while the almost onomatopoeic effect of the rhyming couplet, 'shutters . . . gutters', reflects the lack of lyricism in the perceived sound of the sparrows. The result is particularly satiric.

The monotonous metre evident in the earlier part of Section IV emphasises the drudgery and oppression of this city's life, just as in Section I. The movement of these first nine lines underscores the repetitive routine. They go on and on.

The abrupt shift from the third to the first person in the tenth line dramatises the poet's revelation of himself and his feelings. The strong iambic metre is also relaxed, suggesting a sense of release from tension and strain.

The sense of pathos inherent in these lines is lost in another abrupt shift in the last three lines to a mood of deep cynicism. The simile is intensified by the word choice – 'ancient', 'vacant' – and the slowing down of the rhythm.

MAIN THEMES
- Incessant toil and suffering
- The decay and isolation of twentieth-century life
- Time
- Death-in-life
- Life is mundane, monotonous, repetitive, mechanical.
- Paralysis of the soul/consciousness
- A journey through the mind and senses.

MAIN IMAGES
- The street
- The woman
- Food and drink
- Body parts
- The detritus of the street
- Masquerades
- Rapidly changing images – visual, oral, tactile, olfactory – cinematic style.

Aunt Helen (1915)

Text of poem: New Explorations Anthology page 128

[Note: This poem is also prescribed for Ordinary Level 2010 exam]

INTRODUCTION

This is one of those poems in which Eliot outlines his impressions of genteel society in Boston, to the inner circle of which he was introduced through his uncle.

What the philosopher Santayana referred to as its cultural deadness and smug righteousness left this society open to satire. In this poem Eliot comments on its manners and mores, while also suggesting the emotional and spiritual shallowness behind its conventional beliefs and culture. Aunt Helen is a symbol of a world that ought to be mocked. Eliot himself called it a world 'quite uncivilised, but refined beyond the point of civilisation'.

A READING OF THE POEM

The poem is written in the imagist style. The satiric meaning of the poem, therefore, has to be inferred from the few concise detailed images.

The personal note of the first line is quickly dropped in favour of Eliot's usual device of the detached observer. The banal tone borders on that of a newspaper reporter as a series of apparently objective details are given.

She lived 'in a small house' – a large one would have been vulgar. 'Near a fashionable square' further suggests a genteel refinement. Living *in* the square would be too ostentatious.

The rather contrived and archaic-sounding line 3 conveys the fastidious nature of Miss Helen Slingsby and her self-contained little world: 'Cared for by servants to the number of four.'

Lines 4 and 5 have a satiric edge, which is devastating in its implications. The 'silence at her end of the street' is what is expected out of respect for the dead person. However, the 'silence in heaven' conveys the full contempt of the poet for Aunt Helen's self-serving lifestyle. Faced with this, Heaven has nothing to say. Eliot's contempt is not surprising when one considers how he was raised in a religious environment that promoted unselfish service to the wider community's needs.

The observance of conventions that indicate respect for the dead is also seen in line 6: 'The shutters were drawn and the undertaker wiped his feet –'

However, the dash at the end of the line is almost a challenge to the reader to see the gesture as one of rejection. The reader is reminded of Christ's advice to followers concerning those who reject His and their values – to shake the dust of their towns from their sandals.

The deadpan sarcasm of line 7:

He was aware that this sort of thing had occurred before

reduces the death of this privileged lady to the commonplace. Aunt Helen's death is being dismissed as 'this sort of thing'.

Her decorous but distorted sense of values is seen in the next line:

The dogs were handsomely provided for,

The implied criticism of such values controls our response to line 9, which evokes laughter rather than sympathy. Perhaps the poet is also implying that her values don't survive her any longer than the life of a parrot.

The lifeless, artificial, materialistic world in which she lived is seen in:

The Dresden clock continued ticking on the mantelpiece,

and when we read that the servants resort to behaviour which Aunt Helen would not have tolerated, disregarding both her property and her values, laughter entirely replaces sympathy. The servants' behaviour is not a perversion of ancient values, but a release from their artificial confines.

However, even though we do laugh at and reject Aunt Helen's self-centred values, we are also left with a slight sense of distaste at the vulgarity of the final lines. Satire has not entirely reversed our sense of pathos.

The student may wish to compare Miss Helen Slingsby with the portrayal of women in 'A Game of Chess' and in 'Preludes'.

LANGUAGE AND TONE

The flat, banal tone has been alluded to already. This banal style of narration undermines the seriousness with which Aunt Helen viewed herself and the trivialities that surrounded her.

However, the reader might declare the ultimate tone of the narrator to be quite serious and reject its apparent levity; but, as F.R. Leavis has pointed out, 'It is as necessary to revise the traditional idea of the distinction between seriousness and levity in approaching this poetry as in approaching the metaphysical poetry of the seventeenth century.'

A few random rhymes do little but emphasise the overall absence of lyricism, thus reflecting the general dullness of Aunt Helen's life. Indeed, some lines read almost as prose. This is particularly so of lines 6 and 7. This adds to the sense of boredom and staleness.

The reader could not be blamed for believing initially that this poem is a sonnet. It has the general appearance of one. However, if it does then Eliot is perhaps mocking the attitudes and expectations of the reader, for this is a very distorted 'sonnet', being 13 lines long, with little rhyme and varying rhythm patterns. Thus, this distortion may reflect not only Aunt Helen's distorted values but the reader's also. Satire works in a number of ways.

The contrast between the behaviour of the footman and housemaid and that of Aunt Helen might also be said to add to the humour and introduces a slightly risqué, if not entirely vulgar element.

Finally, Eliot the dramatist is very much in evidence in this poem. Apart from his ability to create a comic type with a few strokes of his pen, he has also created a time and place and most especially, perhaps, he has mimicked the pompous tone of Aunt Helen. Thus quite ordinary words and phrases, such as 'a fashionable square', and 'this sort of thing' echo the bourgeois speech of Miss Helen Slingsby.

The reader will have to decide whether Aunt Helen's life was a tragedy or a comedy.

MAIN THEMES

- Criticism of cultural deadness and self-righteousness
- Emotional and spiritual shallowness
- Distorted values
- Time.

MAIN IMAGES

- Silence
- The undertaker
- The dog and the parrot
- The Dresden clock
- The servants.

A Game of Chess (extract from The Waste Land II, 1922)

Text of poem: New Explorations Anthology page 130

THEMES, ISSUES AND IMAGERY

'A Game of Chess' is section II of Eliot's best-known long poem, 'The Waste Land'. This was first published in 1922 and quickly and enduringly became synonymous with the poet himself.

Just like the full poem, 'A Game of Chess' can be read on the level of a narrative or in its more complicated form, when an understanding of the many references helps to universalise the themes and issues. This use of references concurs with Eliot's belief, expressed in an essay published in 1919 called 'Tradition and the Individual Talent', that literary tradition does not just belong to the past but should be used by the poet to express himself more completely.

This allows Eliot to overtly contrast the marvels of the past with the squalid nature of the present. 'A Game of Chess' is an example of this, where the first 33 lines describe, amongst other things, past grandeur, while the rest of the poem depicts the present.

'A Game of Chess' describes the stunting effects of improperly directed love or of lust confused with love. The poem is constructed as an apparent contrast between the class, wealth and education of the characters in the first part and the lower-class female characters in a pub at closing time. A closer reading will suggest that the differences are superficial in comparison with the fundamental similarities.

The title of the poem is taken from a play by Thomas Middleton (1580–1627), where the action is played out like moves in a game of chess. This play is a political satire which created a furore at the time and which Eliot has described as 'a perfect piece of literary political art'. Middleton's greatest tragedy, *Women beware Women*, is also in Eliot's mind here. In this play a young woman is raped while her mother, downstairs and quite unaware of what is happening, plays a game of chess. The allusion to the rape of Philomel by Tereus, as told in Greek legend, is symbolised later in the poem. All of this is related to the principal theme of the section: the theme of lust without love.

The opening lines place a woman in a room that has been described as full of 'splendid clutter'. This room, or more precisely a rich lady's boudoir, is surrounded by symbols of our cultural heritage. The extreme lavishness of the boudoir is stressed by evoking the opulence of legendary queens like Cleopatra, Cassiopeia, Dido and Philomel.

These opening lines also reflect Enoborbus's description of Cleopatra's ceremonial barge in Shakespeare's *Antony and Cleopatra*. Cleopatra is famous for her love affairs with powerful Roman generals such as Julius Caesar and Mark Antony. However, Eliot substitutes 'chair' for 'barge', thus evoking the Andromeda legend and the story of Cassiopeia, which are also 'waste-land' tales. Lavish wealth is suggested by 'burnished throne', 'marble', 'golden'. The carved Cupidons on the glass standards suggest possible shameful love affairs.

The 'sevenbranched candelabra' (line 6) adds to the richness of the room while evoking further historical and cultural references. The seven-branched candelabra suggests the Jewish Menorah, which in turn reflects a religious sanctuary and the laying waste of much of Judaic culture over the centuries. The candelabra may also be a reference to the constellation of the Seven Sisters (the Pleiades), which is next to the Cassiopeia constellation. Thus the richness of description also becomes a richness of reference.

This superabundance of rich visual details continues. There are glittering jewels, 'satin cases', 'ivory and coloured glass'. However, the greater the accumulation, the greater the confusion in the reader and the less sure we are of what we are seeing or sensing. The woman's perfumes are strange and synthetic (line 11) and they 'lurked' in her vials, suggesting perhaps something illicit or at least decadent. Words such as 'unstoppered' and 'unguent' add to the sense of decadence, as does a phrase like 'drowned the sense in odours' (line 13) and thus the reader also is left 'troubled, confused'.

'The air | That freshened from the window' (line 13–14) doesn't really freshen the room, but stirs the odours into 'fattening the prolonged candle-flames'. Thus the sense of a stifling, decadent sensuality, or indeed sexuality, is further enhanced.

The 'laquearia' (line 16), which is a panelled ceiling, also holds a reference to Virgil's Aeneid, to the scene in Carthage where Queen Dido gives a banquet for her beloved Aeneas. He will eventually desert her. This reinforces the theme of misplaced love.

The patterns on the ceiling continue the notion of almost divine decadence. The colours are rich; the scale is huge and the associations are deliberate. The 'sea-wood' can be linked with the dolphin, which in early Christian times was a symbol of diligence in love, and the word 'framed' prepares us for the pictorial representation of the Philomel story. Even as he introduces the story, Eliot reinforces the theme and tone with a reference to Milton's 'Paradise Lost'. The picture was like a window opening upon 'a sylvan scene', but this sylvan scene is the one which lay before Satan when he first arrived at the Garden of Eden. Thus sexual corruption is introduced in a deceptively beautiful scene. 'The change of Philomel' is a euphemism for what really happens – the violent rape of this girl. The reader is troubled by such violence occurring in such a beautiful place. The story of Philomel, which Eliot takes from Ovid's *Metamorphoses*, is continued in lines 24–27. The barbarity of the sexual violence done to Philomel by King Tereus of Thrace (who was married to Philomel's sister Procne) is compounded by the cutting off of her tongue. Zeus, the king of the gods, took pity on Philomel and turned her into a nightingale – the 'nightingale' of line 24. This classic tragic story is given further voice in this room of the present. The theme of rape, the most immoral and improperly directed love/lust, forces us to react and to see its significance in the 'present' of the poem.

The violated Philomel, her tongue cut out, still manages to express her sorrow in inviolable voice when, as the nightingale, she fills all the desert with song. Perhaps this expresses Eliot's own wish to fill the wasteland, or desert, with song.

However, this may not be possible, for even the sound of the nightingale – the 'Jug Jug' of line 27 was a conventional Elizabethan method of expressing birdsong – becomes merely salacious in the modern world 'to dirty ears'. The move in line 26 from the past tense 'cried' to the present tense of 'pursues' underscores this more prurient perspective.

Lines 28–31 return to a description of the room. The other decorations, presumably outlining scenes from our cultural inheritance, are dismissed as 'withered stumps of time'. The poet is scornful of those who possess but do not appreciate such riches. This further suggests modern people's failure to come to terms with this same cultural inheritance. These 'stumps of time' then, ironically, no longer speak to us, despite being 'told upon the walls'. Perhaps, the 'stumps of time' may also evoke Philomel's stump of a tongue.

The image of the woman brushing her hair in lines 32–34 suggests a nervous person under considerable emotional strain. The rather surreal image of her hair glowing into words suggests her hypersensitivity and her tense speech, while 'savagely still' suggests a truly neurotic silence.

Lines 35–62 are made up of a dialogue between this woman and a male protagonist. The lines between the quotation marks represent the woman's words. The man's are not given quotation marks. Perhaps he is silent, his answers to her questions being unspoken thoughts. Thus the episode is not, perhaps, a full dialogue: just an exchange of sorts, indicating an emotional and communicative stalemate.

While the staccato rhythm of the woman's utterances reveals her nervous tension, the substance suggests her state of purposelessness. The dialogue, if such it be, pivots around aimless questions and nervous imperatives. The answers of the protagonist indicate that his is as desperate a situation as hers is. However, his is a calmer, more resigned despair. He may be in a psychological Hell ('rats' alley') but he is aware of alternatives. He quotes from Shakespeare's *Tempest*: 'Those are pearls that were his eyes.' This suggests the possibility of transformation. Indeed, in *The Tempest* two lovers play a game of chess that may be linked with genuine love.

However, the sardonic counter-perspective immediately intrudes with 'that Shakespeherian Rag' of line 52, an American hit tune of 1912. The words 'elegant' and 'intelligent' deny in this context both true elegance and true intelligence, and perhaps the possibility of finding the true nature of either in this room with these people, despite the grandeur of the room itself.

The overall sense of purposelessness is reinforced by the woman's final questions and the answers to them. Water, which is normally a symbol of life giving, is here without potency. In fact it must be avoided by using a closed car.

The pub scene, apparently set in a working-class urban area from the tone of the narrative, opens in line 63. Much of the essential nature of this scene is its vocalness. We, the readers, have the experience of eavesdropping on a bar-side monologue. The speaker of the narrative is a woman. The difference in class between her and the woman of the earlier lines is quite apparent. There is a sense of immediacy in the setting, with the woman recounting a dialogue between herself and another woman, Lil, some time earlier. The barman's words, in capitals, break into the narrative contributing meanings to the narrative not recognised by its narrator.

The theme of the past haunting the present is again immediately identifiable, as are those of sterility, lust without love, spiritual/emotional illness and emptiness and intimations of mortality and the role of women. The sense of a Waste Land is acute: not the waste of war's destruction, but the emotional and spiritual sterility of modern man.

In a society where appearance means everything, Lil is told to smarten herself up for her husband Albert, who is returning from war. Lil is criticised for looking old before her time (line 82). Indeed Albert had criticised her some time earlier, presumably when he was on leave, and had given her money to get a new set of teeth. She, however, had used the money to procure an abortion (line 85).

The sympathy of the narrator lies with Albert – the 'poor Albert' of line 73 who will want 'a good time' after his four years in the army. Albert may even 'make off' with those who will give him a good time if Lil doesn't.

Lil, meanwhile, is told to smarten up; that she 'ought to be ashamed . . . to look so antique' and that she is 'a proper fool'. Little sympathy is had for her nearly dying in pregnancy (line 86) and a fatalistic attitude is held towards the sexual demands of her husband (lines 90–91). The vulgar insensitivity of it all can be compared to the fate of Philomel in the first section, while the use of the word 'antique' (line 82) also reminds us of the imagery of the first section. In this outline of Lil's life, social satire is in effect evoking sympathy.

The narrative is not concluded. It is disrupted by closing time and there is the suggestion of the speaker leaving the pub (line 98). Time is running out for the characters in the narrative, reinforced by the urgent, constant calling of 'Hurry Up Please It's Time'. Their farewells fade into the Shakespearian final line, drawing us back to one of those stumps of time – Ophelia's madness and her drowning. This reference adds a sense of dignity to the narrative, while also universalising the themes of misplaced love and destruction.

LANGUAGE, TONE AND MOOD

As said, Eliot's poetry is essentially dramatic – from conflict to characterisation, from action to dialogue, from plot to imagery. The student may be well advised to search for examples of these dramatic elements.

The language in 'A Game of Chess' both reflects and is part of the essential drama of the poem. The diction and syntax of the first section reflect the description of the room. Thus words used to describe the 'props' of the dramatic setting could well describe the style also – words such as 'burnished', 'synthetic', or 'rich profusion'. Archaic and artificial-sounding words such as 'Cupidon', 'unguent' and 'laquearia' add to this sense of an urgent, forced style. Overall, the feeling is one of claustrophobia, a sense of being trapped, or 'prolonged' in this gorgeous, cluttered room. The long sentences add to this feeling. (The first sentence is nine lines long.) Similarly, the various subordinate clauses within these long sentences contribute to the sense of being 'troubled, confused'. The lavish opulence of the room and the language in which it is described thus create a feeling of unease.

In the same way there is a glut of active verbs and participles from lines 14–34, almost hypnotising the reader and stifling a response.

At times, however, the language is wonderfully economic. 'Sad light' (line 20) and 'And still she cried, and still the world pursues' beautifully combine both description and emotion.

However, on other occasions the deliberate literariness of the lines hides the brutal reality. This is the case with the description of the rape of Philomel. The rather lofty, Miltonic tone of:

> Above the antique mantel was displayed
> As though a window gave upon the sylvan scene

tends to obscure what is actually happening in the picture. The euphemisms used, 'The change of Philomel' and 'So rudely forced', tend to lessen the enormity of the sexual violence. Thus the sense of sexual decadence is evoked.

The poet's scornful reaction to such opulent decadence is seen in lines 28–29:

> And other withered stumps of time,
> Were told upon the walls . . .

The cold brevity of these lines is in sharp contrast to the aureate earlier descriptions. This economy of expression continues in line 30:

> Leaned out, leaning, hushing the room enclosed.

Here the strained repetitiveness of the line prepares us for the strained emotions of the woman introduced in line 35, while the word 'enclosed' confirms for us the claustrophobia of the room.

The woman's speech reflects her neurotic state. The repetition of one word from earlier on in the line at the end of three of the lines – 'Speak.' 'What?' 'Think.' – emphasises the neurotic state.

The repetition of 'nothing' from lines 44–50 reflects not only the emotional vacancy of the man, but also suggests that this vacancy reverberates in her mind as well. An emotional stalemate is the result.

The unnaturalistic rhythm of the woman's speech, with its deadening, repetitive, nervous questioning, is counterpointed by the smooth rhythm of the quotation from Shakespeare's *Tempest* (line 49). However, the irony here is further compounded by the vulgar ragtime rhythm of 'that Shakespeherian Rag –'

The diction and syntax of the speaker in the pub scene is essentially that of urban English working class. In tone it is an abrupt shift from that of the woman in the room. The word 'said' is repeated some fifteen times in a gossipy fashion. This not only realistically reflects the rhythms and patterns of speech of the working class, but also adds a certain prayer-like intonation.

The barman's sonorous 'HURRY UP PLEASE IT'S TIME' both breaks into and breaks up the speaker's narrative, adding levels of meaning not intended by the speaker. Its repetition contributes to the urgency of the narrative, even introducing a comic, quasi-apocalyptic tone.

The quotation from Shakespeare's *Hamlet*, which ends the passage, has Ophelia's lingering farewell remind us that the time is indeed out of joint. Ophelia's words, which rise out of the mêlée of farewells in lines 100–101, enhance the pathos of these people's lives and remind us again that the past does indeed haunt the present and that music may be made out of suffering.

MAIN THEMES
- The marvels of the past contrast with the squalid nature of the present
- The past haunts the present
- The stunting effect of improperly directed love/lust
- Lust without love
- Sexual corruption may be deceptively beautiful
- The desire to fill the wasteland with song
- Modern people's failure to come to terms with their cultural heritage
- The emotional strain of modern life
- Sense of purposelessness in modern life
- Intimations of mortality.

MAIN IMAGES
- Opulent luxury of the room
- Rape of Philomel
- Nervous gestures of the woman
- The story of Lil and Albert
- The landlord crying 'Time'.

Journey of the Magi (1927)
Text of poem: New Explorations Anthology page 136

This is the first of the Ariel Poems, a set of poems which, beginning in 1927, the year in which Eliot joined the Anglican church, were published by Faber & Faber as a sort of Christmas card. Both this poem and 'A Song for Simeon' (1928) refer specifically to the birth of Christ.

The Magi were the three wise men or kings – commonly, but not scripturally, known as Balthazar, Caspar and Melchior – who journeyed from the east to pay homage to the newly born baby Jesus, according to the gospel of St Matthew 11: 1–12. However, Eliot's inspiration comes not from this well-known gospel story alone but also from a sermon preached by Lancelot Andrews, Bishop in Winchester, on Christmas Day 1622, which Eliot quotes in his 'Selected Essays'. The first five lines of the poem are a direct quotation from this sermon by Lancelot Andrews.

The poem is essentially a dramatic monologue spoken by one of the magi, who is now an old man, recalling and reminiscing on the journey he and his companions made to witness a Birth. Thus the poem is concerned with a quest and those travelling must traverse a type of wasteland to reach the promised land. The Magi's journey is challenging, painful and difficult. It involved giving up old comforts, certainties and beliefs so that it became a 'Hard and bitter agony for us'. Reaching their destination doesn't lead to any great sense of achievement or celebration. Instead the narrator is unsure of the significance of what he has seen. 'It was (you may say) satisfactory.' The narrator remains disturbed and bewildered as he returns to the 'old dispensation' which he and his companions now find strange. He longs for death now, so that he can achieve new life.

The poem can be seen as an analogy of Eliot's own agonising spiritual journey. The quest for a new spiritual life involves rejecting the old life with its many attractions. Thus, the Birth also includes a death; the death of the old way of life. Such a journey involves doubt, regrets and lack of conviction. Maybe 'this was all folly.' This tone of uncertainty leads us to appreciate that rather than asserting his beliefs Eliot is expressing his willingness to believe, which is his present spiritual condition.

THEMES AND ISSUES

The poem is a dramatic monologue in which the magus, the narrator, tells of his and his companions' experiences in their journey to the birth of Christ. The opening five lines are an abbreviation of Andrew's sermon as mentioned above, which Eliot includes as part of the magus's narration.

The journey undertaken is one from death to life. It begins in 'The very dead of winter.' The hardships endured represent the sacrifice the magi must make in order to achieve new birth. Also, before there is a birth there must be a death of the old life.

The hardships undergone include not only the weather and trouble with their camels, but also major regrets for what is left behind:

The summer palaces . . . the silken girls bringing sherbet.

(lines 9–10)

These real attractions cannot be easily overcome.

Exactly how tough the journey was is seen in the sequence from line 11 to line 16. The increasing torment outlined in the matter-of-fact, descriptive statements here is made all the more effective by the repetition of 'And . . . ' The hostility of various communities, symbolic of a disbelieving world, leads them 'to travel all night'. Adding to their discomfort is the realisation that the hostile unbelievers may be right – 'That this was all folly.' (line 20)

The next section, beginning at line 21, seems at first to confirm the death-to-life theme. It is 'dawn'; there is 'a temperate valley', 'a running stream and a water-mill beating the darkness' – all of which can be seen as birth images. However, ambiguity and uncertainty quickly return. The 'three trees' are reminders of the Crucifixion of Christ, as are the 'Six hands . . . dicing for pieces of silver' (line 28). These, coupled with the negativity of the horse galloping away, 'the empty wine-skins' and 'no information', can be seen as furthering the theme of death. However they may also suggest the interrelation between death and birth. Christ's incarnation leads inexorably to His Crucifixion, just as His Crucifixion leads to eternal life.

Ambiguity can also be seen in what should be the joyful climax of the journey and confirmation of belief. However, this is not so. The intense anticipation and anxiety of 'not a moment too soon' is immediately followed by the uncertain reticence of

it was (you may say) satisfactory. (line 32)

No description of the Birth or the One who was born is given.

This sense of uncertainty turns to a degree of confusion in the last section, as the magus tries to work out the meaning of what he saw. Maybe like the knight meeting the Fisher King in the Holy Grail legend, he has failed to ask the right question. While he is convinced that it was significant – 'And I would do it again' (line 34) – and is anxious that no part of his narrative should be overlooked:

. . . but set down
This set down
This: . . .
(lines 34–36)

the Birth doesn't seem to have been what he expected. He 'had thought they [birth and death] were different', but 'this Birth was . . . like Death, our death.' (lines 39–40).

So the Magi return to their kingdoms but feel alienated among their own people. They must continue to live amidst the old way of life – 'the old dispensation' (line 42) – while not believing in it. So their Birth remains a bitter agony while they wait for 'another death' (line 44). Another death is required – the magus's own, or perhaps Christ's – before he can enter a new life.

IMAGERY AND SYMBOLISM

The whole poem is structured around a journey, both real and symbolic. The journey as recalled by the magus is one from death to birth, the imagery of which suggests the inner struggles of the narrator and his companions.

The journey begins at 'the worst time of year' with 'The ways deep and the weather sharp' and ends in 'a temperate valley . . . smelling of vegetation'. The symbolic movement from death to life is clear. Paradoxically, however, there is also a movement from life to death. Here 'The summer palaces . . . And the silken girls bringing sherbet' represent the old life. The travellers make their way through a wasteland of 'cities hostile and the towns unfriendly', until in the valley there is a symbolic death of the old life as the 'old white horse galloped away'. Some critics have seen references to the Fisher King myth in the journey and its symbols.

The second stanza contains a series of death and birth images. 'Dawn', 'temperate valley', 'vegetation' can be seen as birth images, while water is universally acknowledged as symbolising life. However, a flowing river or stream is also a traditional poetic symbol of the passing of time. The action of the 'water-mill' can be seen as beating the darkness of time.* There then follow a series of images foreshadowing the well-known imagery surrounding Christ's death. The 'three trees on the low sky' reflect the three crosses on the Hill of Calvary. The 'hands dicing' suggest the Roman soldiers dicing for Christ's clothes and the 'pieces of silver' remind us of the thirty pieces of silver that Judas was paid for his treachery.

The 'white horse' can be seen as an ambiguous image. It may symbolise the life-giving, triumphant Christ of the Book of Revelations (VI: 2, 19:11). However, as the horse is said to be 'old' and since it 'galloped away' it may also represent the collapse of paganism, 'the old dispensation' of line 42.

LANGUAGE AND TONE

As befits a dramatic monologue the language reflects not only natural speech patterns, which catch the rhythms of speech, but also a particular voice – the voice of the magus, at times both reminiscent and complaining:

> Then the camel men cursing and grumbling
> And running away, and wanting their liquor and women.

Here the emphasis falls into a natural pattern of speech and voice inflection. The prayer-like, incantatory tone also befits both the speaker and the theme. The strong repetition of 'And' in the first two sections reflects this. Overall the purposefully ambiguous symbols and images introduce a tone of uncertainty.

The opening paraphrased uncertainty of Lancelot Andrews' sermon sets the tone of desolation and the bitter environment of the first stanza. The quotation also serves a second purpose for Eliot. It incorporates the poem into a particular tradition. Thus it serves a similar function to the quotation from Dante at the beginning of 'Prufrock' and is part of his efforts to create a synthesis between past and present.

The remainder of the first stanza is quite vitriolic in tone, as the magus criticises both his predicament and his previous life. This criticism is coupled with a tone of regret,

> The summer palaces on slopes, the terraces,
> And the silken girls bringing sherbet.

The sensual sibilant 's' sounds of these lines underscore what is being regretted. A tone of contempt can be seen in the ever-expanding criticism of the remainder of the first stanza.

The second stanza suggests a tone of nostalgia as the magus remembers his arrival at 'a temperate valley'. Then the last three lines of this stanza culminate in an understatement: 'it was (you may say) satisfactory.'

The word 'satisfactory' as seen, reflects the ambiguity and uncertainty of the magi's reaction. Perhaps, they are not completely aware of its relevance. The word is given particular emphasis by the expression in parentheses preceding it and by its irregularity with the set rhythm of the line.

This tone of uncertainty is continued in the next stanza and develops into a tone of anxiety and of urgency:

> . . . but set down
> This set down
> This: . . .

The dislocation and repetition of these lines emphasise this residual tone of uncertainty and urgency. The run-on line:

> . . . this Birth was
> Hard and bitter agony for us, . . .

creates a similar tone of anxiety and perhaps even of self-pity.

The poem ends in a conditioned statement:

> 'I should be glad of another death',

perhaps expressing a tone of resignation.

MAIN THEMES

- The Birth of Jesus Christ
- A quest/journey as an analogy of spiritual searching
- Lack of conviction/uncertainty/alienation
- Birth entails death
- The need for suffering in order to attain a new Birth.

MAIN IMAGES

- A journey
- A wasteland of 'cities hostile'
- Death and birth images
- Biblical images.

Usk (extract from Landscapes III, 1935)

Text of poem: New Explorations Anthology page 138

INTRODUCTION

This is one of Eliot's five 'Landscape poems', three of which are based in America, one in Wales and one in Scotland.

This poem resulted from a ten-day holiday taken by Eliot in Wales in 1935.

In keeping with the term 'Landscape', the poem is a suggestive or evocative sketch in which the poet can be seen as an artist/painter. Like the other 'Landscape' poems, this poem consists of scenes and perceptions of deep significance in the development of Eliot's thinking. In particular, the 'Landscape' poems are definitive pointers in terms of Eliot's developing religious and poetic sensibilities, which are further explored in the 'Four Quartets'.

In this sense, although listed under *Minor Poems*, there is nothing minor about the significance of these poems. Indeed, taken as a sequence of five poems, we can see that Eliot is again evoking drama here, as he did in 'The Wasteland' and in the individual quartets of 'Four Quartets'. The sequence of five is in keeping with the number of acts required by Aristotle for tragic drama. Shakespeare also adhered to this. So both 'Usk' and 'Rannoch' can be seen as two acts in a drama outlining the relationship between human beings and the natural world. As number III, Usk marks a climax in the sequence.

A READING OF THE POEM

'Usk' is a pastoral poem in both senses of the word, i.e. it is descriptive of the countryside and is also spiritually instructive.

The opening of the poem is abrupt, sudden and in the imperative mood. The reader is being instructed:

> Do not suddenly break . . . or
> Hope to find . . .
> . . . do not spell

We are being told *not* to seek images such as 'the white hart', 'the white well', the 'lance'. These are evocative of the classical Arthurian/Celtic legends. As such they are also evocative of the countryside.

Thus Eliot is suggesting that in such a landscape we should not conjure up the past or any notion of romantic fantasy. This he dismisses as 'Old enchantments.' He tells us to 'Let them sleep.' As a sort of second thought he allows us to '"Gently dip, but not too deep"'.

However, having been instructed *against* something, we are now instructed *towards* something. Our relationship with the landscape should not be escapist or full of romantic fantasy, but should be such as to lead us *towards* the spiritual.

In a prayer-like incantation, he tells us to 'Lift your eyes'. We are being sent on a more active spiritual journey – a pilgrimage – 'Where the roads dip and where the roads rise'.

Here we are to seek 'The hermit's chapel, the pilgrim's prayer' which, although conventional images of the spiritual, will not be found in any conventional setting but 'Where the grey light meets the green air'.

A spiritual home will be found in something that is neither human nor animal. Indeed it may not be found in the natural landscape at all, but in the eternal continuum of light and space, i.e. 'Where the grey light meets the green air'.

There is a note of hope here that is not found in 'The Love Song of J. Alfred Prufrock', 'Preludes' or 'A Game of Chess'. It echoes that tiny note of hope, which is to be found in 'The Journey of the Magi' and marks a shift towards a spiritual solution for Eliot in the face of life's difficulties.

USE OF LANGUAGE

The language suggests a certain sense of detachment on the part of the poet. The poem reads as advice to others from someone who has already reached a conclusion or discovered a position with which he is happy. Even though this is a description of a place, the poet is not part of the place. This can be seen as a type of metaphysical detachment.

The negative imperatives and the cacophonous alliterative sounds of the first line introduce us to the poet's attitudes towards the 'Old enchantments.'

These same imperatives also evoke that sense of self-assured, commanding authority we associate with metaphysical poets such as the seventeenth-century poet, John Donne.

In keeping with this robust style the rhythm is quick and irregular. This lively, almost bounding style is furthered by the use of alliteration and repetition in many of the lines. The rhythm, like the road, dips and rises. The use of enjambment, or run-on lines, in the second part of the poem in particular, and the quite intense rhyme, also add to the sense of insistent energy.

The incantatory tones of some of the imperatives have been alluded to already. In fact the tone of the whole poem can be found in the three dimeter lines:

> Hope to find . . .
> Lift your eyes . . .
> Seek only there . . .

The dramatic exhortational tone of an Old Testament prophet is clear and in keeping with one aspect of the pastoral theme.

Finally, the choice of colours in this landscape 'painting' suggests both a sense of peace and invigoration. 'White' is bright, while 'grey light' evokes images of a chill, bracing wind, and 'green' is traditionally seen as a natural, soothing colour. The sense of peace is also evoked by the choice of individual words such as 'sleep', 'gently', 'dip' and 'prayer'.

MAIN THEMES
- A pastoral poem in both senses
- Avoid the 'old enchantments'
- Seek the spiritual
- A journey.

MAIN IMAGES
- Medieval romantic fantasies – 'hart', 'well', 'lance'
- The road
- 'The hermit's chapel'
- 'Grey light', 'green air'.

Rannoch, by Glencoe (extract from Landscapes IV, 1935)

Text of poem: New Explorations Anthology page 140

'Rannoch' is the fourth in the five-poem sequence, 'Landscapes'. (See Introduction on 'Usk'.)

A READING OF THE POEM

The poem explores the relationship between human beings and the natural world. Like 'Usk' it is a pastoral, in the sense of being both a description of a countryside and also containing a message. It may suggest elements of a pastoral elegy to some readers.

In many ways this poem is a stripping away of the idyllic, idealised Golden Age pastoral to reveal a landscape of famine and war.

The poem opens with two death-in-life images – 'the crow starves', 'the patient stag | Breeds for the rifle.'

They are the distressing results of the capacity of humans to condition the landscape. This is a barren landscape full of death. Here all creatures feel constricted and oppressed:

> . . . Between the soft moor
> And the soft sky, scarcely room
> To leap or soar.

The softness here is not of ease or comfort, but a reflection of the sense of oppression. Sky and moor practically meet. If all relationships need space and time, then failure is inevitable here due to a distinct lack of space. This landscape is a burden.

Erosion is the norm here – 'Substance crumbles'; everything is suspended 'in the thin air' of the inexorable movement of time – 'Moon cold or moon hot.'

This psychological topography allows no means of escape. 'The road winds' without apparent purpose. Instead we are offered a journey through 'listlessness', 'languor' and 'clamour'. The sense of direction and invigorating movement evident in 'Usk' is totally absent here. We are stuck in the wretchedness of history and its endless cycles: 'ancient war', 'broken steel', 'confused wrong'. These are the relics of embattled lives, before which the only appropriate response is silence. These old rivalries will not be resolved because 'Memory is strong | Beyond the bone.'

In this landscape of memory where 'Pride snapped', the 'Shadow of pride is long'. In 'the long pass' of a lifetime, there will be no resolution, no reconciliation – 'No concurrence of bone.' This is because even though pride is humiliated (snapped), it holds onto its shadow.

Unlike 'Usk' this poem offers no religious perspective, no sense of hope and direction between life and death – only a sense of 'betweenness', where we are biologically fated to evoke old rivalries. They are of the bone and 'Beyond the bone'.

Living in a state of betweenness, the rational aspect of ourselves is lost amidst the 'Clamour of confused wrong', almost indifferent to suffering, including our own. As is common in Eliot's poetry, the human in its non-rational state is symbolised in animal imagery. Here the human is seen as 'crow' and 'the patient stag' awaiting their fate. They are as unable to understand what they had been reduced to as are the inhabitants of the city street in the 'Preludes'.

The existentialist awareness and its agony are to be found in the speakers and the readers of these poems.

The tragedy of 'Rannoch' may be alleviated by the hope of 'Usk'. However, 'Usk' is not a solution but an indication of the journey that must be taken. But 'Rannoch' is the tragedy that may prevent 'Usk'.

The use of language

This is a dysfunctional landscape and the poet's use of language reflects that.

The end-of-line neatness of strong rhyme and natural pauses in 'Usk' is absent. Instead we are presented with a rather discordant structure. A line or lines run on, only to finish abruptly in the middle of the next line.

There is an emphasis on alliteration, in keeping with Eliot's admiration of medieval English.

This, however, does nothing to even out or smooth the lines. Rather the effect is insistent, if not altogether frenzied when combined with the stutter-like rhythm. This nervous, stutter-like effect is added to by actual close word repetition. All of this creates an unease and a tension in the reader.

Rhyme, where it does exist, is internal or slightly off end – e.g. 'wrong', 'strong' and 'long' and 'sour', 'war'. Again this adds to the sense of a discordant structure.

The sense of constriction explored in the imagery of the first four lines is also present in the language. In the second sentence:

> Between the soft moor
> And the soft sky, scarcely room
> To leap or soar.

there appears to be no room for a main verb.

We are also presented with an anagram as a type of rhyme, i.e. 'moor' and 'room'. The 'moor' turns on itself to become 'room', emphasising the constriction and oppression and becoming an analogy for the retracing and restating of grievances in a closed system of confused wrongs and strong memories.

Main themes
- Death in life
- Time
- Impact of human beings on the natural world
- War, destruction and erosion
- Unresolved rivalries.

MAIN IMAGES

- The crow and the stag
- Moor and sky
- Winding road
- (Images of) war
- Bone.

East Coker IV *(extract from* The Four Quartets, 1940)

Text of poem: New Explorations Anthology page 142

INTRODUCTION

This short piece is part of 'East Coker', the second of 'The Four Quartets'.

'The Four Quartets' is seen by many critics as the most important work of Eliot's career. Helen Gardner has called them Eliot's masterpiece. The new forms and ideas with which he experimented in the 'Landscape' poems ('Usk', 'Rannoch') are developed fully in 'The Four Quartets'.

In keeping with the musical title, the structure of the 'Quartets' is symphonic and thus extraordinarily complex – a complexity which need not trouble the student here.

Time is again one of the central themes – in particular its constant change in contrast with unchanging eternity. The philosophical considerations of the contrast between the real and the ideal, the human and the spiritual, explored in his earlier poetry, are again evident here.

'East Coker' takes its name from the village in Somerset, England, from which Eliot's ancestors emigrated to America. 'East Coker' is concerned with the place of mankind in the natural order of things and with the notion of renewal. This theme of rebirth, which is also found in the 'Journey of the Magi', is part of the spiritual progress of the soul. The soul must yield itself to God's hands and die in order to be born again. Indeed the soul must first suffer in order to be capable of responding fully to God's love. St John of the Cross calls this 'the dark night of the soul'. The saint's writing on this has influenced Eliot here.

A READING OF THE POEM

The poem, written for Good Friday 1940, sees Eliot at his most symbolic and a reading of the poem is, in effect, an interpretation of this symbolism.

The poem is a metaphysical one, structured around metaphysical conceits and paradoxes similar to those which may be found in the poetry of the seventeenth-century poet, John Donne. It lies in the tradition of seventeenth-century devotional verse, such as that of Donne, Herbert and Vaughan.

The 'wounded surgeon' is Jesus Christ, whose suffering and death on the Cross, and whose subsequent Resurrection, ensured mankind's redemption.

The 'wounded surgeon' will cure the soul of its sickness: 'the distempered part'. The surgeon's knife, 'the steel', which operates, or 'questions', is God's love. This is in keeping with St John of the Cross's 'The Dark Night of the Soul', which has influenced Eliot here.

The soul is not unaware of God's love operating on it. It feels 'The sharp compassion of the healer's art'.

The oxymoron that is 'sharp compassion' suggests the idea of a necessary evil, i.e. in order to be cured the soul must suffer first. Suffering is a means of grace. This is 'the enigma of the fever chart'. A physical evil can be seen as a spiritual good. Thus the metaphysical paradox is 'resolved'.

The beginning of the second verse continues this notion of suffering as a means of grace. Thus, 'Our only health is the disease'.

The conceit of a hospital is continued with the image of 'the dying nurse'.

'The dying nurse' is the Church – 'dying' in the sense of the common fate of mankind. The Church's role is not to placate or please us, but to remind us firstly of 'Adam's curse', which is never-ending toil and suffering, similar to the vision of mankind's daily life in the 'Preludes'. The Church's second role is to remind us that, 'to be restored, our sickness must grow worse', meaning that it is only through the fullest suffering that we can be fully cleansed or cleared of our sickness/evil.

The 'hospital' conceit is continued in the third stanza. 'The whole earth is our hospital' in the sense that it is here we can learn the value of suffering and can be cured of our sickness. The 'ruined millionaire' is Adam, whose endowment brought sin into the world – Adam's sin is Original Sin in Christian belief. The 'paternal care' is that of God, under Whose care we would be privileged to die, if we do well as 'patients' in this world. The word 'prevents' is used in its seventeenth-century sense, meaning to go before us with spiritual guidance. God will help us by guiding us towards repentance. The second and modern meaning of 'prevents', that is to stop or frustrate, is also appropriate. God stops our lives everywhere through death.

The notion of cure is continued in the fourth stanza. The cure is a fever one – because 'to be restored, our sickness must grow worse', as stated in the second stanza. The purgation, or cure, must move from a purgation of the flesh, burning away all the sickness and impurities of the flesh, until it ascends to a purgation of the mind:

> If to be warmed, then I must freeze
> And quake in frigid purgatorial fires

The essence of a breaking cold/hot fever, the body shivering and sweating as it rids itself of disease, is achieved here.

The flames of purgation Eliot calls roses, the symbol of both human and divine love. Roses and thorns are also the emblem of martyrdom. So suffering is seen as the basis of the cure – a thorough penitential suffering.

The fifth stanza opens with an image of the 'wounded surgeon' again. It is Jesus Christ on the Cross, whose suffering leads to our Redemption. The image also evokes the Eucharist, the central act of worship for Christians. It may also evoke the need for suffering in ourselves, so that we too will be cured.

The image of flesh and blood is continued in the next two lines in Eliot's criticism of our blindness. We like to think that there is no need for humility and penance with our ideas of our own importance – 'we are sound, substantial flesh and blood'.

The adjectives 'sound, substantial' suggest that we rely too much on the physical, the materialistic.

However, Eliot recognises that behind our materialism, we innately acknowledge our need for repentance and the grace of God. This is why 'we call this Friday good.'

USE OF LANGUAGE

In this poem Eliot has revived the metaphysical poem. He uses many of the features we associate with the seventeenth-century poetry of Donne, Herbert and Vaughan.

In line with metaphysical poetry there is a strong sense of argument throughout the poem. The argument, as outlined above in the READING OF THE POEM, is that we need to reject the demands of the body and achieve redemption through curing its ills. Pain and suffering are means towards achieving redemptive grace or enlightenment.

This argument is presented throughout a series of metaphysical paradoxes, e.g.

> The 'wounded surgeon' will cure us
> 'sharp compassion'
> 'the enigma of the fever chart'
> 'Our only health is the disease'
> 'to be restored, our sickness must grow worse.'
> 'if we do well, we shall | Die'
> 'If to be warmed, then I must freeze'
> 'frigid purgatorial fires'
> 'in spite of that, we call this Friday good.'

Many of these are examples of what is known as metaphysical wit, which is renowned for its clever but serious, incisive, challenging and intelligent puns and paradoxes. The wit of the last stanza in particular removes any sense of emotional religiosity and serves to intensify the devotional mood.

A conceit is an elaborate, sustained comparison. These were much used by the seventeenth-century metaphysical poets. Eliot, in keeping with this, uses conceits in this poem. The 'wounded surgeon' is an example, as are seeing the earth as a hospital and the notion of the fever cure.

The meaning of symbols used is explored above in READING OF THE POEM. However the student should be aware that symbolism is as much a use of language as it is an exploration of meaning. Such usage invigorates both language and meaning.

Similarly, Eliot's precision of language adds depth to the meaning of both individual words and the poem as a whole. His use of the word 'prevents' in the third stanza is an example of this.

Examples of metaphysical wit are seen in the last stanza, in the evocative fused imagery of the first two lines in particular.

Eliot 'reinvented' the alliterated four-stress line commonly found in medieval English. This poem generally follows that pattern, with quite strong medial pauses: e.g. 'The **wound**ed **surgeon plies** the **steel**' or 'B**eneath** the **bleed**ing **hands** we **feel**'.

However, this kind of verse can become monotonous. Eliot's genius was to apply the pattern with sufficient flexibility to avoid monotonous rigidity.

W.B. Yeats once said that rhythm in poetry should be used 'to prolong the moment of contemplation'. Perhaps we can say this of both the rhythm and the strong, definite rhyme patterns in this poem.

MAIN THEMES

- The idea of necessary evil – a physical evil may be a spiritual good.
- Suffering as a means of attaining grace/redemption
- The purgation of evil
- The caring love of God
- Growth towards a new life.

MAIN IMAGES

- The wounded surgeon
- Conceit of a hospital
- The nurse
- The ruined millionaire – Adam
- Play of opposites – 'frigid fires'
- The Cross
- The Eucharist.

T.S. Eliot – An Overview

Not even the most learned critic has said that Eliot's poetry makes easy reading. Yet of all twentieth-century poets he is perhaps the most rewarding. No other poet has better expressed the social condition and psychological state of modern man.

While Eliot's poetry can be read with pleasure at first sight, a full understanding will not come immediately. This is so because quite often, instead of the regular evocative images other poets use, Eliot presents us with a series of literary and historical references. Eliot himself insisted that the reader must be prepared to answer the call for knowledge which poetry demands. Indeed if the reader does persevere, then he/she will be rewarded with a use of symbolism and allusion, and an experimenting with the language and form of poetry, which deepen and intensify the experience of reading it. He/she will feel what Eliot himself called the 'direct shock of poetic intensity'.

INFLUENCES AND THE 'MODERN MOVEMENT'

The 'Modern Movement' is that which effected a revolution in English literature between 1910 and 1930. As the leading poet in the movement, Eliot brought about the break from the poetic tradition of the nineteenth century. Apart from some notable exceptions, such as Hopkins and Hardy, poetry in English had become degenerate in both taste and theme. It appealed to the imperialist prejudices of a smug, self-complacent audience, convinced of its own superiority in just about everything. Poetry flattered rather than educated.

Eliot's achievement, in both his poetry and his critical essays, was in founding new criteria of judgement on what constitutes poetry.

Similar revolutions were happening in the other arts. James Joyce revolutionised prose writing, as did Pablo Picasso painting and Igor Stravinsky music. The First World War (1914–1918) also helped. At first poetry was used for propaganda. Rupert Brooke's saccharine war sonnets were enthusiastically received. However, as the war dragged on public perception was forced to change, as Wilfred Owen and Siegfried Sassoon wrote of the revolting horrors of war. Owen insisted that poetry need not be beautiful, but it must be truthful.

One aspect of the revolution that Eliot effected was the introduction to English of a style of poetry that is known as 'Symbolism'. When he arrived at Oxford in 1914, Eliot brought with him a deep love and admiration for the French nineteenth-century symbolist poets. These included Charles Baudelaire and Jules Laforgue. Eliot's debt to these poets is extensive – from diction to creative remodelling of subject matter, from tone to phrasing.

Eliot adapted from Charles Baudelaire (1821–1867) the poetical possibilities of addressing 'the more sordid aspects of the modern metropolis'. Examples of these are seen in 'Preludes' and in 'The Love Song of J. Alfred Prufrock'.

From Laforgue (1860–1887) he adopted a tone of mocking irony and despair. Eliot said he owed more to Laforgue 'than to any poet in any language'. Laforgue was a technical innovator. He pioneered *'vers libre'*, or free verse, which Eliot also adopted. *'Vers libre'* is verse freed from rigid, conventional forms of regular rhyme and rhythm. Instead Laforgue, and Eliot, use odd or irregular rhyme with varying rhythms to enhance both the theme and tone of the verse. Examples of these can be found throughout Eliot's poetry.

Laforgue also developed a sort of dramatic monologue, a stream-of-consciousness or interior monologue, as it is better known. Eliot adapted this method also, as can be seen in 'The Love Song of J. Alfred Prufrock' and 'Journey of the Magi'. However, Eliot developed the method to a further degree in the distancing and the self-mockery of the dramatic personae of his poems.

Eliot also admired many of the seventeenth-century English poets, seeing in them the emotional intensity and intellectual precision he found in the French Symbolists. Eliot saw a similarity between the seventeenth and twentieth centuries, in that both centuries experienced the disintegration of old traditions and the arrival of new learning. He particularly admired those who came to be known as the Metaphysical Poets and felt that John Donne was closer to him in spirit than most other English poets. Eliot shares with Donne an often robust style, with colloquial language mingling with intellectual language. Like Donne, Eliot's poems contain a sense of argument, unexpected juxtapositions and eclectic references, demanding an intelligent attention from the reader. Even a cursory glance at 'A Game of Chess' or 'The Four Quartets' will confirm this.

However, it was the Italian poet Dante (1265–1321) who was the greatest influence upon Eliot. He saw Dante as greater even than Shakespeare, seeing the Italian poet expressing 'deeper degrees of degradation and higher degrees of exaltation'. The presence of Dante in Eliot's verse extends beyond the epigraph in 'The Love Song of J. Alfred Prufrock' to a recreation of the whole experience of his verse. The hell or purgatory in which both Prufrock and the women in 'A Game of Chess' live reflects this.

Eliot first met Ezra Pound in 1915, another great American poet and critic, who subsequently had a profound influence on Eliot's development both as a poet and as a literary critic. It was through Pound that Eliot came to be influenced by the so-called imagist school of poetry. Imagism promoted the use of common speech in poetry, a complete freedom in subject choice, accuracy, concentration and precise description. The reader need only look at the 'Preludes', 'Rannoch, by Glencoe' or 'Aunt Helen' to see how true all of this is of Eliot's poetry.

THEMES

As said above, Eliot lived in a period that saw the disintegration of old traditions and beliefs and the arrival of new learning and new experiences. As a poet then, he had to find a different way of addressing the new. Pound's famous phrase 'Make it new' was a rallying cry to those who wished to tackle themes relevant to their own experience. For Eliot, this was as much a recovery of a lost tradition in poetry as it was a revolution. Thus we find in Eliot's poetry a *contemplation of the past and an examination of the new* in relation to the past. 'Journey of the Magi' is one such poem.

While Eliot made poetry new, it didn't mean that he approved of everything that was new in contemporary life. On the contrary, there was his belief that much in modern life was a betrayal of civilised values. His poetry is full of his sense of disgust for urban society. 'The Love Song of J. Alfred Prufrock' and 'Preludes' are two such poems. *Modern urban life*, for Eliot, *is an emotional and cultural wasteland*, a world of thoughtless self-gratification and deadening purposelessness. The modern city is a symbol of the nightmare of human decadence. This view is explored in particular in 'Preludes' and 'A Game of Chess'.

This particular notion of *meaningless existence* expands into the wider theme of *death-in-life* and *life-in-death*. Twentieth-century man may be condemned to a living death, but redemption can be achieved. For Eliot this is the answer to how we should live: that is, we need to die to the old life in order to be born into the new. Humanity needs to *journey in search of its spiritual well-being*. This may involve *suffering*, but the cure is at hand. The 'Journey of the Magi', 'Usk' and 'East Coker IV' explore these themes. To redeem itself and construct a new life for itself, humanity must face a painful readjustment of its values and attitudes. Death accompanies a new Birth. Joy follows.

Much of the above reflects Eliot's own *spiritual journey* and his conversion to Anglicanism in 1927. Anglicanism, or more particularly Anglo-Catholicism, appealed to his need for orthodox theological dogma and for an emotional, mystical spirituality.

His conversion to Anglicanism was also a consolation to him during the nightmare that was his first marriage. This too was a living death. His marriage with Vivienne Haigh-Wood may explain the most persistent *personal theme* underlying Eliot's poetry i.e. the *sexual*, whose erotic note is as often as not linked with regret, disappointment, frustration and longing. 'The Love Song of J. Alfred Prufrock' explores this theme most strongly. At the centre of Prufrock's purgatory is a *confusion between love and sexual gratification*. Prufrock is both attracted to and repulsed by women. The theme of *appearance and reality*, or the *real and the ideal*, is explored in Prufrock's love-song, where his fear of women who 'fix you with a formulated phrase' is contrasted with his idealised vision of womanhood as 'sea-girls wreathed with seaweed red and brown'.

Eliot's *portrayal of women* is said to be critically and tortuously realistic, reflecting his attitude towards *human relationships* in general. The girl in the 'Preludes' is physically repulsive and, while the woman in the first part of 'A Game of Chess' may be attractive, she is an emotional wreck. The second part of 'A Game of Chess' explores the tragedy resulting from casual relationships. Miss Helen Slingsby, in 'Aunt Helen', is his 'maiden aunt', whose social foibles suggest a fastidious but repressed character and whose mores are flamboyantly rejected by the behaviour of the footman and maid after her death.

For Eliot, though, it is only the *beauty of divine love* that makes sense of all human relationships. In the 'Preludes' he declares:

> I am moved by fancies . . .
> The notion of some infinitely gentle,
> Infinitely suffering thing.

'The Journey of the Magi' too can be seen as an exploration of divine love or as a struggle to understand the Incarnation of Christ, that moment when divine love made itself manifest.

This theme of *divine love* is made all the more clear in 'East Coker IV', where Christ himself is seen as suffering and dying in order to be reborn. Divine love is linked inextricably with the theme of a journey through suffering to a rebirth.

The Incarnation took place in a moment of time, a moment when historical time and the timelessness of God's eternity met. Eliot's exploration of *time* is central to his poems. It is part of his effort to make sense of life. This is seen in 'Journey of the Magi'.

In 'The Love Song of J. Alfred Prufrock', time is seen as inexorably repetitive, a process which leads ultimately to decay. In the 'Preludes' time is a burden, whose rhythmic patterns beat out the tedium of urban life. Time destroys 'Aunt Helen's' passion for order and restraint, while the result of man's behaviour in times past is seen in 'Rannoch, by Glencoe', where both man and animals are stuck in the wretchedness of history.

IMAGERY, SYMBOLISM AND ALLUSION

While all of the above are dealt with in specific detail in the discussion of the individual poems, a few general points may be useful for the student also.

Eliot's use of *imagery is eclectic*, that is he drew inspiration from a wide tableau of human experience and did not limit himself to nature as a source, something which had become so much a part of the later Romantics. Under French influence and his admiration for seventeenth-century English poets, Eliot trawled widely to ensure an intellectual sharpness and an emotional intensity in his poems.

Much of the meaning and the power of Eliot's poetry lie in his use of images and symbols. *Sordid, seedy images of city life* appear again and again, from 'The Love Song of J. Alfred Prufrock' to 'Preludes' to 'A Game of Chess'. Even in 'Journey of the Magi', cities are seen as 'hostile'. Such use of significant imagery becomes, with repetition, a symbol. It evokes particular ideas and emotions. This is in keeping with Eliot's rather notorious view that poetry communicates before it is understood. Thus the suggestiveness of imagery and symbolism become part of the excitement of discovery when reading Eliot's poetry.

Similarly *journeys, a street or road are common images* throughout Eliot's poetry. These are seen in 'Journey of the Magi', 'Preludes', 'Usk' and 'Rannoch, by Glencoe', for example. These images also become symbolic, evoking Eliot's search or quest for meaning in life, culminating in his achievement of a satisfactory religious perspective.

However, individual images can also be symbolic. Eliot, for example, uses *animal imagery* to reflect the human in its non-thinking, non-rational state. Hence the use of the crab image/symbol in 'The Love Song of J. Alfred Prufrock'. The 'crow' and 'the patient stag' play similar roles in 'Rannoch, by Glencoe'.

Similarly, Eliot's use of *body parts as images*, as in 'Preludes', 'The Love Song of J. Alfred Prufrock' and 'A Game of Chess' becomes symbolic of the depersonalisation, stereotyping and conformity of modern urban society.

Similarly also, the *images of clocks* and the references to *time*, from 'Aunt Helen' to 'Preludes' to 'A Game of Chess' and 'The Love Song of J. Alfred Prufrock', can become a symbol of individual transience and the urgency for renewal.

The student should be particularly aware of Eliot's abrupt transitions in imagery and of his use of images other than visual ones. 'Preludes', for example, explores *aural, tactile and olfactory images* in quickly changing, cinematic-style sequences.

Eliot is the most erudite of poets. He was widely read in *everything from literature to history, from psychology to anthropology, from psychology to philosophy*. This is in keeping with his passion not only for self-discovery, but also for discovering the nature of twentieth-century man. Hence his use of allusion is his way of exploring intellectual traditions and expressing himself more precisely.

In this way, his use of allusion is not just an ostentatious *reference to literary history*, for example, but is a way of making a tradition alive again, while also focusing the present situation in that tradition. So, his epigraph in 'The Love Song of J. Alfred Prufrock' both recalls Dante's work and places Prufrock in an urban Hell. Thus, his allusions universalise his themes and the situations in which his characters' personae exist.

Sometimes his allusions come in the form of more *indirect quotation*, as in his reference in 'The Love Song of J. Alfred Prufrock' to Andrew Marvell's poem 'To His Coy Mistress', or in his references to Hamlet and Lazarus. *Direct quotation* of Shakespeare also takes place in 'A Game of Chess', while indirectly Thomas Middleton, Virgil and Milton are alluded to. All such references and allusions help to build up the picture which tells us some universal truth.

The detailed notes on each poem explain the significance of these allusions and references.

VERSE STRUCTURE

In keeping with the French Symbolists' *'vers libre'*, or free verse, Eliot broke with the regular forms and structures of his immediate predecessors. The suggestiveness of his imagery and symbols demanded that the structures of his verse should be equally suggestive.

If Eliot's imagery often consists of *abrupt transitions*, so also does his verse structure. The structure often reflects both themes and imagery. Thus the *irregular juxtaposition of lines of different length* in 'The Love Song of J. Alfred Prufrock' reflects the agitated nature of Prufrock, while the regularity of lines 23–34 reflects the incantatory tone of the lines. Similarly, the *short lines 33–35* in 'Journey of the Magi' reflect the anxiety of the magus that no part of his narrative should be overlooked.

Eliot also composes his lines to suggest *the natural speech patterns and rhythms of contemporary speech*. This is particularly true of the pub scene, which opens in line 139 of 'A Game of Chess'. The direct speech rhythms of the female narrator give a sense of immediacy to the tone and themes. Into these speech patterns Eliot introduces *colloquialisms and even slang*. The lines do indeed reflect speech patterns, but they also satisfy a metrical pattern.

At times Eliot *repeats particular words and phrases to give a prayer-like or incantatory tone*. This may also effect a reflective mood. This is seen in 'Journey of the Magi' with the strong repetition of 'And'. The strained repetitiveness of lines in 'A Game of Chess' and in 'The Love Song of J. Alfred Prufrock' reflects the nervous tension of the speakers.

Rhyme is used for particular effects in Eliot's poetry. The jingling rhyme of the couplet referring to Michelangelo in 'The Love Song of J. Alfred Prufrock' reflects the shallowness of the women and the mock-heroic tone. Rhyme is used in the 'Preludes' to create a *lyrical effect* in keeping with its title. Both the rhythm and rhyme use in 'East Coker IV' are 'reinventions' of Medieval English verse, which W.B. Yeats, for one, believed helped 'to prolong the moment of contemplation'.

Eliot's interest in music is seen not only in many of the titles of his poems – e.g. 'The Love Song of J. Alfred Prufrock', 'Preludes', 'The Four Quartets' – but *in the very structures of the poems and his use of language*. Some of the verses of 'The Love Song of J. Alfred Prufrock' are composed of single sentences, whose repetitiveness not only reflects the tedium of Prufrock's life but gives a symphonic effect. The heavy stressed *rhythm* of the 'Preludes' suggests the fatigue of the city's inhabitants, while the lyrical sibilant 'S' sounds of lines 9 and 10 of 'Journey of the Magi' evoke the sensuality of the life being left behind. The robust rhythm of 'Usk' suggests the invigorating landscape and underscores the commanding authority of the imperative verbs. The musicality of 'East Coker IV' has been referred to already.

Eliot – a dramatic poet

As can be seen in his poems, Eliot excels in creating characters whose situations reflect the universal condition of man.

Eliot's greatest *verse drama* is, without doubt, 'Murder in the Cathedral', but many of his poems are verse dramas in themselves. The use of *internal monologue*, or stream-of-consciousness speech, is a particularly effective device in *creating drama* in verse.

'The Love Song of J. Alfred Prufrock' has all the elements of drama. The main character is in *conflict*, within himself and with society in general. In his monologue he develops his conflict and demonstrates his *character*, while also creating both the characters and speech of others. Characters are placed in *particular times and places* where the drama unfolds. A *plot*, or storyline, is developed and comes to a conclusion. The reader (or audience) becomes interested in the fate of this character – one who reflects the reader's own predicament, perhaps. Overall, *dialogue* is either direct or implied, advancing the plot and enhancing the reader's understanding of the character.

In this way, 'Aunt Helen', 'Preludes', 'A Game of Chess' and 'Journey of the Magi' are also verse dramas. The pub scene in 'A Game of Chess' is a dramatic reflection of the world in miniature. The student may enjoy reading it out loud in 'an appropriate accent'.

Many of Eliot's poems are 'spoken' by created personae or else detached observers. The latter, as in 'Preludes', has been called a cinematic style. For the student interested in film these may prove especially rewarding. It may also be worth noting how many of Eliot's characters are grotesque in the literary sense. In Prufrock, Miss Helen Slingsby and the women in 'A Game of Chess', Eliot has created characters as memorable as those of Shakespeare or Dickens.

Questions

1. Write a personal response to the poetry of T.S. Eliot. Support your answer by reference to the poetry of Eliot that you have studied.
2. 'The poetry of T.S. Eliot appeals to modern readers for various reasons.'

Write an introduction to Eliot's poetry in which you suggest what these reasons might be.

3. Imagine you have been asked to give a reading of T.S. Eliot's poetry to your class. What poems would you choose and why would you choose them?

4. Suppose someone told you that he/she found T.S. Eliot's poetry too obscure. Write a response to this person in which you outline your understanding of Eliot's poetry.

5. What impression did the poetry of T.S. Eliot make on you as a reader? In your answer you may wish to address the following:
   - your sense of the poet's personality
   - his major themes
   - the poet's use of imagery and language
   - the poem/poems that appealed to you most.

6. 'Eliot's major achievement is as a verse dramatist.'
   Write out a speech you would make to your class on the above topic.

Bibliography

Gardner, Helen, *The Art of T.S. Eliot*, Faber and Faber: London 1985.

Moody, A.David, (editor), *The Cambridge Companion to T.S. Eliot*, Cambridge: Cambridge University Press 1994.

Braybrooke, Neville, (editor), *T.S. A Symposium for His Seventieth Birthday*, London: Garnstone Press 1958.

Donoghue, Denis, *Words Alone: The Poet T.S. Eliot*, Yale University Press 2000.

Steed, C.K., *The New Poetic: Yeats to Eliot*, Pelican Books 1967.

Herbert, Michael, *T.S. Eliot Selected Poems*, York Notes, Longman York Press 1982.

Southam, B.C., *A Student's Guide to The Selected Poems of T.S. Eliot*, London: Faber and Faber 1968.

Press, John, *The Chequer'd Shade: Reflections on Obscurity in Poetry*, London: Oxford University Press 1963.

Leavis, F.R., *New Bearings in English Poetry*, Pelican Books 1972.

* If the 'water-mill' represents Christ then 'darkness' could represent death, which Christ conquers by the Resurrection. On the other hand the water-mill could represent the superior forces of those in the world who put Christ to death.

4   *Patrick* KAVANAGH

John McCarthy

Kavanagh Overview

Kavanagh was born on 21 October 1904, in the village of Inniskeen, Co. Monaghan. His father was a shoemaker and had a small farm of land. Kavanagh received only primary school education and at the age of thirteen, he became an apprentice shoemaker. He gave it up 15 months later, admitting that he didn't make one wearable pair of boots. For the next 20 years Kavanagh would work on the family farm, before moving to Dublin in 1939. From his early years on, he was a man who was out of place. When in Monaghan Kavanagh was a dreamer in a world of realists who were concerned with what seemed to him to be the mundanities of life. In Dublin he stood out as the man up from the bog, who didn't understand the complexities of city life. He was seen as gauche and unrefined. Ironically in Monaghan he was seen as effeminate for having an interest in poetry.

Kavanagh's interest in literature and poetry marked him out as different from other people in his local place. In a society that was insular and agricultural, a man's worth was measured by the straightness of the furrow he could plough, rather than the lines of poetry he could write. Kavanagh's first attempts to become a published poet resulted in the publication of some poems in a local newspaper in the early 1930s, and in the publishing of his autobiographical novel, *Tarry Flynn*, in 1939. Urged by his brother Peter, who was a Dublin-based teacher, Kavanagh moved to the city to establish himself as a writer. At that time, the Dublin Literary Society was dominated by an educated Anglo-Irish group with whom Kavanagh had nothing in common; among them were Oliver St John Gogarty and Douglas Wylie. They saw Kavanagh as a country bumpkin and referred to him as 'that Monaghan boy'.

Kavanagh's early years in Dublin were unproductive as he struggled for recognition. In 1947 his first major collection, 'A Soul for Sale', was published. These poems were the product of his Monaghan youth. In the early 1950s Kavanagh and his brother Peter published a weekly newspaper called *Kavanagh's Weekly*; it failed because the editorial viewpoint was too narrow. In 1954 Kavanagh became embroiled in an infamous court case. He accused *The Leader* newspaper of slander. The newspaper decided to contest the case and employed the former Taoiseach, John A. Costello, as their defence counsel;

Kavanagh decided to prosecute the case himself, and he was destroyed by Costello. The court case dragged on for over a year and Kavanagh's health began to fail. In 1955 he was diagnosed as having lung cancer and had a lung removed; he survived, and the event was a major turning point in his life and career. In 1958 he published *Come Dance with me Kitty Stobling.* In 1959 he was appointed by John A. Costello to the faculty of English in UCD. His lectures were popular, but often irrelevant to the course. In the early 1960s he visited Britain and the USA; in 1965 he married Katherine Maloney. He died in 1967 from an attack of bronchitis. Kavanagh's reputation as a poet is based on the lyrical quality of his work, his mastery of language and form and his ability to transform the ordinary and the banal into something of significance. He is an acute observer of things and situations, and this allows him to make things that may seem ordinary and unimportant into something deserving of a place in poetry.

He is constantly using his work to make sense of the natural world, be it in Dublin or Monaghan. More importantly, Kavanagh is always trying to assess his own place in this world. He often approaches a poem from a point of doubt, where he is unsure about where he belongs, and uses the poem to come to a resolution. The best example of this is in the poem 'Epic'. He is also trying to praise God and Nature in his poems. Indeed his Monaghan poems are not so much about the area, but about how it affects him and his work. It would not be unfair to say that Kavanagh is very self-obsessed. But on the other hand, he is writing about what he knows best.

Technique and Style

Language

In attempting to create a sense of the mystery and magic of a child's mind, Kavanagh's use of language is a vital ingredient in his work. He uses words in a new fashion. He fuses words together, such as 'clay-minted' and most famously 'leafy-with-love'. These phrases and words give extra energy to his poetry and provide it with vigour.

Imagery

Kavanagh's use of imagery is a very important aspect of his language. In 'Advent' he alludes to the Nativity: '. . . old stables where Time begins'. In 'Inniskeen Road' he refers to Alexander Selkirk. Colloquial language is an intrinsic element of Kavanagh's style. His phraseology is conversational and many of his phrases owe their origin to his Monaghan background: 'Among simple decent men too who barrow dung . . .'; 'he stared at me half eyed'; '. . . every blooming thing'.

Structure – Form

The poems on the course display Kavanagh's ability in the sonnet form, which is a structural feature of 'Inniskeen Road', 'Advent', 'Lines Written . . .' and Canal Bank Walk'. In 'Inniskeen Road', Kavanagh combines features of the Petrarchan and Shakespearean forms. Stanzaic pattern reflects the Petrarchan subdivision of a sonnet into an octet and a sestet. In the octet a picture is painted by the poet and the problems are posed. The poet's own personal response is contained in the sestet. The opening stanza can be subdivided into two quatrains, each containing a separate picture of Monaghan life. The sestet also can be divided into a quatrain and couplet, therefore mirroring the Shakespearean division into three quatrains followed by a rhyming couplet. The rhyme scheme of the poem is also Shakespearean: *abab, cdcd, efef, gg*. 'Advent' represents Kavanagh's particular use of the sonnet form. The poem is an amalgam of two sonnets, and the stanzaic pattern is neither Petrarchan nor Shakespearean. The opening two stanzas each contain seven lines, with the third stanza representing an entire sonnet. The division of the sonnet into two septets is unusual and Kavanagh formulates a rhyme scheme to parallel this: *aabbccbd, aab, aacc*. Stanza three is again different as Kavanagh reverts to the Shakespearean rhyming technique: *abab, cded, fgfg, hh*. The thought pattern of the third stanza follows that set out by the opening two stanzas, with a natural pause occurring at the end of the seventeenth line. The reason why Kavanagh does not create a fourth stanza is that the rhythm of the third one reflects the excitement that he associates with having rediscovered '. . . the luxury of a child's soul'. The three stanzas in the poem reflect the three stages in Kavanagh's bid to regain this position – penance, forgiveness, grace.

'Canal Bank Walk' is written in the traditional 14-line sonnet form with no stanzaic separation. In this poem, Kavanagh combines both the Petrarchan and Shakespearean sonnets, using the same methods as in 'Inniskeen Road'.

'Lines Written . . .' is fashioned completely in the Petrarchan style. Both the thought pattern and the rhyming scheme follow an octet–sestet sublimation.

'Memory . . .' and 'On Raglan Road' are reminiscent of ballad technique in that they each feature four-line stanzas; however, Kavanagh doesn't stick rigidly to the rhyming schemes of the ballad, displaying again his ability to individualise a fashion or feature.

Religion

Religion is a dominant feature in Kavanagh's poetry, both as a theme and as a source of imagery. Religion features thematically in 'Advent', 'Canal Bank Walk' and in a minor way in 'Stony Grey Soil'. 'Advent' derives from religion in both its theme and its main source of imagery. The theme of the poem is penance–forgiveness–grace, which reflects the Catholic church's seasons of

Advent, the Nativity and the beginning of the new church year. Kavanagh formulates his wish to return to the state of innocence as a child within the imagery of religion, using original sin to represent acquired knowledge, penance as a main act of contrition and the grace of the forgiven soul as the newly required state of innocence. In 'Canal Bank Walk' the theme is one of redemption reflecting baptism, as Kavanagh draws analogies between the waters of the baptismal font and the water of the canal.

RURAL AND URBAN

Although Kavanagh arrived in Dublin in 1939, leaving behind his sixteen acres of stony grey soil, it was not until the mid-1950s that his adopted city provided the environmental background to his work. The summer of 1955 and the banks of the Grand Canal in Dublin are the time and place which moved Kavanagh to write 'Canal Bank Walk' and 'Lines Written . . .'.

Kavanagh's attitude to the environment changed dramatically following his operation for lung cancer. He said, 'As a poet I was born in or about 1955, the place of my birth being the banks of the Grand Canal.' This new appreciation of the environment, his vision of Eden, is evident in his novel *Tarry Flynn*, where he wrote: 'O the rich beauty of the weeds in the ditches, Tarry's heart cried: the lush Nettles and Docks and tuffs of grass. Life pouring out in critical abundance.' In the novel he also wrote, 'Without ambition, without desire, the beauty of the world pared in thought his unresting mind.' These two sentences describe exactly the moods of Kavanagh in 'Canal Bank Walk' and 'Lines Written . . .' Here the environment is glorified in a pantheistic manner. Kavanagh uses hyperbole and many neologisms in an attempt to demonstrate the magnificence of Nature, as experienced by the innocent mind of a child or of the poet reformed to the state of grace. The opposing attitudes expressed by Kavanagh to the environments of Monaghan and Dublin reflect more on his state of mind than on the environments themselves. In 1963 he did recognise the beauty of the Monaghan countryside:

> Thirty-years before, Shank Duff's water-fill could of done the trick for me, but I was too thick to realise it.

Bibliography

PRIMARY SOURCES

Ploughman and Other Poems	1936
The Green Fool	1938
The Great Hunger	1942

A Soul for Sale	1947
Tarry Flynn	1948
Recent Poems	1958
Come Dance with me Kitty Stobling	1960
Self Portrait	1964
The Complete Poems	1972 (Posthumous)

SECONDARY SOURCES

John Nemo	*Patrick Kavanagh*
Alan Warner	*Clay is the Word*
Antoinette Quinn	*Patrick Kavanagh: Born Again Romantic*
Peter Kavanagh	*Sacred Keeper*
Anthony Cronin	*Dead as Doornails*

Inniskeen Road: July Evening

Text of poem: New Explorations Anthology page 146

Kavanagh self-visualises himself in this poem. The poem is all about him, even though he spends over half the poem appearing to be concerned with others. In the poem Kavanagh attempts to describe where he sees his position in society; this question is central to all of his work. His position is at best on the fringes of the society he chooses, and at worst completely outside it and isolated. Another question central to Kavanagh's work is: where does he want to be? Is this role, as the outsider looking in, one that he has decided suits him? Does he need the tension of being different to stimulate his work?

The poem may or may not be based on a real event, but the first thing that Kavanagh does is make everything seem real. He does this by giving us real places and time. The poem's title presupposes a reality. It is 'Inniskeen Road', not a road in Monaghan. It is a 'July Evening', not some time in his youth. Kavanagh seems to be looking for sympathy in this poem, and by making things real he adds to this emotional appeal. He even mention's 'Billy Brennan's barn', which is a real place owned by a real person. The premise is that if Kavanagh is using fact here, then everything else that he says must also be true.

In fact the truth may matter little, and what may be most important in this poem is how Kavanagh sees himself and how he wants to be seen.

This part is simple. To Kavanagh, he is '*l'étranger*'. He is the outsider who can observe his own community's actions from the inside, yet still look objectively. The major question for a reader is, 'Is Kavanagh objective enough?' The answer to this question must be 'no'. Even when he's outside the action of the poem, his observing is still central to the poem.

WHAT DOES KAVANAGH SEE?

He sees society passing him by. He sees local people passing him by on the way to a dance. They don't look at him or stop to talk to him. They are in 'twos and threes'; he is on his own. They are on their way to something too important. This is a regular occurrence.

> There's a dance in Billy Brennan's barn tonight.

This is not *the* dance. It's just *a* dance. It is a regular thing that he takes no part of. It appears he never will. The alliteration in this line suggests optimism and a childlike sense of fun, and these sit uneasily with Kavanagh. The alliteration of the B's is inapposite with the spat-out sounds of desperation that come in the final stanza.

Kavanagh sees a means of communication that he does not understand. He hears 'half-talk' and 'wink and elbow language'. This frustrates him. He is not allowed to be part of this society. There is even a hint of knowingness and sexuality in this way that people are communicating.

As full of people and life and communication as the first quatrain was, the second quatrain is quickly depopulated. Kavanagh spends four lines telling us that there is nobody to be seen. Even the coded language he complained about in lines three and four is gone for there is:

> . . . not
> A footfall tapping secrecies of stone.

As much as he complained about the people passing him by, he seems to feel that it was better than the silence.

This quatrain is full of the language of spy movies. It is almost like a scene from the movie *The Third Man*, with its silence and secrets and footfalls and shadows. Again there is a frustrated isolation evident here. Kavanagh is convinced that he is incapable of decoding the language and the nuances that these people use.

In the sestet, Kavanagh gets to the nub of the matter. The people that populated the octet are gone and now he turns to himself. He addresses his audience in an aggressive and prosaic manner. He is direct and uncompromising in the first two lines. He then makes direct reference to a much older poem by William Cowper, 'Verses supposed to be written by Alexander Selkirk'. Cowper's Selkirk has the following to say:

> I am monarch of all I survey.
> My right there is none to dispute;
> From the centre all round to the sea,
> I am lord of the fowl and the brute.
> O solitude! Where are the charms

That sages have seen in thy face?
Better dwell in the midst of alarms
Than reign in this horrible place.

Kavanagh takes these sentiments and adapts them to his own situation. He is more concerned with the bogs and farms of county Monaghan than with a deserted island where Selkirk was supposed to have been abandoned. He nevertheless shares the sentiment that his 'gift' brings bitter fruits with it. Is this too extreme a metaphor? Selkirk was abandoned and left on a deserted island. In circumstances beyond his control, he had to live the life of a hermit on a deserted island, with no hope of communicating with anybody for years. Kavanagh is in self-enforced exile, unless you submit to his own theory that he has no choice but to be a poet, and to be a poet meant exiling himself from the society that he felt closest to. The irony is that he still needs to write about these people and include them in his poetry. There is a complete contradiction between trying to stay away from these people and still writing about them centrally.

He finishes his rant with the wonderful pun on the curse 'blooming thing'. The double meanings are a euphemism for 'bloody' and another word for 'growing'. If he says 'bloody', you can understand this: he is angry at his exile. If he is talking about 'growth', then he is saying that there is room for growth in a land where there should not be hope for any type of growth, an area 'Of banks and stones . . . '; maybe this is like his poetry, an area were he sees little of hope, but that little amount of hope is enough for a poem to grow.

LANGUAGE, STRUCTURE AND SOUNDS

Kavanagh works within the confines of the sonnet and this seems to suit his purpose well. The structure moves from the first quartet, which is well populated, to the second quartet where everybody is now off the road and in the barn, presumably enjoying themselves. The sestet brings us Kavanagh and allows him to pontificate on what all this means to him.

The rhyming sequence is *abab cdcd efefgg*. The effect of this is a highly exalted poetic sense. By working with a Shakespearean structure, he seems to imply a sense of accuracy and truth, that everything that is reported is correct.

The sonnet's sense of false balance is also used well. There is no 'I' in the first eight lines, yet it dominates the sestet.

The prominent sounds in the poem suggest anger and bitterness. The heavily prominent 'B' sound at the beginning is spat out like an unwanted taste by his use of alliteration. Importantly, he brings this sound back right at the end of the poem, when he writes about '. . . every blooming thing.'

Epic

Text of poem: New Explorations Anthology page 148

This poem has a grandiose title, a grandiose first line and an even more grandiose last sentence. Kavanagh's favourite poetic theme has always been poetry and the role of the poet. He is constantly self-conscious. Often in his poetry he will use a specific real event from his own life or the lives of the people who surrounded him in order to make a more direct point about poetry, the job of the poet or aesthetics.

In this poem he uses a real incident: a row between two families over a plot of land. In the notes to the collected poems, Kavanagh's brother Peter gives the background to the incident:

> I recall the row over the half a rood of rock in 1938. The row was temporarily settled when the contestants agreed to arbitration by the local schoolmaster who was also unofficial surveyor. Neither side was fully satisfied and the row smouldered for some years. Today all the surrounding farms including the disputed rock are owned by the same farmer.

Kavanagh starts the poem in what might seem to be an ironic mood. Words such as 'important places' and 'great events' can hardly be appropriate when referring to something as trivial as a dispute between two families over a 'half a rood of rock' or 'iron stones'. But when relativity kicks in, then these retrospectively trivial occurrences can seem gigantic to the protagonists. This, according to Kavanagh, is the stuff of poetry. This is where his concerns are, because this is where his people's concerns are. The 'Munich Bother' might as well have been happening on another planet as far as the Duffys and the McCabes were concerned. It would be easy for Kavanagh to mock or patronise these people, but he doesn't. Or at least he doesn't any more. Kavanagh admits that he was:

> . . . inclined
> To lose my faith in Ballyrush and Gortin

But he was inspired by a fellow artist, the great Greek poet Homer, whose 'Ghost came whispering to my mind'. Kavanagh says that if it was good enough for Homer and Greece, then it must be good enough for himself and the parishes of County Monaghan.

In the action of the poem, Kavanagh sets up a drama between the two sides and reports about it directly to us. He even tells us what each side said. The fierceness of the dispute is typified by the warlike declaration of 'Damn your soul'.

He shows us one of the protagonists stepping on the disputed land and declaring a new border between the families – the iron stones being like Hitler's Iron Cross.

It then looks as if he is delving into farce, as he compares this dispute with one of the twentieth century's most important events, the beginning of World War Two. He even dismisses this event as 'the Munich bother'.

When he finally decides on which one was more important, he says he has changed his mind. He tells us that once he dismissed the local matter, but then after he did some reading of Homer's 'Iliad' (and more importantly, E.V. Rieu's biography of Homer), he came to change his mind.

In Kavanagh's poem 'On Looking into E.V. Rieu's Homer' he describes the Greek poet's vision:

> For only the half-god can see
> The Immortal in things mortal.

And later he observes of Homer:

> The intensity that radiated from
> The Far Field Rock – you afterwards denied –
> Was the half-god seeing his half-brothers
> Joking on the fabulous mountain-side.

In 'Epic' he is talking to Homer to justify the idea that nothing is beyond a poet's telling of it. A literary classic may begin in a simple local event, but it is the poet's telling of it that makes it immortal. It is not the event but the reporting of the event that gives immortality. By proposing this thesis Kavanagh makes this not a poem about a local dispute, but a poem about poetry itself.

Kavanagh's ego comes through twice. First of all he shows no shyness in comparing himself with Homer. Remember that this poem was published in the early 1940s, before Kavanagh's reputation was in any way established in the way it is today. To compare himself with one of the most important poets of all time seems incredibly presumptuous. He also seems to compare a poet with a God in this poem and in the other Homer poem. He says that a poet is a creator of worlds. There may be some sense to this; a poet does have control of the world that he reports on. He is allowed to influence his readers' thoughts. It seems that Kavanagh is acknowledging the importance of this role. He is saying that what a poet reports on will last and become important.

At the end of the poem the reader is left to wonder whether the events are important or not, because Kavanagh uses those events to make a point about poetry itself, rather than the events the poem is describing.

Shancoduff

Text of poem: New Explorations Anthology page 150

[*Note: This poem is also prescribed for Ordinary Level 2010 exam*]

According to the critic Antoinette Quinn, 'Shancoduff is a north-facing hill farm depicted at its wintry worst, frostbound, starved of grass, swept by sleety winds.' Yet this is a love poem to it.

Kavanagh had a love–hate relationship with the countryside of his youth. One of his most famous poems is 'Stony Grey Soil'. In that poem the poet accused the area where he was reared of burgling 'his bank of youth'. He describes the area as being one that is lifeless and soulless, and he questions how he managed to survive in a place where even plant life struggled to maintain an existence. Yet in this poem his attitude is different; he is more interested in finding the good in his 'black hills'. He turns any notion of something negative into something positive. He transforms the faults of Shancoduff in the same way that a lover transforms his partner's faults into something to be loved. The immediate question that must be asked is: Why would anybody write a love-poem to Shancoduff?

The answer must be because the hills are his. He claims ownership four times. He calls them '*My* black hills' twice in the first verse, and then '*My* hills' and '*my* Alps' in the second. Possession of this land is obviously very important to Kavanagh. After all, they are 'eternal'. Shancoduff will last long after he has gone and more importantly, they will still be there after the people who sneer at them are gone. He also personifies them. They are given a personality like a lover would have. The hills can 'look', they are 'incurious', they are 'happy', they 'hoard'.

Kavanagh relishes their drabness. Anything that might be confused as being something negative can be construed into a positive: for example, the fact that the hills are so incurious or inactive that they can't even be bothered to look at the sun. This is seen as a good thing when Kavanagh compares it with the fate of Lot's wife, who was turned into a pillar of salt for looking back as she left Sodom and Gomorrah.

Kavanagh puts a lot of emphasis on the local place names. He lists them with pride: Glassdrummond, Rocksavage, Featherna Bush; these are as important as the Alps. The names themselves have mythic qualities. They sound tough and treacherous. They have a resonance of something from an action movie, in which a hero stands proud above the hills. They all have a grandness granted to them by being multisyllabic.

Kavanagh's own importance in the poem is also highlighted here as the person who has:

> . . . climbed the Matterhorn
> with a sheaf of hay for three perishing calves.

This act itself seems heroic, as if he had climbed the most dangerous mountain face in the world – whereas all he has done is walk up a hill to feed the cows. This use of hyperbole shows the love that Kavanagh has for this place. The rebellious nature of the hills is also shown as they refuse to conform to the usual structures of nature. They are oblivious to the changes in the seasons and the weather. Their immortality is stressed by the fact that they are unchanged by the travails of time Springtime cannot catch up with them as his

> . . . hills hoard the bright shillings of March
> While the sun searches in every pocket.

The poem turns at this point; the poet has come to the realisation, albeit after being told, that his mountains are not the glorious thing of beauty that he may have thought they were. The farmers who are in a more sheltered, wealthier place sneer at him. Even though his hills are personified with their 'rushy beards', nobody else declares them worth looking after. When he is acknowledged as a poet, it is almost done as a form of derision. A poet may be someone who is seen as poor.

Kavanagh departs with a rhetorical question that is forced on him by the comments of the other men. This affects him deeply, just as if his wife or lover were to be described as ugly or disgusting. He asks himself: 'Is my heart not badly shaken?' The love that he felt for the hills is broken by the piece of reality forced on him.

The Great Hunger

Text of poem: New Explorations Anthology page 152

'The Great Hunger' could well be Kavanagh's most important work; the format of the poem is certainly the most unique and ambitious. One of Kavanagh's biggest influences (although their subject matter was often completely different) was the English poet W.H. Auden. Auden was one of the best and most frequent practitioners of the long poem. 'The Great Hunger' is quite different from Auden's dramatic poems, or his 'Letter to Lord Byron' or 'New Year Letter', which are meditations on a specific time. Even poets who were in turn influenced by Kavanagh, like John Montague and Seamus Heaney, knitted together a series of poems to make up 'The Rough Field' and 'Station Island' respectively. This long poem is almost divided as a novelist would divide a book into chapters, with different parts coming together to give us a more rounded view of the life, times and opinions of Patrick Maguire.

Kavanagh takes on a narrative structure in this poem. The narrative allows him to use a cinematic technique to develop the central character in the poem. 'The Great Hunger' is focalised completely around the character of Patrick Maguire. It allows us to see what he sees, feel what he feels and hear what he says and hears. However, it also allows us some time to look at Maguire objectively.

Kavanagh seems to be on a voyage of discovery in this poem, and he seems to be enjoying bringing his reader with him. He uses a 'cinematic technique' to do this, by helping the reader to visualise what's going on as it happens. He is always shifting the angle, even though we are constantly viewing the character of Maguire. In the middle of the first section he reaffirms this by imploring the reader to:

> Watch him, watch him, that man on a hill whose spirit
> Is a wet sack flapping about the knees of time,

This poem sees Kavanagh with his most negative attitude towards his own background. The poem begins with lifelessness and a sense of biblical foreboding where the Word is not made Flesh, a symbol of the beginning of Life. Instead all is turned to where Death exists. We are pointed to where the dead go; in Kavanagh's landscape we begin with a lack of life.

> Clay is the word and clay is the flesh.

It is already obvious that this terrain that Kavanagh is about to map out is one that sees little chance for hope. When we see the

> . . . potato-gatherers like mechanised scare-crows move
> Along the side-fall of the hill –

it feels like being stuck in a purgatorial vision from Dante. Then Kavanagh gives his instruction and his despair as he asks:

> If we watch them an hour is there anything we can prove
> Of life as it is broken-backed over the Book
> Of Death?

There appears to be no hope in this landscape at all. There appears to be no sympathy between the inhabitants of the landscape, between wind and worms and frogs and seagulls. And then he gets to the question that must be asked: why write this poem? What is the point in examining this seemingly desolate terrain? He tells us that he is searching for the 'light of imagination'. He is searching for something worth searching for.

He finds what he is looking for in a character who seems different from the other bleak people who live on the terrain. The rest of this first section of the poem attempts to show us Patrick Maguire. Kavanagh promises us a view of his life:

> Till the last soul passively like a bag of wet clay
> Rolls down the side of the hill,

This life is in a terrain where accuracy and intent are dismissed, things seem to happen with routine – but if they don't, it doesn't seem to matter too much. Kavanagh litters this early part of the poem with places where the plough missed, dogs lie lazily and horses pull rusty ploughs. This languorous air seems to suit Maguire, or at least that's the impression that he likes to give. He shrugs off the idea that experience of a broader life would be preferable – but the narrator of the poem tells us differently when he tells us that Maguire 'pretended to his soul'. Maguire convinces himself that children would only get in his way and be a nuisance even more than crows are. There is a sense here of regret; that something is missing from his life.

Central to this is the idea that Maguire is married to the land. The land dominates his life: he is in love with it and he hates it. He is committed to it, but the commitment may be too much. It is causing a deficit in other areas of his life. The narrator shows us Maguire bent among the potato fields, turning over the clumps of root. He asks *the* most important question: 'What is he looking for there?' The answer tells us that Maguire is a man lost; a man who thinks he is in control of his own life and destiny, but isn't. We know this from his answer: 'He thinks it is a potato, but we know better . . .' This seems like condescension from the omniscient narrator, but we now get a chance to examine Maguire in his own voice. The narrator is almost saying to us, 'If you don't believe what I'm saying, then listen for yourself.'

At this point the narration changes to allow us to listen to Maguire. When we hear him speak, he sounds like a man in charge of his own affairs. He is giving instruction to his workers, he is ordering people to 'move', 'balance', 'pull', 'straddle'. He is a man in touch with Nature:

> The wind's over Brannagan's, now that means rain.

He is capable of planning for the future:

> And that's a job we'll have to do in December,

and capable of getting angry when he sees 'Cassidy's ass'.

So perhaps he is not the solitary stand-still figure that we saw in the first 40 lines. But if we believed that thesis, then the narrator brings us back to earth by putting Maguire back in the 'cloud-swung wind'. He is married to the land: a man who is living his life for the future not of his children, but of the crops that will grow in his fields even when he:

> Is spread in the bottom of a ditch under two coulters
> crossed in Christ's Name.

This poignant vision of his own future, as no future at all, is even more depressing with the symbol of the Cross being represented by two parts of a plough. There is also the element of martyrdom here. He has sacrificed his own life for the good of others.

We are shown his distance from a regular youth by the way he sees girls of his own age. If they laughed, they laughed at him. When they screamed, he regarded them as animals. He knew that life was showing him a difficult path ahead, and it seems that perhaps he was aiming for it.

The next piece, from lines 67 to 79, is probably the most harrowing of the poem. Maguire seems depressingly regretful here; he is not able to shake 'a knowing head | And pretend to his soul'. He acknowledges that he is trapped by his undying commitment to the land; he knows that there is no easy way out from here, but that perhaps there was a time when a way out was possible. He sighs in despair twice: 'O God if I had been wiser!' The only thing that lifts him temporarily from his despair is the knowledge that he could be part of a bigger picture, that he and his life are part of Nature and God's will, because 'God's truth is life', even the hardship that he has to endure. The trick that Maguire has learned is to find ways of coping with Nature. He has taught himself compensatory skills, such as when to avoid life's obstacles, when to avoid climbing over boulders that will make him bleed.

The poem begins its end with universal natural images – the sun, rain, wind, light – blending in with more local, specific images like Donaghmoyne and Brady's farm, reinforcing the earlier thesis that 'God's truth is life,' no matter where it is.

Finally an invitation is issued to look at the beginnings of this story (we have already seen the end). The narrator asks us to detach ourselves and listen to the grim story that he wants to tell.

It must be remembered that this poem is part of a larger piece. There are dominant themes in the poem of self-sacrifice and of the relationship between man and Nature, and more specifically of the relationship between man and The Land. It would be wrong, however, to see this poem as one of Kavanagh's lyric poems, that have an exact structure and a single dominant theme. It is more wide ranging in its scope and aspirations. It genuinely attempts to provide a truthful, honest and – most importantly – full picture of a man at a particular time. By doing that Kavanagh gives us an insight into a whole society. He is presenting a vivid portrait of rural Ireland in the prewar years by focusing us on the character of Patrick Maguire.

A Christmas Childhood

Text of poem: New Explorations Anthology page 157

[Note: *this poem is also prescribed for 2010 Ordinary level exam*]

In 'A Christmas Childhood', Kavanagh seems to be very conscious of his voice and the voice that he is using in the poem. Kavanagh adopts an innocent, naïve attitude in this poem and that seems to be central to both the style and the substance. It is the merging of what he is saying and how he is saying it that gives the poem real quality. It uses simple, direct language and this simplicity is also important in what the poet is attempting to say. It is, however, in this reader's eyes a poem of two halves, to use the football cliché. Indeed it was originally published as two separate pieces, the first part being published in 1943, and what is now the second part a full three years earlier. This reader feels that the later addition was unnecessary.

PART I

The poem begins with a simple description of a potato field, where one side was in the sun and was beginning to thaw out. The other side was still frozen over and 'white with frost'. Nature dominates everything; it takes over and liberates inanimate objects. The paling-post that was once merely supporting a fence now sends music out through it:

> And when we put our ears to the paling-post
> The music that came out was magical.

The way that Nature attacks all the senses is important to Kavanagh. He goes through sight, taste and hearing in order to give us a holistic vision of how the Christmas spirit invades everything.

He then inserts an 'over-the-top' repetition of his emotions. Hyperbole pervades this part, with even the fence providing 'magical' music. He continues with this mixture of the simple and the marvellous when comparing a gap of light with 'a hole in Heaven's gable.' Even an apple tree reminds him of the temptation of Adam.

The death of innocence, and a longing to return to innocence, is a familiar theme in Kavanagh's poetry and it is reinforced here. The world has taken him, like Eve took Adam from what he supposed was a better life:

> O you, Eve, were the world that tempted me
> To eat the knowledge that grew in clay
> And death the germ within it!

He then sets up the second part of the poem by leaving us tranquil symbols of the 'gay garden that was childhood's', the most important being the final image: 'Of a beauty that the world did not touch.'

There is a longing here to return to a better time for himself. That time is when people were more dependent on Nature. This closer interaction with Nature is epitomised and made clearer by the amount of religious imagery that runs through the first section. There is plenty of religious imagery present, such as 'Heaven's gable' and Eve and the apple. The time was more sacred to Kavanagh; he saw it as a time that was also good and holy.

PART II

The second part of the poem continues with the religious imagery, making striking comparisons between an Irish town and Bethlehem with its 'stars in the morning east'. There is a genuine excitement pervading this part and it is less diluted by adult knowingness than the first part was. There are simple descriptions of what was going on in his childhood, and this allows him to retain an attitude of childlike wonder. The voice in the second half of the poem is certainly more full of clarity.

The setting for the second half of the poem is almost completely outdoors, and this natural open setting allows him to go from the local to the universal – or even biblical – with ease. There is a seamless intertwining of the personal and the public. Again, the significance of the fact that the father was playing his music outdoors cannot be underplayed. He finds harmony with Nature and allows it to influence his playing. The stars manage to recognise his father's music and are so captivated that they decide to dance to it.

Rapidly Kavanagh brings us back to his own townland and remarks on the unspoken signs between the families. Where in 'Epic' he describes local rivalries, here the unspoken language of music is a uniting force as 'his melodion called | To Lennons and Callans.' Kavanagh remarks that he 'knew some strange thing had happened.' The harmonising power of his father's music is highly significant when one reflects on the first verse, where the music from the paling-post is described as magical.

His mother's daily ritual of milking the cows becomes inspired by 'the frost of Bethlehem'. The religious imagery continues here. Bethlehem brought new hope to Christians, and this time of year, with its sense of a new start, also suggests rebirth. Nature in the form of ice and wind and the water-hen is recalled. It is the sense of 'wonder of a Christmas townland', where even the dawn is personified and winks, which makes this poem one of the most beautiful that Kavanagh wrote. Yet again he tries to show how the senses are affected: sight with the 'child-poet (who) picked out letters'; the sound of the melodion and of when:

> A water-hen screeched on the bog,
> Mass-going feet
> Crunched the wafer-ice on the potholes,

In the sixth verse he shows exquisite skill at mixing the northern constellation Cassiopeia with 'Cassidy's hanging hill', using run-through lines with clever use of alliteration to expose the child's sense of awe at Christmas. This also introduces the religious notion again and suggests the Eastern Star that guided the Three Wise Men towards the birth of Christ; instead, the stars guide people towards his father's house.

There is one wise man who proves his intelligence by commenting on the poet's father's fiddle playing. His father is working just like Nature, when the inanimate is brought to life as the man says, 'Can't he make it talk.'

Pleasant childhood memories of Christmas are exposed graciously throughout the poem: his father's way of making the melodion talk, his mother's commitment to the daily work on the farm, his presents, and an overall satisfaction that Nature had provided all of these things.

Advent

Text of poem: New Explorations Anthology page 160

'Advent' is a poem made up of two sonnets. The sonnet itself is a structure that gives way to easy division. It is usually divided into an octet followed by a sestet. Kavanagh abandons this convention in the first sonnet, dividing his sonnet into two even halves of seven lines each. It is no coincidence that in this poem he seeks an equality. (That initial octet is often divided into two quatrains.) So the idea of stitching two separate sonnets together should immediately suggest some sort of linear progression of ideas. Kavanagh does that in this poem. The journey that he decides to adopt is a peculiar one; he sets out his new poetic manifesto in this poem. To do so, he decides that in order to go forwards, he must first go back. The poem was originally called 'Renewal', and to this reader that title was certainly a more direct approach.

The poem starts with a world-weary reminiscence to somebody familiar:

> We have tested and tasted too much, lover

He then returns to an earlier poem, 'A Christmas Childhood'. In that poem he states:

> The light between the ricks of hay and straw
> Was a hole in Heaven's gable.

Here he points out that you can overexpose yourself. He decides that it is more worthwhile to search for the minutiae of life than for true wonderment. So he has to go back to real basics in a genuine and ascetic way, because 'Through a chink too wide there comes no wonder.'

He advocates returning to simple sustenance, because he feels that this will garner a truer sense of spiritual purity. When he talks about penance he attributes no negativity to it, but rather sees it as part of a process towards self-fulfilment. He promises himself that he will give back the negativity of useless knowledge. Experience for its own sake is not enough for him now – just as it wasn't when he was younger. Back then he did not appreciate it:

> The knowledge we stole but could not use.

In the second half of the first sonnet he spells out his own poetic manifesto. He needs to return to a state where he finds wonder in simple things. He makes a list of the lifestyle he has abandoned, and he obviously feels that he has suffered from being without this feeling. He wants to have his spirit shocked; he needs to feel a 'prophetic astonishment'. If he can find these things again, then he will have a poetic rebirth.

It is all very well Kavanagh talking about these things; the proof will come in whether or not he puts them into practice.

> And the newness that was in every stale thing
> When we looked at it as children.

Kavanagh uses hyperbole again and again in his poems, to great effect. So when he talks about 'the spirit-shocking | Wonder in a black slanting Ulster hill', the sense of uniqueness is certainly very heightened, even though it seems mundane now. He is longing for a time when these hills were comparable to the Alps. It is perception that is important here, and the ability to see things as though for the first time. Again Kavanagh is never content with dealing with one of the senses, just in case we might think that sight is the only sensation that is allowed to be heightened. To a child, even what is heard seems different. What can seem now to an adult like 'the tedious talking | Of an old fool' can be relayed to the child as 'prophetic astonishment'.

The imagery that he uses in the poem is one clear indication that he is capable of doing this. He uses apparent opposites to achieve it. When he breaks a paradox he sets out his poetic philosophy, so he can reconcile 'newness in every stale thing', 'astonishment in the tedious talking of an old fool . . .', and he can find 'old stables where Time begins'. This brings to mind a connection reminding us that Jesus himself was born in a an 'old stable'. There is a strong note of caution here: don't take things like 'bog-holes, cart-tracks, old stables' for granted.

The second sonnet allows Kavanagh to say what he's going to do about all of this. He is saying that the poetry is dependent on his attitude. If he opens himself to a new way of reacting to Nature, then the poetry will come to him. There is a lot of emphasis on faith and fate in the second verse; he seems determined to change his ways now. He says, 'We'll have no need to go searching', or he insists we don't have to listen for it: 'We'll hear it . . . .' It is almost as if the hearing is enough and that the hearing will come naturally, too. If he gives way to God.

Where this new inspiration comes from is an important element. It will be in simple places and from simple people doing simple things, such as:

> . . . in the whispered argument of a churning
> Or in the streets where the village boys are lurching.

And especially:

> Wherever life pours ordinary plenty.

This shall be reward in itself. The inspiration will come to him. Indeed, too much analysis by him could destroy the beauty of the act. He makes this clear when he insists to his lover:

> Won't we be rich, my love and I, and please
> God we shall not ask for reason's payment,
> The why of heart-breaking strangeness . . .
> Nor analyse God's breath in common statement.

This is a Catholic poem, accepting without question God's goodness and simplicity, and Kavanagh insists that 'pleasure, knowledge and the conscious hour' should be 'thrown in the dust-bin'. He must open himself to the glory of God and constantly praise the vision that he has been given.

The poem is partly an obituary for the past, and partly an incantation to a new celebratory aesthetic. Kavanagh says that by learning the lessons of self-sacrifice and rebirth that are taught during Advent, he will re-emerge reinvigorated and more in understanding with Christ, like a 'January flower.'

On Raglan Road

Text of poem: New Explorations Anthology page 162
[Note: this poem is also prescribed for 2010 Ordinary level exam]

Note: This poem is better known as a song, made most famous by Luke Kelly of the Dubliners. It is worth the reader's effort to hear a recorded version of this song.

This is a love poem. In itself this is rare in Kavanagh's poetry. It is a love poem tinged with regret. Kavanagh sometimes prided himself on his innocence in his poems; indeed, in a number of them he advocated a sensibility that encouraged it. In this poem he expects the reader to see him as completely naïve.

He begins the poem with a specific place. This is very similar to many of his poems. Of the poems in this anthology, however, this is the first poem set in Dublin rather than in Monaghan. When Kavanagh names a place he does so not only because

> Naming these things is the love act,
> ['The Hospital']

but also because the naming of these places helps to ground the poems. It allows the reader to believe them and him. The perception may be that if this is a real place and time ('an autumn day'), then it must be true.

From the beginning of the poem, Kavanagh puts himself in the place of an innocent who has been dragged into a situation that he did not want but could not avoid. Kavanagh sees the inevitable pitfalls ahead but cannot resist. He admits that he

> . . . knew
> That her dark hair would weave a snare that I might one day rue;

He acknowledges that he 'saw the danger', yet still walked into her path. Indeed, the image created by Kavanagh of himself is of an innocent hypnotised by a Medusa-like creature who forces him to do her will. Kavanagh admits to giving in to temptation, but like Othello he only admits in his own way that he 'did not love too wisely but too well'. He says that he '. . . loved too much and by such and such is happiness thrown away.'

The Queen of Hearts image is a curious one. There is an element here that suggests Kavanagh was gambling and it didn't pay off. He certainly didn't end up 'making hay'. He seems to be complaining that the woman was too quiet and spent her time doing homely things, rather than making hay with him.

In the third verse he declares that he gave and she took. This may seem like an arrogant attitude to a contemporary reader:

> I gave her gifts of the mind I gave her the secret sign that's known
> To the artists who have known the true gods of sound and stone
> And word and tint.

He declares that he has brought her to Parnassus and has given her that which every intelligent person would want: an insight into his mind. He was even gracious enough to name her in some of his poems. What more could any woman want?:

> I did not stint for I gave her poems to say
> With her own name there ...

He does this even though she may have ruined his talent and killed the sunshine that should have fallen on him:

> . . . her own dark hair like clouds over fields of May.

In the fourth verse Kavanagh sees his 'ex' and rationalises why she would turn away from him. He comes to the final damning conclusion that she did not deserve his love. He describes himself as an angel and his ex as a gargoyle. The angel made too much of a sacrifice, by trying to love somebody so base that they are made of clay. The net result of this encounter has been inevitable; the angel was injured:

> . . . I had wooed not as I should a creature made of clay –
> When the angel woos he'd lose his wings at the dawn of day.

As a poem, 'On Raglan Road' is certainly presented from the poet's point of view. Should he be expected to give more balance? He is not writing a piece of journalism. Poetic licence with the truth is allowable, but it is important to see that this is one side of the argument and maybe Kavanagh loses some of the impact that he might have had.

Some of the imagery that Kavanagh uses is worth remarking upon. He seems to be referring to himself in a passive mode and as somebody who is angelic and taken by Nature, whereas the woman in the poem is associated with darkness: 'her dark hair', 'a deep ravine', 'Clouds over fields of May', 'made of clay'.

The long, winding lines of the poem are often associated with poetry written *as gaeilge* and they fit in with many of the poems written in the bardic tradition. Many of these poems were also about women, but saw a woman in a vision poem and as someone who was pure, representing Ireland to the poet and encouraging him to eulogise rather than lament (although Kavanagh's lament seems to be more for himself). These long lines fit into the pattern of the song-line; they flow dreamily and sweetly.

He uses a lot of mid-line rhyme in this poem, too, which also encourages a lament-like atmosphere. There are examples of this all the way through the poem. In the first verse: 'hair' and 'snare' and 'grief' and 'leaf'. In the second verse he uses 'ravine' and 'seen', 'hearts' and 'tarts' and 'much' and 'such'. The third verse has 'mind' and 'sign', 'tint' and 'stint' and 'there' and 'hair'; while finally the fourth has 'street' and 'meet', 'me' and 'hurriedly', 'wooed' and 'should' and 'woos' and 'lose'.

The Hospital

Text of poem: New Explorations Anthology page 164

This is yet another sonnet, obviously Kavanagh's favourite form; yet again its content is what makes this sonnet different from other poets' versions of the same form. This is a love poem. That must be clear from the fact that he uses the word 'love' or 'lover' five times in the space of the five sentences that make up the poem. The main question that should be going through the reader's mind is: why would anybody want to write a love poem to a building? For it is the building that he is in love with, not what has been done to him within the building. He does not seem to be writing a poem about being grateful for being cured. He seems to be referring in this paean to just the hospital itself. Or is he yet again writing a poem about poetry?

The octet begins in a matter-of-fact manner. There is nothing austere or profound about this place. It is not a miraculous healing place; it is a 'functional ward'. It seems incredibly uniform and without personality:

> . . . square cubicles in a row
> Plain concrete, wash basins –

Immediately it is dismissed as 'an art lover's woe'. Surely a poet should know something about art. Is his dismissal a contradiction, or does he hate art? Not only is the room drab, but also the other occupants are not exactly people to be revered. Rather than populate his hospital with healing angels, Kavanagh inserts a 'fellow in the next bed (who) snored'.

Kavanagh uses that first quatrain to describe the place. The next two lines explain the motivation for his love. There is nothing that cannot be loved. He reassures himself that by loving something:

> The common and banal her heat can know.

There is nothing that cannot be used as a subject for poetry; this is the essence of much of Kavanagh's work. The same theme is directed at us in 'Epic' or in 'Shancoduff'. It is not enough just to write about them, however. It must be done well and in a proper poetic genre. Therefore it is also not enough to 'just love' the Hospital: it must be done with passion, as he tells us about 'her heat'.

This poem was written during a period of transition for Kavanagh. It is one of the first of his poems that was written during what is known as his Canal Period. It is appropriate, therefore, that just as his period of illness led him to a new period of poetic freedom, then he should also point out that the hospital is not just the building itself, but outside there is 'the inexhaustible adventure of a gravelled yard.' He doesn't tell us what the adventure is, but he tells us some of the things that go on there.

He then goes on to tell us what type of things have not just happened, but have existed. Kavanagh, by naming them in his poem, has now given them immortality. They exist outside themselves now. They exist in his poem; this is the love that he can give to them. Indeed he sees it as his duty to name them.

The naming is an act of love; it is personal and intimate between Kavanagh and the hospital.

He is giving it a life 'out of time'. He feels it is important to give immortality to that which has affected him. Because he has been affected by a particular place or situation, he feels that he has a duty to explain about it and to give it life. Places are the lifeblood of his poetry; he always names them. The venues of his life make up the different stages of his life – his time in Monaghan, his illness in the hospital, and afterwards his time at the Grand Canal.

The time that he spent in the Rialto Hospital was obviously a very important time for him. It did mark a turnaround in his poetic oeuvre. This poem is important for him because it is a time when he began to have a self-realisation about his own future, and about the direction in which his poetry should go.

Canal Bank Walk

Text of poem: New Explorations Anthology page 166

If in 'Advent' Kavanagh was looking for a renewal of his way of looking at things, he seems to have found it in this sonnet. He found his spiritual renewal, or rather it found him, when he fell ill in 1955. This poem was written during his convalescence. As his health was improving, Kavanagh became more and more grateful for his gifts and for life itself. This poem is a clear celebration; indeed, one critic has described it as a hymn. It is not perhaps a hymn to God, but to the world that God has created. This is important in the overall context of Kavanagh's new poetic philosophy. He felt that poetry was a gift, and he believed that poets had a duty to use that gift.

The predominant images in the poem are natural ones, and he starts with a beautifully crafted neologism: 'leafy-with-love' gets the mood of the poem right almost immediately. This place, after all, is a little piece of the country in a city setting. The area and the canal are inspiring him to do the 'will of God'. When the poet says that God would wish him to wallow, he does not mean that he should lie and do nothing, but rather that he should cherish and enjoy the glory of being with Nature and that he should celebrate it fervently.

Kavanagh sees redemption coming with water and he wishes to grow 'as before'. The image of the stick represents himself 'immobilised and helpless, but radiant'. His new way of living will be populated by romance and he wants to feel comfortable with Nature, as the couple on the bench do. He wants to use the energy of moments such as these and to add 'a third | Party to the couple kissing on the old seat'. But he wants to be infused with the knowledge that Nature will have a controlling influence. His poetry will take off into a different sphere of thought and it will be 'Eloquently new and abandoned to its delirious beat.'

The sestet is a prayer that reaches out for inspiration and like 'Lines written . . .', it reaches out with a poetic invocation to Nature to allow him to become a better poet and to envelop his senses. It is when surrounded by Nature that he can paradoxically be most free. Kavanagh wants to be both enraptured and encaptured. He expects Nature to do this to him; all he has to do is to submit to it.

What he desires is to abandon himself to another power which will allow him to become a medium for the glory of Nature:

> Feed the gaping need of my senses, give me ad lib
> To pray unselfconsciously with overflowing speech

Kavanagh has needs in this poem, just like a baby might have. The 'new dress woven' is like a baptismal gown that will bring him and his poetry to a place where his spiritual and poetic rebirth can take place.

The rhythm and structure of the poem suggest fluidity and use enjambment or 'run-on lines', subtle rhyme and assonance to produce an incantation that flows like the canal which he describes.

There are a lot of differences between this poem and 'Advent'. They are both about the importance of being grateful to God; the difference between them is simple. 'Advent' urges a sense of solemn ascetic devotion, whereas 'Canal Bank Walk' is in favour of a more glorious outpouring of emotion where the poet is urging himself to praise God in a more open and vigorous manner. The verbs that Kavanagh uses are much more aggressive: 'enrapture', 'encapture', 'gaping'. He wants to lose control here, rather than keep things under control like he did in 'Advent'. He feels that the qualities of the water can have an invigorating effect on him, just as they did on Jesus when he met John the Baptist.

Lines Written on a Seat on the Grand Canal, Dublin
'Erected to the Memory of Mrs Dermot O'Brien'

Text of poem: New Explorations Anthology page 168

'Lines Written . . .' is the second of the Canal poems, and is a plea from the heart for poetry to be given the tribute that he feels it deserves. There are some questions raised by the idea of such a poem in the first place. The first one is: does a poet deserve commemoration in the first place? To answer this we must understand Kavanagh's ideas behind the role of a poet. The second obvious question is: why set the poem on a seat overlooking a canal? The third is: why does he leave the subtitle in?

To answer the last point first, he seems to admire the idea of having a seat as a memorial. He thinks it is a good idea, so he includes it in his poem. He also includes it perhaps to instigate an idea of mortality in the reader of the poem. This poem may be seen as the poet's requiem for himself. It is worth it, at this point, for the reader to reread the poem in that context.

The poem begins in a gloriously poetic manner; the first word is the declaring 'O'. The 'O' sets up an intensely poetic mood. If it is left out, what difference does it make? One of the effects it definitely has is that it sets up the poem as a grand exercise. We have seen in Kavanagh's poems up to this point that he likes using simple, even colloquial language, but this declaration is something new and unusual for him. There is also a sense of death in this opening phrase, and Dr Antoinette Quinn has remarked that the opening and its mirror phrase at the end 'frame the sonnet like a black mourning border'. This introduces an element of finality in the poem again and goes back to the inscription on the seat.

So Kavanagh continues through the poem and reflects that the place for people to remember him should be where there is water. Water suggests life, but it also suggests birth and in the Christian tradition it suggests rebirth. A rebirth of the imagination was important to Kavanagh's poetic thesis. He felt that a poet should not just accept what he could see, but should constantly re-inspect his perception of what was seen to be present.

It is Kavanagh's belief that a poet should seek out the wonder of the ordinary that brings him to see the water as something that was capable of many lives: and perhaps so, too, a poem can have many different readings for its readers. The idea of a simple lock in Dublin roaring like Niagara Falls is a use of hyperbole that backs up Kavanagh's belief that perception and attitude are everything. If you wish to see the Niagara Falls, you can. The inspiration that comes from this sight is what is important to him. Kavanagh also wants this attitude to be his legacy to other poets:

> No one will speak in prose
> Who finds his way to these Parnassian islands.

Nature and the seemingly banal as muse is an important theme in Kavanagh's work. He uses an image that was previously used in 'Advent' and 'Shancoduff', where light can find its way through any hole and bring life to a place where previously it was thought that there was none. In 'Advent' we are told:

> Through a chink too wide there comes in no wonder.

Here we are reminded that:

> Fantastic light looks through the eyes of bridges –

Hyperbole is used throughout this poem. His references to Parnassus, Niagara and 'fantastic light' are in an exaggerated manner, and now Athy is a place where mythologies are born.

He siphons this hyperbole by coming back at the end of the poem with a simple, modest, heartfelt plea that we would not commemorate him with a 'hero-courageous | Tomb – just a canal-bank seat for the passer-by.'

This poem is Kavanagh's last great poem, and it is entirely appropriate that in it he tries to find a place for himself in the whole scheme of the world. He desperately seeks a return to the natural world of his youth – the difference being that he is now in a position to enjoy what he sees and what goes on around him. He has found modesty in this poem, not just with God, because he had found that already; he has found his place among regular people and seems to be much more aware that this is where life is at its most vibrant. Seeing things becomes very important to him here. He wants to acknowledge the greatness and majesty of the ordinary things that go on around him. By recognising them, he makes things seem far more magnificent. He transforms the Grand Canal into Parnassus quite naturally, because this is the place that transforms him and gives him his inspiration. This inspiration to his art is awe-inspiring to him, and it is for that reason that he feels free to make the comparison.

Again it is the sense of place that influences Kavanagh. In the Gaelic tradition 'Dinnseanchas' is the term given to the poetry written about a sense of place. In this tradition, the act of describing a place left behind was very important to the poets. In Kavanagh's case, he tries to bring his craft a bit further. He has already acknowledged the influence that County Monaghan and the past have had on him, for better or for worse; now he wants to pay tribute to his present.

5   *Adrienne* RICH

Carole Scully

The poetry of power and revolution

EARLY LIFE

> My own luck was being born white and middle-class into a house full of
> books, with a father who encouraged me to read and write.
>
> (Adrienne Rich, *When We Dead Awaken: Writing a Re-Vision*)

This brief description by Adrienne Rich of her childhood suggests that her
formative years were spent in a secure and solid home where she was
intellectually stimulated by a supportive parent. Indeed, there is a truth
in this interpretation, but equally truthful is the fact that, in later years, Rich had
to struggle to come to terms with certain features of her early life.

Adrienne Rich was born in Baltimore, USA, on 16 May 1929, in the hospital
where her father, Arnold, worked as a doctor. He was also a teacher and a
researcher in the Department of Pathology in Johns Hopkins Medical School. It
was only as she grew older that Rich fully appreciated just how unique her
father was in the academic world of Baltimore. Arnold was one of a very small
number of Jews who taught in the Medical School and, as such, he had to
endure a lengthy delay in his appointment to the Professorship of Pathology at
Johns Hopkins simply because no Jew had ever held the chair before.

Arnold's attitude to his Jewish heritage was a complex one that proved to be
one aspect of her childhood that Rich struggled to reconcile in later years.
Arnold did not hide the fact that he was a Jew, once commenting to Adrienne,
'You know that I have never denied that I am a Jew . . . I am a scientist . . . I
have no use for organized religion . . . I am a person, not simply a Jew.'
(Adrienne Rich, *Split at the Root*). Ironically, according to Rich, Arnold's
appearance very definitely revealed his ethnic roots because he had dark hair
and eyes and a large, hooked nose.

However, it is clear that Arnold deliberately created a family and social
environment where Jewishness, although not denied, was certainly avoided in
favour of Christian values. He married a Protestant woman and his two
daughters were sent to an Episcopalian school. He and his family mixed with
people who considered it impolite to mention such words as 'Negro' and 'Jew'.

Arnold expected his wife and daughters to behave 'correctly' at all times in the belief that, as Rich put it, 'With enough excellence, you could presumably make it stop mattering you were Jewish. . . .' (Adrienne Rich, *Split at the Root*).

Rich's mother, Helen, was ideally suited to such a lifestyle. From a once-wealthy southern family, Helen had been reared in a world where the Christian ethos was the foundation of good social behaviour and where the old-fashioned, genteel values of white, middle-class good breeding were prized above all else. To be seen as 'common' was the greatest sin of all for any woman. Rich's mother diligently attempted to pass on these values to Adrienne and her sister, advising them, that in relationships with men, 'It was in the woman's interest to cultivate "mystery", conceal her actual feelings.' (Adrienne Rich, *Split at the Root*). This was another aspect of her early years that Adrienne Rich would later struggle to reconcile.

Yet, Helen was more than simply a 'southern belle'. Prior to her wedding, she had been a gifted pianist and composer. At one point, she had even considered becoming a concert pianist, but had decided against it because of the predominantly male nature of the classical-music world at that time. Once she met Arnold Rich, Helen gave up any career ambitions and devoted herself to caring for her husband and daughters. She did continue to play the piano and taught both of her children to play, but her exceptional musical talent was only ever expressed in private. Rich's experience of the way in which marriage had forced her mother to abandon the open expression of her ability proved to be another feature of her childhood that would affect her adult life.

Adrienne's parents instilled a respect for education in their daughters. Indeed, both girls were educated at home for some time before joining the school system. Adrienne was particularly close to her father. He gave her access to his large library of books and continually encouraged her to develop her intellect and to write poetry. Adrienne was a bright child who enjoyed such pursuits. She worked hard to impress her father and to produce the type of views and the style of poetry that would gain his approval. However, Arnold's approval was not gained easily. In later years, Rich vividly described the rigours that he put her through as a young girl: 'He prowled and pounced over my school papers, insisting I use "grown-up" sources; he criticized my poems for faulty techniques. . . .' (Adrienne Rich, *Split at the Root*).

Adrienne more than fulfilled her father's hopes with her brilliant academic career. In 1947, she went from high school to the all-female Radcliffe College, part of the prestigious Harvard University. Yet, ironically, it was here that she began to encounter ideas that would challenge her to reassess her childhood experiences, ideas that would ultimately lead her to a prolonged and bitter break from her parents.

RICH'S JEWISH HERITAGE

At Radcliffe, Rich met with young Jewish women who were not only her equals intellectually and academically, but who were also fiercely proud of their Jewish culture and religion. In Rich's own words, ' They took me on.' They taught her 'the names of holidays and foods, which surnames are Jewish and which are "changed names"; about girls who had their noses fixed. . . .' Although she knew that she would be unacceptable as a Jew to strict Jewish families because her mother was non-Jewish, Rich found something within her that responded to these revelations. She knew that she was 'testing a forbidden current', because she was deliberately going against her father's wishes. But even more dangerously, Rich was aware that she 'was flirting with identity' (Adrienne Rich, *Split at the Root)* .

Up until this point in Rich's life, because of the efforts of her father and mother, her Jewish heritage had not really impinged on her existence. During her childhood, she had the view that 'Jews were in the Bible and mentioned in English literature . . . but they seemed not to exist in everyday life.' (Adrienne Rich, *Split at the Root*). In 1946, at the age of sixteen, she had gone to a cinema to watch films showing the Allied liberation of the Nazi concentration camps, but when she had told her parents what she had seen they were 'not pleased. I felt accused of being morbidly curious, not healthy, sniffing around death for the thrill of it.' (Adrienne Rich, *Split at the Root)*. The confusion and guilt that Rich felt as a result of this experience restrained her from engaging in any such similar incidents for a long time.

Now, however, the more independent Rich would not be so easily diverted. She did struggle to reconcile her own desires with her wish to please her parents but, finally, she decided to address the unresolved issue of Jewishness that had lingered from her childhood years. Gradually, she came to see her father's lack of concern for his Jewish heritage as a veneer that covered an ambivalent mixture of 'self-hatred' and 'Jewish pride'. He 'lived in an increasingly withdrawn world, in his house up on a hill in a neighbourhood where Jews were not supposed to buy property.' (Adrienne Rich, *Split at the Root*). Her determination to embrace her Jewish roots marked the beginning of her separation from her parents and from the social and cultural mores and conventions that they had worked so hard to instil in her. In 1953, she married Alfred H. Conrad, a Jewish economist who was teaching at Harvard. Her parents did not attend the wedding. It was to be several years before she would communicate with them again.

DOMESTICITY AND RICH'S POETRY

This separation, particularly from her father, caused Rich not only to reassess her relationship with him but also his influence on her writing. It is undeniable that Arnold Rich had a profound effect on his daughter's early intellectual and creative development. As we have seen, he pushed her to achieve academically and he drove her to refine her writing skills. He had given her books dealing with the technical aspects of poetry, such as metre and rhyme, in order to guide her writing towards a style that he regarded as being 'correct'. In Arnold Rich's view, 'correct' poetry was poetry that demonstrated a knowledge and mastery of traditionally accepted poetic forms.

Indeed, when Rich's first book of poetry was published in 1951, in her final year at Radcliffe, it was widely praised for its technical quality. The poet W. H. Auden, who chose the book for the Yale Younger Poets Award, wrote of it:

> Craftsmanship includes, of course, not only a talent for versification, but also . . . an intuitive grasp of much subtler and more difficult matters like proportion, consistency of diction and tone, and the matching of these with the subject at hand; Miss Rich's poems rarely fail on any of those counts.

In later years, Rich was to view such poems as 'Storm Warnings', 'Aunt Jennifer's Tigers' and 'The Uncle Speaks in the Drawing Room' as having a 'conscious craft' about them. Each of them was 'an arrangement of ideas and feelings, pre-determined, and it said what I had already decided it would say.' (Adrienne Rich, *Poetry and Experience: Statement at a Poetry Reading*). Indeed, there is an undeniable elegance of form and a gracefulness of expression about such lines as:

And set a match to candles sheathed in glass

('Storm Warnings')

When Aunt is dead, her terrified hands will lie
Still ringed with ordeals she was mastered by.

('Aunt Jennifer's Tigers')

Some have talked in bitter tones,
Some have held and fingered stones.

('The Uncle Speaks in the Drawing Room')

However, the radical alterations that took place in Rich's life following the publication of her first anthology began to change her approach to her writing. After the acrimonious and bitter split from her parents, she struggled to escape from her intense desire to please her father both in her life and her writing. Freed from the constraints and preconceptions of her father's view of poetry, Rich began to explore other ways of expressing her thoughts and feelings, so that she was not simply recreating a 'male' style of poetry, but finding a way of expressing her own 'female' experience in poetic terms.

In addition, she began to think about the way that her relationship with her father had been influenced by the fact that he was male and she female:

In my separation from him, in my realization at what price that once-intoxicating approval had been bought, I was learning in concrete ways a great deal about patriarchy, in particular how the 'special' woman, the favoured daughter, is controlled and rewarded.

(Adrienne Rich, *Split at the Root*)

Thus, once again, her early childhood experiences – in particular her relationship with her father – affected her later development. She began to examine the patriarchal nature of her society where, she believed, the hierarchical form of relations between men and women ensured that men were allocated the dominant, powerful role in family and society, while women were kept in a subservient and powerless position.

However, it was not only Rich's childhood experiences that influenced her at this point in her life. Her marriage to Alfred opened up a new world to her, one that would profoundly change not only her writing but also her whole way of living. As with many modern poets, Adrienne Rich has coupled her writing of poetry with extensive prose writings describing her intellectual and emotional development, thereby enabling her readers to directly connect her poetic development to her life. Consequently, she has written openly and honestly about the early years of her marriage, tracing the emotional confusion and the ambivalence that she felt about her role as a wife and mother.

From her childhood experiences, Rich already had some doubts about the effects that becoming a wife had on a woman's position in the world. She had witnessed her mother's surrendering of her career as a pianist and her submission to the role of dutiful wife. It is clear from her writing that Rich did love her husband, Alfred, but there was a very deliberate aspect to her decision to marry him. She saw it as a way of enabling her to participate in the Jewish culture of home and family, that culture that had been denied to her by her parents: ' I longed to embrace that family, that new and mysterious Jewish world.' Furthermore, she regarded her marriage as a statement about her position as a female poet:

Because I was determined to prove that as a woman poet I could have what was then defined as a 'full' woman's life, I plunged in my early twenties into marriage and had three children before I was thirty.

(Adrienne Rich, *Split at the Root*)

It may seem a rather confusing choice for her to make, given her growing questioning of the patriarchal nature of society, but, at that point in her life, marriage seemed to answer many of the questions that Rich was facing. Yet there was still a sense of uneasiness about her situation that haunted Rich, an uneasiness that she felt unable to express openly in her writing:

> In those years, formalism . . . like asbestos gloves . . . allowed me to handle materials I couldn't pick up barehanded.
> (Adrienne Rich, *Poetry and Experience: Statement at a Poetry Reading*)

Thus, the image of the storm in her poem 'Storm Warnings' and the disenchantment felt by the female character in 'Living in Sin' are Rich's veiled references to the increasing turmoil that she felt within herself. Another device that Rich used to mask her expression of her confusion was the use of a male character, as in 'The Roofwalker'.

She considered this uneasiness as somehow unnatural, an act of disloyalty to her husband and, as her family grew, to her three sons. She struggled on with her writing in the context of her roles of wife and mother. Her second book of poetry was published in the same month that she gave birth to her first son. Again, it was received positively, and her poetry was judged to have a 'gracefulness' about it. Rich, however, was not satisfied with these poems. On the one hand, she recognised the positives in her life: a well-received second book of poems; a loving husband and a new son. On the other, she had times when she felt ' doubts', 'mild depression' and 'active despairing'.

By the time her third son was born, Rich's writing had almost ground to a halt. She experienced a terrible weariness, 'that female fatigue of suppressed anger and loss of contact with my own being'. She found that her daily routine of housewifely and motherly duties left her little or no time to actually write. Above all, she felt a terrible sense of failure: failure as a wife and mother, and failure as a poet. She came to the conclusion that she either had to accept 'failure' as her lot in life and continue on with the way things were, or to find some way of making sense of what she was experiencing and what she was feeling. She decided that she would have to find 'some synthesis by which to understand what was happening to me' (Adrienne Rich, *When We Dead Awaken: Writing a Re-Vision*).

FINDING A SYNTHESIS

The 1950s and 1960s were a time of great political upheaval in America. As you may have learned from your CSPE course, during this time a number of movements developed with the aim of bringing about greater freedom for particular sections of American society. Along with many other academics and intellectuals, Adrienne Rich and her husband became actively involved in civil rights groups. Later in her life, Rich expressed the view that the impetus for this involvement grew out of her early experiences of 'a social and familial world in which there was a great deal of splitting'. (Adrienne Rich: *An Interview with David Montenegro*). In other words, she felt that she had lived her formative years in a family split between Jewish and Gentile (non-Jewish) cultural roots and in a society split between black and white. For her, the civil rights-based movements seemed to offer some way of uniting all of the split parts of her identity.

One such movement was founded to coordinate the struggle of American blacks to bring about an end to segregation and to achieve full rights of citizenship. For a time, Dr Martin Luther King was its leader.

The film entitled *The Rosa Parks Story* shows the types of social restriction that black people endured at the time and the methods that they used to change their position in American society. It tells of Rosa Parks' refusal to give up her bus seat to a white passenger in 1955 in Alabama. At the time, such an action was considered to be a violation of the segregation laws. Rosa Parks was arrested and, as a protest against this action, Dr Martin Luther King led a boycott of the bus system. Finally, in 1956, the buses were desegregated.

Rich found herself responding to this movement because it gave black people the opportunity to voice how they felt about their position in American society. It was this development of a language to express a sense of oppression that struck a chord with Rich. As she said in her interview with David Montenegro, 'That was the first place where I heard a language to name oppression. And it was an enormous relief. . . .' For Rich, this marked the beginnings of her open acknowledgement of her own sense of oppression and her awareness that language and power are inextricably linked.

At the same time, the anti-war movement was steadily growing following the involvement of United States troops in Vietnam. Many American universities, such as Berkeley, witnessed large student demonstrations where intellectuals and musicians expressed the deep dissatisfaction that a large number of Americans felt at the time. One such musician was Joan Baez, whose rendition of the song 'We shall not be moved' became a popular anthem. Here again, we can experience something of the atmosphere of these times in the film *Born on the Fourth of July*. In this film, Tom Cruise portrays the life of Ron Kovic, who was paralysed fighting in Vietnam and subsequently became an anti-war activist.

As with the black civil rights movement, Rich found that the anti-war movement also challenged accepted forms of expression, because they were seen as conveying only the views of the pro-war political establishment. Consequently, a new language gradually arose out of anti-war protests, one that expressed a rejection of America's position in Vietnam and questioned the balance of political power in the world.

However, it was Rich's involvement with one group in particular that was to have the most profound effect on her life and her work: that of the women's liberation movement. The concept of women's liberation, or feminism, developed in the United States alongside the other civil rights movements. It challenged the traditional roles allowed to women in American society. As the film *Mona Lisa Smile* with Julia Roberts illustrates, in 1950s America a college education for women was available only to well-off, white women. However, even among these women, the roles of wife and mother were generally considered to be far more important that any career. Consequently, as had happened with Rich's own mother, marriage usually meant that a woman focused on supporting her husband, running her home and caring for her children, and abandoned any career aspirations.

Until she encountered the women's liberation movement, Adrienne Rich had thought of herself as isolated and alone in her feelings of frustration and dissatisfaction. Now, she met women who felt the same as she did. She threw herself into the movement. She revelled in the debates and the conversations with women who, like her, had experienced a profound despair arising out of the boundaries and expectations that society placed upon them because they were women. She found that not only did she relate to women on an intellectual level, but she also responded to them physically and sexually:

'The suppressed lesbian I had been carrying in me since adolescence began to stretch her limbs. . . .' (Adrienne Rich: *An Interview with David Montenegro*).

After seventeen years of marriage, Rich left her husband and then fell in love with a Jewish woman. At last, she had found the connection, that synthesis, that which would reconcile and unite all the 'split' elements that she had absorbed in her childhood.

LANGUAGE AND POWER

As we have seen, Rich's involvement with civil rights movements had awakened her to the intimate relationship that exists between language and power. She realised that the language that we use in everyday life is more than simply a means of communication enabling each one of us to survive and function.

Humans are, in general, social animals who live with other human beings. Clearly then, on one level language is used to ensure that our individual basic survival needs are met within a group situation: we each communicate in order to obtain the food, clothing, shelter and any other objects that are needed for day-to-day living. But there is more to human life than this. We are highly complex creatures, both emotionally and psychologically. To live fully we need to be able to express our thoughts and our feelings successfully and satisfactorily.

However, it has long been recognised that individual expression is potentially a disruptive element to the continuing good order of the group or society in which humans live. Therefore, human societies have tended to institute some form of social hierarchy where there is an ultimate governing power whose role is to ensure that the society continues to function successfully, even if this means that the needs of individuals or groups within that society are not always met. In practice this means that those who hold the governing power in a society decide what is socially acceptable, that is, what is good for the continuance of that society; and what is socially unacceptable, that is, what is damaging to the continuance of that society.

The language that is used by the people who govern and the people who live in a society reflects and supports what is socially acceptable in that society, while also expressing rejection and disapproval for that which is deemed to be unacceptable. The governing power will frequently take steps to suppress or eliminate language that expresses views running counter to acceptable thinking, since this represents a threat. This suppression or elimination can be conducted subtly or overtly. History provides us with many examples of such overt actions, for instance, the book burnings conducted by the Nazis.

Indeed, our own recent Irish history is a perfect illustration of the connection between language and power, since English control of Ireland meant that a social situation was constructed where the ability to speak English was considered to be an advantage. In 1831, the Irish National School System was established, with English as the only acceptable 'school' language even in totally Irish-speaking areas. Conversely, when it came to constructing a Constitution for the new Irish Free State, one of its very first articles, Article 4, emphasised the connection between language and power when it stated: 'The national language of the Irish Free State (Saorstat Eireann) is the Irish language. . . .'

For the civil rights movements in America, the language that was used in their society did not reflect either their beliefs or values; rather, it embodied the beliefs and values of those in power. In this way, each word that they spoke in their everyday lives served to emphasise their lack of power and to represent their submission to those governing. At that time, those who were governing were stereotypically and overwhelmingly white, financially secure, heterosexual males. Thus non-white people, poor people, workers, pacifists, homosexuals and women decided that part of their movement towards gaining power had to be the development of a language that did truly reflect what they regarded as important.

Adrienne Rich's participation in feminism, and her lesbianism, led her to view the very language that she had used so 'gracefully' and with such 'craftsmanship' as representing both the chains that held women in captivity in a male-controlled, patriarchal society, and the rope that they could use to climb to power and liberty. She understood 'how our language has trapped as well as liberated us, how the very act of naming has been till now a male prerogative, and how we can begin to see and name – and therefore start afresh.' (Adrienne Rich, *When We Dead Awaken: Writing a Re-Vision*). Together with other feminist writers, Rich set about finding words to express their new identities; to dismantle a language that they felt echoed with the message that men held all the power in society; to allow women to access power and to revolutionise the very structures of society:

> Women are speaking to and of women in these poems, out of a newly released courage to name, to love each other, to share risk and grief and celebration. . . . The creative energy of patriarchy is fast running out. . . . (Adrienne Rich, *When We Dead Awaken: Writing a Re-Vision*)

Thus, from the late 1950s on, Rich began to recognise that not only should her writing have a political dimension to it, but also that her very life should embrace a political stance. For her, politics was 'not something "out there", but something "in here" and of the essence of my condition'. Rich believed that the time had come for women to focus on the role that they had played in previous societies, their role in the present society, and the role that they could play in the society of the future.

Nor was this going to be an easy task, either for women or men. On the one hand, women had no models on which to base their vision of a new 'woman-driven' world. So, there were bound to be feelings of fear and confusion in some women, when faced with the sufferings of women in the past and the uncertainty surrounding women's roles in the future. Thus in 'Power', about Marie Curie's denial of the cause of her dreadful physical condition, can be seen a representation of the reluctance of some women to acknowledge the truth of the female/male relationship. On the other hand, men would also experience fear and confusion, as they had to confront this challenge to the traditional, patriarchal society that had served them so well for so many centuries.

Most difficult of all, however, was the fact that women and men were now beginning to speak a different language, because women were no longer content to use the words that had been formed by and for a male-centred society. Her later poems, such as 'Our Whole Life', 'Trying to Talk with a Man' and 'Diving into the Wreck' express many of those concerns.

RICH'S LATER LIFE AND POETRY

Although Rich had finally found the 'synthesis' that she had been looking for to draw together the 'split' elements of her life into an understandable whole, she still had to endure some very difficult times. In 1968 her father died, and in 1970 her husband Alfred committed suicide. Rich was deeply upset and her poem 'From a Survivor' communicates her profound sense of loss with an uncompromising honesty. In addition, she has had to undergo a series of operations for arthritis and in 1992 she had spinal surgery.

However, Rich has also had happier times. In 1976, she began living with another writer, Michelle Cliff. She has continued to write both poetry and prose while lecturing in a number of American universities, including Columbia, Cornell and Stanford. The quality of her work has been frequently acknowledged, ranging from the National Book Award in 1974, through two Guggenheim Fellowships and the Brandeis Creative Arts Medal in Poetry, to the Lannan Foundation Lifetime Achievement Award in 2000. In 1997 her principles led her to decline a National Medal for the Arts from the then President of the United States, Bill Clinton, commenting, 'I do know that art . . . means nothing if it simply decorates the dinner table of the power that holds it hostage. The radical disparities of wealth and power in America are widening at a devastating rate. A president cannot meaningfully honour certain token artists while the people at large are so dishonoured.'

Rich's later poetry is clearly very different from her earlier work in appearance, structure, expression and content. The tight elegance of 'Aunt Jennifer's Tigers' is strikingly opposed to the cluster of words and spaces used in 'Power'. The refined clarity of language in 'The Uncle Speaks in the Drawing Room' contrasts with the challenging connection of words found in 'Trying to Talk with a Man'. The hesitant, careful expression of uneasiness in 'Storm Warning' gives way to the confident heroism of 'Diving into the Wreck'.

The manner in which Rich has continually and uncompromisingly wrestled with the poetic form reflects the way in which she has wrestled with the experiences of her life. Initially, she learned her poetic craft from men: her father and the male poets that she studied. She strove to write in a way that had 'occasional surprises . . . but control, technical mastery and intellectual clarity were the real goals' (Adrienne Rich, *Poetry and Experience: Statement at a Poetry Reading*). In doing so, she received great praise for her ability from such distinguished male writers as W. H. Auden, but she also had to suppress aspects of her identity, of her womanhood.

It was this act of suppression that caused Rich to feel a terrible sense of confusion and, for a time, the ordered formality of her poems provided her with a comforting means of escape from this confusion. Inevitably, she was driven to face the reality of the conflict inherent in her life and the lie of the order that she had so frantically tried to make a truth. As her life experiences expanded, so too did her poetry. She began to re-form her writing, so that there was still that refinement in her choice of words and phrases but there was also an openness to 'let the unconscious offer its materials', to allow her imagination to work on experience. She no longer hid behind her writing; instead she used it to engage directly with her life. Thus her poems became 'experiences, that contribute to my knowledge and my emotional life' (Adrienne Rich, *Poetry and Experience: Statement at a Poetry Reading*). It is notable that she characteristically writes in the present tense, so that her poems appear as processes in action.

With immense bravery and an unbroken determination to be truthful, Adrienne Rich opens up the process of her act of living to us, her readers – not to provide answers, nor to supply solutions, but simply to share and acknowledge the value of a life experience, in the hope that we too will move towards a greater sharing and acknowledgment of the value of all life experiences:

> '. . . in the more recent poems something is happening, something has happened to me and, if I have been a good parent to the poem, something will happen to you who read it.'
> (Adrienne Rich, *Poetry and Experience: Statement at a Poetry Reading*)

There is, indeed, a heroic quality about the role that she has assigned for herself and the task that she has undertaken, but there is also an underlying sense of unremitting solitariness. For like Aunt Jennifer, like the woman 'Living in Sin', like the 'naked man fleeing' and like 'the Algerian', Rich writes as a figure on her own. Although occasionally she may, like the diver in 'Diving into the Wreck', feel a sense of wholeness or she may celebrate the fact that she is a 'Survivor', the wholeness and the celebration never totally nullify the image of Rich standing alone with her fists raised against the society that surrounds her. And yet she fights on, encouraging her readers to witness her struggle to find a language that will have the power to change the world that she inhabits. She is driven to do this in the hope that each of us will be impelled to seek words for our worlds and, in so doing, empower ourselves to revolutionise society so that humanity can enter into a new age, where all have the power to speak and the right to be heard.

Aunt Jennifer's Tigers

Text of poem: New Explorations Anthology page 272
[*Note: This poem is also prescribed for Ordinary Level 2010 exam*]

BACKGROUND NOTE
Along with 'The Uncle Speaks in the Drawing Room' and 'Storm Warnings', 'Aunt Jennifer's Tigers' comes from Rich's first collection of poetry, published in 1951 while she was in her final year at Radcliffe College. At this time, Rich was writing in a way that was influenced by her father's opinions on poetry and the

work of the male poets that she had studied. These poems are notable for their ordered appearance on the page, their tight structure, their elegance of expression and their management of tone.

In later years, Rich saw this mastery of the technical aspects of writing poetry as providing her with a way of subtly expressing her sense of unease about the world that she inhabited because, at that time in her life, she felt unable to declare it openly. Thus, her poems should be seen as multi-layered. They often appear on the page as vivid descriptions of a dramatic moment or situation. However, a careful reading of these descriptions reveals the intricate connections that Rich has built into her images, so that the reader gradually comes to understand the issues and themes that lie at the heart of her pieces. Thus, in spite of the control that she exerted on the poems, they do have an emotional resonance that vibrates within each word, so that the feelings expressed in these pieces linger hauntingly.

TECHNICAL QUALITY

'Aunt Jennifer's Tigers' is made up of three stanzas, each of four lines. The rhyme scheme is tight and regular: *aabb ccdd eeff*. However, Rich has mastered these structural elements to such a degree that they do not interfere with either the reading or the meaning of the poem. Rather they control the pace, so that the reader is encouraged to take time over reading the poem. Indeed, Rich's skilful use of her vocabulary merits careful reading, as she invests a considerable depth of meaning and implication into her use of colour, nouns and verbs. Rich also uses the sounds of her words most effectively, to reinforce the images that she creates. So, the alliteration (where two or more words close together begin with the same letter) in the words 'fingers fluttering' (line 5) emphasises the nervous anxiety of Aunt Jennifer. Similarly, the alliteration of 'prancing, proud' (line 12) conveys the assured certainty of the tigers.

A READING OF THE POEM

The opening image of this poem bursts off the page, filled with colour and excitement. Rich describes an embroidered scene of golden tigers moving confidently through their natural environment. They gleam like gems against the lush, green vegetation. There is a wonderful feeling of life and energy about this opening image: the strong, beautiful animals surrounded by the growing, flourishing jungle. The verbs that Rich uses to describe the tigers, 'prance' and 'pace', indicate that these creatures are totally free in their surroundings. They are masters of their territory who fear nothing, and because of this freedom and power, they have a dignity and confidence that is in marked contrast to the behaviour of the men, who huddle under a tree.

Thus, in the four lines of her opening stanza, Rich has effectively established a number of key elements that will reappear again in the poem: the colour gold, the concepts of freedom and power and the image of the male figure.

In the second stanza, Rich shifts the focus of the poem away from the wonderful tigers and the cowering men, and onto the hands of the person who created them, Aunt Jennifer. It quickly becomes clear that Aunt Jennifer is very different from the tigers. Her movements suggest anxiety and nervousness. Her hands 'flutter' like panic-stricken little birds. They are so delicate, so lacking in physical strength, that her fingers have difficulty with the ivory needle that she is using to embroider the picture. Unlike the tigers, Aunt Jennifer is struggling to cope with her environment. The creamy white of the ivory conjures up an image of the pale, almost bloodless, skin of Aunt Jennifer's fingers, as if her struggle is sucking all life out of her. The fact that the needle is made of ivory is significant, since man obtains ivory by killing elephants. So, the ivory of the needle represents man's triumph over the strength and freedom of the elephant and the power of life and death that he holds over this wild animal.

But the ivory needle is not the only object that is causing difficulties for Aunt Jennifer's hands. What is really weighing them down is her golden wedding ring. In the first stanza, gold was associated with the beautiful, powerful, free tigers; in the second stanza, gold is linked with a cold, heavy piece of metal that drags down the light, agitated movements of Aunt Jennifer's fingers. Interestingly, the Latin word 'oppressare', meaning 'to weigh down', gave rise to the word oppression. For although Aunt Jennifer wears it, this is very definitely 'Uncle's' ring – a means of oppression. Like a harness or a yoke, the ring symbolises the control and power that Uncle obtained over Aunt Jennifer by marrying her. Just as the ivory needle indicated the subjection of the elephant, so the ring testifies to the enslavement of Aunt Jennifer by a male figure. The fearful male figures in the first stanza are no more. The male figure in the second stanza brings death, uses creatures for his own ends and exerts a powerful control over his female partner. It is notable that the Uncle has no name. It is his oppressive bulk and presence that loom not only over fragile Aunt Jennifer, but also over the second and third stanzas.

The image of the golden wedding ring reappears again in the first line of the third stanza, along with Aunt Jennifer's fingers. In direct contrast to the first stanza, where energy and life filled every word, the third stanza evokes death. Aunt Jennifer is motionless, her creamy-white fingers, now finally drained of the blood of life, have been stilled by death – but the ring is still upon them. So, even in death, Aunt Jennifer still carries the emblem that signifies her lack of power and freedom. Rich's use of the words 'ordeals' and 'mastered', in connection with the ring, link back to the image of the ring in the second stanza. In Rich's view, Aunt Jennifer's marriage to the 'Uncle' committed her to a life of oppression and subjection to the power of her husband. For Aunt Jennifer, marriage forced her to yield up her own power, to surrender her control of her life and to suppress her own feelings and wishes. For Rich, the wedding ring is not a symbol of love or mutual commitment, but of male oppression and female repression.

In the final two lines of the poem, Rich returns again to the tigers that Aunt Jennifer struggled in life to embroider. They are still free and powerful. They are everything that Aunt Jennifer gave up once she entered into marriage with the Uncle. They celebrate their living, while Aunt Jennifer simply endured hers. Yet what we must not forget is the fact that it was Aunt Jennifer who created the tigers. It was she who chose the coloured wool and worked it through the screen. Do the tigers represent a small act of rebellion by Aunt Jennifer against the control and mastery of her husband? Are they the symbols of a tiny flame of freedom and power that endured deep within this anxious, delicate, birdlike woman? Could the small and rather cowardly male figures in the first stanza represent the apparently submissive Aunt Jennifer's real opinion about her husband? It would be wonderful to think that Aunt Jennifer was, indeed, a rebel with a needle, that her embroidered screen was a gesture of her defiance.

But perhaps there is not such a positive ending to the poem. Aunt Jennifer's tigers are splendid in their freedom and power. However, they are not truly alive. They are creatures woven in thread and fabric, stretched within the frame of a screen; like captured and preserved butterflies they are stuck on a panel. Perhaps this is the true tragedy that Rich sees in Aunt Jennifer's life: marriage to the domineering, male Uncle broke her spirit to such an extent that even if some small flame of freedom and power did survive within her, it was neither flickering nor active but static and unmoving, frozen and fixed by her own powerlessness in the face of the Uncle's all-consuming, all-powerful oppression.

IMAGERY AND THEMES
The following are simply suggested relationships between images and themes in this poem; you may find others in your reading:

Aunt Jennifer:	Female
	An oppressed figure
	Unable to express herself openly
	Timid and lacking in confidence
The Tigers:	Free
	Powerful
	Confident figures
Uncle:	Male
	The oppressor
The Wedding Ring:	An instrument of oppression

The Uncle Speaks in the Drawing Room

Text of poem: New Explorations Anthology page 275

BACKGROUND NOTE

See Background Note on 'Aunt Jennifer's Tigers'.

TECHNICAL QUALITY

This poem exhibits the same skilful mastery of the technical features of poetry as is displayed in 'Aunt Jennifer's Tigers'. It is made up of four stanzas, each consisting of six lines. The rhyme scheme of *abbacc* provides an ordered substructure to the poem, while not interrupting the natural arrangement or the sense of the everyday language. Therefore, the piece reads naturally, as if we are simply engaged in a conversation. However, this simplicity and naturalness should not be mistaken for a lack of craft on Rich's part. A closer analysis indicates that she has combined everyday words into a series of stunningly dramatic images reinforced by appropriate musical phrases. So, in the first stanza, she brings the mob to life with their 'sullen stare', their 'bitter tones' and, most disturbingly of all, their 'stones'. Rich uses alliteration to strengthen the vividness of this image. Her use of 's' sounds and repetition in the phrases 'Standing sullen' and 'sullen stare' evoke the rebellious whispering and murmuring of the hostile crowd. Similarly, the assonance (where two or more words close together have the same vowel sound) and rhyme in lines 17–18 'ruby/thunder' and 'bowl/roll' effectively convey the vibrations that threaten the grandfather's precious bowl.

A READING OF THE POEM

The title of this poem, ' The Uncle Speaks in the Drawing Room', establishes the tone of the piece. Rich's use of a nameless persona (an assumed character), known only by his title of Uncle, makes this male character seem distant and unapproachable, someone who is aware of his position and proud of his status. Similarly, the setting of the 'Drawing Room' gives the whole scene a formal, rather ceremonial quality, since this room was traditionally reserved for entertaining guests to the house. Consider how different our expectations would be if the title read 'Uncle John Speaks in the Kitchen'. This title is an excellent example of the way in which Rich uses apparently simple, everyday words to imply a multitude of suggestions to her readers. That is why, with Rich's poetry, we should read and reread in order to capture and appreciate the fullness of her work.

In the first stanza we hear the Uncle speaking about the 'mob'. He describes their simmering discontent in a calm, rather detached manner. It is clear that, as befits his venerable position as 'Uncle', he is determined to maintain a 'stiff upper lip', to provide a steadying influence over the rest of the family. He is a man who lives in a comfortable world where houses are arranged around squares and have the architectural luxuries of balconies and gates. He recognises that it is this world that the mob resents and, given the courage, would like to destroy. However, he remains steadfastly unperturbed, even in the face of their stones.

His dismissive attitude continues into the second stanza, where he describes the behaviour of the mob as 'follies that subside'. He deliberately reduces their concerns and actions down to nothing more than foolishness that will soon pass away. Up until this point, Rich has managed the tone of the Uncle's speech very skilfully, so that it is consistently controlled and steadily dignified. However, in line 8, the Uncle's confident assurance seems to slip a little. He begins to undercut his speech with phrases that suggest some doubt on his part, as with 'none the less'. His use of 'us' indicates that he still regards himself as a leading figure in a particular group, but there is a growing disquiet in the tone of his voice. He even uses the word 'fear' in line 11. But the 'fear' that he feels does not arise out of a concern for himself or the others who belong to his group; rather, he is fearful for the elegant objects that fill his prosperous world: the delicate, glass vases and chandeliers. The threat of the mob's stones to such breakable items cannot be ignored.

Hastily, the Uncle recovers himself in the first two lines of the third stanza. He seeks to reassure his listeners that nothing will be thrown, no violent acts will occur. However, once again, his underlying disquiet seeps through his words. Almost in spite of himself, he is drawn to remember an incident where the 'grandsire' of the group 'stood aghast'. Clearly, Rich's use of 'grandsire' is a deliberate one on her part, conveying a male person who is both respected and held in high esteem. The image of such a figure standing transfixed by dismay must be a disturbing one both for the Uncle and for those others who have descended from such a man. Once again, it is an object that has led to such a shocking reaction – a red glass bowl vibrating in a thunderstorm. This is a particularly effective image that conveys the depth of the Uncle's anxiety. The ruby-red colour of the bowl conjures up images of blood; while a thunderstorm is an unstoppable, uncontrollable force that sweeps away man's power in an instant. In spite of all his efforts, the Uncle's 'stiff upper lip' is quivering and he reveals his worst fears.

With the fourth stanza, the Uncle tries to recover his position. He gives up his attempts to dismiss the potential threat of the mob and, instead, seeks to urge his listeners to stand together in the face of the threat. Rather like a military leader in wartime, such as Sir Winston Churchill during World War II, the Uncle exhorts his group to remember the ties that bind them. He reminds them of the special 'treasures' that they have inherited from their shared past: a past when mobs did not gather and murmur threateningly against the order of society. These 'treasures' which surround them are not only the beautiful objects from a 'calmer age', but also their genetic inheritance from their ancestors who lived in the 'calmer age' that enables them to appreciate fully the beauty and worth of these objects. For they, along with the Uncle, are of a 'kind' that is better than the mob, because they value the elegance of objects such as the balconies and gates, glass bowls and chandeliers.

The final two lines of the poem vibrate with a confusion of emotions. We could interpret the Uncle's image of his 'kind' positioning themselves between the beautiful glass objects and the mob as a positive and inspirational one, revealing his supreme confidence that his 'kind' will survive. Indeed, his attitude has validity in that many feel that beautiful works of art should be above political upheaval and ought to be protected no matter who is in power. However, his confidence does seem to be rather brittle. In line 13, the Uncle had categorically stated that the mob would not throw 'missiles'. Tellingly, in the final line of the poem he describes the mob as 'missile-throwers'. Could these lines be simply the hysterical ravings of a man who knows that, in spite of all the bravado of his 'stiff upper lip', the end has come for his 'kind'?

IMAGERY AND THEMES
The following are simply suggested relationships between images and themes in this poem; you may find others in your reading:

The Uncle: Male
                  The oppressor
                  A member of the ruling section of society
                  At the top of the hierarchy
                  Has the power to express views/opinions
                  Desires to maintain the status quo

The Mob: The oppressed
                  At the bottom of the hierarchy
                  No power to express views/opinions
                  Violence the only means of expression
                  Figures of revolution
                  A threat to the established social order
                  Desires to change the status quo

Balcony	
Gate	Objects that represent the values of the dominant,
Crystal vase	oppressive section of society
Chandelier	
Ruby bowl	

Storm Warnings

Text of poem: New Exploratins Anthology page 278

[*Note: This poem is also prescribed for Ordinary Level exam in 2010*]

BACKGROUND NOTE

See Background Note on 'Aunt Jennifer's Tigers'.

TECHNICAL QUALITY

Initially this poem appears to be very similar to 'Aunt Jennifer's Tigers' and 'The Uncle Speaks in the Drawing Room'. It has the same regularity of appearance, with four stanzas, each made up of seven lines. However, on closer inspection we begin to notice an important structural difference: rhyme is not a feature of this poem. Whereas 'Aunt Jennifer's Tigers' and 'The Uncle Speaks in the Drawing Room' both had strong, regular rhyme schemes, this poem has not. Instead, Rich relies on metre and rhythm, along with assonance and alliteration, to give her writing a technical elegance and grace.

An excellent example of her technical mastery of these elements is line 6: 'And walk from window to closed window, watching'. To appreciate the metre of the line read the following highlighted letters slightly louder: 'And **walk** from **wind**ow **to** closed **wind**ow, **watch**ing'. There are five stressed syllables (the highlighted letters). This gives the line a rhythm that conjures up the sound of the wind buffeting against the windows. Her use of alliteration, with the repeated 'w', creates a similar effect of wind blowing in gusts: 'And **walk** from **window** to closed **window**, **watching**'. Rich employs assonance to further reinforce the impact of this line. She interweaves 'a', 'o' and 'i' sounds to convey the impression of the ever-changing cadence of the gusts: 'And walk from window to closed window, watching'.

You might like to compare and contrast Rich's approach to conveying the movement of the wind with that of John Montague in his poem 'Windharp', also in this anthology.

THE DRAMATIC LYRIC

This poem is written as a dramatic lyric. A lyric poem has a strong personal element in that it communicates the feelings or state of mind of an individual. The individual who is speaking can be either the poet, engaging in a direct communication with the reader, or an imaginary individual, a persona created by the poet who expresses certain thoughts or feelings. A lyric poem is not concerned with telling a story. However, some poets do create a context or setting for the individual, as Rich does in this poem, and this approach is known as a dramatic lyric.

A READING OF THE POEM

The first stanza of the poem creates an image that sweeps from an instrument that measures pressure, a barometer, held inside the windows and walls of the house, out into a sky filled with 'gray unrest' and 'walking winds' hauling at the trees. The effect of this image is to convey the smallness of the house that is protecting the barometer and the speaker, and the uncontrollable vastness of the sky and wind. The apparent tranquillity that is contained within the house, where the speaker is reading a book while sitting on 'a pillowed chair', seems to be very vulnerable and fragile. The walls and windows offer some protection against the violence of the wind. Unlike the trees, the speaker, her book and her chair are not being physically pulled about by the wind. Nevertheless, the wind does have an effect on them in that the speaker abandons the book and the chair and is drawn, it seems irresistibly, to look out at the turmoil.

The second stanza is an important one. Up until this point, it seems as if Rich is simply writing a description of an approaching storm. However, as we know from her other poems, Rich uses dramatic situations and concrete images to give expression to abstract and complex thoughts, feelings and beliefs. Thus, in the second stanza, the focus of the piece shifts away from the weather elements signalling change in the physical world, and on to the idea that emotions are also subject to such changes. Just as a calm, blue sky can become a turbulent grey, so a calm heart can become troubled. In both cases, we humans are largely unable to foretell exactly when this alteration will occur. In the first stanza, the barometer had indicated a fall in pressure 'all the afternoon', but it did not give a precise time for the storm's arrival. The air currents that carry the weather move invisibly, uncontrollably and unpredictably in the skies above us, swirling into calm areas. So it is with emotions. They too move invisibly, uncontrollably and unpredictably into hearts that were once quiet. Yet, there is a suggestion that the speaker's heart may not have been completely calm. Rich establishes a connection between the image of the 'silent core of waiting', in line 9, and the heart, in line 13. Is she suggesting that this heart too was a 'silent core of waiting'?

In the third stanza, Rich again returns to the image of the barometer used in the first stanza. She links it to the image of a clock. Both are man-made instruments that seek to give us some feeling of control in the world. A clock indicates how time is passing; a barometer indicates how the weather is altering.

But they can only indicate. Neither of them has any control over the elements that they are linked to: the clock cannot stop time passing; the barometer cannot stop the weather changing, nor stop the wind from shattering it into fragments. In the final image of the third stanza Rich creates an image of futility in the face of inevitability. The closing of window shutters, nothing more than strips of wood joined together, is essentially a pointless action when set against the uncontrollable, destructive power of the wind. Clearly, she is suggesting that it is the same with emotions. We may run around closing our emotional 'shutters', attempting to suppress emotional alterations, but we are simply wasting our time. The emotional change will occur inevitably.

The fourth and final stanza of the poem returns to where the poem began: inside the house with the wind raging outside. The speaker sets about shutting out the storm as it increases in its intensity. She pulls the curtains and lights a candle. Again we have frailty set against overwhelming power, futility set against inevitability. The curtains are nothing more than thin fabric; the candle, despite apparently being protected by glass, can be extinguished in an instant. These instruments of 'sole defense' are pathetic. Despite all the speaker's actions, the turbulent wind still manages to penetrate into the tranquillity of the house. It squeezes in through the gaps that exist in this seemingly solid structure: the 'keyhole' and 'the unsealed aperture'.

The final two lines of the poem are stunning. The simplicity of the words contains a wealth of expression that is breathtaking. The 'I' of the speaker becomes 'we', releasing the poem from the limitations of individual expression into the communication of a political position. Rich swings the impact of the poem away from the single 'heart' and onto the concepts of power and powerlessness. The speaker stands with others who have had to learn to suppress their desire for change, to reject their awareness that change is necessary. This suppression and rejection may well have come partly from their own fear as well as from external forces, but they indicate a powerlessness about the group. However, for all the power of the factors that force this group to put up a 'sole defense against the season', there is an ominous inevitability about the phrase 'troubled regions'. The calm that the learned defensive actions bring about is a limited one. The actions do not calm the 'troubled regions'; they simply temporarily resist the trouble. The clear implication is that just as the wind infiltrates its way into a house, just as emotional change creeps into the heart, so groups who behave in a 'learned' way finally, and inevitably, break free to gain the power to behave as they want to behave.

IMAGERY AND THEMES
The following are simply suggested relationships between images and themes in this poem; you may find others in your reading:

The Storm:	Change/alteration
	Emotional change
	Social change
The Wind:	The force of change
The House:	A construction that appears to contain calm tranquillity
	It appears to offer protection against the turbulence of change.
Weatherglasses Clocks Curtains	Objects within the house that appear to offer control and power, but in reality offer only an illusion of control and power.

Living in Sin

Text of poem: New Explorations Anthology page 282

BACKGROUND NOTE

During the 1950s Adrienne Rich began to change the way that she wrote poetry. She moved away from the more formal style evident in 'Aunt Jennifer's Tigers', 'The Uncle Speaks in the Drawing Room' and 'Storm Warnings'. Rich saw this progression as developing out of her growing understanding that her poetry and her life experiences were intimately bound together. She felt that the demands of formal poetry restricted her expression, noting in later years, 'Experience itself had become too much for that.' (Adrienne Rich: *An Interview with David Montenegro*).

Thus, she began to write poetry where she allowed her readers to witness the ways in which her imagination acted on her life experiences. Rich has characterised her early poems, as represented by 'Aunt Jennifer's Tigers', 'The Uncle Speaks in the Drawing Room' and 'Storm Warnings', as poems that were written with precision '*about* experiences' (Adrienne Rich, *Poetry and Experience: Statement at a Poetry Reading*); while her later poems, as represented by the remaining seven poems in this selection, were actual experiences, written in the present tense, where a process was happening.

STRUCTURE

It is immediately evident that the structure of this poem is radically different from Rich's earlier pieces. The ordered appearance created by regular stanzas has been abandoned in favour of 26 uninterrupted lines of varying lengths. Similarly, rhyme is no longer a feature of her writing. The punctuation is much looser, with sentences spilling over a number of lines and the use of dashes and dots. This approach gives the piece an unresolved, open quality and a sense of immediacy. Whereas her earlier poems sought to put some sort of form on experience, Rich is now comfortable simply allowing experience to stand on its own. It is important to note, however, that this does not imply less effort on Rich's part. In many ways the abandonment of the rules of formal poetic writing demands more effort from the writer, since the language used must be shaped, not according to a series of accepted rules, but by a sense of honesty and integrity.

A READING OF THE POEM

Rich again uses the device of situating her poem within a dramatic situation. We are introduced to 'She' in the opening line of the poem. 'She' is clearly a woman who has decided to rebel against the accepted norms of social behaviour in 1950s America, as is indicated by the title of the poem, 'Living in Sin'. This phrase was used to describe a couple cohabiting without being married. The couple live in a 'studio'. There are suggestions of an unconventional, artistic lifestyle about the word 'studio'. It is just the sort of place where two people would 'live in sin'. But the second line of the poem introduces a note of emotional conflict. There is the rather romantic reference to 'the furniture of love', but 'She' no longer sees the romance: her main concern is with the dust that covers 'the furniture of love'. Her emotional conflict continues into lines 3 and 4, where we learn that dust is not the only difficulty that 'She' faces: the taps in the 'studio' are noisy and the windows are dirty. 'She' feels guilty about her disenchantment. After all, the decision to 'live in sin' was a brave one at that time, and required great faith that the love that was shared would conquer all. In this way, her irritation at these less-than-perfect objects seems to her to be an act of disbelief in their love.

Lines 4–7 present the reader with a description of how 'She' imagined 'Living in Sin'. It is a vision of perfection, with perfect pears on a perfect plate, a perfect piano draped in an exotically perfect shawl, and a perfect cat chasing a perfectly 'amusing' mouse.

The contrast between this idealised perfection and the grubby reality of the 'studio' is evident in lines 8–14. It echoes to the heavy footsteps of the milkman in the early morning; it is chilly and it is untidy, with bits of cheese and empty bottles left lying around. Rich's use of the word 'sepulchral' conveys the gloominess that 'She' feels. As if all of this were not depressing enough, we encounter a beetle on one of the kitchen shelves, evidently only one of many that scuttle around the flat. The three dots convey a sense that 'She' is plunging downwards on a waterfall of depression.

However, line 15 interrupts these gloomy thoughts: 'he' is getting up. This is the 'he' with whom 'She' chose to 'live in sin'. Unfortunately, the reality of the situation that 'She' finds herself in is embodied in the description of 'her man'. He does not look at her and smile, nor enfold her in a loving embrace. On the contrary, he does not even seem to notice her. He yawns, fiddles about on the piano, scratches his chin and goes out to buy cigarettes. This is hardly the stuff of a great Romantic Love.

Unable to withstand the irritation of the untidiness of the flat, 'She' embarks on a frenzy of housework: making the bed and dusting. Unfortunately, the objects in the flat seem determined to thwart her efforts to impose something of the perfection that she imagined onto them. Annoyingly, she is so intent on her cleaning that she forgets to watch the coffee-pot and it boils over, causing more mess for her to clean up. Perfection seems to be slipping further and further away.

In line 23, the tone becomes slightly more hopeful, as we learn that during the day 'She' regains her love. Perhaps 'he' brought her back some flowers, or wrote a song for her on the piano, or held her close. Whatever happened, 'She' manages to escape from the harshness of the reality of their situation and to immerse herself once more in their love. But, sadly, this escape is only temporary. Her feelings of disenchantment never really go away. Although the darkness of the night hides the grubbiness of their flat, her sleep is disturbed by her awareness that the light of day will once more reveal it in all its depressing untidiness.

THE THEME
By simply referring to the couple as 'She' and 'he' Rich enables the theme of the poem to develop from a single situation into the expression of her political viewpoint. Thus, the theme of this poem addresses the fundamental differences that Rich sees as existing between men and women because of the radically different roles that they are allocated by the social structure of the traditional, patriarchal society. Love may draw them together, but these profound differences prevent them from communicating on a meaningful level and, consequently, prevent the couple from developing their love.

Coupled with this, Rich acknowledges that women are in many ways their own worst enemies when it comes to breaking free from the traditional roles allowed to them by a patriarchal society. Rich takes the view that women are programmed from birth to behave in certain ways that reinforce their own subservience and the dominance of males in society. So the 'he' in the poem is totally unmoved by the condition of the flat, because his traditional training does not involve anything to do with housekeeping. On the other hand, the 'She' cannot resist her learned responsibility for housekeeping and she succumbs to the urge to clean the flat. However, it is significant that these actions do not provide her with any lasting sense of fulfilment. Nor, indeed, does the love that drew her to the man. The final image of the poem conveys the recurring disquiet and disenchantment that she feels about her role.

Perhaps within the context of Rich's political viewpoint, the title of the poem

'Living in Sin' might be more concerned with the endless compromises and disappointments that she feels women are forced to endure in a male-dominated society, rather than the sexual connotation that this phrase normally suggests.

The Roofwalker
Text of poem: New Explorations Anthology page 286

BACKGROUND NOTE
See Background Note on ' Living in Sin'.

STYLE AND STRUCTURE
With 'The Roofwalker, Rich continues to push back the poetic, intellectual and emotional boundaries that she had struggled with for so long.

In poetic terms, 'The Roofwalker' is significant for two main reasons. Firstly, there is a further loosening of punctuation. In this respect, Rich was influenced by the work of Emily Dickinson. Here, she uses dashes in lines 16–21 and in line 32. Whereas full stops and commas give a sense of definite structure and composition, the use of dashes conveys the immediacy and openness of developing thoughts. Rich writes in a 'stream of consciousness'. This means that the poet tries to retain the immediacy and the energy of the way that personal thoughts and feelings blend and merge, rather like an intellectual 'lava lamp'. Rich's dedication of this poem to the poet Denise Levertov is significant, since Levertov focused on the development of such a style where the thinking process was reflected in line and image.

Secondly, Rich's use of the ' stream of consciousness' technique is connected to her belief that poetry should be a process, in that it empowers both the poet and the reader to engage in the act of becoming, to be changed. The dashes reinforce the sense of process that underlies the poem, since they appear to be more open, more transitional, than the closure and finality of full stops.

Despite this loosening of style, Rich maintains a strong sense of coherence in the poem. Much of this coherence stems from the comparison she establishes between herself and the builders. This metaphor acts most successfully as a structural support for the piece.

A READING OF THE POEM
Although this poem is significantly different from Rich's earlier poems, it does contain familiar features. It is a dramatic lyric, so we have the piece located in a dramatic context, with an individual figure expressing thoughts and feelings. In this respect Rich's poems often seem to be like condensed plays, or scenes extracted from a film.

Lines 1–12 are a masterpiece of descriptive writing. As readers, we see the gathering gloom of night with the last streaks of daylight silhouetting the figures of the builders and illuminating the roof. We hear the stillness now that their work is finished: the hammers lie still and the pulleys rest. Rich's comparison of the builders on the roof to sailors on board a ship effectively communicates her emotional response to these men. She is impressed by them, as they move about high above the ground with the same confident balance that experienced sailors have on board ship. She sees them as 'Giants' in that they seem to be greater, more heroic, than normal human men. A 'wave' hovers above their heads; they walk on a 'burning deck', but they do not panic. For these men, danger is to be embraced and conquered, rather than feared and avoided. And yet, the presence of the 'wave' and the 'burning deck' could be indicative of a threat to the builders and their world. They may not be aware of it – indeed, they may be 'indifferent' to it – but the threat is still there.

The space that is placed at this point, between the first and second section, is important, since it acts as a bridge drawing the reader across from one context to another. Lines 13–15 mark a movement away from the external setting of the poem to the internal world of thought and emotion. Rich establishes a connection between herself and the builders in that she, too, is exposing herself to danger. Like the builders, she is 'up there', but, unlike them, there is a feeling of isolation and vulnerability about Rich's position.

The second space, between the second and third sections, again acts as a bridge to the final section of the poem. We are drawn further into Rich's 'stream of consciousness' as she reflects on the reality of her position. Continuing to make references to the 'builder' metaphor, Rich sees her life as being one of great effort that has achieved very little. Having struggled to make a 'roof' she finds that she 'can't live under' it, unlike the builders who stride about confidently on top of it. The 'roof' is seen as an object that oppresses Rich, while, conversely, it supports the male builders in all their assured confidence. Furthermore, her hard work of calculating and adjusting to create a good, strong structure appears to have been fruitless. For the problem lies not with her effort, nor indeed with what she was attempting to construct, but with her lack of choice.

Rich regarded the ability to choose as being an essential aspect of living as a human being with power. To be denied choice is to have the rights of one's humanity denied. Therefore, the fact that 'A life' chose the speaker in this poem, rather than her choosing it, doomed her efforts to failure. Rather like an electrician being forced to fix a burst water-pipe, Rich recognises that she has skills, she has abilities, but she is being obliged to use them in a situation where they are not suitable. Unlike the builders on the roof, who are perfectly 'at home' in their situation, Rich feels exposed and terrified.

Her use of the 'naked man fleeing' image to express her feelings may seem rather surprising in view of the way that she portrays male figures in her earlier poems. Indeed, her use of this image is open to a variety of interpretations. At times in her writing, Rich employs a male character to mask her expression of her own confusion. Thus, the 'naked man fleeing' is a 'safe' way for her to write about her innermost thoughts and feelings, because they are linked to a male figure who is clearly very different from the female Adrienne Rich. At other times, the male figure is a way of representing her intellectual experimentation with alternative ways of being. So she presents us with the image of the 'naked man fleeing', who could be engaged in the alternative existence of sitting in a peaceful room reading. The implication is that it could be just so with Rich's own life, if things were very slightly different. Such a slight difference would mean that instead of experiencing deep unhappiness with her life, she could be happy with it.

Rich establishes a pointed connection between the words 'difference' (line 29) and 'indifference' (line 32). Difference is suggestive of the recognition of the need for, and the ability to initiate, change. Indifference suggests unwillingness and a lack of the ability to change. Rich is aware of the need for change in her life, the need for things to be different in the world. But, as yet, she is unable to initiate this change. She is powerless and panicking, trapped within a way of living that she has tried so hard to make successful. Rich may long for the calm quietness of being comfortable with her life, but the fact that she once again returns to the image of the 'naked man fleeing' in the final two lines of the poem is significant. Her final use of the 'naked man fleeing' image suggests that Rich knows, only too well, that such comfort will never be found in her present way of living.

IMAGERY AND THEMES
The following are simply suggested relationships between images and themes in this poem; you may find others in your reading:

The Builders:	Male
	Powerful
	Confident
	In control
The Roof:	An object that oppresses and represses Rich
	An object that supports and empowers the builders
The 'naked man fleeing':	Male
	Powerless
	Vulnerable
	Afraid
	Representing Adrienne Rich?

Our Whole Life

Text of poem: New Explorations Anthology page 289

Text of poem: New Explorations Anthology page 289

BACKGROUND NOTE

By the early 1970s Adrienne Rich was very much involved in civil rights movements. She felt increasingly drawn to groups who, because of the social structures at the time, were powerless to give expression to their beliefs and values. Such groups as non-white people, pacifists, homosexuals and women joined together in order to challenge the dominance of white, financially secure, heterosexual males.

As a result of her experiences with these groups, Rich developed the view that language and power are inextricably linked. She felt that as most human societies are traditionally male-dominated, with men holding power, then the words that are developed and accepted into everyday use by all those who live in those societies must also be male-dominated, in that they reflect male-centred values and beliefs. Rich saw this male-dominated language as a method of preventing other groups both from injecting their values and beliefs into the language of their society, and from having access to power. Therefore, she advocated that for disempowered groups to gain access to power, so that they could bring about a societal acknowledgment of their rights and needs, they had to develop an alternative language that was not male-dominated.

STRUCTURE AND STYLE

The appearance of this poem is very different from the ordered compactness of, for example, 'Aunt Jennifer's Tigers'. Instead there is an apparently loose grouping of phrases, sometimes with three or two or even just one line.

The absence of punctuation gives the passage a continuous, unbroken feeling that effectively creates the 'stream of consciousness' technique. This, along with her use of conversational language, gives the impression that we, as readers, are actually inside Rich's head, witnessing her thoughts connecting and interconnecting. However, this connecting and interconnecting does not take place in a haphazard or disordered manner. In spite of the rather loose appearance of the poem, Rich creates a strong sense of coherence by carefully placing words in a sequence of meaning, as with 'translations', 'fibs' and 'lies', and by using an intricate web of echoed images based on 'eating' and 'burning'.

A READING OF THE POEM

The main thrust of this poem is evident from the first four lines, where Rich connects three words that are of fundamental importance to her theme: 'translation', 'fibs' and 'lies'. There is a deliberate and significant progression in the meanings of these words. Translation means that a word in one language is interpreted into another language. A fib is a trivial or unimportant lie. Lies, however, are deliberately untrue statements. Thus we move from a straightforward act of changing one word into another language without any alteration in its 'truth' of meaning, through a slight adjustment to its 'truth' of meaning: until, finally, the word loses all of its 'truth' of meaning. Rich's imagery of the 'knot' of lies, self-destructing in its attempted 'eating' through its own tangle, indicates that when a word loses its truth, when it becomes a lie, it becomes fossilised, because it is no longer able to communicate meaningfully. Clearly, for Rich, the lifeblood of a word lies in its 'truth' and honesty of expression. Indeed, Rich's revulsion for words that are lies is effectively conveyed by the rather nightmarish image of something 'eating' itself.

The image of 'eating' is carried forward into line 5, where we have the word 'bitten'. Here Rich suggests a tremendous feeling of tense repression, where words are not spoken through an open mouth but come out through clenched teeth. Her use of the 'blowtorch' image introduces the concept of 'burning', suggesting that words may form inside the mind and the mouth, but somewhere between this and actually saying them aloud, some force burns off their original meaning and shapes them into completely different words with completely different meanings. Thus the words, like 'dead letters', never get to deliver their original meaning. Instead, they are burned and remoulded into words that are lies, words that express the values and beliefs of those who hold power: of the oppressors.

The group represented by Rich's use of the term 'Our' may struggle to resist such a force. But, irresistibly, they will find themselves lured by it: initially by the apparently innocent act of 'translation'; then by the seemingly harmless use of 'fibs', until they find that they are engaged in telling lies, using the 'oppressor's language'. In this way the group has no language of its own, and therefore it has no power.

In lines 10–15 Rich introduces an image that is both vivid and disturbing: that of 'the Algerian'. This unfortunate man is 'burning' with pain. Yet he is powerless to express his incredible suffering because he cannot use the language of the man in power, the doctor. The 'Algerian' can do no more than simply stand wordless, displaying his terrible wounds. In these five lines and with this final image, Rich draws together the sequence of meaning and webs of imagery that hold this poem together. Thus the progression from 'translation', to 'fib', to 'lies' that cause injury leads to 'a cloud of pain'; the 'eating' and biting become the guttural sounds emanating from the dried mouth of the 'Algerian' and the burning of paint mutates into the burning of a human body.

Most horrifying of all, Rich links the mutilated body of the 'Algerian' with those whom she writes for, the 'Our' in the opening line of the poem. Her message is clear: both she and this group have spent their collective life trying to communicate what they honestly thought and felt to their oppressors. Their lack of success has not only increased their powerlessness, but it has also caused them to suffer intensely. They stand alongside the 'Algerian', mute with pain.

IMAGERY AND THEMES
The following are simply suggested relationships between images and themes in this poem; you may find others in your reading:

Translation } Fibs } Lies }	A sequence representing the steady erosion of the 'true' meaning of a word so that it loses its 'honesty' of expression
The Algerian:	Male Trying to communicate but unable to be understood Powerless Suffering Representing a powerless social group
The Doctor:	Male Unable to understand Powerful – can heal and banish pain Representing a powerful social group

Trying to Talk with a Man
Text of poem: New Explorations Anthology page 292

BACKGROUND NOTE
Between 1939 and 1945, the United States of America spent some $2 billion on developing the atomic bomb, in a project known as 'The Manhattan Project'. This research was carried out in a laboratory specially constructed by the government in the geographically isolated Los Alamos, New Mexico. Scientists engaged in the project, along with their families, were obliged to move close to the laboratory and to live in temporary housing. Their work culminated with the explosion of an atomic bomb on the morning of 16 July, 1945.

STRUCTURE AND STYLE
Rich employs a rather loose clustering of lines, a conversational style of language and the lyric form to give this poem a wonderful sense of immediacy.
   Her arrangement of the lines of this poem into groups of varying lengths

might at first appear to be almost accidental. However, on closer reading it becomes evident that each group pivots around a central concept that contributes to developing the theme of the poem.

Similarly, her use of conversational language is deceptively natural. This natural quality is underpinned by Rich's masterful use of punctuation. It is significant that some groups of lines in the poem have little or no punctuation, while others are peppered with a variety of punctuation marks. In this way, Rich successfully captures the variety of pace that is evident in everyday speech, while at the same time skilfully using punctuation to control the speed at which theis poem is read, so that key words are emphasised as in the line 'they reflect lights that spell out: EXIT'.

Finally, this poem is written as a dramatic lyric. For a discussion of this literary technique, read the note on 'The Dramatic Lyric' attached to the analysis of 'Storm Warnings'.

A READING OF THE POEM

The opening two lines of this poem create a dramatic environment that immediately captures the reader's interest. Rich seems to be writing about scientists experimenting with bombs out in the desert. The references to the United States' development of the atomic bomb are evident.

Initially, the second group of lines, 3–7, seem to be no more than a description of the geography of the desert with 'an underground river' moving around 'deformed cliffs'. Rich suggests the free-flowing nature of the river by her omission of punctuation, resulting in this section being read without interruption. Significantly, Rich shifts the overall meaning slightly by introducing the concept of 'understanding' in line 5. This linking of the river with 'understanding' presents the reader with a challenge, since at this point in the poem the connection between the two is not clear.

Lines 8–14 do little to help the reader to resolve this challenge. Instead, we encounter a list of apparently unconnected items. However, on closer examination we see that this list is a collection of snapshots, images that express aspects of the type of society left behind by those who came to the desert. So, there are 'LP collections' alongside 'the language of love-letters'. The insertion of the 'suicide notes' in the middle of the list creates a jarring effect, rather like a wrong note in the middle of a phrase of music. It carries an unsettling implication: this society may not have been quite as pleasant as the other items on the list suggest.

The fourth section, lines 15–19, is also undercut with a sense of unease. The image of the 'ghost town' and the sound of the 'silence' give the desert an overwhelming feeling of desolation. There is no sign of growth or development here. The 'dull green succulents' appear as jagged forms that simply endure. The once busy town is empty and silent. In spite of the speaker's declaration that they intended to 'change the face' of the desert, it is evident that change will never come about in such a place as this.

Disturbing as the expansive silence of the desert is, Rich introduces an even more frightening type of silence in lines 20–25. The speaker reveals that the vast silence that filled lines 15–19 did not actually come from the desert, but from within the speaker and her companion. This silence exists between them. Try as the couple might to cover up this silence by talking, it remains ever-present: a continual reminder of how they are unable to communicate in any honest, true or meaningful sense.

It is at this point that the reader solves the challenge that Rich had presented with her use of 'understanding' in line 5 of the poem. The setting for this poem may appear to be two people, who have moved to the area to test bombs, out walking in the silent desert. However, it now becomes clear that the silent desert is simply an image, a metaphor, to express the terrible lack of communication that lies between the couple.

The implication of the poem's title becomes clear: the couple are a woman, – the speaker – and a man. At times, these two people may almost arrive at a point of understanding, just like the underground river forces its way around cliffs. At times, they have each given up aspects of their lives in an effort to be united as a couple. But in the present moment of the poem, this woman and man are caught in incomprehension: like the cactuses, they simply endure. There is nothing flourishing or developing between them. Their relationship is nothing more than a 'ghost' of what it might have been.

For this is the tragedy that Rich explores in the final two sections of this poem: the possibilities, the potential of their relationship that the woman and man are unable to seize. In lines 26–36 we learn how their inability to communicate denies them the joy of being a 'true' couple. There is no mutual support, no shared caring. Instead, they say words that speak of support and caring, but mean nothing. The speaker notes her companion's uneasiness. Like a caged animal he paces about restlessly and his eyes are haunted by the desire for escape, to find the 'EXIT'. He is simply unable, or even perhaps unwilling, to respond to her.

In the final three lines of the poem, Rich draws the piece together. As she had opened it with the concept of testing, she now returns to this concept again. In line 1, the speaker had referred to 'testing bombs'. In line 39, the testing is now of 'ourselves'. The speaker watches and listens helplessly as the man talks of the 'danger' in a frantic attempt to avoid confronting it. In the face of his avoidance, her use of 'we' in the final line has a hollow ring to it. For this couple 'we' is a lost possibility. They are each doomed by their inability to communicate with the other on any meaningful level. In a brilliantly damning phrase, we learn that the woman feels 'more helpless' when she is with her male partner than when she is apart from him. Equally, he regards her with panic as a bringer of danger. Try as she might to 'Talk with a Man' the speaker is, most definitely, not with the man, and nor is he with her.

THE THEME
Rich deliberately avoids personalising the characters in this poem. We learn very little about them other than that one is female and the other male. In this way, the two become representatives for all women and all men. In a similar way, her list of aspects of the world that they had left behind stands for society as a whole rather than one local society.

Thus, she uses the confrontation between the two to represent the political confrontation that she sees as existing between all women and all men. As her woman speaker seeks to talk on a meaningful level to the man, so Rich regards this as reflecting the efforts of feminists to engage with men, the holders of power in society. Equally, the man's reluctance, and indeed panic, when faced with what he sees as the 'danger' inherent in the woman's attempts to talk with him meaningfully, represents the reluctance of men in power to consider an alternative social structure to the traditional patriarchal hierarchy.

Diving into the Wreck
Text of poem: New Explorations Anthology page 296

BACKGROUND NOTE
See Background Note on 'Living in Sin'.

STRUCTURE AND STYLE
This poem is surprising because of its length, and there is no doubt that, initially, the 94 lines can be quite off-putting for the reader. However, Rich's mastery of the technical aspects of writing poetry enable her to provide a strong sense of sequence and coherence that serve to maintain the focus of the piece throughout the 94 lines.

The sense of sequence partially arises out of her moving the action of the poem in a logical and natural manner from the solid deck of the schooner, above water, down to the fantastical depths of the wreck under water. Thus, the narrative element in the poem, the story that it tells of diving into the sea, adds to the establishment of a sense of sequence.

Rich's careful arrangement of the different sections of the poem also contributes to the sense of sequence. The first five sections begin with a capital letter and end with a full stop. This reflects the way in which each of these sections deals with a specific action and experience. Although Rich loosens this capital letter – full stop arrangement in the sixth to the tenth sections, where it is extended over two and three sections, the sense of sequence is successfully maintained.

The coherence is established by Rich's linking and repetition of images and words. For example, the first section of the poem describes the preparations that the diver makes. Once again, there is a logical link between the items that she puts on (the wet-suit, the flippers, the face-mask) that gives this section a coherence, a sense of unity. Similarly, her repetition of the words 'came' and 'wreck', in the opening lines of the sixth and seventh stanzas, forms a clear connection between the two, as does her use of the image of the wreck as a body with the linked parts of a 'flank', a 'face' and 'ribs'.

It is this careful attention to such technical details on Rich's part that enables her to maintain the focus of this extended piece. She never allows her reader to forget that we are indeed 'Diving into the Wreck'. However, this poem is more than simply the story of a dive under the sea. It is far more complex, in that the story of the dive tries to represent, or illustrate in a concrete way, the process of Rich's search for alternatives to the hierarchical society that will enable her to more fully understand the true nature of its traditionally accepted social and political rules.

A READING OF THE POEM

In an effort to unravel the complexity of this poem we will look first at the narrative, concrete aspect of each section in the poem. In each case, that will be followed by a consideration, in italics, of what political messages are represented by the narrative.

Adrienne Rich has frequently observed that her later poems are concerned with 'process' and 'Diving into the Wreck' is a wonderful illustration of this, since it focuses on the process of an exploratory dive into the sea. The connection that Rich establishes in the first line between this dive and myth is a significant one, in that it alerts her readers to the fact that this poem is more than simply a narrative telling a story of a diver diving down to a wreck.

In section 1, lines 1–12, Rich outlines the preparations that the diver has made for the dive. She has done her reading; put film into her camera; made sure that her knife is sharp. All these preparations have taken her some time. She then 'dresses' herself for her journey into an alien environment. With all the deliberate care of a warrior preparing to go into battle, the diver puts on her wet-suit, flippers and mask. Again, this all takes time. As readers, we can't help but wonder what it is that drives the diver to go through all this. We then learn that she must undertake this exploratory dive alone. One of the main rules in sub-aqua diving is that, for safety reasons, divers should never dive alone. The fact that the diver is unable to adhere to this rule introduces an unmistakeable feeling of danger into this section. If we look again at all the diver's preparations we see that there are hints of danger there, too. Worryingly, we learn that the book that the diver read is a 'book of myths' and myths have a large element of fiction about them. Surely the diver should be reading books filled with facts. The images of the knife and the 'body-armour' also suggest that there is some threat to her safety.

Section 1 can be interpreted as illustrating the way in which Rich felt compelled to undertake the task of exploring alternatives to our traditional social structures, in order to see more clearly the true nature of our society. Careful preparations were necessary before this task because it was potentially dangerous, not so much physically but psychologically and emotionally, since it would lead to the destruction of what had long been accepted as the 'right' way for human beings to live as a group. Bravely, Rich undertakes this task alone. This section conveys her determination even in the face of the loneliness of her role.

The second section, lines 13–21, begins innocently enough with the image of a ladder. This ladder seems to be something that will help the diver to enter the water as safely as possible, and in this way it appears as a positive object. However, Rich makes the point that the ladder is useful only if the user knows how it should be used: without that knowledge, the ladder becomes no more than a gathering of rope and wood. Rather like ' the book of myths' in the first section, the ladder offers a form of help to the diver that is not entirely reliable or trustworthy.

Section 2 introduces the 'ladder' in order to represent Rich's awareness that there are ways to investigate alternative social and political structures to the one that we use. There is a sense of confidence and assurance arising out of the knowledge acquired by those who have set about such an investigation.

The third section, lines 22–33, is an excellent example of the technical mastery in Rich's writing. Her repetition of the short phrase 'I go down' conveys not only the depth, but also the distance of the diver's journey down the ladder. Her progress is slow and difficult: her fingers become disabled and she is reduced to crawling. These vivid images capture the tremendous effort that the diver has to make, and the suffering that she has to endure, in order to go into this other environment. Once again, the loneliness of her exploration is emphasised in lines 31–33. The diver forces herself onwards, not knowing when she will break through from her familiar environment into the new one. It is a dangerous situation for her as she is clearly tiring, and yet she is unwilling to give up.

Section 3 illustrates the tremendous effort required to explore these social and political alternatives to the traditional, hierarchical society. The 'ladder' that had appeared to offer help is not really of any help at all: this process of exploration is still hard and difficult. Again, Rich feels that she is undertaking this task on her own. This section expresses feelings of exhaustion, frustration and loneliness, balanced by the determination and courage to continue with the task.

At first the opening lines of the fourth section, lines 34–43, seem to suggest that the danger has vanished, as the diver finally enters the water. She is enveloped by a wonderful mixture of blue and green far more vivid than the air that she has left behind. But suddenly, the feeling of danger returns when the diver begins to black out. Her body is finding it hard to cope with this watery environment. Still, rather than giving up, the diver reassures herself about the safety of her equipment and decides that she will learn how to deal with this new world.

Section 4 depicts the way in which Rich initially feels overwhelmed by her engagement with social and political alternatives to her society. Her feeling of panic and her near-blacking out represent the challenge that she faces when she decides to abandon the traditionally accepted social and political rules of living. Nevertheless, this section once again ends on a note of determination: she will learn to cope.

In fact, her efforts to learn how to cope are so successful that in the fifth section, lines 44–51, she admits that she has almost forgotten the reason why she is diving. She is filled with such wonder by the beauty around her that her determination to engage in a process of exploration weakens.

Section 5 once again portrays the difficulties Rich faces in her task. She is so fascinated by these alternative ways of living, and those who actually live according to them, that she begins to lose her determination to explore the true nature of our traditional society.

In the sixth section, lines 52–70, the diver forces herself to put into words the purpose that drives her: 'I came to explore the wreck.' This sentence is more than a simple collection of words: it expresses both the reason for her process of exploration and the aim that she hopes to achieve. In this way, the six words 'I came to explore the wreck' are indeed 'purposes' and 'maps' that both drive and direct her. The diver tells us that she wants to see the truth of the wreck, both bad and good, the 'damage' that it has suffered, and 'the treasures'. She is no longer satisfied by 'the book of myths'; she wants to see the 'real' thing. Rich very carefully employs a series of images to suggest the ambivalent feelings that the diver has towards the wreck. On the one hand, she feels respect for it and is careful to 'stroke' it with her torchlight. Similarly, she feels sympathy for it trapped beneath the water, separated from the warmth of the sunlight. She regards it as having a 'threadbare beauty'. On the other hand, she recognises that the wreck was a 'disaster'.

Section 6 introduces the problematic image of the wreck, which has been interpreted in a number of ways. However, if we set it within the context of our overall interpretation of the political messages that lie behind this poem then the wreck, logically, stands for our traditional form of society. Although Rich feels

some affection for this traditional society, since she is familiar with it, her
determination to confront the true nature of this society returns.

The final section of the poem, lines 71–94, begins on a note of triumph: 'This is the place'. The diver has achieved her goal of exploring the wreck. She has survived the dangers that faced her and she has done so alone. It is at this point that Rich introduces the rather perplexing image of the androgynous, male/female figure. This image seems to suggest that, because of her success, the diver is transformed into an alternative way of existing, one that is not restricted by narrow definitions, one that banishes her sense of being alone. She is no longer 'I' or 'she' or 'he', but 'we'. In this androgynous body the diver is empowered to explore and analyse the true nature of the wreck, in order to work past the glittering surface and confront the 'rot' that lies underneath. Suddenly, the realisation is grasped: the diver, and all of those others who are like her, are connected to the wreck because it has played a part in their formation, and they have played a part in its 'course'. Although they may reject and abandon the wreck, they will return to it frequently, carrying the same objects that featured in the first section of the poem: a knife, a camera and a book of myths. Thus the poem does not really end by offering a definite alternative to the traditional social structure. Instead it emphasises the importance of the process of exploration of those alternatives, in order to understand fully the true nature of our existing society.

Section 7 brings together the representations that we have encountered earlier in the poem. The arrival at the wreck and the exploration of it suggest the success of feminists and other civil rights movements in highlighting the terrible inadequacies and the unjust distribution of power that lie at the base of the traditional, male-dominated, patriarchal society. This section also expresses one of the major difficulties facing all those who reject the traditional society. Try as they might, they will never fully erase the influence of that traditional society. Rich proposes that there are two ways to view this indestructible link to a despised society: it could be born out of 'cowardice', a reluctance to totally sever all connections; or, alternatively, it might indicate 'courage', a willingness to confront the past.

The androgynous figure is the direct opposite to the lonely diver in the earlier six sections: 'I' has become 'we'; restrictive definitions such as 'she' and 'he' do not apply to it. The underlying sense of danger and the need to learn how to cope with this alternative environment have been transformed into feelings of empowerment and understanding.

THE THEMES
The themes addressed in this poem are open to a variety of interpretations.
The following is one of the more widely accepted interpretations. However, you

may wish to consider alternatives:

- The diver is determined to dive into an alternative environment, indicating that Rich considers the exploration of alternative social structures as being politically vital.

- The dive itself is a dangerous undertaking, suggesting that this social exploration is also difficult and dangerous, because it threatens the stability of the existing, traditional social structure.

- The diver manages to conquer fear and becomes transformed into a different form of being, an androgynous figure. This implies that Rich believes that if this social exploration is undertaken with courage and determination, then it will open up new ways of living where there is greater freedom and power for all.

- The wreck has a superficial beauty but underneath, in the ship's hold, there is decay. Rich uses this image to convey her political stance regarding the society that she lives in: on the surface it appears to be good and fair but, in reality, this traditional social structure keeps power in the hands of a few and denies power to groups who disagree with aspects of the society.

- The poem ends with an image of the wreck being revisited time and time again by those whose 'names do not appear' in the 'book of myths'. This illustrates Rich's awareness that, although she and others like her may seek to abandon this traditional social structure and to create an alternative one, they will never be able to escape completely from its influences. Nevertheless, it is politically vital that the exploration of alternative social structures continues.

- Rich does not offer any concrete alternative to the wreck, implying that once again it is the exploration process that is of political importance. She believes that we should not be diverted from this simply because we are uncertain about the exact form of these alternatives to the existing, traditional social structures, since such an exploration will lead to a better understanding of our existing society.

From a Survivor

Text of poem: New Explorations Anthology page 301

BACKGROUND NOTE

In 1953, Adrienne Rich married Alfred H. Conrad, a Jewish economist who was teaching at Harvard. The couple went on to have three sons. Along with Adrienne, Alfred became actively involved in many of the civil rights movements that emerged in America in the 1960s. After seventeen years of marriage, Rich separated from her husband. Soon after, Alfred committed suicide. This poem is a reflection on their marriage and Rich's feelings for her late husband.

The poignancy of this poem lies in Rich's use of straightforward, everyday, conversational language to express her reaction to her husband's suicide. She makes no attempt to soften the emotional impact by the use of such technical devices as clever rhymes, beautiful imagery or musical language. Instead, she simply uses ' the 'stream of consciousness' technique, allowing her thoughts to develop and connect on the page. (For an explanation of 'the 'stream of consciousness' technique, see the notes 'Style and structure' for 'The Roofwalker'.)

The appearance of the poem, with one, two, three and more lines interrupted by spaces, reinforces the sense that we are reading her thoughts and experiencing her feelings as they are actually occurring. However, this approach to structure does not represent a lack of effort on Rich's part. Her careful use of highly significant words to communicate a wealth of implications and suggestions indicates that a considerable amount of time and thought went into this piece.

A READING OF THE POEM
Rich opens the poem with a reference to their marriage, calling it an 'ordinary pact'. Her use of the word 'pact' is significant since it suggests that, in Rich's view, the ceremony of marriage is like a treaty between two opposing forces. The two opposing forces are, of course, a man and a woman.

In an incredibly immediate and natural style of writing in lines 3–5, she expresses her amazement at the fact that when they married, both she and Alfred actually believed that they could make a success of it. However, Rich does not suggest that any lack, or fault, on their parts caused the failure of their marriage. Instead, she states that the marriage was doomed because of 'the failures of the race'. In other words, their marriage failed because of the society in which they lived. As we have seen previously, Rich came to see the traditional, male-dominated, patriarchal society as an oppressive one that sought to eliminate and reject any person or group who did not believe in the values of that society.

In lines 6–9, we learn that both she and Alfred simply did not know that their marriage would be destroyed by the social structure within which they lived. Her comment that this ignorance on their part could be seen as either 'Lucky or unlucky' indicates the ambivalence of her feelings about her marriage. It could have been 'lucky' in the sense that if they had known that their marriage would be destroyed by their society, then they would never have married. Clearly, Rich feels that there was something of value in the time that they spent together. On the other hand, their lack of knowledge could be seen as being 'unlucky', because when their marriage ended they had the dreadful emotional upset and heartbreak that occurs with the failure of a relationship.

With the benefit of hindsight, Rich looks back at her young self and the young Alfred and is amazed at their innocent and naïve belief that they were 'special', that they were different from all the other men and women who also tried to make a 'pact' and were equally unsuccessful.

Line 10 marks a change in the tone of the writing. Up until this point, the tone has been one of slightly puzzled amazement that she and Alfred could have actually believed that a marriage between a man and woman might be successful. With line 10 the tone becomes much more intense. The shorter lines indicate the strength of Rich's feelings. She remembers her husband's body and the way that her feelings towards both him and his physical presence changed over the years. Initially, she accepted the traditional male/female roles dictated by the patriarchal society. Thus Alfred was the dominant figure, 'a god' who had 'power' over Rich's life. But as time passed she began to see that both the body and the man were, in fact, limited and vulnerable. Indeed, it is fair to say that we all have the tendency to idealise our partner in the first exciting days of a new love affair. It is only as the excitement and novelty wears off that we begin to see that this person is just as human as we are.

Rich uses simple words and phrases, in lines 17–20, to give a vivid and moving description of her relationship with Alfred. Their lives had been connected for almost twenty years. The fact that Rich remembers the exact number of years indicates the level of importance that she attaches to their time together. We can almost hear the sob in her voice when she talks of Alfred being 'wastefully dead'. Once again her use of one word, 'wastefully', proves to be deeply significant. It is evident that Rich valued her late husband's existence. His death represents the 'waste' of the contribution that she clearly believes he would have made to the development of a new and better way for all men and all women to live together. The closeness of their relationship is revealed in her reference to the conversations that they had about making a 'leap' into this other way of living.

The final four lines introduce a more positive tone into the poem. Rich still feels a sense of loss because Alfred is dead, but she can acknowledge the fact that she, herself, has succeeded in embarking on the process of finding a new way of living. This process is much slower and happens in 'brief, amazing moments' rather than in the dramatic and sudden 'leap' that she and Alfred had spoken about. Nevertheless, the process is still immensely valuable and worthwhile because it is ongoing. It is these lines that reveal the reason why Rich entitled this poem 'From a Survivor' – for she is the survivor. Unlike Alfred and unlike their marriage, both regarded by Rich as casualties of the repressive and destructive forces of the traditional, patriarchal society, Rich has managed to survive. Even more importantly, her survival is not based on her resigned acceptance of that traditional, patriarchal society. Instead, her survival is driven by the determination to explore alternative social structures that will fill the lives of both women and men with 'amazing moments' that promise the freedom of endless possibilities.

PUNCTUATION AND MEANING

Rich's use of punctuation plays a very important part in the successful communication of meaning in this poem. It is noticeable that she uses very little punctuation in the piece, in order to reflect her use of 'the stream of consciousness' technique. Here Rich's thoughts and feelings, largely uninterrupted by punctuation, have such immediacy and honesty that her words are filled with a great depth and intensity of meaning. As readers, we know that she is speaking to us from the heart.

It is highly significant that this poem, ending as it does with a celebration of the joy and freedom that comes from living a life filled with 'amazing moments' of possibilities, does not have a full stop after the final word. In this way, Rich reinforces the sense of endless possibilities that lead on in a never-ending and empowering process.

Power

Text of poem: New Explorations Anthology page 305

BACKGROUND NOTE

Adrienne Rich frequently writes about individual successful women from history, such as the poet Emily Dickinson. However, although these women did achieve success, it was often accompanied by a lonely lifestyle. This poem deals with one such woman: Marie Curie.

Marie Curie (1867–1934), along with her husband Pierre, worked on isolating radioactive elements from a type of uranium ore known as pitchblende. At the time, it was most unusual for a woman to be a scientist and to engage in scientific research. The Curies isolated two radioactive elements from the pitchblende: polonium and radium. The couple were awarded the Nobel Prize for Physics in 1903. Later, in 1911, Marie was awarded the Nobel Prize for Chemistry, making her the first person ever to win two Nobel Prizes. Unfortunately, owing to her constant exposure to high levels of radiation, Marie developed leukaemia and died in 1934.

The structure of this poem makes it a rather challenging one to get to grips with on a first reading. Rich again uses the 'stream of consciousness' technique. Therefore, we see a varied arrangement of the lines of poetry, ranging from a single line to clusters of lines and images that do not immediately appear to be connected.

However, there is a further structural development evident in this poem. Rich not only surrounds her lines with space, but she also inserts space into the very lines of poetry themselves. In this way, she deconstructs the traditional compact poetic line as used in 'Aunt Jennifer's Tigers', for example, and turns it into a loosely connected grouping of phrases. This, allied with her minimal use of punctuation, can make it difficult to understand, on a first reading, what Rich is expressing.

A READING OF THE POEM

Rich's reference to history in the first line suggests that the present and the past are very closely linked. It seems as if there is only a thin skin of soil that separates them from each other. Rich sees the soil as a kind of storage space for our past history. This image calls up pictures of archaeologists digging down and finding artefacts that have survived from previous ages. It is interesting to note that Rich has conveyed all of this meaning in just eight words.

The next image, of the digger digging up an old bottle, follows on from the first line in that the bottle is an example of one such item that has been stored in the soil. However, it is not an archaeologist who finds it but a large mechanical digger. Rich's use of the word 'flank' to describe the bank of earth where the discovery takes place connects back to the first word of the poem, 'Living'. She sees the mound of soil as a living thing, like a huge figure lying on its side. The present and past meet, as the modern mechanical digger lifts the old medicine bottle out of the earth. In doing so, the digger has punctured the thin skin that separates the present from the past. The bottle is still intact, even after one hundred years, and contains a liquid that promises to cure everything from a high temperature to depression. It is clearly not possible to develop a medicine that could do all those things: therefore the bottle obviously came from one of the many 'quack doctors', unqualified medical practitioners or con-men, who used to travel around America in the nineteenth and early twentieth centuries selling fake medicines.

There is a sudden shift of focus in the next section of the poem, lines 6–17, where Rich explains that she has been reading about Marie Curie. Along with her husband, Curie worked extensively with radioactive substances. As a result of her exposure to these radioactive elements she began to suffer physically. Rich refers to Curie's 'radiation sickness' causing her eyes to be blinded by cataracts and the skin on her hands to crack and ooze pus.

However, the main focus of Rich's attention does not fall on Curie's wonderful discoveries that earned her two Nobel Prizes, nor on the fact that Marie Curie was one of the few female scientists in the late nineteenth and early twentieth centuries and, as such, was treated with suspicion by the predominantly male world of science. Rich is much more concerned with Curie's reaction to her 'radiation sickness': her denial that it was the radioactive substances that had made her sick. Rich is amazed by Curie's refusal to acknowledge the truth and is certain that Curie 'must have known' that it was 'radiation sickness'.

The final four lines of the poem, lines 14–17, can be interpreted in a number of ways. This ambiguity arises out of Rich's use of spaces between the words and her lack of punctuation.

One interpretation sees these lines as a reference to Marie Curie's steadfast denial, right up to her death from leukaemia, that the radioactive substances that had made her famous had also doomed her to death. In this way, she refused to accept that her physical injuries were caused by 'the same source as her power': that is, by her position of fame in society.

An alternative interpretation sees these lines as being related to Rich's belief that women have long been prevented from gaining any meaningful power by the traditional, patriarchal society that has been dominant for much of history. The image of the bottle containing the fake medicine that helps with 'living on this earth' refers to the way that this traditional social structure has fooled women into thinking that they do have some power. Thus, the final four lines can be seen as expressing Rich's view that Curie, as a woman, was unable to cope with the power that she gained because she came from a gender unused to dealing with 'real' power and, as a result, she was destroyed by it.

A third interpretation suggests that the emphasis should be placed on the act of denial. For women to gain 'real' power, they have to deny the identity that has been forced on them by the traditional, patriarchal society. In other words, they have to stop behaving according to the male view of how a woman should behave, and they have to stop using words about themselves that have been formed by men. In Rich's opinion, this behaviour and language have done nothing for women but cause them to feel wounded and damaged because they have been imposed on them by a completely different gender. So women have to sacrifice this identity, this selfhood, and struggle to find their own behaviour and words. In this context, Curie's denial that her 'wounds' were caused by 'the same source as her power' means that Curie refused to accept that she, as a woman, had been deeply injured, and ultimately would be destroyed, by the same male-dominated world that had also made her famous by giving her awards.

The final interpretation to be considered here rests on Rich's ongoing analysis of the differences between men and women. In 'Power' the female figure on the one hand, Marie Curie, gains power through hard work and the sacrifice of her health. On the other hand the male figure, represented by the bottle containing the fake medicine developed by 'quack doctors', tries to gain power through deception and trickery.

In the final analysis, it is up to you, as the reader, to choose whether you agree or disagree with these interpretations. Indeed, you may choose to develop an interpretation of your own for this poem. Adrienne Rich sees the power of choice as a fundamental element in becoming an empowered human being. The power of choice is also part of the pleasure that comes from being a reader of poetry.

An overview of selected themes and aspects of Adrienne Rich's poetry

RICH'S PORTRAYAL OF THE FEMALE ROLE IN SOCIETY
   Aunt Jennifer's Tigers
   Living in Sin
   The Roofwalker
   Our Whole Life
   Trying to Talk with a Man
   Diving into the Wreck
   From a Survivor
   Power

RICH'S PORTRAYAL OF THE MALE ROLE IN SOCIETY
   Aunt Jennifer's Tigers
   The Uncle Speaks in the Drawing Room
   Living in Sin
   The Roofwalker
   Our Whole Life
   Trying to Talk with a Man
   From a Survivor

RICH'S PORTRAYAL OF THE RELATIONSHIP BETWEEN MEN AND WOMEN
   Aunt Jennifer's Tigers
   Living in Sin
   Our Whole Life
   Trying to Talk with a Man
   Diving into the Wreck
   From a Survivor

POWER AND LANGUAGE
   The Uncle Speaks in the Drawing Room
   Our Whole Life
   Trying to Talk with a Man

POWER AND WOMEN
   Aunt Jennifer's Tigers
   Living in Sin
   Our Whole Life
   Trying to Talk with a Man
   Diving into the Wreck
   From a Survivor
   Power

IMPENDING REVOLUTION AND CHANGE
   Aunt Jennifer's Tigers
   The Uncle Speaks in the Drawing Room
   Storm Warnings
   Diving into the Wreck
   From a Survivor

RICH'S USE OF THE DRAMATIC LYRIC FORM
   Storm Warnings
   The Roofwalker
   Trying to Talk with a Man
   Diving into the Wreck
   From a Survivor
   Power

RICH'S USE OF THE 'STREAM OF CONSCIOUSNESS' TECHNIQUE
   The Roofwalker
   Our Whole Life
   Trying to Talk with a Man
   Diving into the Wreck
   From a Survivor
   Power

RICH'S EARLY 'MALE-INFLUENCED' POEMS 'ABOUT EXPERIENCES'
   Aunt Jennifer's Tigers
   The Uncle Speaks in the Drawing Room
   Storm Warnings

Questions

1. Read 'Aunt Jennifer's Tigers' and answer the following questions:
   1. (a) What picture do you get of Aunt Jennifer from the poem?
      (b) 'Aunt Jennifer's tigers prance across a screen'.
         Describe in your own words how you imagine the screen that Aunt Jennifer embroidered.
      (c) Based on your reading of the poem, what impression do you get of the nature of Aunt Jennifer's relationship with Uncle?
   2. Answer **ONE** of the following:
      (a) Why do you think Aunt Jennifer embroidered the screen?
         Refer to the poem in your answer.

         OR

      (b) Imagine that you have been asked to make a short film of this poem. Outline the overall atmosphere that you would like to achieve and the images, sound effects and music that you would use to create this atmosphere.

         OR

      (c) 'The tigers in the panel that she made
         Will go on prancing, proud and unafraid.'

         What do you understand these last two lines of the poem to mean?

2. Read 'Storm Warnings' and answer the following questions:
   1. (a) How, in the first stanza of the poem, does Rich help us to imagine the stormy weather? Refer to the poem in your answer.

      (b) How does the person in the poem react to the oncoming storm?

      (c) '... Weather abroad
         And weather in the heart alike come on
         Regardless of prediction.'
         What is Rich saying about emotions in these lines?

2. Answer **ONE** of the following:
    (a) What does this poem tell you about Rich's state of mind?
        Refer to the poem in your answer.
    OR
    (b) 'I draw the curtains as the sky goes black.'
        Do you think that the person in the poem will be successful in her
        attempts to keep the storm out of the house? Give reasons for your
        answer.
    OR
    (c) Can you suggest another title for this poem? Support your
        suggestion by reference to the poem.

3. Read 'Power' and answer the following questions:
    1. Which **ONE** of the following phrases do you feel best suggests Rich's
        reaction to the digging up of the old bottle:?
        −   She is not interested in it
        −   She is fascinated by it
        −   She is frightened by it.

Support your choice by reference to the poem.

2. What impression do you get of Marie Curie's life from your reading of
    the poem?
3. Answer **ONE** of the following:
    (a) What does this poem tell you about Rich's attitude to Marie Curie?
        Refer to the poem in your answer.
    OR
    (b) 'her wounds came from the same source as her power'
        What do you understand this last line of the poem to mean?
    OR
    (c) Write a paragraph in which you outline the similarities **and/or**
        differences between 'Power' and 'Aunt Jennifer's Tigers'.

4. With reference to **at least six** poems by Adrienne Rich that you have studied:
    (a) Outline her portrayal of the position in society held by **either** women **or**
        men.
    (b) Do you agree or disagree with this portrayal?

5. 'Power is a central concept in the poetry of Adrienne Rich.' Respond to this
    statement, referring to the poetry by Rich on your course.

6. 'Adrienne Rich's poetry consistently reveals her mastery of the technical

aspects of writing poetry.' Discuss this statement, with reference to **at least six** poems by Rich.

7. 'Rich's view of the world is firmly based in 1960s America, and has little to say to present-day Irish readers.' Write an essay in response to this statement, quoting from or referring to the poems on your course.

8. 'An Introduction to Adrienne Rich.'
    Write out the text of a public talk that you might give on the poetry of Adrienne Rich. Your talk should make reference to the poetry on your course.

9. *Dear Adrienne Rich . . .*
    Write a letter to Adrienne Rich, telling her how you responded to some of her poems on your course. Support the points you make by detailed reference to the poems you choose to write about.

10. 'Why read the poetry of Adrienne Rich?'
    Write out the text of an article that you would submit to a journal in response to the above title. Support your response by quoting from, or referring to, the poetry on your course.

Bibliography

Cooper, Jane Roberta (editor), *Reading Adrienne Rich: Reviews and Revisions, 1951–81,* Michigan: The University of Michigan Press 1984.

DeShazer, Mary K., *Inspiring Women: Reimagining the Muse,* New York: Pergamon Press 1986.

Dickie, Margaret, *Stein, Bishop and Rich: Lyrics of Love, War and Place,* North Carolina: The University of North Carolina Press 1987.

Erkkila, Betsy, *The Wicked Sisters: Women Poets, Literary History and Discord,* Oxford: Oxford University Press 1992.

Gamble, Sarah (editor), *Feminism and Postfeminism,* London: Routledge 2001.

Gelpi, Barbara Charlesworth and Gelpi, Albert (editors), *Adrienne Rich's Poetry and Prose,* New York: W. W. Norton 1993.

Keyes, Claire, *The Aesthetics of Power: The Poetry of Adrienne Rich,* Athens and London: The University of Georgia Press 1986.

Kolmar, Wendy K. and Frances Bartkowski, *Feminist Theory: A Reader,* Boston: McGraw Hill 2005.

Rich, Adrienne, *On Lies, Secrets and Silence: Selected Prose 1966–1978,* New York: W.W. Norton 1979.

Rich, Adrienne, *What is Found There: Notebooks on Poetry and Politics*, New York: W. W. Norton 1993.

Roberts, Neil (editor), *A Companion to Twentieth Century Poetry,* Oxford: Blackwell 2003.

Sunstein, Cass R. (editor), *Feminism and Political Theory,* Chicago: The University of Chicago Press 1990.

6 Derek WALCOTT

Carole Scully

Derek Walcott: the Island of Poetry

EARLY LIFE

Derek Alton Walcott was born in Victoria Hospital in Castries, the capital city of St Lucia, on 23 January 1930. He was followed a few minutes later by his twin brother Roderick. His parents, Warwick and Alix, soon brought their two new sons back home to meet their older sister Pamela (born 1928) and the servants who looked after the family. Home was a two-storey wooden house with gothic gables and a porch draped with vines, situated in a middle-class area on the eastern side of Castries. Warwick, a civil servant, worked in the Registry Department in Castries and Alix was a teacher in the nearby Methodist Infant School.

But this traditional middle-class home was set in a society that had been made complex by the turbulent history of the Caribbean region. The small island of St Lucia is part of the cluster of islands known as the Antilles, which make up a large part of the West Indies. Although only 616 sq. km. in size, during the seventeenth and eighteenth centuries the island was at the centre of a power struggle between France and Britain because of its magnificent natural harbour. During the one hundred and fifty years when control of the island alternated between France and England, many African people were brought by force to St Lucia to provide slave labour on the sugar plantations owned by Europeans. The original native population of the island, who could have served as a workforce, had been quickly wiped out by the early European settlers.

Although the first towns on the island had been established by the French, and French cultural influences remained strong, St Lucia finally became part of the British Empire in the nineteenth century. Following the emancipation of the slaves in the 1830s, Asian Indians were brought in to work on the plantations as indentured servants ('indentured' meaning that they signed contracts with their master to work for an agreed number of years), but the sugar market collapsed and St Lucia became a very poor island.

By the 1930s, when Derek Walcott was born, the society of St Lucia was rigidly hierarchical with colour, property, family and education dictating one's social position. At that time, only two per cent of the population were white; they comprised Old French families, some estate owners and civil servants. Largely based in Castries, they spoke, read and wrote in English. They looked to England for their codes of behaviour, education system and culture. So too did the middle class of the island, a sizeable number of whom were of mixed parentage. These two groups formed the upper levels of the society and had access to education. The remainder of the population, made up of servants and rural communities, spoke Creole, a dialect with French and African influences. Indeed, the largely oral culture of this lower class also had its origins in France and Africa.

Walcott was a member of the upper echelon because of his family connections. Both of his grandfathers were white estate owners. The Walcott family was originally English and Alix's father was Dutch. His two grandmothers had brown-coloured skin and were local women. In a society where shades of skin were immensely important, Derek's mother was particularly proud of the fact that her father had blonde hair and blue eyes and, later on, that her children had inherited 'light' skin. Derek's father was very much an English gentleman: quiet, cultured and with impeccable manners. He delighted in opera; had an extensive library; wrote poetry and was a gifted painter of watercolours. In 'A Letter from Brooklyn', Walcott recounts Mable Rawlins' description of his late father:

> Your father was a dutiful, honest,
> Faithful, and useful person.

Derek's mother, a great lover of literature, trained as a teacher and by 1918 was the head teacher of the Methodist Infant School. Indeed, as Methodists, the Walcott family were part of another small group, since the vast majority of the population of St Lucia were Roman Catholics.

Sadly, in 1931, Derek's father, Warwick, died suddenly. Alix was determined that her young children would maintain their position in society in spite of the severe economic problems caused by her husband's death. She supplemented her small teaching salary by taking in sewing, but the family lived in what can only be described as 'genteel poverty'. Nevertheless, she ensured that Derek, Roderick and Pamela developed the intellectual and artistic skills appropriate to those who were in the upper social level. Derek was academically bright and succeeded in winning a scholarship to St Mary's College, the school that educated the sons of the elite.

DEVELOPING A FORM OF CREATIVE EXPRESSION

From a very early age, Derek showed considerable artistic talent. He had a facility for language and painting. When he entered St Mary's College, he met Dunstan St Omer, who had a wonderful natural talent for drawing and painting, and the two boys became friends. Luckily, Derek and Dunstan were encouraged and nurtured in their development by Harold Simmons, one of the first important painters from St Lucia and an old friend of Derek's father. Harold allowed them to use his studio and his equipment while he taught them a variety of techniques. As Walcott describes in his poetic autobiography, 'Another Life', the two boys became determined to capture creatively the essence of the island of St Lucia:

> But drunkenly, or secretly, we swore,
> . . . that we would never leave the island
> until we had put down, in paint, in words,
> . . . all of its sunken, leaf-choked ravines.

However, gradually the young Walcott came to the realisation that, while he was technically an extremely proficient artist, he would never be quite as good as Dunstan. He held on to the idea of 'putting down' St Lucia, and he continued to paint, but he focused his efforts on writing, using his 'artist's eye' to create amazingly vivid word pictures to portray his island home.

Alix was particularly keen that her three children would follow their father's lead and become poets. However, as Bruce King notes in his book *Derek Walcott: A Caribbean Life*, she expected Derek to be the one who would 'fulfil his father's aborted artistry'. She constantly encouraged him to work hard at developing his God-given talent for words by reading, analysing and imitating the great writers of English literature. It was she who found the $200 to pay for the private publication of Derek's first volume of poetry, *25 Poems*, when he was eighteen years old. Walcott also received tremendous support for his writing from his late father's friends and his teachers. Indeed, a general feeling had quickly developed following the publication of his first poem in 1944 that the then fourteen-year-old Derek Walcott would one day become a great poet who would write of and for the West Indies.

WRITING ABOUT THE WEST INDIES

The young Derek embraced the idea that his literary development was intimately linked to his home island of St Lucia, the Antilles and the wider West Indies. He recognised that 'no one had written of this landscape': any pieces that had been written about the region were by outsiders who 'looked at a landscape furious with vegetation in the wrong light and with the wrong eye'. He saw himself as being perfectly suited to taking on the role of expressing the 'reality of light, of work, of survival' because he was part of it all. Thus, his desire to 'put down' the world that he inhabited evolved into a belief that he, like the biblical Adam, was embarking on the 'task of giving things their names'. What he meant by this was that he, Derek Walcott, born out of the complex history of the West Indies, inheritor of the ambiguous past of the West Indies, would undertake the role of writing about the West Indies. For like Shabine, the hero of 'The Schooner Flight', Walcott sees himself as a 'hybrid' product in flesh and blood and mind of the West Indies:

> I had a sound colonial education,
> I have Dutch, nigger and English in me,
> and either I'm nobody, or I'm a nation.

The time was right in the West Indies for such a writer and the literary works that he produced in the 1940s, both poetry and plays, were seen not only as the voice of a young, gifted West Indian, but as the cry that signalled to the British Empire the emergence of an independent West Indian nation.

POST-COLONIAL LITERATURE IN THE WEST INDIES AND IRELAND

In many ways, the process that literature was undergoing in the West Indies in the middle of the twentieth century echoed the developments that had taken place in Ireland at the beginning of that century with the Irish Literary Revival. Indeed, Walcott himself has commented:

> I've always felt some kind of intimacy with the Irish poets because one realized that they were also colonials with the same kind of problems that existed in the Caribbean.

Both Ireland and St Lucia were indeed 'colonial' countries in that they were part of the British Empire, and as such there was no room in either place for a separate national identity linguistically, culturally or politically. Thus the two countries were remarkably similar. Standard English was used in the classroom, schoolbooks presented a British Empire view of the world, and the great classics of English literature were taught. The ruling elite modelled their social practices on English society, wrote and conversed in English and delighted in all aspects of English culture. At the other end of the social scale, the lower classes spoke a different language (Irish in Ireland, Creole in St Lucia); had a different, largely oral culture and were often regarded by the upper classes as incapable of being educated since they were 'childlike' or, more negatively, 'intellectually limited'. However, as with all great empires, this state of affairs could not go on for ever.

Towards the end of the nineteenth century and into the early twentieth century the dominance of the British Empire was steadily eroded by an increasing demand for political independence for the colonies. Generally, the appearance of this political direction in a colony was accompanied by a growing appreciation in the arts of the unique identity and native culture of the particular country, as opposed to the identity and culture of the British Empire. The literary aspect of this artistic movement has come to be known as 'post-colonial literature'.

The term 'post-colonial literature' is a wide one since it embraces literature from all the countries where colonialism existed but, for the purposes of this piece, we can say that it includes writing that expresses different aspects of the consequences of colonialism. In the case of St Lucia, these would include: the enforced movement and brutal treatment of African slaves by European plantation owners; the influx of the Asian Indians and the efforts of the colonial power, the British Empire, to eradicate the native cultures of these groups by imposing English culture and the English language on the society.

Thus, post-colonial literature in this region, as in Ireland, involves finding the words to express the value of the culture and the language that the British Empire sought to eliminate or, at the very least, regarded as primitive and inferior. The dilemma for writers such as Walcott is that they are literate in English and have developed an understanding and appreciation of literature from reading English works, so English is the language they would be expected to use to communicate their nation's essential individuality. But English is the language that represents the colonising dominance of the British Empire and, as such, carries with it echoes of the oppression from which they are trying to free themselves.

FINDING A LANGUAGE OF EXPRESSION

One of the main issues facing Walcott in his early attempts to find a uniquely West Indian language of expression was the fact that he loved the English language and English literature. He found himself torn between this love and his desire to return to the language of his ancestors:

> I who have cursed
> The drunken officer of British rule, how choose
> Between this Africa and the English tongue I love?
> (from *A Far Cry from Africa*)

Walcott wanted to use some of the English literary forms and structures that he had imitated so carefully in his younger days, not because he was unable to create new ones but because he felt that they would make a positive contribution to his development of a West Indian language of expression. Walcott has compared this process of imitation leading to creation to an artist developing his own unique style as a result of copying the styles of other artists; or to a child who begins by imitating the gestures, behaviour and speech of the parent but then becomes a distinct individual. This thinking has led him to a personally satisfactory resolution of the dilemma of writing in English:

> I hate all that nonsense about not touching the colonialist's language. All that about it being corrupting and belonging to the master . . . That thinking just denies you an outlet. You deny everything that is great from a language . . .

Despite criticism from some quarters, Walcott simply refuses to allow the language of his writing to be restricted by the history of his region:

> In the New World servitude to the muse of history has produced a literature of recrimination and despair, a literature of revenge written by the descendants of slaves or a literature of remorse written by the descendants of masters.
>
> (The Muse of History)

In doing this, Walcott does not deny this history, but he 'refuses to recognize it as a creative force'. Instead, he works to construct an expanded and enriched form of language that is accessible for those whose primary language is English and for those whose mother tongue is Creole. He believes that he can achieve this by ensuring that his language of expression has a 'true' tone: 'The aim was that a West Indian or an Englishman could read a single poem, each with his own accent, without either one feeling that it was written in a dialect.'

Interestingly, Walcott has frequently expressed his admiration for a number of Irish writers from Synge to Joyce and on to Heaney in that 'tonally, they are Irish'. Consequently, Walcott is not merely engaging in a 'cut and paste' approach in his poetry. He does not simply take English poetic structures and slot in Creole words or phrases. Because of the 'true' tone of his words there is a finely balanced interweaving of the two, resulting in Creole breathing new life and energy into English structures. In this way, Walcott aims to create a poetic language of expression that will transcend differences in culture and create a unity among his readers. Indeed, although Walcott is also an accomplished playwright, he feels that poetry is particularly suitable for such an endeavour since it is 'an island that breaks away from the main'. What he means by this is that poetry has the capability to allow language to function in a creative context that ignores the confines of space and time. For this reason, poetry enables the living variety and vitality of the language of the present to refresh the words and forms of the past so that a uniquely appropriate language of expression is created:

. . . it conjugates both tenses simultaneously: the past and the present
. . . There is the buried language and there is the individual vocabulary,
and the process of poetry is one of excavation and of self-discovery.

The opening lines of the extract 'From *Omeros*' are an excellent example of how Walcott succeeds in coherently blending different vocabulary and syntax from different worlds and different times so that all his readers can respond to his language of expression in an unbroken and natural way:

He yawned and watched the lilac horns of his island
lift the horizon.
           'I know you ain't like to talk,'
the mate said, 'but this morning I could use a hand.
Where your mind was whole night?'

Because of his determination to remain open to influences, Walcott is able to celebrate and embrace the linguistic variety that he encountered in his colonial education: 'We knew the literature of Empires, Greek, Roman, British, through their essential classics; and both the patois of the street and the language of the classroom hid the elation . . . of discovery.'

Thus, he sees the space between the two languages of his society, English and Creole, as presenting him not with the need to choose one as superior to the other; but with the opportunity to discover a language of expression to fill that space by choosing both as equally superior and equally contributory, 'If there was nothing, there was everything to be made.'

In the lecture that he gave on receiving the Nobel Prize in Literature in 1992, Walcott used the image of a broken vase to represent how he has arrived at a positive resolution of the language dilemma:

Break a vase, and the love that reassembles the fragments is stronger than that love which took its symmetry for granted when it was whole . . . It is such love that reassembles our African and Asiatic fragments . . . Antillean art is this restoration of our shattered histories, our shards of vocabulary . . .

For Walcott, poetry is not 'making', it is 'remaking', because in its language of expression it carries 'the past and the present', the African, the Asian, the French and the English. Thus, he does not shy away from using poetic elements from the 'coloniser's' language, nor elements from the language of the 'colonised', nor elements from the past, nor elements from the present, if these elements will further his aim of successfully completing 'Adam's task of giving things their names'.

THE MIGRANT WRITER

After graduating from St Mary's College in 1947, Derek continued his association with the school by becoming a junior master there, teaching Latin and art. During this time, he continued to write both poetry and plays. In 1950, he won a scholarship to study at the University College of the West Indies in Jamaica and left St Lucia. Having completed his degree, he took a postgraduate education course and taught for a few years in Grenada, St Lucia and Jamaica. In 1957, he travelled to the United States for the first time, for a brief stay in New York. He then settled in Trinidad and founded the Trinidad Theatre Workshop, an immensely successful group to this day. By the early 1960s, the wider world was beginning to take note of his work. In 1962, his collection of poetry entitled *In a Green Night* was published in the UK and in 1964 *Selected Poems* was published in the USA. In the years that followed, his poetry and plays were increasingly well-received and won a number of awards. In 1981 he was appointed Professor of Creative Writing at Boston University where he founded the Boston Playwrights' Theatre. The publication in 1990 of *Omeros*, Walcott's spectacular Caribbean epic, was followed in 1992 by the award of the Nobel Prize in Literature 'for a poetic oeuvre of great luminosity, sustained by a historical vision, the outcome of a multicultural commitment'.

Walcott divides his time between the Caribbean and the USA and travels widely throughout the world. There is an undeniable irony in the fact that the young Derek Walcott set out to write about St Lucia, the landscape that 'no one had yet written of' and the very success of his work has led him to leave that landscape. Yet, in a way, this is exactly what had to happen, since migration has always been a part of the West Indies. For Walcott, St Lucia is still 'a life older than geography' and he always carries the essence of that 'life' within him no matter where he goes:

> Make of my heart an ark
> Let my ribs bear
> All

But to see Walcott's poetry as simply a record of one man's experience of island life in the West Indies is to ignore the universality of it. Love, death, hope, sadness, the search for a sense of identity and a celebration of the vivid visual beauty of life vibrate with an intense energy through his words. These are issues that each one of us encounters, whether we are in Ireland on a cold, wet, wintry November day or on a sun-bathed beach in St Lucia. Even more significantly, Walcott's poetry offers us the chance to stand with him on a tropical cliff and to gaze out on the bay that 'shines like tinfoil', then up along 'the asphalt's worn-out ribbon' until we turn and look into his heart and understand how and why he has come, like the biblical figure of Adam, to name his world. And as we stand beside him the realisation dawns that, in an age where individual cultures and languages are dissolving in a wave of economic globalisation, each one of us has a unique life experience and a unique language born out of a cradle of interwoven personal, social and historical influences. But, most importantly of all, Walcott reminds us that we each have the privilege and the right to be as Adam once was, to experience a world that exists for no one else in the way that it exists for each one of us, and to name it by choosing our own words.

A Letter from Brooklyn
Text of poem: New Explorations Anthology page 310

A READING OF THE POEM

Walcott's considerable poetic ability is evident from the outset. The opening two lines of the poem immediately create a realistic and dramatic setting for the piece, while at the same time establishing an intimate relationship between Walcott and his reader. His conversational tone and use of the present tense, 'An old lady writes me' and his vivid description of the 'spidery style' of the old lady's handwriting give the impression that we are there with him, leaning over his shoulder, as he unfolds the letter and comments on its topic and on the writer. In addition, he uses the first two lines to provide a platform for his fragmented memories of the old lady. The 'veined hand' that he imagines is followed by snap-shot images of 'small, buttoned boots' and 'Grey-haired, thin-voiced, perpetually bowed'. This is a very realistic and natural portrayal of how memory works in that we tend not to remember perfectly people's physical make-up, but rather recall the parts that have made an impression on us. Consequently, Walcott admits 'I forget her face'. Similarly, we often remember people in the context of their habits or actions. So, Walcott recalls how the old lady had a 'place' in the church where she usually sat. The overwhelming impression is that this lady is very old. Initially, Walcott links her ageing body to a similar deterioration in her mental abilities. Thus, he sees the delicate transparency of her old skin 'Pellucid as paper' as being suggestive of 'frail thoughts' that become easily 'broken'.

In keeping with the realism and dramatic immediacy of the first section of the poem, Walcott begins the second section by quoting directly from the letter. Again, we seem to be actually there with him as reads aloud and reacts with an amused but slightly dismissive tone, 'He is dead, Miss Rawlins, but God bless your tense'. On the one hand, Walcott seems to be touched by the fact that Mable Rawlins still remembers his father as a living person, while on the other, he seems to be taking the view that the old lady is simply confused about what is present and past in her life. However, as he reads on, his reactions begin to change. He sees the simple truthfulness of her description of his father's good qualities as having a value beyond 'fame'. In the same way, her reference to his father contentedly painting reminds him that 'The peace of God needs nothing to adorn | It'. But it is her phrase 'he was called home' that really stops Walcott in his tracks. Suddenly, he realises that Mable Rawlins' frail, ageing body and mind are sustained by a strength that defies age: a spiritual faith in God as the original creator. Mable may be 'Alone' sitting 'in a dim room' in Brooklyn, far removed from her home of St Lucia, and her beauty may be 'withered', but she has not 'withdrawn' from the world. Because of her faith she still 'spins the blessings of her years'. Similarly, although she has 'such short time to live' she does not fear death because she believes in a life after death in a heaven 'where painters go'. Through her words, Walcott suddenly sees heaven as Mable does. It is the source of creativity, where all is made, from where man derives his creative inspiration and to where all will eventually return. It is this insight that restores Walcott's own faith so that he is able to 'believe it all' and, like Mable, he too sees death as a 'return to do work that is God's'. Walcott understands that all humans are artists in the sense that they each have a God-given ability for some form of creativity and so he can declare, 'for no man's death I grieve'.

THEME

Through the letter from Mable Rawlins concerning the death of his father, Walcott is brought to a greater understanding of the way in which a belief in God, as the source of creativity, and in a life after death can eliminate the grief that is normally felt in response to bereavement.

Walcott was only a baby when his father Warwick died suddenly. Although his mother portrayed Warwick as a perfect role model for the three children, Walcott had mixed feelings about him: he admired his father's intellectual and creative abilities but he was angry that his father had left him and his brother and sister. It is evident from the poem that his father's death was a difficult and significant issue for Walcott. Initially, he tells us that he always remembers the anniversary of his father's death, although he can never really have known him. But he cannot remember the face of a woman who was part of his life as he was growing up:

> . . . I forget her face
> More easily than my father's yearly dying

Then, his rather brief and dismissive comment 'He is dead, Miss Rawlins' suggests that he is uncomfortable with the emotions that references to his father's death provoke in him and therefore tries to suppress them by stating the fact briefly. However, by the end of the poem Walcott's attitude has been altered by the words and example of Mable Rawlins. He now has the faith to believe that death has enabled his father to return to heaven, the place where both he and his creative inspiration originated. In this way, Walcott comes to accept his father's death and to understand that death itself should not be viewed as a negative or destructive experience signalling an end. Rather, it is positive in that human beings, who have an innate God-given capacity for creativity, are enabled to 'return' to the source that created them.

STRUCTURE

As we have seen in the consideration of Walcott's life and literary development, he believes that, for him, the most effective language of poetic expression is a 'remaking' of both English and Creole. Thus, he often uses traditional English literary forms in his poetry but revitalises them with the uninhibited energy that is found in West Indian culture and Creole.

Walcott uses the elegy form in this poem. Since the seventeenth century, in English literature an elegy was a formal lament for someone's death, and it often included an element of consolation. An elegy can also involve a general reflection on death in the context of human life.

In a brilliant move, Walcott combines this form with the arrival of a letter, an important feature of West Indian life because, for so long, many West Indians have been forced to emigrate to the USA and Europe in search of employment. This combination has the effect of reducing the formal aspect of the elegy and bringing it into the real world of human emotions. Walcott still retains the element of 'lament' in the description of his father's positive qualities and in the sense of loss. However, the 'consolation' that appears at the end of the poem is both genuine and believable, not just a part of a literary formula. Similarly, his move from a personalised consideration of his father's death into a general reflection on death is unforced, seeming to develop naturally out of Walcott's own thoughts and feelings.

IMAGERY

As with many of Walcott's poems, there is a subtle but beautifully constructed substructure of images in this poem. In line 1, he introduces the image of a 'spidery' style of writing. This is followed in lines 3–7 by images of a 'skein', a 'thread', a 'filament' that 'shines like steel', all of which mesh into a 'whole web' that links back to the spider image in line 1. Here, he is conveying the process of writing, a creative act, where thoughts are put down on paper, sometimes to form a coherent and suggestive piece of expression, but at other times in a disjointed and unsuccessful way.

Walcott returns to this image of a 'thread' made of 'steel' in line 35, in his description of the link between God's heaven, the source of creativity, and human beings. But significantly, whereas the 'thread' between thoughts and written words described earlier in the poem is liable to be 'broken', in this case, the steel thread is now 'resilient' and, although temporarily 'Lost', ultimately succeeds in guiding a return to God's heaven.

Endings
Text of poem: New Explorations Anthology page 313

A READING OF THE POEM

Walcott opens this wonderfully vivid poem in a dramatic and arresting manner with his declaration:

> Things do not explode,
> they fail, they fade,

The contrast that he achieves between these two short lines arises out of his exceptionally effective use of assonance and alliteration. Thus, the assonance in line 1, where he repeats the broad vowel o ('do not explode') creates a dramatically sudden and explosive sound. But in line 2, the alliteration of f along with the assonance of the long a ('they fail, they fade') are suggestive of a much more long-drawn-out process. In this way, Walcott appeals to his reader's senses of sight and hearing to make the images in these eight words immensely real and vivid.

Walcott follows this opening with a series of incredibly condensed yet amazingly effective illustrations of the processes of failing and fading. They appear rather like a piece of time-lapse photography in which, for instance, clouds are filmed by taking one frame at intervals over a six-hour period. When the film is run, the clouds appear to move across the screen in a matter of seconds. So Walcott presents us with a tan fading from skin and sea foam draining into the sand. Again, his use of sound is remarkable. For instance, his control of the pace of his words in the line 'as the foam drains quick in the sand' reinforces the image of the white bubbles momentarily poised on the sand. Then the word 'quick' suggests their sudden disappearance. There is nothing that can escape this fading and failing process. Even love, which begins with the loud crack of the 'lightning flash' of connection and attraction, 'dies' as quietly as 'flowers fading'. In turn, these flowers fade as easily as tiny pieces of hard skin are washed off the pumice stone that has been used to remove them.

The final lines of the poem are both haunting and enigmatic. Walcott declares 'everything shapes this', meaning that all things finally and inevitably end by fading or failing. Then he presents us with a remarkable image: 'till we are left | with the silence that surrounds Beethoven's head'. The great composer Beethoven did, indeed, gradually lose his hearing until he became profoundly deaf. But what is Walcott trying to convey here? The whole poem has hinged on the idea that 'Endings' do not involve the dramatic action and noise of an explosion, but rather, the understated and essentially silent movement of fading and failing. Is Walcott using the image of 'Beethoven's head' surrounded by silence to communicate the profound and empty silence that Beethoven must have felt when he could no longer hear his wonderful music being played? Or is it a bust of Beethoven's head that Walcott is describing? Could Walcott be suggesting that when Beethoven's head, which in life was filled both inside and out by his amazing music, finally died his vibrant genius did not explode in some dramatic musical crescendo but faded to being no more than a silent stone bust?

STRUCTURE

The appearance of this poem suggests that it is a simple and brief piece of writing. The lines are short and arranged in six pairs of two, known as unrhymed couplets. The poem consists of only twelve lines, some 59 words, one long sentence beginning with a capital letter and ending with a full stop. However, once the poem has actually been read, it is clear that it is far from simple and its short appearance is deceptive.

The two most obvious aspects of the poem are the tight cluster of intensely vivid images centred on the concept of 'Endings', and its construction as one continuous sentence. Both of these are indicative of Walcott's interest in modernist writing. The first modernists appeared early in the twentieth century. They rejected tradition and realism in the arts in favour of more radical and experimental approaches. One of their innovations was to change the purpose of imagery in poetic writing. Instead of simply using the traditional approach of creating images that appeal to the reader's five senses so that the reader understands the sensory realism of the object, modernists aim to enable the reader to be fully 'there' with the object, to be completely aware of it and to understand clearly the nature of its being. This is called realisation. Walcott presents us with a variety of images, each conveying something of his understanding of the essence of the concept of 'Endings'. His arrangement of these images in two lines followed by a space, then two more lines and so on is reminiscent of an art exhibition dealing with a particular theme. So, we look at:

as sunlight fades from the flesh,
as the foam drains quick in the sand

Then there is a pause before we move on to:

> even love's lightning flash
> has no thunderous end,

This has the effect of slowing down the pace at which we read the poem and building in the sense that these images should be savoured and appreciated in a thoughtful way. Indeed, his images do need to be thought about in order to appreciate their full impact because Walcott has really pared down the language that he uses to express them. For instance, the final image of 'the silence that surrounds Beethoven's head' consists of only six words but it takes a great many more to explain what this image has to do with 'Endings'.

Modernist poets frequently link realisation to a technique known as the 'stream of consciousness'. This is where the poet tries to represent the continuous and spontaneous way that his thoughts and feelings blend and merge within him. Thus Walcott uses one continuous sentence that flows without a break from the first word to the last. It is clear that although this poem consists of only 59 words, it conveys an amazing complexity of thought, an exceptional mastery of language and a great deal of hard work on Walcott's part.

The Sailor Sings Back to the Casuarinas (from The Schooner *Flight*)

Text of poem: New Explorations Anthology page 316

BACKGROUND NOTE

This is an extract from a long poem entitled 'The Schooner *Flight*', included in Walcott's volume of poetry *The Star-Apple Kingdom* published in 1979. The central character of the poem is Shabine, Walcott's West Indian version of Homer's Greek hero Ulysses. Shabine is closely linked to Walcott in a number of ways. They both have 'mixed blood'. In fact the word 'shabine' means a person of mixed black and white parentage who has reddish hair and a rather freckled tan. The Shabine in this poem is a sailor and poet who feels unsure about where he belongs: 'I have no nation now but the imagination.'

Walcott feels a similar sense of dislocation, caught somewhere between his European and African roots. Indeed, Shabine's physical journeying around the seas of the Caribbean can be seen as representing Walcott's emotional and creative journey in search of a sense of identity. Both men feel a deep connection to the Caribbean landscape and ocean, and see a link between these and their personal and national identities. Perhaps most significantly of all, Walcott and Shabine share the recognition that language is a powerful force.

A READING OF THE POEM

Shabine's description of the Casuarina trees is at once breathtakingly beautiful and deeply moving as his genuine love for his environment fills every word that he uses. So, he enables us to 'see' the Casuarinas on 'the low hills of Barbados' and, through his hauntingly appropriate similes, to share his appreciation of their strength and gracefulness as they stand 'bracing like windbreaks' and 'trailing, like masts, the cirrus of torn sails'. The connection that he feels with them is illustrated in his use of the phrase 'when I was green like them' to describe when he was young. But this wonderfully evocative moment is interrupted by Shabine's references, in lines 5–10, to the different names by which the trees are known. He recalls how as a boy he felt that they were 'not real cypresses but casuarinas'. Now his captain calls them 'Canadian cedars'.

Shabine's thoughts move on to the power that resides in the language of men and in the act of naming. He realises that the trees are unaffected by whatever name is applied to them: 'since they were trees with nothing else in mind | but heavenly leaping or to guard a grave'.

This indifference stands in marked contrast to the influence that names can have on human beings, 'but we live like our names'. As we have seen in the consideration of Walcott's life and literary development, he is concerned with finding a language of expression that will reflect the unique complexity of what it is to be West Indian. As a young poet, he consciously took on the task of 'naming' his world. In a similar vein, Shabine considers the negative effects that colonialism had on the language of the West Indies by its introduction of 'the pain of history' into words. This 'pain' arises out of the way in which the oppressor, in this case the British Empire, made the West Indian oppressed feel subordinate and inferior, that their feelings and thoughts were of less value than those of the oppressor. As a result, they felt that they could only express 'an inferior love'. Shabine understands that the 'masters', by imposing their choice of name, or language, on a human being subject to their authority, were dictating the way in which that human being perceived himself and, consequently, his development as a person: 'if we live like the names our masters please, | by careful mimicry might become men.'

For since this language did not come naturally, or by choice, from the minds and hearts of the oppressed it could never express their sense of identity or their human dignity. Thus, the tone of these lines conveys 'the pain of history' that haunts the languages of the Caribbean in a deeply moving and real way. Shabine's emotional declaration, 'you would have | to be colonial to know the difference', has a particular relevance to us, who live in Ireland, for we, too, were once 'colonial' and we, too, ought to 'know the difference'.

LANGUAGE

Walcott has Shabine express his thoughts and feelings in a vital and energetic language that, while not being an exact copy of Creole, vibrates with some of its words, rhythm and syntax. This is particularly evident in such lines as: 'Now captain just call them Canadian cedars.'

Walcott handles this aspect of the piece with considerable skill so that the Creole elements mesh smoothly and naturally with English. There is no interference with the flow of his writing, or with the sequence of the thinking. Instead, they subtly add depth and realism to the extract. Consequently, we come to understand that Shabine's determinedly non-standard English, and the development of Creole dialects in the West Indies, is indicative of resistance, of a refusal to accept this attempt at linguistic oppression. It is a sign of hope that, in spite of the best efforts of the 'masters', the people of the West Indies will one day be able to transcend the 'pain of history that words contain' and choose their own names and their own destinies.

To Norline

Text of poem: New Explorations Anthology page 320

[*Note: This poem is also prescribed for Ordinary Level 2010 exam*]

BACKGROUND NOTE

In 1982, Walcott married his third wife, Norline Metivier, a dancer and choreographer. The marriage ended in 1993 after a lengthy separation.

STRUCTURE

'To Norline' is a lyric poem. This form of poetry does not attempt to tell a story, nor does it portray either characters or actions. The main aim of the lyric poem is for the poet to share his innermost emotions, thoughts and perceptions with the reader. The speaker in the lyric poem may be the poet or a persona, a character created by the poet to express his feelings and views. Lyric poems are usually short. 'To Norline' consists of twelve lines, divided into three groups of four lines, known as quatrains.

A READING OF THE POEM

As is usual with the lyric form, Walcott makes no attempt to explain the situation that inspired him to write this beautiful poem. There are only a few clues as to the circumstances: the poem's title mentions Norline, who was his third wife, and we learn that they have an intimate relationship from the line 'as my body once cupped yours'.

But really, the details of the situation are largely unimportant since Walcott is more concerned with communicating what he feels through the mood and tone of the poem. Similarly, the place and the things that Walcott mentions in the poem are only important in that he uses them to convey his emotional and intellectual state to his readers.

So, in the first quatrain, Walcott's emotional state is revealed in the way that he portrays the beach as an unchanging paradise that will always be restored to unmarked smoothness by the surf and lit by wonderful 'slate-coloured dawns'. He clearly feels that this is a moment of perfect, unspoiled tranquillity and happiness. The second quatrain introduces an imaginary figure in the future onto the beach:

> and someone else will come
> from the still-sleeping house

These lines suggest that this is just what Walcott has done – come from a beachside house out onto the empty beach to watch the dawn. But unlike Walcott the figure only has 'a coffee mug' with him. It becomes clear that Walcott is not alone, as he says to his companion 'as my body once cupped yours'. Walcott obviously feels sorry for the imaginary figure because the warmth that he feels is limited to only the 'palm' of his hand and comes from the mug of coffee that he is holding. Walcott implies that he has a much deeper and far more precious type of emotional and spiritual warmth: a sense of loving and being loved arising from the tender intimacy that he shares with his companion. In the third quatrain, Walcott suggests that he and the imaginary figure share the same reaction in that, like Walcott, he will also want to 'memorize this passage | of a salt-sipping tern'. This indicates that they both want to hold on to the perfection of the moment, although the implication is that the experience of the man with the coffee will be of less emotional depth than Walcott's. Walcott uses a vivid image to convey their reluctance to leave the perfect moment, comparing it to an unwillingness to turn a page in a book.

But a second reading of the poem suggests that Walcott's moment may not be quite as perfect as he would like it to be. His references to 'more slate-coloured dawns' and the way in which 'the surf continually erases' the beach imply time passing. Similarly, the appearance of the imaginary figure in the future suggests a time when Walcott and his companion will no longer be there. While the 'salt-tipping tern' is only in their field of vision for a moment and then disappears. And the reluctance that is felt about turning the page cannot last as, finally, the page must be turned to finish the book. But perhaps most tellingly of all, the warmth that comes from the coffee mug will inevitably grow cold. Is Walcott implying that the wonderful emotional and spiritual warmth that he feels may be equally transient? Or perhaps he is suggesting that his special moment, like all special moments, is made all the more perfect by an awareness of the fact that it cannot last.

LANGUAGE

Walcott's use of language is particularly impressive in the poem and makes an important contribution to the success of the piece. He establishes subtle connections through his careful choice of words. For instance, in line 3 he uses 'lines' to suggest the marks in the sand; while in line 11, 'line' refers to the print in a book. This repetition creates a sense of unity in the poem. But it also encourages the reader to think about how the two forms of 'line' relate to each other. Similarly, his use of the word 'tern' in line 10 and 'turn' in line 12 sets up a kind of sound echo that serves to highlight the words and thereby stimulates a consideration of their meaning and possible connection. Another extremely elegant example of establishing a connection between words in order to evoke a more thoughtful response in the reader is in his use of 'mug' in line 7 and 'cupped' in line 8. As we have seen, Walcott suggests that the 'perfect moment' that the imaginary figure will experience will not as special, either emotionally or spiritually, as his own 'perfect moment'. Thus, the mug is suggestive of a more basic functionality, while 'cupped' implies the refinement and delicate grace of a special china teacup.

Summer Elegies I

Text of poem: New Explorations Anthology page 323

[*Note: this poem is also prescribed for Ordinary Level 2010 exam*]

LANDSCAPE AND NATURE IN WALCOTT'S POETRY

As we have seen in the consideration of Walcott's life and literary development, the island of St Lucia plays a very important part in his creativity. However, his attitude towards its landscape and nature is rather complex. In his use of the word 'landscape' Walcott generally includes both land and sea because he sees the Caribbean region as having 'a sea culture'. He also feels that the sea has the capacity for 'renewal' because it can wash away the debris of the past. He frequently links this landscape to Eden, the paradise that God created for Adam and Eve, because 'It is still a place where you can find a beach that is totally deserted, and it still looks as primal, Edenic, as when it first happened.' He feels that the geography is truly magnificent: 'we have three things going that create that sense of awe . . . a very vast sky, a really large sea and, of course, the landscape . . .'

But this 'awe' is haunted by the way in which the British Empire tried to force the people of the colonies to regard their native cultures and environments as inferior to European cultures and environments: 'What we were taught as young colonials, is that our awe was inferior. We were taught that the sky in Italy was superior, that the light of their sky was really superior . . .'

Even the plants that were native to the West Indies, such as mangos and pineapples, were considered inferior to fruit, such as apples and peaches, that were native to Europe. Indeed, a number of European plants were brought to St Lucia by European settlers, such as apple trees and almond trees, and Walcott sees them as representing the coloniser's determination to impose a supposedly superior environment and culture on all the colonies, so that they become nothing more than 'little Englands' or 'little Frances', little facsimiles of whatever European country is acting as the coloniser.

A READING OF THE POEM

Walcott uses a very natural and conversational language from the very opening of this piece. It is as if we are actually beside Walcott and Cynthia listening to them as they recall a very special experience:

Cynthia, the things we did,
our hands growing more bold

The description that follows of the couple's 'changing shapes of love' is both sensual and charming. For instance, in lines 3–4, Walcott's use of the word 'slithered' and the alliteration of the letter 's' suggest the actual sensation of Cynthia's top sliding down her skin. While the image of the dove that 'gurgled astonished "Ooos"' at their activities is charmingly amusing. There is a marvellous sense of innocent joy and a natural delight in their intimacy. It was such an amazing experience for the couple that they felt as if they were the only people on the island. There are subtle echoes of Adam and Eve in the Garden of Eden in all of this. Walcott manages both the tone and the mood of this passage so beautifully that we, the readers, are also caught up in the sense of nostalgia. However, line 14 signals a change in the mood: 'now heat and image fade'.

Walcott's use of the word 'fade' not only suggests the fading of the sensory memory of what they did but also of the emotional memory. Rather like his approach in 'Endings', he uses two wonderfully appropriate similes to convey the concept of fading: 'like foam lace, like the tan | on a striped shoulder blade'. There is a gentle delicacy about these images, almost as if the last shadows of nostalgia are gently dissolving.

The fifth stanza makes it clear that the nostalgia is definitely gone. The tone and mood become much more brittle and brisk as Walcott uses assonance, repetition of the vowel **i**, and **s** and **r** sounds to convey the sensation of the grainy salt trapped uncomfortably: 'Salt dried in every fissure'.

The sunburn and tan now change to 'dead flesh'. There is something self-consciously dismissive about the lines, 'feeling love could renew it- | self, and a new life begin'. Walcott now seems to be embarrassed about his remembered innocent joy and unthinking delight. Significantly, the tense changes from past to present and the pace of his words becomes clipped and jagged as if he is forcing down his emotions: 'A halcyon day. No sail.'

He seems deliberately to choose images that indicate his sophisticated worldliness, as with the 'cigarette paper' and the 'red thumbnail'. The images of the sea being a 'cigarette paper' that is 'creased to a small square' serve to reduce its expanse. Walcott condenses down 'the whole island' of his memory into a bay that 'shines like tinfoil, | crimps like excelsior'(surprisingly cold and jagged similes for such deeply blue warm waters) and a beach that is furnished with (civilised) 'beach chairs'. This furniture that keeps people separated from the sensation of the hot, and irritating, sand of the beach contrasts with the uninhibited immersion of Walcott and Cynthia 'in water'. His comment 'but the beach is emptier' indicates that, in spite of his sophistication, he feels that both he and the landscape have lost something. Indeed, the title of the poem further reinforces this sense of loss, since an elegy is a poem usually written about the death of someone. But in this case, Walcott connects it to the 'death' of the carefree, happy summer days of his youth.

The final stanza of the poem begins with a vivid and rather complex image:

> The snake hangs its old question
> on almond or apple tree

The 'snake' certainly links back to the suggestions of Eden in Walcott's memories of his time with Cynthia. The 'old question' that it poses is rather puzzling until we look at the remainder of the stanza. It is significant that Walcott places both snake and question 'on almond or apple tree', trees that were introduced to the island by the colonisers. The line 'I had her breast to rest on' recalls his intimacy with Cynthia but the 'we' of the past has turned into the much more separate 'I' and 'her'. Is the 'her' Cynthia? Is it the snake? The key word in all of this is 'History', since it is this word that causes the change of mood in line 14. For Walcott, his time with Cynthia represents his youthful, unthinking and uninhibited celebration of what it was to be West Indian. He and Cynthia, both children of St Lucia, shared their wonderful love in the marvellous landscape of St Lucia. Reminders of their colonised position were ever-present but they did not see them because they were so focused on what they were sharing. Inevitably, however, as Walcott matured he was increasingly affected by 'the snake' and 'History'. He, like many other West Indians, took on the attitudes of the colonisers and began to regard the world of the West Indies as inferior. But poignantly for Walcott, he realises that this act of surrender by him, and the West Indies, involved not only the loss of something from their landscape, but also the loss of something from within themselves.

For Adrian
Text of poem: New Explorations Anthology page 327

STRUCTURE

As with 'A Letter from Brooklyn', Walcott again takes the traditional English literary form of the elegy and infuses it with a deeply moving and personal quality. He retains the elegance of the traditional elegy in his beautifully balanced unrhymed couplets (two successive lines of poetry). Similarly, in keeping with the elegiac form, some thoughts are expressed on the transient and passing nature of life, although he does this in a delicately positive way, as in the lines:

> . . . and what, in your sorrow . . .
> you call a goodbye
>
> is – I wish you would listen to me – a different welcome
> which you will share with me . . .

But Walcott does reject one of the key principles of the traditional elegy: that it should be about the death of someone of great importance, such as a political leader. Instead, he writes about the untimely death of a young boy, who may not have been famous or powerful, but whose importance to his family is distressingly evident in the poem.

A READING OF THE POEM

The opening couplet of this poem is simple and apparently straightforward. A general statement is made about 'furniture' and 'a wardrobe' dissolving. Given that this poem is an elegy, it is to be expected that some comments will be made on the transitory nature of life. However, the second couplet introduces something of a surprise with the comment, 'I can see through you'. Suddenly, it becomes clear that the speaker of this poem is Adrian, the eight-year-old boy for whom the elegy is written. This is a daring approach for Walcott to take because, in his efforts to bring comfort, the tone of his writing could easily become emotionally awkward as he portrays a young boy grappling with what it means to be dead. However, he manages to maintain a beautifully natural and 'boyish' spontaneity of tone throughout, without sliding over into sentimentality, while at the same time addressing the family's terrible grief and the implications of death. Thus, Adrian's childlike acceptance of his altered state makes his death less terrible: '. . . I have now entered a wisdom, not a silence.'

Indeed, Walcott is immensely successful in conveying Adrian's new 'wisdom', that is his understanding of life and death, without losing the childlike tone. Thus, such weighty phrases as 'vestal authority' are balanced by Adrian's typically boyish delight at how 'easy' it is to be an angel. In a similar way, Adrian's recognition of the levelling power of death:

> . . . I share the secret that is only a silence,
> with the tyrants of the earth, with the man who piles
>   rags
> in a creaking cart . . .'

is followed by his expression of the frustration felt at some stage by every child: '– I wish you would listen to me –'. Likewise, his desire to reassure his family is expressed with the unrestrained and excited honesty of an eight-year-old boy, who has not yet learned the art of discretion: 'Why do you miss me? I am not missing you, sisters'. Walcott does not mean us to see this statement as being heartless or callous. Rather he wants to show us how Adrian's state of being is very different to that of his family. Indeed, Adrian's genuine love for his family is revealed in the way that he affectionately notes special features about them, as when he speaks about his aunt 'with the soft eyes'. But the contrast that Walcott draws between Adrian's composed recognition that death is as much a part of the natural universe as the 'stars' and the 'sea', and his family's great distress represents the way in which Adrian has moved 'beyond' his 'eight years' and beyond his living family. However, Walcott never lets us forget that, in spite of this 'wisdom', Adrian is still very much a boy. This is nowhere more evident than in the final images that Adrian uses to describe his altered being to his family. He rejects the standard, rather sentimental and, it has to be said, 'girly' image of the 'bud I snipped before it flowered' in favour of images filled with the vigorous physicality that usually characterises an eight-year-old boy: '. . . I am part of the muscle I of a galloping lion, or a bird keeping low over I dark canes'.

Walcott has handled this piece brilliantly as he moves us, the readers, through confronting the death of a young boy, the sense of loss experienced by his family and the belief that there is a form of being after death. Thus, when we read the final couplet of the poem urging us to see the grave that registers the end of Adrian's brief life as 'the smile of the earth', this is not a trite remark but an image that captures and celebrates the positive and unique contribution that

Adrian made to his family during his brief life on earth and will continue to make to the universe now that he has 'entered a wisdom'.

LANGUAGE

Walcott frequently uses the sounds of his words to add extra depth to his images. For example, he uses alliteration (two or more words close together begin with the same letter) in line 1: 'Look, and you will see that the furniture is fading'.

His repetition of the **f** effectively reinforces the sense of objects dissolving. Equally successful is the assonance (two or more words close together have the same vowel sound) in lines 5–6: 'The days run through the light's fingers like dust | or a child's in a sandpit.'

The recurring narrow 'i' sound reflects the image of tiny particles trickling through fingers. Finally, the alliteration in the phrase 'creaking cart' along with the rhythm of the words brilliantly evoke the sounds of an old cart as it moves noisily along.

The Young Wife

Text of poem: New Explorations Anthology page 331

[*Note: this poem is also prescribed for Ordinary Level 2010 exam*]

A READING OF THE POEM

Walcott uses a natural, conversational tone and language in this poem, but he deals with some very difficult and challenging topics. It is clear from the first line that he is addressing another person: 'Make all your sorrows neat.'

This is an unusual phrase in that it is difficult to understand how 'sorrows' could be made 'neat'. But as the piece moves on, Walcott reveals the connection. We see the person 'Plump pillows' and smooth down the 'coverlet', almost as if he is tidying in an effort to suppress his emotions. In an echo of the 'sorrows' of the first line of the stanza, the fourth line of the stanza introduces 'mourners'. Although Walcott has not clearly stated what this poem is about, it is evident from the title and his clues in the poem that he is addressing a man who has just lost his wife. Indeed, as the poem progresses, we learn more about this man and the way he is attempting to cope with his wife's death. After working in 'the office', he sits alone in the sitting room. Walcott very successfully conveys just how alone the man feels by using words like 'ridge' and 'valley' to make it seem as if the room is a huge and empty space. Even more depressing, there is the suggestion of death in the pattern of the curtains since it looks like 'dead foliage'.

This mood of loneliness and sadness continues as we see the man desperately trying to clean a cloudy mirror. Walcott seems to be suggesting that the 'clouds' are really tears in the man's eyes. This is followed by his 'muffled sobbing' and, another clue, a reference to 'the children'. So this man has been left to look after their children. He is clearly trying his best, but he has not yet reconciled himself to the loss of his wife. He is unable to open certain drawers because he is afraid of how he will react to seeing her belongings inside.

However, Walcott then changes the focus of the poem from the bereaved man to his late wife. In an image that conveys his wife's acceptance of her death, we see her going away quietly and gently 'arm in arm' with 'that visitor'. There is some small comfort in that she seems to have accepted her death. But, Walcott once again returns to the bereaved husband. He feels that all that he has left is a wedding photograph in 'its lace frame' and the telephone 'without a voice'. Both of these suggest a terrible sense of emptiness, of something painfully absent. The man clearly has a terrible 'weight' to bear because he misses his dead wife dreadfully. Sadly, her death has forced him to cope with 'the very edge', or the last part, of the promise that they made to each other on their wedding day: 'till death do us part'. The contrast between 'the drapes' dead foliage' in line 8, and the hawthorn that breaks 'happily into blossom' in this stanza, indicates that his difficulty in coping with her death is added to by the fact that it has happened in the spring, when the world of nature is filled with new life.

Once again, we see the man doing the household chores. This time he is setting the table. Movingly, he still puts out a knife and fork for his wife. This suggests that he is trying to keep some feeling of connection with her. But, in contrast, their children 'close in the space' where their mother's chair once was and they laugh. This does not mean that they no longer miss their mother, but rather that they, unlike their father, have come to terms with her death because they know, with the instinctive wisdom of children, that they are permanently connected to her by their love: 'and nothing takes her place, I loved and now deeper loved.'

The final two lines of the poem imply that their father has also finally found some comfort: 'She sits there smiling that cancer I kills everything but Love.'

There is the suggestion that he feels less alone as he realises that their children sitting around the table carry something of his wife in them. He understands that she is still there in a physical sense because each one of their children has inherited genes from her. But she is also there in a more abstract spiritual sense in that she created a happy and loving home both for her children and her husband, and in this way they will always have her love, and the memories of the joy that they shared, in their hearts. So, he can now stop tidying and sit at the table with their children and know that 'cancer I kills everything but Love.'

This is a beautifully crafted poem, from the way in which it appears on the page to the images and rhymes that Walcott has woven through it. Structurally, the eleven stanzas, or quatrains (four lines of poetry), with their short lines give the impression of neatness, reflecting the husband's attempts to suppress his desolation by 'tidying' and keeping busy. Occasionally, Walcott does lengthen a line to better represent its meaning, as with 'the valley of the shadow in the sofas', where the longer line contributes to the feeling of a huge empty space. The language of the poem is equally impressive. Although it is written in a conversational style using everyday words, Walcott creates a subtle network of connections between some of the words. Thus, the 'lace' framing the wedding photograph in line 22 appears again in line 28 where the image of the couple making their wedding vows is described. This image of delicate white laciness is echoed in line 31 with the 'hawthorn hedge'. This serves to hold the piece together, both in terms of imagery and by contributing to the overall theme of the poem: the enduring force of love and life in the face of death. Walcott uses rhyme in a similar way, as in the final lines:

> The children accept your answer.
> They startle you when they laugh.
> She sits there smiling that cancer
> kills everything but Love.

The rhyming of 'answer' and 'cancer' adds to the positive tone of this stanza and provides a platform for what the answer is to the death from cancer of this young wife and mother. This answer is, of course, found in the two similar sounding words: 'laugh' and 'Love'.

Saint Lucia's First Communion

Text of poem: New Explorations Anthology page 335

BACKGROUND NOTE

For much of the twentieth century, religion was linked to social position on St Lucia. When Walcott was born in 1930, ninety per cent of the population was Roman Catholic, and most spoke Creole. The elite ruling class was predominantly Protestant and English-speaking. As a Methodist, Walcott belonged to a very small religious sub-group, numbering only a few hundred. However, the English-speaking Methodist school was regarded as the best school on the island since it taught in English and provided the opportunity for social advancement through contact with the ruling class and a 'British' style of education. For this reason, many of the better-off Roman Catholics were prepared to risk excommunication to send their children there.

A READING OF THE POEM

Walcott opens this wonderfully vivid poem with an image vibrating with startling visual contrasts. We see the light of the dusk deepen the 'asphalt's worn-out ribbon' to a black inkiness and irradiate the white of the communion 'frock' and the 'cotton stockings' against the black skin of the young girl. Walcott's image of the 'small field' of communicants suggests their natural energy and movement, rather like a field of swaying corn. As a non-Catholic, he is momentarily puzzled by what is happening but then he remembers, 'Ah, it's First Communion!'

The second stanza introduces one of the key ideas in the poem: restraint. The little girl's 'stiff plaits' restrain her hair. We also meet the 'moth' image for the first time when Walcott uses it to describe the bows on the little girl's plaits. Walcott develops this moth image to represent his feelings about the essence of religion. He sees it in terms of a caterpillar, an immature moth, continuously pumping out silk. The religious 'myth' is constantly pumped out and transferred through the 'wafer pod', a reference to the host or consecrated bread, to the congregation who totally believe it, 'without an 'if'!'

In the third stanza, Walcott imagines the 'thousands of innocents' who are receiving their First Communion 'all across Saint Lucia'. In an image that once again expresses a feeling of being restrained, the children are 'arranged on church steps'. Although Walcott portrays the children as being 'erect' with pride because they feel grown up following the ceremony, there is an underlying sense of uneasiness. This arises out of his use of the word 'innocents' to describe the children, his portrayal of the parents 'squinting' and his prediction that all of them will soon be engulfed by 'darkness'. The implication is that the children are unaware of what awaits them and so they gaze wide-eyed at the 'sun's lens', still filled with a natural spontaneity and uninhibited energy, both physically and intellectually. However, the ceremony has begun the process of restraining these qualities. Walcott implies that it will not be long before they too become like their parents, in that they will begin to 'squint' in an intellectual sense, to restrain their natural independence, until, ultimately, they will blindly follow the precepts of their religion.

The last eight lines of the poem are filled with an almost heartbreaking evocation of exquisite beauty and a sense of drama reminiscent of the best television thrillers. Walcott is clearly horrified by his view of what will happen to the 'innocents'. He longs to be able to help them to escape, before it is too late, by swerving his car up onto the verge and using it as a getaway vehicle. He brings together the two separate strands of images, the children and the moths, in order to convey the essential fragility and vulnerability of these young communicants. So the children become moths. His repetition of 'delicately' as he guides the child-moths into his car conveys his care and concern for them. The image of his car filled with 'their blizzard' is visually spectacular but it also suggests that his enclosing of the child-moths is very different to the restraining force of their religion. For, as snowflakes swirl around in a blizzard, so the child-moths can fly within the car, gently and only temporarily restrained. Walcott's final image is breathtaking as we see him standing 'on some black hill' and releasing the child-moths to freedom. Their wings are 'undusted' and they 'stagger | heavenward', momentarily overwhelmed by it all. But Walcott has succeeded in enabling them to escape the 'darkness' that 'came on' their parents through their interactions with religion. He has saved them from 'the prejudice, the evil!'

THEME

Walcott takes a very strong position in this poem. Through his incredible imagery he conveys his pity and concern for the 'innocents' because they have embarked on a relationship with religion that, he feels, will lead to them being physically and intellectually restrained and 'blinded' by prejudice and evil.

IMAGERY

Walcott's use of imagery in his poetry is always exceptional. Many critics believe that this is because he is also a talented painter and playwright: they see his images as being visually memorable and dramatically realistic. Certainly, the imagery of this poem exhibits both of these qualities. But Walcott does more than simply paint word pictures or insert short scenes into his poetry.

He creates images that are infused with a poetic quality that enables him to convey their very essence. Thus, the structure, sounds and rhythm of his words play a vital role. An excellent example of this is line 19: 'their pulsing wings undusted, loose them in thousands to stagger'.

First, the longer length of this line reflects the image of the thousands of child-moths fluttering upwards into the dusky sky. Second, Walcott's brilliant use of assonance with his repetition of the broad vowel u in the phrase 'pulsing wings undusted' conveys the idea of the thin little moth wings (note the narrow 'i') unfolding and spreading out. Similarly, the alliteration of the th sound in 'them in thousands' serves to emphasise the huge numbers of the child-moths. In this way, we not only read Walcott's description, we feel and understand it as if we were there.

Walcott also uses his ability to marry the visual, the dramatic and the poetic to communicate extremely complex and abstract ideas in immensely accessible and memorable ways, as in line 6: 'The caterpillar's accordion, still pumping out the myth'. The metaphor of the 'caterpillar' and the 'accordion' being used to represent a fundamental feature of religion is irreverently amusing. However, the 'accordion' dramatically portrays the repetitive squeezing movement of a caterpillar as it moves along a branch. Along with the steady rhythm of the phrase 'still pumping out that myth' this line vividly suggests the mechanical quality that Walcott sees as being inherent in the production and dissemination of religious teachings.

Pentecost

Text of poem: New Explorations Anthology page 339

BACKGROUND NOTE

As we have seen in the discussion of Walcott's life and development as a poet, one of his main aims is to construct a language that will uniquely speak of and for the West Indian experience. In his Nobel lecture he described his work in this area as 'this process of renaming, of finding new metaphors'. Walcott sees this language as a positive and unifying force drawing together the disparate peoples and cultures of the region. Furthermore, this 'renaming' also involves a transforming action in that it aims to reveal the extraordinary in the ordinary so that the commonplace becomes elevated into something special. On occasions, Walcott has used Pentecost to represent these aims. Pentecost commemorates how, ten days after Jesus ascended into heaven, the disciples gathered in Jerusalem and the Holy Ghost came to them in the form of tongues of fire resting over their heads. They began to preach the gospel and they were able to speak in the language of the person who was listening to them.

STRUCTURE

Walcott is determinedly open to literary influences because he feels that such an openness provides the best foundation for developing one's own writing style. In this poem, Walcott uses the modernist 'stream of consciousness' technique. This means that the poet tries to retain the immediacy and energy of the way his thoughts and feelings blend and merge within him. This can prove to be both the pleasure and the pain of modernist poetry. Sometimes the connections between the images mesh and we, as readers, experience an insightful understanding of what it is that the poet seeks to convey. But there are occasions when, try as we might, the links remain unclear and all that we are left with is a feeling of bewilderment. Although modernists do accept bewilderment as a valid response, in such instances it is often helpful to simply allow the images to float around inside your head until the link reveals itself.

In this poem, it seems to me that Walcott is considering the theme of 'trying to find the right way', possibly in connection with writing his poetry. He conveys this complex and abstract concept by using accessible and familiar imagery. Thus, he begins the poem by declaring that it is better to have a 'jungle in the head than rootless concrete'. The lush living density of the jungle could be seen as representing a confusion of vibrant ideas and connected influences. In contrast, the concrete may represent a much more ordered state but it is 'rootless' because it has no life and is not connected to anything. Perhaps Walcott could be thinking about his role as a writer. He may feel that it is better, although it makes his task more difficult, that he has allowed his writing to acknowledge the confused and often brutal past of the West Indies rather than covering over that past by either ignoring or rejecting parts of it. In a similar way, it is better to 'stand bewildered' in the face of the unpredictable and confusing light patterns of 'the fireflies' because they represent how real life can often be unpredictable and confusing, rather than be guided by unnaturally still and steady 'winter lamps'. Walcott then introduces the image of a language that is cold and unable to communicate. So we have the 'tongues of snow' that, unlike the tongues of fire, are unable to speak 'for the Holy Ghost'. This refers back to the poem's title, 'Pentecost'. He also presents a wonderfully vivid image of words falling off roofs like lumps of ice:

> the self-increasing silence
> of words dropped from a roof

However, this cold and lifeless language does indicate a 'direction' for him, in that it shows him the type of language that he does not want to create.

In the final eight lines he describes what does help him to find his way: the 'night surf' and the 'scriptures of sand'. There are obvious echoes of St Lucia in the words 'surf' and 'sand', and Walcott has always linked his literary inspiration to the geography of the West Indies. Indeed, the way in which he uses these terms, normally linked to heat and sun, to describe the snow falling establishes a vivid connection between this wintry environment and his native home. This has the effect of elevating the ordinary in both situations into the realms of the extraordinary because we see the images in a completely new way. Another connection is established between the two places with the appearance of 'a late cormorant', a bird found in the West Indies. There is a touch of dry humour in Walcott's comment that it is 'not quite a seraph', for he is all too aware that he does not inhabit the biblical world of Pentecost where angels of the Lord appear. Brilliantly, Walcott describes the cormorant, normally found on shorelines waiting to feed on shoals of fish, flying above a glowing 'phosphorescent shoal' of snowflakes. It is the cry of this bird, the memory of his island home, that calls up a response in Walcott's soul. He has now found his way and can now sit and write in a language of his own.

From Omeros *Chapter XXX*
Text of poem: New Explorations Anthology page 342

BACKGROUND NOTE

This is the poem that helped Walcott win the Nobel Prize in Literature in 1992. It was described as 'a majestic Caribbean epos in 64 chapters . . . a work of incomparable ambitiousness'. *Omeros* is indeed ambitious: Walcott set about writing it in order to define and assert what it is to be West Indian. The brutal history of the region had interrupted the natural development of the culture with the massacre of the indigenous natives, the importation of slaves from Africa and of indentured servants from India. In addition, the presence of a colonial power led to the imposition of an alien culture. Consequently, when the West Indies gained independence, the essence of what made the West Indies distinct and unique had to be addressed. Walcott understood that unless this question was answered the West Indies would be unable to move forward in a united and positive way. But it was a daunting task. Milton commented on his great epic *Paradise Lost* that he had written of 'things unattempted yet in prose or rhyme'. So it was with Walcott, who was working in a cultural vacuum, with no history of West Indian literature to provide him with a reference point or indication of direction. He chose the only poetic form that would enable him to deal with such complex and demanding issues: the epic poem. Traditionally, the epic poem has been seen as a form that expresses essential truths about the society for which it is written. Walcott felt that there were many similarities between the Caribbean region and Homer's world of ancient Greece:

> In terms of *Omeros,* I felt totally natural, without making it an academic exercise or some justification or an elevation of St Lucians into Greeks . . . because of the harbours of the Caribbean, the work of the people in the Caribbean, the light of the Caribbean . . . that sense of elation you get in the morning, of the possibility that is always there, and of the width of the ocean . . .

As the title of the poem indicates, there are connections between Walcott's epic and the work of the classical Greek writer Homer. Perhaps the most obvious links are Walcott's use of the Homeric names Achille, Philoctete and Helen, and the centrality of a sea journey. But Walcott is adamant that his epic is not simply an imitation of Homer's *Odyssey*. As a great lover of Irish literature, he is all too aware that James Joyce's *Ulysses* has already set an incredibly innovative and exceptionally successful literary precedent in this respect. Quite simply, as Walcott points out in his essay 'Reflections on *Omeros*':

> *The Odyssey* is the story of some man who wandered around, and the story of wandering is the classical epic. Epic is about wandering in search of something and finding (or not finding) it . . . For Achille, the journey is back in time, to find out his name . . .

Thus, what Walcott does in *Omeros* is what we have seen him do in a number of his other much smaller-scale poems. He takes a recognised literary form, in this case the epic, and pushes back the boundaries by infusing it with his own unique West Indian culture, history and language. Thus, it takes on a universality that transcends time and space so that it becomes not merely a new and great piece of West Indian epic poetry but a new and great piece of epic poetry for the world.

A READING OF THE POEM

This extract is an excellent illustration of Walcott's aim, discussed in the consideration of his life and poetic development, to weave together the two languages of his island, English and Creole, in such a way that each retains its true tone. In this way, neither language is given precedence but instead they interact in a skilfully crafted relationship to expand and enrich the quality and depth of the poetic expression. Walcott opens this extract using standard English to convey a beautifully vivid image of the early morning: 'He yawned and watched the lilac horns of his island | lift the horizon.' This is quickly balanced by the mate's Creole: 'I know you ain't like to talk'.

Together, these lines convey something of the true essence of this uniquely West Indian scene. The extract continues in this way, but Walcott controls the interaction of the two carefully so that we, the readers, move easily from one to the other without being distracted by the changes in language. Thus, in lines 8–9 we register the humour of the image rather than the dialect in which it is written: 'The mate held up his T-shirt, mainly a red hole, | and wriggled it on.'

Furthermore, Walcott's use of Creole rhythms and words when Achille and the mate are speaking, alongside significant pieces of information about them, expressed in standard English, convey a strong sense that these men are real 'flesh and blood' human beings. He manages this linguistic blending so beautifully that it enables us, the readers, to engage more fully with the mate and Achille, to understand the essence of their complex humanity. So the tough, strong mate who fights hard to land 'One *mako* size "ton"' and stays awake all night on watch, reveals a genuine affection for and loyalty to his captain, Achille:

'Africa, right! You get sunstroke chief. That is all.

You best put that damn captain-cap back on your head.'
All night he had worked the rods without any sleep,
watching Achille cradled in the bow . . .

but he owed it to his captain, who took him on

when he was stale-drunk.

Achille, Walcott's 'hero', represents the West Indian people as he searches for his name, his history and his true home. He, like the nation itself, needs to establish a sense of identity. But Walcott does more than present us with a cardboard cut-out, emblematic figure. At the beginning of the passage Achille appears to be rather gruff and uncommunicative, reacting in monosyllables, or with silence, to the mate's comments. The mate even says 'I know you ain't like to talk'. But the one word he does speak, 'Africa', is significant because it reveals how he is trying to reconcile himself with the brutal dislocation of his own past, this past that he shares with the rest of his nation. Gradually, we begin to see Achille's vulnerability as he struggles with this act of reconciliation: 'Achille had slept through the fight. Cradled at the bow I like a foetus, like a sea-horse'.

In spite of his heroic role, Achille is trapped in an unfinished state because of the history of his region. It is hard not to be moved by the image of this 'captain' curled 'like a sea-horse' at the bow of the ship. So, when Achille feels his spirits rise in response to the 'black magnificent frigate', we are fully there with him. He celebrates the power that the bird embodies because he sees it as symbolising the dignity that is inherent in his own spirit and history; that dignity that had for so long been denied to him, and the West Indian people:

'Them stupid gulls does fish
for him every morning. He himself don't catch none,

white slaves for a black king.'

As he watches the bird, Achille finally achieves a sense of reconciliation and peace:

'The black bugger beautiful

though!' The mate nodded, and Achille felt the phrase lift

his heart as high as the bird . . .

He is able to accept his history, and in doing so he can release it and allow his African ancestor to return to Africa, where he belongs:

'The king going home,' he said as he and the mate
watched the frigate steer into that immensity
of seraphic space whose cumuli were a gate
dividing for a monarch entering his city.

In the face of such purity and intensity of expression we can only celebrate Achille's triumph on behalf of the West Indies, and Walcott's genius. The question of Creole or standard English seems unimportant.

It is not only the people of the West Indies who Walcott wishes to represent with dignity in *Omeros*. In his essay 'Reflections on *Omeros*' he explains: '. . . what I was trying to do was express my gratitude for the island -- for the people of the island, the beauty of the island.'

As was discussed in the note 'Landscape and Nature in Walcott's Poetry' (under 'Summer Elegies', above), Walcott wants to elevate the natural flora and fauna of his island in his writing so that they are considered equal to the flora and fauna celebrated in English literature. In this way, he is further representing the importance and worth of the West Indian region, which the literature of the coloniser had tried to diminish. In an interview in 1978, he explained his position:

'. . . sculpturally a breadfruit is infinitely more interesting as a shape than, say, a cantaloupe. But the colonial looking at it, having been taught that there's a literature that talks about the cantaloupe, the melon, the apple, the peach, knows there's no poem about breadfruit. Then you begin to feel, well, despite the fact that this particular fruit sculpturally is more interesting, it carries with it an inferior kind of association.

Consequently, in this extract from *Omeros* we meet wonderfully vivid descriptions of the kingfish and the man-o'-war. Walcott applies all his ability to convey the magnificence of these creatures. So the kingfish lies before us:

gaping,
its blue flakes yielding the oceanic colour

of the steel-cold depth from which it had shot, leaping'

while the man-o'-war flies above us,

tracing the herring-gulls with that endless gliding
that made it the sea-king.

In an interview with Hilton Ales, printed in the *New Yorker*, reference is made to Walcott's explanation for his empathy with the epic form:

I come from a place that likes grandeur. It likes large gesture; it is not inhibited by flourish; it is a society of physical performance; it is a society of style.

With *Omeros*, Walcott has enabled us all to share in that grandeur and style.

An overview of selected themes and aspects of Derek Walcott's poetry

DEATH
A Letter from Brooklyn
For Adrian
The Young Wife

LOVE
A Letter from Brooklyn
To Norline
Summer Elegies
For Adrian
The Young Wife

FAITH AND RELIGION
A Letter from Brooklyn
For Adrian
The Young Wife
Saint Lucia's First Communion

CREATIVITY
A Letter from Brooklyn

Endings
Pentecost

CELEBRATING THE WEST INDIES

The Sailor Sings Back to the Casuarinas (from The Schooner *Flight*)
To Norline
Summer Elegies
From *Omeros*

WALCOTT'S WEST INDIAN LANGUAGE OF POETIC EXPRESSION

The Sailor Sings Back to the Casuarinas (from The Schooner *Flight*)
From *Omeros*

VIVID IMAGERY

A Letter from Brooklyn
Endings
The Sailor Sings Back to the Casuarinas (from The Schooner *Flight*)
To Norline
Summer Elegies
For Adrian
The Young Wife
Saint Lucia's First Communion
Pentecost
From *Omeros*

USE OF TRADITIONAL LITERARY FORMS

The elegy:
    A Letter from Brooklyn
    For Adrian
    The Young Wife
The lyric:
    To Norline
    Summer Elegies
    Saint Lucia's First Communion
The epic:
    From *Omeros*

'STREAM OF CONSCIOUSNESS' TECHNIQUE

Endings
Pentecost

USE OF MUSICAL LANGUAGE

Endings
To Norline
Summer Elegies
For Adrian

Questions

1. Read 'Summer Elegies' and answer the following questions:
    1. (a) What, in your view, do we learn about the beach from reading this poem? Support your answer by reference to the text.
       (b) 'Time lent us the whole island.' What does this tell you about the way that Walcott and Cynthia felt about each other?
       (c) Write out the phrase or line from the poem that particularly appeals to you and explain what you especially like about it.
    2. Answer ONE of the following:
       (a) Imagine that you have been asked to write a short piece for a holiday brochure promoting this beach as a holiday destination. Write the piece making use of some of the details from the poem.

            OR

       (b) Explain how the poet's attitude to the beach changes as he grows up. Refer to the words of the poem in your answer.

            OR

       (c) Do you like this poem? Give reasons for your answer.

2. Read 'Norline' and answer the following questions:
    1. (a) How does the poet show us that this is a very special moment for him? Support your answer by reference to the poem.
       (b) Write out one phrase or line from the poem that you particularly like and explain why it appeals to you.
       (c) What picture of the beach do you get from this poem? Refer to the poem to support your answer.
    2. Answer ONE of the following:
       (a) Imagine that you are Norline and Walcott has just given you this poem. Write out what you would say to him.

            OR

       (b) You have been asked to choose a poem to be included in a collection of poems called A Perfect Moment. Explain why you would or would not recommend this poem.

            OR

(c) You want to make a short film of this poem. Describe the sort of atmosphere you would like to create, and say what music, sound effects and images you would use.

3. Read 'The Young Wife' and answer the following questions:

   1. (a) What impression does the poet give us of the husband's reaction to his wife's death? Refer to the poem in your answer.

      (b) Are you surprised by the description of the behaviour of the children in the last two stanzas? Give reasons for your answer.

      (c) Here are some phrases that might describe the young wife:
      - she had great courage
      - she was a very loving person
      - she was a happy person.

      Explain which one is closest to your impression of her.

   2. Answer ONE of the following:

      (a) Imagine that the husband writes a short tribute to his wife to be carved on her tombstone. Suggest what he would write and explain your suggestion.

      OR

      (b) In your opinion, is this a happy or a sad poem? Refer to the poem in your answer.

      OR

      (c) Imagine that you have been asked to provide music that would accompany a reading of this poem. Describe the kinds of music that you would choose and explain your choice by referring to the words and ideas in the poem.

4. 'Derek Walcott's poetry is a vibrant combination of vivid images and intense emotions.' Discuss this statement, with reference to **at least five poems** by Walcott.

5. 'For Derek Walcott language is both the means of expressing his brilliant poetic abilities and a significant theme in his poetry.' Respond to this statement with reference to the poetry by Walcott that you have studied.

6. 'Derek Walcott takes both traditional and modern poetic forms and techniques and makes them uniquely his own.' Write out the text of a talk that you would give to your class in which you discuss and illustrate this statement.

7. 'Landscape is more than simply a backdrop to Derek Walcott's poetry, it is both a theme and a source of creative inspiration.' Write an essay in response to this statement, quoting from or referring to a selection of Walcott's poems.

8. Write an introduction to the poetry of Derek Walcott for new readers. Refer to the poems by Walcott that you have studied.

9. 'Although Derek Walcott writes of a place far away from Ireland, he still has a great deal to say to present-day Irish readers.' Write out the text of an article that you would submit to a journal in response to this statement. Support your response by quoting from, or referring to, the poetry on your course.
10. *Dear Derek Walcott . . .*
Write a letter to Derek Walcott telling him about your experience of studying his poetry. Use references or quotations from the poems that you have studied to support the points that you make.

Bibliography

Bobb, June D., *Beating a Restless Drum*, New Jersey: Africa World Press Inc. 1998.

Brown, Stewart (editor), *The Art of Derek Walcott*, Wales: Seren Books 1991.

Callahan, Lance, *In the Shadows of Divine Perfection*, New York: Routledge 2003.

Davis, Gregson (editor), 'The Poetics of Derek Walcott: Intertextual Perspectives', *South Atlantic Quarterly*, vol. 96, no. 2, Spring 1997.

Fumagalli, Maria Cristina, *The Flight of the Vernacular*, New York: Rodopi 2001.

King, Bruce, *Derek Walcott: A Caribbean Life*, Oxford: Oxford University Press 2000.

O'Reilly, Christopher, *Post-Colonial Literature*, Cambridge: Cambridge University Press 2005.

Pollard, Charles W., *New World Modernisms*, Charlottesville: University of Virginia Press 2004.

Schmidt, Michael, *Lives of the Poets*, London: Phoenix 1999.

Terada, Rei, *Derek Walcott's Poetry: American Mimicry*, Boston: Northeastern University Press 1992.

Thieme, John, *Derek Walcott*, Manchester: Manchester University Press 1999.

Walcott, Derek, *Another Life*, London: Jonathan Cape 1973.

7 *Michael* LONGLEY

John G. Fahy

Life and writings

Michael Longley was born in Belfast on 27 July 1939, of English parents. His father, Richard – who features in the poems 'Wounds', 'Wreaths' and 'Last Requests' from this selection – fought in the First World War and was gassed, wounded, decorated, and promoted to the rank of captain. Between the wars the Longleys moved to Belfast, where Richard was a commercial traveller for an English firm of furniture manufacturers. He enlisted again in the Second World War, ending with the rank of major.

In *Tuppenny Stung,* a short collection of autobiographical chapters, you can read of Michael Longley's childhood: of his twin brother, Peter, and older sister, Wendy; of his ingenious and versatile war-veteran father ('that rare thing, an Englishman accepted and trusted by Ulstermen'); of his crippled and temperamental mother ('It has taken me a long time to forgive her that atmosphere of uncertainty, its anxieties, even fears'); of his irrepressible English grandfather, 'Grandpa George'; and the usual menagerie of eccentric relatives we all accumulate. You can read of his primary and secondary education and the forces on his early cultural formation: Protestant schoolboy fears of the dark savageries supposedly practised by Catholics; an English education system dismissive of Irish culture and history; Protestant Belfast's fear and resentment of the Republic. His early education and local socialisation made him aware of conflicting classes and religions and of the duality of Irish identity.

Later he was educated at the Royal Belfast Academical Institution and in 1958 went to Trinity College, Dublin, where the student population at that time consisted in the main of Southern and Northern Protestants, middle- and upper-class English, and a scattering of Southern Catholics who defied the Catholic Church's ban on attendance. Longley studied classics and wrote poetry but felt very under-read in English literature until taken in hand by his friend and young fellow-poet Derek Mahon:

> We inhaled with our untipped Sweet Afton cigarettes MacNeice, Crane, Dylan Thomas, Yeats, Larkin, Lawrence, Graves, Ted Hughes, Stevens, Cummings, Richard Wilbur, Robert Lowell, as well as Rimbaud, Baudelaire, Brecht, Rilke – higgledepiggledy, in any order. We scanned the journals and newspapers for poems written yesterday. When

Larkin's 'The Whitsun Weddings' first appeared in *Encounter*, Mahon steered me past the documentary details, which as an aspiring lyricist I found irritating, to the poem's resonant, transcendental moments. He introduced me to George Herbert who thrilled me as though he were a brilliant contemporary published that very week by the Dolmen Press. Herbert, thanks to Mahon, is a beneficent influence in my first collection and provides the stanzaic templates for two of its more ambitious poems.

Longley first worked as a teacher in Dublin, London and Belfast. From 1964 he was one of the group of young writers fostered by Philip Hobsbaum at Queen's University, though Longley felt that his poetry didn't fit in particularly well.

From the beginning Hobsbaum made it clear that his stars were Séamus Heaney and Stewart Parker, who was teaching in the States at this time. Hobsbaum's aesthetic demanded gritty particularity and unrhetorical utterance. Heaney's work fitted the bill especially well: at the second or third meeting which I attended a sheet of his poems was discussed – 'Digging' and 'Death of a Naturalist' (it was called 'End of a Naturalist' then).

By this time I was beginning to enjoy what was for me as a lapsed Classicist a new experience – practical criticism. But I didn't much care for the Group aesthetic or, to be honest, the average poem which won approval. I believed that poetry should be polished, metrical and rhymed; oblique rather than head-on; imagistic and symbolic rather than rawly factual, rhetorical rather than documentary. I felt like a Paleface among a tribe of Redskins. Although I have since modified my ideas, I still think that despite the rigours of practical criticism and the kitchen heat of the discussions, many Group poems tended to be underdone.

Longley worked for the Arts Council of Northern Ireland between 1970 and 1991, when he took early retirement. His work for the arts was driven by a number of guiding principles, among which were the nurturing of indigenous talent (he used to ask, 'How much of what we are doing differentiates us from Bolton or Wolverhampton?'), support for the artists, not just the arts, and the need to transcend class barriers and bring the arts, at an affordable price, to the working class.

He was always a champion of cultural pluralism, fostering the artistic expression of both sides of the religious and political divide. In fact the first event Longley organised for the Arts Council was 'The Planter and the Gael', a poetry-reading tour by John Hewitt and John Montague, in which each poet read poems exploring his particular experience of Ulster. So it was not surprising that Longley should be invited to join the Cultural Traditions Group at its launch in 1988. Its aims are, as he has written, 'to encourage in Northern

Ireland the acceptance and understanding of cultural diversity; to replace political belligerence with cultural pride'.

His vision of Ulster culture has always sought to include its many different strands and influences and so encourage a unique hybrid rather than separate, antagonistic cultures. As he has said elsewhere, 'Imaginative Ulstermen (and by extension, Irishmen) could be the beneficiaries of a unique cultural confluence which embraces the qualities of the Irish, the Scottish, the English and the Anglo-Irish' (quoted by Michael Parker).

Longley fostered a great range and diversity of artists, from traditional singers and fiddlers to painters, photographers and drama groups. For the last nine years of his career with the Arts Council he was combined arts director, overseeing traditional arts, youth arts and community arts, while concentrating on his chief preoccupation, literature. Here he directed Arts Council money towards publication, attempting to ensure that as many writers as possible got into print.

Michael Longley is a fellow of the Royal Society of Literature and a member of Aosdána. He is married to the critic and academic Edna Longley.

No Continuity City (1969), Longley's first volume, is known for its technically accomplished and learned poetry. Among its concerns are poets and poetry and nature, but it is best known for the learned, witty and sophisticated love poetry, almost in the metaphysical tradition. *An Exploded View* (1973) continues to deal with poetry and poetic issues. Nature is also a preoccupation. 'Badger' is from this volume. This book does respond briefly to the upsurge of violence around this time; in 'Wounds' the violence is seen from the broad perspective of international conflict. A great number of the poems focus on an alternative life in the west of Ireland; 'Carrigskeewaun' and 'Poteen' are among these. This attachment of Longley's for County Mayo also forms the focus of his third volume, *Man Lying on a Wall* (1976).

The Echo Gate (1979) demonstrates Longley's now established bifocal view: on Belfast and Mayo. He confronts the political violence in its stark, everyday settings in 'Wreaths' and explores the war experiences of his father as a perspective on this violence in 'Last Requests'. He also explores the folklore, ethos and culture of the west of Ireland and finds a bleak, unconscious parallel between its crude violence and that of Belfast in 'Self-Heal'.

Gorse Fires (1991) is centred on Longley's adopted second home of Carrigskeewaun in County Mayo. But it also includes poems on the Holocaust, the Second World War and the Spanish Civil War. Interspersed with these are some free translations from Homer's *Odyssey*, focusing on Odysseus's return to his home and interpreted by some critics as having strong if oblique references to Longley's own home province. 'Laertes' is from this sequence.

In *The Ghost Orchid* (1995) Longley continues to write perceptively and sensitively about the delicacy of nature: the long grasses by the lake like autumn lady's tresses; sandpipers; the sighting of otters and dolphins; birdsong; and of course the flowers that give the volume its title. These are not so much nature studies in the usual sense as intimate encounters that are shared with the reader in the style of a personal diary. And the locations are wide-ranging, from the west of Ireland to the stone gardens of Japan.

This volume not only celebrates the natural beauty of the world but also affirms the sexuality of life, whether manifested in nature's flowers or in artwork, from sheela-na-gigs to Japanese erotic art. A variety of styles of language is employed, ranging from the simplicity and precision of Haiku-style description to the phonic thunder of Ulster dialect.

In this volume also Longley continues with his very creative free translations, from the Roman love poet Ovid, from Virgil, and also from Homer. 'Ceasefire' is one of these, featuring the meeting between King Priam and Achilles at the end of Homer's *Iliad*.

Tuppenny Stung (1994) is a collection of autobiographical chapters, previously published in periodicals or delivered as lectures from 1972 to 1992.

POETRY COLLECTIONS

	In this selection
No Continuing City (1969)	
An Exploded View (1973)	'Badger'
	'Wounds'
	'Poteen'
	'Carrigskeewaun'
Man Lying on a Wall (1976)	
The Echo Gate (1979)	'Wreaths'
	'Last Requests'
	'Mayo Monologues 3: Self-Heal'
Gorse Fires (1991)	'An Amish Rug'
	'Laertes'
The Ghost Orchid (1995)	'Ceasefire'
Broken Dishes (1998)	

Badger

Text of poem: New Explorations Anthology page 380

A READING OF THE POEM

This nature poem celebrates that nocturnal woodland creature, the badger, but it also questions humankind's interference in nature.

The badger's legendary strength is evoked both in the descriptions ('the wedge of his body') and by his activities ('He excavates . . . into the depths of the hill'), which personify him as a muscular miner. There is a sense of uncompromising directness and dependability about his 'path straight and narrow' that contrasts with the deceptiveness of the fox and the giddiness of the hare. That ruggedness is also evident from his indiscriminate diet: he can cope with the poisonous dog's mercury and the tough brambles as well as the gentler bluebells.

But it is his relationship with the earth that is most interestingly portrayed. Longley sees the badger as a sort of horticulturalist: he 'manages the earth with his paws'; he facilitates the growth of great oak trees ('a heel revolving acorns'). The picture comes across of an animal at one with the earth, the caretaker of the hill, which in turn takes care of him in death. The animal's close association with prehistoric tombs lends him an even greater aura of significance. Somehow he becomes a symbol of the earth's ancientness, its longevity and mythological power. Longley himself has said that he thinks of animals as spirits. He tries to have an animal in each of his books.

The poem also deals with humankind's destructiveness and cruelty, our interference in the natural world. The poet's criticism of this is communicated through the bleak ironies of section III: digging out the digger, the bitter euphemism of this process being described as a forceps birth, the irony of being 'delivered' to his death:

> It is a difficult delivery
> once the tongs take hold.

There is sympathy for the 'vulnerable . . . pig's snout' and implicit condemnation of the brutal treatment ('his limbs dragging after them') and also of the environmental disturbance:

> So many stones turned over,
> The trees they tilted.

This treatment is in marked contrast to the badger's careful management of the earth, unaided by machines or 'tongs' of any kind! A clear environmental statement is made here, but it is subtly put across through the contrast rather than by any kind of didactic statement.

TONE

This is a tough, unsentimental poem, recording the perennial secret workings of nature. True, it does romanticise the badger somewhat:

> Night's silence around his shoulders,
> His face lit by the moon.

But it also records the violence, the suffering and the destruction of nature and creatures.

Behind that wealth of observed details and naturalist knowledge we can detect a tone of admiration for the animal's strength and its management of the woodland ('His path straight . . . not like the fox's zig-zags . . .') and we can certainly feel the poet's sympathy for the vulnerable animal in section III.

Wounds

Text of poem: New Explorations Anthology page 382
[*Note: this poem is also prescribed for Ordinary Level 2010 exam*]

BACKGROUND NOTE

In his autobiographical book *Tuppenny Stung,* Longley elaborates on his father's wartime experiences:

> Having lived through so much by the time he was thirty, perhaps my father deserved his early partial retirement. At the age of seventeen he had enlisted in 1914, one of thousands queuing up outside Buckingham Palace. He joined the London-Scottish by mistake and went into battle wearing an unwarranted kilt. A Lady from Hell. Like so many survivors he seldom talked about his experiences, reluctant to relive the nightmare. But not long before he died, we sat up late one night and he reminisced. He had won the Military Cross for knocking out single-handed a German machine-gun post and, later, the Royal Humane Society's medal for gallantry: he had saved two nurses from drowning. By the time he was twenty he had risen to the rank of Captain, in charge of a company known as 'Longley's Babies' because many of them were not yet regular shavers. He recalled the lice, the rats, the mud, the tedium, the terror. Yes, he had bayoneted men and still dreamed about a tubby little German who 'couldn't run fast enough. He turned around to face me and burst into tears.' My father was nicknamed Squib in the trenches. For the rest of his life no-one ever called him Richard.

A READING OF THE POEM

The figure of his father features prominently in Michael Longley's poetry. The father is graphically and sympathetically realised and the father–son bond asserted in such poems as 'In Memoriam', 'Wounds', 'Last Requests', and 'Laertes'.

The poet's relationship with his father in 'Wounds' is characterised by intimacy and tenderness. There is an intimacy about their style of communication. 'Two pictures from my father's head' suggests a perfect nonverbal understanding, which the poet has kept 'like secrets'. The caress is tender, repetitive and comforting: 'I touched his hand, his thin head I touched.' The father's sense of humour, even if a little grim, indicates the easiness of the relationship: 'I am dying for King and Country, slowly.' (This refers to the link between his final illness and the old war wounds; see 'In Memoriam': 'In my twentieth year your old wounds woke | As cancer.')

In these repeated father–son exchanges Longley is probing his own identity and defining his background. Much has been written about the supposed identity crisis of the Ulster Protestant writer, shakily situated between the conflicting claims of the English and Irish literary traditions and outlooks. As Terence Brown points out in another context, Longley is a lyric poet nurtured in the English and classical traditions 'attempting to come to terms with the fact that he was born in Ireland of an English father and that he now lives in a Belfast shaken almost nightly by the national question, violently actualised.' This family experience of immigration might be seen to mirror the experience of the Ulster Protestant as immigrant. We catch some of this confusion, this incomprehension of the local view in the father's bemused reaction to the Ulster soldiers' sectarian battle cries:

> 'wilder than Gurkhas' were my father's words
> of admiration and bewilderment.

He expresses admiration, presumably for their courage, but complete bewilderment at the sectarian sentiment. Something of the same bewilderment is evident in the poet's own reaction to present-day violence when he describes the murder of the bus conductor:

> . . . shot through the head
> By a shivering boy who wandered in
> Before they could turn the television down

The air of incomprehension, this slight sense of distance from local realities, which may be the inheritance of the immigrant, is shared by father and son.

In summary, the poet is establishing his identity as the son of a courageous English soldier. There is no direct discussion of an identity crisis, either literary or political; but we do register a sense of bewilderment, something of the outsider's air of detachment in the attitudes of both father and son towards Ulstermen at war.

Longley is using his father's First World War experiences as a perspective on present-day atrocities. Patricia Craig says that the violence of the trenches is 'brought up smack against the dingier violences of present-day Belfast'. Whether it is more or less dingy in the poet's eyes is debatable. The grotesqueness of the slaughter and the indignities of violent death are emphasised in both the world war and the present-day killings. The 'landscape of dead buttocks' that haunted his father for fifty years is hardly less bizarre than the recent image of

> Three teenage soldiers, bellies full of
> Bullets and Irish beer, their flies undone.

What is different and shocking about the portrayal of modern violence in the poem is its invasion of the domestic scene:

> Before they could turn the television down
> Or tidy away the supper dishes.

It is casual, perpetrated by a boy who 'wandered in'. The shocking ordinariness of the violence is underlined by the ridiculous apology, 'Sorry, missus.' It is as if he had just bumped into her in the street. Death is delivered to your home with a casual, polite apology.

ISSUES RAISED IN THE POEM

Longley's sense of identity
- The poet is defining himself by describing his family background.
- The English military background is an important and accepted facet of the poet's identity.
- The sensitive and humorous portrait of his father communicates an easy and tender father–son relationship.
- The importance of that father-figure generally in the poet's life: the long-dead man is still a powerful reality.
- The violent city is part of his identity also.

Violence
- The 'wounds' of the title refers to old war wounds, lingering psychological wounds (haunting images), and new wounds.
- The universality of killing: the world of the poem is a world of violence, whether legitimised as war or condemned as illegal. Does the poem differentiate between war violence and present-day atrocities?
- The less-than-glorious reality of war
- The indignity of violent death
- The increasing ordinariness of violence: terror at the heart of the domestic scene
- The wanton nature of present-day violence.

Tone
The opening is conversational, personal. The speaker is sharing a confidence, inviting us in: 'Here are two pictures . . . secrets.' There is evidence of a certain wry humour, which successfully deflates any possible attempt at glorifying either

his father or the war ('I am dying for King and Country, slowly'; 'A packet of Woodbines I throw in, | A lucifer').

Is there a note of critical irony detectable in the parson's fussiness about dress in the face of death, and a hint of religious cynicism in the apparent indifference of God to human suffering and evil ('the Sacred Heart of Jesus | Paralysed')? The emotional impact is frequently disguised behind the relentless listing of details, but it is there, for example in 'heavy guns put out | The night-light in a nursery for ever'. And the understatement of the last line packs quite an emotional punch.

Visual impact

This particularly visual style relies heavily on Longley's eye for incongruous details, such as the sectarian battle-cries as the soldiers go over the top; the chaplain with the stylish backhand; the domestic details of the three teenage soldiers, lured to their deaths by the promise of sex; the bus conductor who 'collapsed beside his carpet-slippers,' etc. And they all make the point about how brutally unglorious death is.

Poteen

Text of poem: New Explorations Anthology page 385

A READING OF THE POEM

The description of illicit whiskey-making turns into a statement about national identity. The primitive, superstitious act of 'one noggin-full | Sprinkled on the ground' as a sort of votive offering to the spirits opens up other atavistic echoes and race memories. It conjures up images of other illegal activities, rebel plottings, also carried on in remote bogland and similar inaccessible areas. Poitín-making becomes a symbol of historical Ireland, the Ireland of the dispossessed, of the rebel, with all the paraphernalia of secret societies, stored weapons, and furtive plottings (souterrains, sunk workshops, cudgels, guns, the informer's ear, blood-money).

So it becomes a poem about 'the back of the mind' (suppressed race memory), and the racial consciousness evoked is one of furtive living, blunt violence ('cudgels, guns'), and seamy betrayals ('the informer's ear'). It is not exactly an idealised picture, but rather a bleak and realistic psychological portrait where greed and romantic aspiration go hand in hand ('Blood money, treasure-trove').

Carrigskeewaun

Text of poem: New Explorations Anthology page 387

A READING OF THE POEM

We notice that Longley's view of County Mayo is certainly not the romanticised one of the tourist or holiday weekender, but more like the realistic perception of the native who sees the landscape in all its harshness and its beauty. He presents its arid face to us, a landscape of boulders and dry-stone walls, a harsh territory inimical to human and animals alike, the graveyard of many.

> This is ravens' territory, skulls, bones,
> The marrow of these boulders supervised
> From the upper air:

But he also presents the serene beauty of nature, in the image of the lake 'tilted to receive | The sun perfectly'. His interest is primarily in the physical landscape and the flora and fauna rather than in the people; in fact he seems to enjoy his solitary, Crusoe-like existence, dislodging mallards, discovering cattle tracks, etc., in this sparsely populated place.

He has a keen naturalist's eye, as we can see from his perceptive descriptions of the birds in 'The Path'. Kittiwakes 'scrape' the waves; mallards' necks 'strain' over the bog; and the 'gradual disdain' of the swans is captured. He understands both their movements and their psychology. And his treatment of them is gentle, as evidenced by the verbs used to describe his actions: 'dislodge', 'to nudge', etc. There is a sensitive and perceptive naturalist at work here.

For all the harshness of the scene, Longley is at ease with it. In a primitive and slightly crude way he shares a sense of identity with the people's forebears, who also 'squatted here | This lichened side of the dry-stone wall'. He feels that he is part of the life cycle of the place, part of the process of erosion, as when he notices the effect of his footprints in the strand:

> Linking the dunes to the water's edge,
> Reducing to sand the dry shells, the toe –
> And fingernail parings of the sea.

And he enjoys the atmosphere of serenity and acceptance in 'The Lake', as if he too were one of the 'special visitors'.

Family and the human community are but a shadowy presence here. Ghost-like memories of his children are conjured up ('my voice | Filling the district as I recall their names'), or they are registered merely as footprints in the sand. Images of family domesticity he carries in his head, as one might carry a photograph of loved ones:

Smoke from our turf fire
Recalls in the cool air above the lake
Steam from a kettle, a tablecloth and
A table she might have already set.

So, in some ways, the image of the poet here is the traditional romantic one of the figure alone in the landscape, communing with nature. Yet this poet's home and family are never far away, a constant presence in his mind. Peter McDonald sees Carrigskeewaun as Longley's home from home and says that here Longley is 'bringing one home into contact with another through naming the elements that are missing. Here, it is the family "home" that is named in the stern solitude of a mountain landscape.'

THEMES

- The poet's appreciation of this western landscape, its elemental harshness and its quiet welcoming beauty, its solitude, its abundance of wildlife, etc.
- An exploration of the relationship between humans and nature: the calm sense of belonging, etc.
- Yet an awareness that humankind is but a tiny part of the process of nature's cycle, helping to dispose of 'the dry shells, the toe | And fingernail parings of the sea.' This generates a sense of philosophical perspective.
- The love of family, children and domesticity that is somehow inspired by this wild place.

THE SIGNIFICANCE OF THE WEST OF IRELAND IN LONGLEY'S POETRY

Longley's preoccupation with the west of Ireland can be traced throughout his poetry. 'Carrigskeewaun' and 'Poteen' are from his second collection, *An Exploded View,* which contains poems from 1968 to 1972. So even as he was focusing on the erupting violence of the times (in such poems as 'Wounds') he was also contemplating an alternative. His attachment to the west grew as a result of long summers spent in County Mayo, and this is evident from Longley's third volume, *Man Lying on a Wall* (1976). And his fifth volume, *The Gorse Fires* (1991), is centrally focused on Carrigskeewaun, which had become his second home.

Critics have interpreted this fascination with the west in various ways. Terence Brown asks: 'Which is the poet's Ireland – Belfast or Mayo?' He believes this relates to the poet's confused sense of national identity, in attempting to be an Ulsterman and an Anglo-Irishman. Brown believes that the problem of confused identity 'can partially be solved in an identification with the Irish landscape'. And he notes how unusual 'Carrigskeewaun' is in Longley's work for the sense it creates of a person 'at ease with himself and his fellows'.

Peter McDonald takes a slightly different approach, regarding the west as an issue of perspective rather than identity. He feels that the west is in fact a way of undoing the settled nature of the poet's identity and that what it does is provide a new sense of perspective, an angle from which home can be reappraised, 'can be reapproached without the encoding of tribal claims to certain territories'.

Gerald Dawe argues that while Longley accepts his northern roots, the ties of family, home, class and country, he is also searching for an alternative, imagined ideal, 'a compensatory order to transcend these'. He says: 'For Longley, the west of Ireland is seen as an embodiment of some kind of alternative life, a fictional life that compensates for certain values and attitudes missing in the real, given, historical world . . . Longley itemises that vision into the simple sights of landscape and nature which, common to the west of Ireland, take on in his work a symbolic potency all of their own.'

What values and attitudes are embodied in 'Carrigskeewaun', and what is symbolised by the landscape? What values are missing from Longley's real, historical world?

Wreaths

Text of poem: New Explorations Anthology page 391

A READING OF THE POEM

In 'Wreaths' Longley deals directly with what is euphemistically described as the 'Troubles'. He describes the violent killings, in graphic detail, in their ordinary, everyday settings: a kitchen, a shop, the roadway. In each case his focus of attention is the human consequences of this violence, the loss of life, the deranged grief of relatives, or the psychological effect on the general population as it forces people to relive memories of family deaths.

'The Civil Servant' was written in memory of Martin McBirney QC, a lawyer and friend who was murdered by the IRA. This poem shows violence invading the heart of domestic life: the kitchen. It is the contrast between the ordinariness and intimacy of the setting and the incongruity of the violence that makes the greatest impact in this poem.

> He was preparing an Ulster fry for breakfast
> When someone walked into the kitchen and shot him . . .
> He lay in his dressing gown and pyjamas
> While they dusted the dresser for fingerprints

The language rhythms too record that incongruity. The prosaic, conversational rhythms of the first line leave us unprepared for the violence of lines 2 and 3.

The insignificance of life is recorded. It is regarded as of temporary and symbolic importance only, like the transitory outing of a red carpet, walked on and forgotten:

> They rolled him up like a red carpet and left
> Only a bullet hole in the cutlery drawer;

The emotional control of the narration adds to the strangeness of this piece. The killing is described in a matter-of-fact tone, in the neutral and precise language of a police witness ('A bullet entered his mouth and pierced his skull'). The loss is recorded in cultural terms only ('The books he had read, the music he could play'). The only indication of feeling comes in the disturbed actions of the widow, who 'took a hammer and chisel | And removed the black keys from his piano.' And even that is narrated in measured, controlled language: 'Later his widow . . . and removed . . .' It is this control of feeling that is one of the most chilling aspects of this poem.

Matter-of-fact descriptions and conversational rhythms of language also characterise the narration of 'The Greengrocer', written about a local shopkeeper, Jim Gibson. Yet the tone here is laced with a bleak irony:

> He ran a good shop, and he died
> Serving even the death-dealers
> Who found him busy as usual . . .

The ironic timing of the violence is emphasised. The Christmas wreaths, celebrating a birth, become his burial wreaths and also provide the general title for the pieces. We register the inappropriateness of this death amid the Christmas fare and the exotic fruit ('Dates and chestnuts and tangerines'). It is ironic too that the killing is overtly linked to the Christmas story ('Astrologers or three wise men'). Is there a bitterness towards the powerlessness of religion here?

'The Linen Workers', based on the Bessbrooke sectarian murders, has a more psychological focus, exploring how public political violence impinges on private thoughts and memories. Strangely, it is also the most personal of the three poems, written in the first person and dealing with the poet's personal memories.

The setting for the massacre of the linen workers is once again an ordinary everyday venue: the roadside. Death is seen as the scattering of the personal bric-a-brac of living:

> . . . spectacles,
> Wallets, small change, and a set of dentures:
> Blood, food particles, the bread, the wine.

While some of these images have symbolic value (for example the bread and wine, symbolic of self-sacrifice, renewal and eternal life), it is the set of dentures that resonates in the poet's mind, triggering bizarre memories of his dead father.

The effect is surreal: the Christ figure, like some giant hoarding, 'fastened for ever | By his exposed canines to a wintry sky' in a parody of the Crucifixion. The father, once a victim of world-war violence, is disinterred to witness the fruits of violence yet again ('Before I can bury my father once again | I must polish the spectacles . . . And into his dead mouth slip the set of teeth'). The images are of victims, religious and familial. Also we see the ubiquitous nature of violence, stretching through history, erupting in the modern community and reaching into the individual psyche, where it shakes up disturbing past and private memories.

THEMES

- The casual 'ordinariness' of violent death in the community
- The ubiquitous nature of violence, in kitchen, shop or street, in the mind
- Human insignificance in the face of violence ('The Civil Servant')
- The bitterness of unseasonal death ('The Greengrocer')
- The psychological effects of violence, reaching right through people's lives, invading the psyche, interlacing public horror and private memory ('The Linen Workers')
- The ineffectiveness of religion in the face of this onslaught ('The Greengrocer'; 'The Linen Workers').

IMAGERY

For the most part the images consist of background details of domestic living, of insignificant private possessions: an 'Ulster fry', dressing-gown, pyjamas, dresser, cutlery drawer, holly wreaths for Christmas, spectacles, etc. They evoke ordinariness, urban banality, and the insignificance of ordinary lives.

Details of the killings are restrained, devoid of horror or gory detail. They are either rendered in stark simplicity ('A bullet entered his mouth and pierced his skull') or conveyed in general terms ('he died,' 'they massacred'). The impact is always in the consequences, conveyed through the telling details, such as the pathetic list of personal bric-a-brac ('spectacles | Wallets, small change, and a set of dentures'). The surreal images of a gap-toothed Christ and a long-dead bespectacled father convey the psychological disturbance of violence.

TONE

The deadpan, largely unemotional tone of the narration, particularly in 'The Civil Servant' and 'The Greengrocer' (see 'A READING OF THE POEM' above), serves to emphasise the air of unreality and the incongruity of violent death in these everyday settings. 'The Linen Workers' is less controlled. For example, 'massacred' has overtones of horror and revulsion. In this poem there is more evidence of the poetic voice involved in the drama, commenting, not just recording details but interpreting also. 'Blood, food particles' are seen as 'the bread, the wine'.

But Longley does not approach this violence from any sectarian or political point of view, or indeed with any moral attitude. Certainly there is no sympathy for the violence, no attempt to explain or understand the killings. Neither is there outraged condemnation, just a patient recording of the facts. And through these facts, this list of intimate consequences, we see the pointlessness of the violence. Longley's slightly disengaged attitude and neutral tone allow the reader a clear view.

Last Requests

Text of poem: New Explorations Anthology page 394
[*This poem is also prescribed for Ordinary Level 2010 exam*]

A READING OF THE POEM

This poem focuses on death and once again on the death of his own father. The two parts are complementary, part I dealing with the father's earlier brush with death in the trenches and part II focusing on his actual death-bed scene. Perhaps the earlier scene is meant to serve as a comfort: he could have died so many years before.

The death-bed scene is treated with a mixture of pathos and humour. The sense of separation, the impenetrable distance of death is physically illustrated: 'I . . . Couldn't reach you through the oxygen tent.' The onlooker's feeling of helplessness and inadequacy is recorded in the wry comment by the poet: 'I who brought you peppermints and grapes only'. Yet there is humour occasioned by the speaker's misinterpretation of the father's hand movement. The poet needs to interpret it as a last romantic gesture, a kiss, whereas it signifies the dying man's more prosaic need for nicotine, like the need for that last sacramental cigarette before a battle. Perhaps this can be read as yet another sign of the separation wrought by death: a mental as well as a physical distance from loved ones.

Despite the humour, we are in no doubt of the effect of the scene on the poet. Every detail is etched into his mind: 'the bony fingers that waved to and fro'. The memories carry not only the gesture but the mood of the moment.

> The brand you chose to smoke for forty years
> Thoughtfully, each one like a sacrament.

There is real feeling here behind the façade of wit. The seamier side of war is also adverted to ('Your batman . . . Left you for dead and stole your pocket watch'). Once again Longley views military exploits with a jaundiced eye.

Mayo Monologues – Self-Heal

Text of poem: New Explorations Anthology page 396

CONTEXT OF THE POEM

This is one of the sequence of four poems – 'Brothers', 'Housekeeper', 'Self-Heal' and 'Arrest' – collectively entitled 'Mayo Monologues' from the volume *The Echo Gate* (1979). They deal with the pathetic and flawed relationships of some isolated and lonely people.

A READING OF THE POEM

The poem deals with the tragic consequences of an inherently flawed relationship between the young female narrator, a teacher, and a mentally retarded boy. At first the relationship was one of innocent education, centring on the communication of beauty.

> I wanted to teach him the names of flowers,
> Self-heal and centaury; on the long acre
> Where cattle never graze, bog asphodel.

But it is an unequal pairing, incompatible intellectually and physically, the delicacy of the flowers contrasting strangely with the grotesque figure of the boy-man whose 'skull seemed to be hammered like a wedge | Into his shoulders, and his back was hunched, | Which gave him an almost scholarly air.'

The intellectual frustration is described in the natural image of the butterfly:

> Each name would hover above its flower
> like a butterfly unable to alight.

But the only delight he can comprehend and reach for is sexual. A community taboo is broken, and enormous and brutal consequences, out of all proportion to the deed, fall on him with the weight of a Greek tragedy, souring beauty and stunting humanity further. The savage treatment meted out to him unleashes a terrible savagery within himself.

THEMES

- A view of the dark undercurrents in rural society, involving sullied innocence, thwarted sexuality, ignorance and prejudice, and the crude violence and brutality just beneath the surface
- Insensitive treatment of the mentally retarded
- The almost insignificant origins of tragedy.

A POEM OF PRIMITIVE ENERGIES

This poem is highly charged with elemental human passions. The female narrator, exhibiting a dangerous innocence, was taking risks. Though innocent of any complicity, she is sensitive enough to question her motivation –

> Could I love someone so gone in the head
> And, as they say, was I leading him on?

– and, discounting what was a reasonable reaction on her part, she does not completely exonerate herself from her role in precipitating the consequences:

> I wasn't frightened; and still I don't know why,
> But I ran from him in tears to tell them.

So there is a traumatic, sexually charged moment, a sense of sullied innocence, and a hint of regret that perhaps things could have been handled differently.

We are confronted with the basic animal nature of humankind, lurking just beneath the surface; the unexpected sexual advance is later represented in animal imagery: 'I might have been the cow . . . and he the ram'. The primitive animal brutality, coupled with ignorance and lack of any tolerant insight into this condition, is shocking.

> He was flogged with a blackthorn, then tethered
> In the hayfield.

The belief that violence is effective begets a cycle of wanton cruelty: the cow's tail docked with shears and 'The ram tangled in barbed wire | That he stoned to death when they set him free.' And one cannot help but be overawed by the disproportionate nature of the consequences, as if one were viewing a world out of control.

AS A VIEW OF THE WEST OF IRELAND

The poem paints an unflattering picture of the dark undercurrents, the barely tamed savagery, the pain of ignorance and prejudice just beneath the surface of rural society.

TONE

Sympathy, revulsion and anger all swirl beneath the surface of this poem. Yet all feelings are controlled by Longley's matter-of-fact descriptions, by the quiet, conversational rhythms of the language and the balanced point of view of the narrator. The narrator herself is the victim of sexual advances, yet in many ways she is a detached and sympathetic observer. She both questions her own motives and understands the actions of the retarded man. So we are drawn in to sympathise with both parties. We understand her sense of regret and her bewilderment at it all: 'and still I don't know why, I But I ran . . .' We cannot help but be revolted by the brutality, narrated in matter-of-fact, unadorned language: 'He was flogged . . . tethered . . . dock with shears . . . the ram tangled . . . he stoned to death . . .'

But overall we register the deep irony of these events. A worthy desire to educate, enlighten and beautify has created instead a dark, brutal monster. And we note the irony of the title: the plant produces no healing properties on this occasion; there are no immortal flowers for his mind, or indeed for hers.

Longley relates these dark deeds not with condemnation and bitterness but with a quiet understanding that this is how things are.

RELEVANCE TO NORTHERN IRELAND?

Séamus Heaney's comment on this poem follows a psychological approach in Jungian terms and argues that poetry is the symbolic resolution of lived and felt conflict. He accepts that Longley had no deliberate notion of writing a poem relevant to the 'Troubles'; yet he suggests that the innocent and yet not quite detached female voice in the poem might be the voice of poetry, understanding the victim and the violence and embellishing it with her vision. This is the role of the poet in a violent society; this is how the poet deals with the conflict.

> So she might be an analogue for the action of the poetic imagination as we have been considering it: by comprehending and expressing the violent reactions of the victim in relation to the violent mores of the community, by taking all this into herself and embalming it with flowers and memory, she turns a dirty deed into a vision of reality.

The action of poetry, he says,

> is a self-healing process, neither deliberately provocative nor culpably detached.

An Amish Rug

Text of poem: New Explorations Anthology page 398
[Note: This poem is also prescribed for Ordinary Level 2010 exam]

A READING OF THE POEM

The Amish rug, a gift from the speaker to his lover, carries with it his memories of that culture and community and so enriches the poet's life and love.

The Amish experience of the world is deliberately limited ('a one-room schoolhouse') and calls for simplicity and lack of adornment ('as if . . . our clothes were black, our underclothes black'). Mechanisation and industrialisation are avoided ('boy behind the harrow,' etc.) and marriage is signified by its religious element and its simplicity rather than any ostentation ('Marriage a horse and buggy going to church'). Children are a natural, elemental part of the landscape ('silhouettes in a snowy field'). The predominant black-and-white colouring emphasises the simplicity of the culture and the uncompromising nature of the moral values.

The rug, symbol of cultural encounter, and very different from indigenous Amish artefacts, yet transmits the Amish values of naturalness and religious belief. Its colours are described in images from nature, 'cantaloupe and cherry'. Depending on its placing in the room it can be either 'a cathedral window' or 'a flowerbed'. The unspoken wish seems to be that it may bring something of its natural beauty into their lives.

This is a love poem of great charm and elegance. The lover's gift is a simple patchwork quilt. The lovers' desire is for a simple life and uninhibited naturalness in their relationship:

> So that whenever we undress for sleep or love
> We shall step over it as over a flowerbed.

Laertes
Text of poem: New Explorations Anthology page 400

BACKGROUND NOTE

This poem is based on an episode from Homer's Greek epic poem 'The Odyssey'. Odysseus, king of the island of Ithaca and one of the Greek heroes of the Trojan war, was for ten years prevented from returning home, blown hither and thither by the storms of Poseidon. Many in Ithaca presumed him dead. Suitors seeking to marry his faithful wife, Penelope, gathered at his palace and wasted his estate in continuous feasting.

Odysseus returned, disguised to all at first except to his son, Telemachus, and killed all the suitors in a great and bloody slaughter. As these were the sons of local princes and prominent nobles, there were likely to be repercussions. Before facing these, Odysseus slipped out to the hill country to visit his father, Laertes, who had retired to his vineyards. And this is where the poem is set.

Longley rendered a number of episodes from the *Odyssey* in a fairly free translation, as he explained in the notes with *Gorse Fires*:

> In differing proportions and with varying degrees of high-handedness but always, I hope, with reverence, I have in seven of these poems combined free translation from Homer's 'Odyssey' with original lines.

A READING OF THE POEM

Here Longley returns to his recurring theme of father–son relationships, this time in the classical context of Homer's *Odyssey*. The poem offers interesting psychological insights into the roles people fulfil in a relationship and how these roles alter over time. Odysseus's memories of his childhood centre on a dependent, persistently questioning child–parent relationship, 'traipsing after his father | And asking for everything he saw'. Despite the fact that he now returns as the conquering hero, his first instinct is to revert to his child role and run to the parent for comfort, blurting out his tale. But now the roles have been reversed. The father is now a fragile old man ('So old and pathetic'), and the erstwhile child has become the protector and comforter:

> Who drew the old man fainting to his breast and held him there
> And cradled like driftwood the bones of his dwindling father.

Another interesting aspect of the encounter is the son's need to be recognised. The dramatic delaying tactic practised by Odysseus – the drawing out of the old man to see if he remembered – may seem pointlessly cruel to a modern reader. 'So he waited for images . . . Until Laertes recognised his son'. But, psychologically, Odysseus seems to need to be recognised, at least in the outward physical aspect. Perhaps this could be read at a deeper level also and seen to refer to the son's need for a father's recognition of his deeds, his achievements, his independent separate self. In Homer's original version, as we can see from the extract, old Laertes is made to undergo a more formal, rigorous testing, and so the recognition becomes highly significant.

The father–son relationship in this poem, as in the other Longley poems on the same theme, is emotional and tender:

> Odysseus sobbed in the shade of a pear-tree for his father
> So old and pathetic that all he wanted then and there
> Was to kiss him and hug him and blurt out the whole story,

The need for comfort, for emotional closeness, for recognition, for protection and the joy of meeting are at the heart of this father–son relationship.

The poem also makes a statement about home. Home here is a place of familial love, psychological and emotional support and affirmation. But, taking the broader context of the Homeric allusion into account, we cannot evade the awareness that home is also a place of strife and intrigue, civil wars and bloody retribution. And we can hardly avoid drawing parallels between the Homeric world of Ithaca and Northern Ireland. Perhaps this is the greatest value of the allusion. It allows Longley to contemplate the perplexing realities of background, obliquely and from a distance.

Odyssey

BOOK 24 (EXTRACT)

(Translated by E.V. Rieu)

When they reached the spot, Odysseus said to Telemachus and his men: 'Go into the main building now and make haste to kill the best pig you can find for our midday meal. Meanwhile I shall try an experiment with my father, to find out whether he will remember me and realise who it is when he sees me, or fail to know me after so long an absence.'

As he spoke, he handed his weapons of war to the servants, who then went straight into the house, while Odysseus moved off towards the luxuriant vineyard, intent on his experiment. As he made his way down into the great orchard he fell in neither with Dolius nor with any of the serfs or Dolius' sons, who had all gone with the old man at their head to gather stones for the vineyard wall. Thus he found his father alone on the vineyard terrace digging round a plant. He was wearing a filthy, patched and disreputable tunic, a pair of stitched leather gaiters strapped round his shins to protect them from scratches, and gloves to save his hands from the brambles; while to crown all, and by way of emphasising his misery, he had a hat of goatskin on his head. When the gallant Odysseus saw how old and worn his father looked and realised how miserable he was, he halted under a tall pear-tree and the tears came into his eyes. Nor could he make up his mind at once whether to hug and kiss his father, and tell him the whole story of his own return to Ithaca, or first to question him and find out what he thought. In the end he decided to start assuming a brusque manner in order to draw the old man out, and with this purpose in view he now went straight up to his father.

Laertes was still hoeing round his plant with his head down, as his famous son came up and accosted him.

'Old man,' said Odysseus, 'you have everything so tidy here that I can see there is little about gardening that you do not know. There is nothing, not a green thing in the whole enclosure, not a fig, olive, vine, pear or vegetable bed that does not show signs of your care. On the other hand I cannot help remarking, I hope without offence, that you don't look after yourself very well. In fact, what with your squalor and your wretched clothes, old age has hit you very hard. Yet it can't be on account of any laziness that your master neglects you, nor is there anything in your build and size to suggest the slave. You look more like a man of royal blood, the sort of person who enjoys the privilege of age, and sleeps on a soft bed when he has had his bath and dined. However, tell me whose serf you are. And whose is this garden you look after? The truth, if you please. And there's another point you can clear up for me. Am I really in Ithaca? A fellow I met on my way up here just now assured me that I was. But he was not very intelligent, for he wouldn't deign to answer me properly or listen to what I said, when I mentioned a friend of mine and asked him whether he was still in the land of the living or dead and gone by now. You shall learn about this friend yourself if you pay attention to what I say. Some time ago in my own country I befriended a stranger who turned up at our place and proved the most attractive visitor I have ever entertained from abroad. He said he was an Ithacan, and that Arceisius' son Laertes was his father. I took him in, made him thoroughly welcome and gave him every hospitality that my rich house could afford, including presents worthy of his rank. Seven talents of wrought gold he had from me, a solid silver wine-bowl with a floral design, twelve single-folded cloaks, twelve rugs, twelve splendid mantles and as many tunics too, and besides all this, four women as skilled in fine handicraft as they were good to look at. I let him choose them for himself.'

'Sir,' said his father to Odysseus, with tears on his cheeks, 'I can assure you that you're in the place you asked for but it's in the hands of rogues and criminals. The gifts you lavished on your friend were given in vain, though had you found him alive in Ithaca he would never have let you go before he had made you an ample return in presents and hospitality, as is right when such an example has been set. But pray tell me exactly how long ago it was that you befriended the unfortunate man, for the guest of yours was my unhappy son – if ever I had one – my son, who far from friends and home has been devoured by fishes in the sea or fallen prey, maybe, to the wild beasts and birds on land. Dead people have their dues, but not Odysseus. We had no chance, we two that brought him into the world, to wrap his body up and wail for him, nor had his richly dowered wife, constant Penelope, the chance to close her husband's eyes and give him on his bier the seemly tribute of a dirge.

'But you have made me curious about yourself. Who are you, sir? What is your native town? And where might she be moored, the good ship that brought you here with your gallant crew? Or were you travelling as a passenger on someone else's ship, which landed you and sailed away?'

'I am quite willing,' said the resourceful Odysseus, 'to tell you all you wish to know. I come from Alybas. My home is in the palace there, for my father is King Apheidas, Polypemon's son. My own name is Eperitus. I had no intention of putting in here when I left Sicania but had the misfortune to be driven out of my course, and my ship is riding yonder by the open coast some way from the port. As for Odysseus, it is four years and more since he bade me farewell and left my country – to fall on evil days, it seems. And yet the omens when he left were good: birds on the right, which pleased me as I said goodbye, and cheered him as he started out. We both had every hope that we should meet again as host and guest and give each other splendid gifts.'

When Laertes heard this, he sank into the black depths of despair. Groaning heavily, he picked the black dust up in both his hands and poured it onto the grey hairs of his head. Odysseus' heart was stirred, and suddenly, as he watched his dear father, poignant compassion forced its way through his nostrils. He rushed forward, flung his arms round his neck and kissed him. 'Father,' he cried, 'here I am, the very man you asked about, home in my own land after nineteen years. But this is no time for tears and lamentation. For I have news to tell you, and heaven knows there is need for haste. I have killed the gang of suitors in our palace. I have paid them out for their insulting gibes and all their crimes.'

Laertes answered him: 'If you that have come here are indeed my son Odysseus, give me some definite proof to make me sure.'

Odysseus was ready for this. 'To begin with,' he said, 'cast your eye on this scar, where I was wounded by the white tusk of a boar when I went to Parnassus. You and my mother had sent me to my grandfather Autolycus, to fetch the gifts he solemnly promised me when he came to visit us. Then again, I can tell you all the trees you gave me one day on this garden terrace. I was only a little boy at the time, trotting after you through the orchard, begging for this and that, and as we wound our way through these very trees you told me all their names. You gave me thirteen pear trees, ten apple, forty fig trees, and at the same time you pointed out the fifty rows of vines that were to be mine. Each ripened at a different time, so that the bunches on them were at various stages when the branches felt their weight under the summer skies.'

Laertes realised at once that Odysseus' evidence had proved his claim. With trembling knees and bursting heart he flung his arms round the neck of his beloved son, and stalwart Odysseus caught him fainting to his breast. The first words he uttered as he rallied and his consciousness returned were in reply to the news his son had given him. 'By Father Zeus,' he cried, 'you gods are still in your heaven if those suitors have really paid the price for their iniquitous presumption! But I have horrible fear now that the whole forces of Ithaca will soon be on us here, and that they will send urgent messages for help to every town in Cephallenia.'

'Have no fear,' said his resourceful son, 'and don't trouble your head about that; but come with me to the farmhouse here by the orchard, where I sent on Telemachus with the cowman and swineherd to prepare a meal as quickly as they could.'

Ceasefire

Text of poem: New Explorations Anthology page 401

BACKGROUND NOTE

This poem was first published in the *Irish Times* on 3 September 1994, two days after an IRA ceasefire was announced. It is another 'free translation' of an episode from Homer's classic poem *The Iliad,* which tells the story of Troy's siege by the Greeks. *The Iliad* begins in the tenth year of the Trojan conflict and ends with the burial of Hector, shortly after this episode.

During the conflict, Achilles sulked in his tent and refused to fight, because of a dispute with Agamemnon over a woman. However, with the Greeks in danger of being routed by Hector, Achilles allowed his close friend Patroclus to borrow his armour and his men to defend the Greek ships. But Patroclus was killed by Hector. In a fit of grief, rage and guilt, Achilles went back to the battle and after great slaughter pushed the Trojans back and killed Hector. In a frenzy of vengeance he dragged Hector's body in the dust behind his chariot, round the walls of Troy, and for eleven days thereafter round the tomb of Patroclus. Finally, old King Priam, prompted by the gods, came to the Greek camp bearing a huge ransom to redeem the body. He clasped the knees and kissed the hands of Achilles, urging him to remember his own father of similar age and also separated from his son.

You can read a translation of the original scene below.

THEMES

This poem deals with the aftermath of war. It explores the sadness of mourning, the feelings of those left behind to pick up the pieces, the emotions of the victors as well as the bereaved. It faces squarely the compromises people make when necessary, the self-abasement that even proud people will suffer for love and grief. And it signals the building of a reconciliation of a sort. So it relates quite aptly to the needs of a post-conflict Northern Ireland. Indeed, Longley himself has said that he kept Gordon Wilson's face as Priam in front of him while he wrote this poem.

VISUAL GESTURES

This dramatic episode is built around extravagant visual gestures: the kneeling; kissing hands; pushing the old king gently away. The set-piece meal also acts as a visual tableau, performed with eyes and looks, more reminiscent of a romantic scene than of a meal between deadly enemies. Much of the poignancy of this poem is communicated through gestures and looks.

The most exciting thing about the imagery is the unusual nature of the similes. 'Wrapped like a present' is shockingly inappropriate. Yet the very lightheartedness of that image seems to heighten the pathos of the scene, the awfulness of that old man's burden, just as an insensitive comment would increase the sympathy felt in such a situation. The hint of eroticism in 'To stare at each other's beauty as lovers might' is equally inappropriate for the recently mortal enemies. Indeed the reversal of roles in the image of the king's self-abasement – on his knees, kissing the hand of his son's killer – is visually shocking.

All this disturbing imagery punctures the heroic concept of war and conveys something of the true discomfort of the moment, the uncertainty and tension of this scene.

The Iliad

BOOK 24 (EXTRACT)

(Translated by Robert Eagles)

Priam found the warrior there inside . . .
many captains sitting some way off, but two,
veteran Automedon and the fine fighter Alcimus,
were busy serving him. He had just finished dinner,
eating, drinking, and the table still stood near.
The majestic King of Troy slipped past the rest
and kneeling down beside Achilles, clasped his knees
and kissed his hands, those terrible, man-killing hands
that had slaughtered Priam's many sons in battle.
Awesome – as when the grip of madness seizes one
who murders a man in his own fatherland and flees
abroad to foreign shores, to a wealthy, noble host,
and a sense of marvel runs through all who see him –
so Achilles marvelled, beholding majestic Priam.
His men marvelled too, trading startled glances.
But Priam prayed his heart out to Achilles:
'Remember your own father, great godlike Achilles –
as old as I am, past the threshold of deadly old age!
No doubt the countrymen round about him plague him now,
with no-one there to defend him, beat away disaster.
No-one – but at least he hears you're still alive
and his old heart rejoices, hopes rising, day by day,

to see his beloved son come sailing home from Troy.
But I – dear god, my life so cursed by fate . . .
I fathered hero sons in the wide realm of Troy
and now not a single one is left, I tell you.
Fifty sons I had when the sons of Achaea came,
nineteen born to me from a single mother's womb
and the rest by other women in the palace. Many,
most of them violent Ares cut the knees from under,
But one, one was left to me, to guard my walls, my people –
the one you killed the other day, defending his fatherland,
my Hector! It's all for him I've come to the ships now,
to win him back from you – I bring a priceless ransom.
Revere the gods, Achilles! Pity me in my own right,
remember your own father! I deserve more pity . . .
I have endured what no-one on earth has ever done before –
I put to my lips the hands of the man who killed my son.'

Those words stirred within Achilles a deep desire
to grieve for his own father. Taking the old man's hand
he gently moved him back. And overpowered by memory
both men gave way to grief. Priam wept freely
for man-killing Hector, throbbing, crouching
before Achilles' feet as Achilles wept himself,
now for his father, now for Patroclus once again,
and their sobbing rose and fell throughout the house.
Then, when brilliant Achilles had his fill of tears
and the longing for it had left his mind and body,
he rose from his seat, raised the old man by the hand
and filled with pity now for his grey head and grey beard,
he spoke out winging words, flying straight to the heart:
'Poor man, how much you've borne – pain to break the spirit!
What daring brought you down to the ships, all alone,
to face the glance of the man who killed your sons,
so many fine brave boys? You have a heart of iron.
Come, please, sit down on this chair here' . . .
But the old and noble Priam protested strongly:
'Don't make me sit on a chair, Achilles, Prince,
not while Hector lies uncared for in your camp!
Give him back to me, now, no more delay –
I must see my son with my own eyes.
Accept the ransom I bring you, a king's ransom!

Enjoy it, all of it – return to your own native land,
safe and sound . . . since now you've spared my life.'

A dark glance – and the headstrong runner answered,
'No more, old man, don't tempt my wrath, not now!
My own mind's made up to give you back your son.
A messenger brought me word from Zeus – my mother,
Thetis who bore me, the Old Man of the Sea's daughter.
And what's more, I can see through you, Priam –
no hiding the fact from me: one of the gods
has led you down to Achaea's fast ships.
No man alive, not even a rugged young fighter,
would dare to venture into our camp. Never –
how could he slip past the sentries unchallenged?
Or shoot back the bolt of my gates with so much ease?
So don't anger me now. Don't stir my raging heart still more.
Or under my own roof I may not spare your life, old man –
suppliant that you are – may break the laws of Zeus!'

The old man was terrified. He obeyed the order.
But Achilles bounded out of doors like a lion –
not alone but flanked by his two aides-in-arms,
veteran Automedon and Alcimus, steady comrades,
Achilles' favourites next to the dead Patroclus.
They loosed from harness the horses and the mules,
they led the herald in, the old king's crier,
and sat him down on a bench. From the polished wagon
they lifted the priceless ransom brought for Hector's corpse
but they left behind two capes and a finely woven shirt
to shroud the body well when Priam bore him home.
Then Achilles called the serving-women out:
'Bathe and anoint the body –
bear it aside first. Priam must not see his son.'
He feared that, overwhelmed by the sight of Hector,
wild with grief, Priam might let his anger flare
and Achilles might fly into fresh rage himself,
cut the old man down and break the laws of Zeus.
So when the maids had bathed and anointed the body
sleek with olive oil and wrapped it round and round
in a braided battle-shirt and handsome battle-cape,
then Achilles lifted Hector up in his own arms

and laid him down on a bier, and comrades helped him
raise the bier and body onto the sturdy wagon . . .
Then with a groan he called his dear friend by name:
'Feel no anger at me, Patroclus, if you learn –
even there in the House of Death – I let his father
have Prince Hector back. He gave me worthy ransom
and you shall have your share from me, as always,
your fitting, lordly share.'
                              So he vowed
and brilliant Achilles strode back to his shelter,
sat down on the well-carved chair that he had left,
at the far wall of the room, leaned toward Priam
and firmly spoke the words the king had come to hear:
'Your son is now set free, old man, as you requested.
Hector lies in state. With the first light of day
you will see for yourself as you convey him home.
Now, at last, let us turn our thoughts to supper' . . .

They reached out for the good things that lay at hand
and when they had put aside desire for food and drink
Priam the son of Dardanus gazed at Achilles, marvelling
now at the man's beauty, his magnificent build –
face-to-face he seemed a deathless god . . .
and Achilles gazed and marvelled at Dardan Priam,
beholding his noble looks, listening to his words.
But once they'd had their fill of gazing at each other,
the old majestic Priam broke the silence first:
'Put me to bed quickly, Achilles, Prince.
Time to rest, to enjoy the sweet relief of sleep.
Not once have my eyes closed shut beneath my lids
from the day my son went down beneath your hands . . .
day and night I groan, brooding over the countless griefs,
grovelling in the dung that fills my walled-in court.
But now, at long last, I have tasted food again
and let some glistening wine go down my throat.
Before this hour I had tasted nothing' . . .

Some themes and issues in Michael Longley's poetry

NOTE 1

For the purpose of acquiring an overview, it might be useful to re-read the poems in thematic groupings rather than in chronological order. For example:

(1) 'Wounds', 'Last Request' and 'Laertes' deal with the poet's father and thereby with his sense of his own identity and family background.

(2) 'An Amish Rug' features intimate love and home and family values and contributes to our understanding of the poet and his identity.

(3) 'Wreaths', 'Wounds' and 'Ceasefire' deal with violence, past and present, with violent myths, official war, and the 'Troubles'.

(4) 'Carrigskeewaun', 'Poteen', 'Badger' and 'Self-Heal' feature the Mayo landscape, Longley's second home and alternative culture.

NOTE 2

Consider each general point made, and return to the relevant poems for supporting evidence and quotation. If you disagree, make your argument with supporting reference also. Either way, build up a knowledge of the poetic detail. Make notes for yourself, perhaps in spider-diagram form.

EXPLORATION OF IDENTITY: POEMS OF SELF-DEFINITION

We can interpret a number of the poems in this selection as pieces exploring the poet's own background, environment, and values. These areas are not covered in any broad and systematic way, but selected subjects serve as anchor points of his identity.

- Family identity is anchored on the figure of his father in these poems. Acknowledgment of his soldier father helps clarify his own identity. As the critic Edna Longley summarised it, 'The father focuses questions of belonging rather than longing: an Englishman who fought twice for his country.'

- Honouring and remembering the dead is a part of this identity: see 'Last Rites', 'Wounds' and 'Laertes'. (The father–son relationship is examined separately, page 277).

- The violent society also is part of that identity: see 'Wounds' and 'Wreaths'.

- Family values, intimate love and a yearning for simplicity are part of this tapestry of identity: see 'An Amish Rug'.

- An alternative culture, the native Irish identity, is explored in 'Poteen', with its emphasis on the rebel race memory: see the critical commentary of 'Wounds' (pages 252–5) for a discussion of conflicting identities.

VIOLENCE

- A stark treatment of violence in its ordinary, everyday reality: see 'Wreaths'.
- The pervasive nature of violence in society; death invades the home: see 'The Civil Servant' and 'The Greengrocer'; it even invades the psyche: see 'The Linen Workers'.
- Human insignificance and powerlessness in the face of this violence: see 'Wreaths' and 'Wounds'.
- The 'Troubles' are dealt with against a background of wars and other human conflicts; this gives a sense of perspective to present-day violence: see 'Wounds', 'Wreaths', and 'Last Request'. 'He is able to analogise between different kinds and theatres of human conflict in a personal and historically informed and mediated treatment of the troubles' (Peacock).
- Longley presents the pictures of violence in a neutral, non-partisan way and with a slight air of detachment. He concentrates on presenting detailed pictures rather than conveying emotions: see 'Wounds' and 'Wreaths'.
- Examine what Longley himself has to say (in *Tuppenny Stung*) about the relationship between a poet and the 'Troubles':

> I find offensive the notion that what we inadequately call 'the Troubles' might provide inspiration for artists; and that in some weird *quid pro quo* the arts might provide solace for grief and anguish. Twenty years ago I wrote in Causeway: 'Too many critics seem to expect a harvest of paintings, poems, plays and novels to drop from the twisted branches of civil discord. They fail to realise that the artist needs time in which to allow the raw material of experience to settle to an imaginative depth where he can transform it . . . He is not some sort of super-journalist commenting with unflattering spontaneity on events immediately after they have happened. Rather, as Wilfred Owen stated fifty years ago, it is the artist's duty to warn, to be tuned in before anyone else to the implications of a situation.'
>
> Ten years later I wrote for the Poetry Book Society about what I was trying to do in my fourth collection, The Echo Gate: 'As an Ulsterman I realise that this may sound like fiddling while Rome burns. So I would insist that poetry is a normal human activity, its proper concern all of the things that happen to people. Though the poet's first duty must be to his imagination, he has other obligations: and not just as a citizen. He would be inhuman if he did not respond to tragic events in his own community, and a poor artist if he did not seek to endorse that response imaginatively. But if his imagination fails him, the result will be a dangerous impertinence. In the context of political violence the deployment of words at their most precise and most suggestive remains one of the few antidotes to death-dealing dishonesty.']

OTHER CONFLICTS

- War: he deals with the seamier side of war, the grave-robbing, anti-heroic view in 'Last Request'; see also 'Ceasefire'.
- Violence in society: see 'Self-Heal'.

THE WEST OF IRELAND

- A different landscape, another ethos, alternative values
- Is he claiming kinship with an alternative national identity, as in 'Poteen'; merely fleeing home; or finding a good place of perspective from which to look north? See the critical commentary on 'Carrigskeewaun'.
- Identifying with the Irish landscape? See 'Carrigskeewaun'. 'The sense of a man at ease with himself and his fellows' (Brown)
- The sheer enjoyment of nature, feeling part of the process: see 'Carrigskeewaun'.
- A genuine naturalist's pleasure, the preoccupation with creatures: see 'Badger'.
- The lonely, isolated nature of his western experience, the absence of community, family, and people: see 'Carrigskeewaun'.
- Not a romantic view of the west; he records the harshness, the pain, the violence and the ignorance as well as the beauty: see 'Badger', 'Carrigskeewaun', and 'Self-heal'.
- Again the precise description, the keen eye for detail: see 'Carrigskeewaun', 'Badger'.
- A view of the west as a place of compensatory values: 'a community of realisable values that are personally authentic and yet generally available, such as there seems to be present in nature: particularly in the redemptive landscapes of the west of Ireland' (Dawe).

THE FATHER FIGURE

- Honouring and acknowledging the dead is part of the process of self-definition: see 'Wounds' and 'Last Requests'.
- But Longley seems preoccupied with the father's dying, his almost-dying in the trenches and then his actual death: see 'Last Requests' and 'Wounds'. Then his psychological disinterment happens in 'The Linen Workers'. Is this becoming a fixation?
- Images of his father are of a frail old man, such as in 'Laertes' and 'Ceasefire', or focus on his teeth and glasses, images of his imperfection: see 'The Linen Workers'. But they are of a man with endearing human frailties, such as the cigarette addiction. And he has a sense of humour: see 'Wounds'.
- Intimacy of the father–son relationship: see the imagery of 'Wounds': 'I touched his hand, his thin head I touched.'

- Interesting reversal of father–son roles in 'Laertes': the hero slipping back into the child's role, the adult still needing recognition or affirmation from the father.
- A father's love and the lengths to which he will go to reclaim a son are evident in 'Ceasefire'.

THE ELUSIVE 'HOME' IN LONGLEY'S POETRY

- Very few concrete images of home feature in these poems. A bedroom features in an 'An Amish Rug'.
- The father figure, used by the poet to define his identity, is never pictured at home but only in the trenches, in his grave, in the hospital bed: see 'Wounds' and 'Last Requests'.
- Carrigskeewaun is the poet's home from home, yet it produces no concrete home, merely an imagined image: 'Recalls . . . a tablecloth and | A table she might have already set.'
- The passages from Homer that struck a chord with Longley are about a man longing for home, prevented for years from returning and on his return finding it taken over by others.

THE SENSE OF PERSPECTIVE IN LONGLEY'S POETRY

- Peacock talks of Longley's ability to look beyond the immediate issues of his own society and personal circumstances to other historical times and literary traditions. Notice the range of settings and times: present-day Ulster; the west of Ireland; the trenches in Europe, 1914–18; the classical Greece of Homer. The result is 'a catholicity of culture and political outlook which fosters objectivity, non-partisan human sympathy and historically informed understanding' (Peacock).
- The past and present are placed in juxtaposition to achieve a sense of perspective: violence in the First World War and present-day Belfast; the classical past of Ithaca has parallels with modern Ulster ('Laertes' and 'Ceasefire').
- Is present-day violence dingier? Or is all killing pointless?
- Past and present, life and death are no longer distinct: the dead father is ever present in 'The Linen Workers'.

A GENERALLY UNROMANTIC VIEW OF LIFE

- Dominated by war and violence: see 'Wounds', 'Last Requests', 'Wreaths', and 'Ceasefire'.
- Country life is rendered in all its realistic harshness ('Carrigskeewaun'), its brutality and pain ('Badger'), its ignorance and prejudice ('Self-Heal').

- The exception in this selection is 'An Amish Rug', with its yearning for simple values and loving intimacy.

- For the human condition: see 'Self-Heal'
- For grieving parents and dead heroes: see 'Ceasefire'
- For nature's creatures: see 'Badger'
- For victims of violence, ancient and modern: see 'Wounds' and 'Ceasefire'.

Style and technique: some points

FIRST-PERSON NARRATIVE
- The personal voice lends an air of intimacy to many of the poems: see 'Self-Heal', 'Carrigskeewaun', and 'An Amish Rug'.
- He uses a female voice in 'Self-Heal'.
- There is a strong autobiographical element in some of the poems: see 'Last Requests' and 'Wounds'.

DETAILED DESCRIPTIONS
- The use of precise detail creates the realism, whether dealing with violence or the beauties of nature: see 'Wreaths' and 'Carrigskeewaun'.
- Longley has an eye for incongruous detail. Often the point of the poem is made through this visual style rather than through any explicit comment: see 'Wounds' and 'Ceasefire'. For example, he views violence in the context of world wars and other violent contexts, and he views love in the context of the Amish culture.

TONE
- The tone is unemotional for the most part, neutral and slightly detached: see 'Wreaths'.
- The concentration is on precise, matter-of-fact descriptions, objectively rendered: see 'Wreaths' and 'Self-Heal'.
- Yet the tone is not callous; he is full of sympathy for the human condition: see 'Self-Heal'.
- The indications of emotion occur in the poems dealing with his father: see 'Wounds' and 'Last Requests'.
- The balanced tone is achieved through this wide perspective he takes up. For example, he views violence in the context of world wars and other violent contexts, and he views love in the context of the Amish culture: see 'Wounds' and 'An Amish Rug'.

INDIRECT TECHNIQUE

- He approaches subjects obliquely at times: for example, he uses his father's war experience to forge a perspective on Northern violence: see 'Wounds'. Or he uses classical Greek poetry to explore the psychological and emotional relationship with his father: see 'Laertes' and 'Ceasefire'.
- This attempt at contrast and comparison is sometimes reflected in the structuring of the poem in two halves, resonating off each other: see 'Wounds'.

SHAPE

- Shape and form are important in Longley's poems. See, for example, the thin, longish poem 'Poteen', resembling a tube; the rectangular picture-postcard sections of 'Carrigskeewaun'; or the rock-like, unbeautiful oblong of 'Self-Heal', immovable as ignorance. Explore the relationship between shape and meaning in the poems.

Forging a personal understanding of Longley's poetry

1. Which poems do you remember most sharply?
2. Which images have remained in your mind?
3. Choose any poem of Longley's. Place yourself in the scene; view it with the poet's eye. What do you see, hear, smell, etc.? How are you feeling? Why write that poem?
4. What are the poet's main preoccupations? What does he love, hate, fear, etc.? What interests him?
5. What do you discover about the personality of the poet? What do you think are his attitudes to life?
6. What does he contribute to your understanding of Ireland and of human nature?
7. What would you like to ask him?
8. What do you notice that is distinctive about the way he writes?
9. Compare his work with that of Séamus Heaney. What similarities and differences do you notice with regard to themes and styles of writing?
10. Why read Michael Longley?

Questions

1. Outline the main issues dealt with in this selection of Longley's poetry.
2. 'Violent events are seen in all the pathos of their everyday settings' (Peacock). Would you agree?
3. 'Longley views all military exploits with a jaundiced eye.' Comment on this statement, with reference to at least two poems from the selection.

4. 'The truth of human relationships is an important issue in the poetry of Michael Longley.' Comment on this aspect of his poetry.
5. 'One of the strengths of Longley's poetry is its descriptive detail.' Examine this element of his style, with particular reference to at least two of the poems.
6. Examine the treatment of death in the poetry of Michael Longley.
7. 'The west of Ireland is seen as the embodiment of some kind of alternative life' (Dawe). What aspects of this alternative life does Longley deal with in the poems you have read?

Michael Longley: writings

No Continuing City, London: Macmillan 1969.
An Exploded View, London: Victor Gollancz 1973.
Man Lying on a Wall, London: Victor Gollancz 1976.
The Echo Gate, London: Secker and Warburg 1979.
Poems, 1963–1983, London: Secker and Warburg 1991.
Gorse Fires, London: Secker and Warburg 1991.
Tuppenny Stung: Autobiographical Chapters, Belfast: Lagan Press 1994.
The Ghost Orchid, London: Jonathan Cape 1995.

Bibliography

Allen, Michael, 'Rhythm and development in Michael Longley's earlier poetry' in *Contemporary Irish Poetry: A Collection of Critical Essays,* edited by Elmer Andrews, London: Macmillan 1992.

Brown, Terence, *Northern Voices: Poets from Ulster,* Dublin: Gill and Macmillan 1975.

Craig, Patricia, 'History and retrieval in contemporary Northern Irish poetry' in *Contemporary Irish Poetry: A Collection of Critical Essays,* edited by Elmer Andrews, London: Macmillan 1992.

Dawe, Gerald, *Against Piety: Essays in Irish Poetry,* Belfast: Lagan Press 1995.

Eagles, Robert (translator), *Homer: The Iliad,* New York: Viking Penguin 1990.

Heaney, Séamus, 'Place and Displacement: Reflections on Some Recent Poetry from Northern Ireland' (first Pete Laver Memorial Lecture, Grasmere, 1984) in *Contemporary Irish Poetry: A Collection of Critical Essays,* edited by Elmer Andrews, London: Macmillan 1992.

McDonald, Peter, 'Michael Longley's homes' in *The Chosen Ground: Essays on the Contemporary Poetry of Northern Ireland,* edited by Neil Corcoran, London: Seren Books 1992.

Parker, Michael, 'Priest of the masses' [a review of Longley's Poems, 1936–83], *Honest Ulsterman*, no. 79, autumn 1985.

Peacock, Alan, 'Michael Longley: poet between worlds' in *Poetry in Contemporary Irish Literature* (Irish Literary Studies, 43), edited by Michael Kenneally, Gerrards Cross (Bucks.): Colin Smythe 1995.

8   *Eavan* BOLAND

Mary Shine Thompson

A literary life

Eavan Boland was born in Dublin in 1944. Her mother was the painter Frances Kelly and her father was the diplomat Frederick Boland, whose career moves resulted in her roving childhood and youth. From the age of six to twelve she lived in London, then in New York for a number of years, to return to Dublin when she was fourteen.

She was educated at Holy Child Convent, Killiney, County Dublin, then went on to Trinity College, first as a student and later as a lecturer in the English Department. After a few years she embarked on a career as a literary journalist with the *Irish Times,* and she also presented a regular poetry programme for RTE radio.

'New Territory'

New Territory, her first book of poetry, published in 1967, contains the early poems, written between the ages of seventeen and twenty-two, which were critically acknowledged at the time as talented, well-crafted work. Among its main concerns, this volume showed some preoccupation with the role of the poet, in pieces such as 'The Poets' and 'New Territory'. It also contained the first of her poems about paintings and so introduced what was to become an important theme of Boland's work: the stereotyped view of women in art and literature. 'From the Painting *Back from Market* by Chardin' shows the peasant woman, defined by love and domestic duties, 'her eyes mixed I Between love and market.'

The poet feels that artists throughout the centuries have ignored the real lives of women:

> I think of what great art removes:
> Hazard and death, the future and the past,
> This woman's secret history and her loves ...

In general this volume is in the mainstream of the Irish political – romantic poetic tradition, with its themes of exile ('The Flight of the Earls') and political martyrdom ('A Cynic at Kilmainham Jail'); poems about Irish poets ('Yeats in

Civil War' and 'After the Irish of Aodhagán Ó Rathaille'); and the retelling of legends ('Three Songs for a Legend' and 'The Winning of Etain'). But her outlook was soon to change, under pressure of the unfolding political situation.

Religious and political antagonism in Northern Ireland exploded into violence from 1969 onwards. Few people were unmoved or unaffected by this. The violence spread southwards with the bombing of Dublin and Monaghan in May 1974. Eavan Boland conducted a series of interviews in the *Irish Times* with Northern writers concerning their views on the situation, its effects on the work of the writer, and in general concerning the function of art in a time of violence. In a seminal article on 7 June 1974 entitled 'The Weasel's Tooth', she questioned the whole notion of cultural unity and accused Irish writing, influenced by Yeats, of fostering lethal fantasies for political activists:

> Let us be rid at last of any longing for cultural unity in a country whose most precious contribution may be precisely its insight into the anguish of disunity … For there is, and at last I recognise it, no unity whatsoever in this culture of ours. And even more important, I recognise that there is no need whatsoever for such a unity. If we search for it we will, at a crucial moment, be mutilating with fantasy once again the very force we should be liberating with reality: our one strength as writers, the individual voice, speaking in tones of outcry, vengeance, bitterness even, against our disunity but speaking, for all that, with a cool tough acceptance of it.

'The War Horse'

The second volume of poetry, *The War Horse*, published in 1975, reflects Boland's concerns with violence and conflict in both private and community life. She deals with many types of conflict: the Irish–English struggle, worrying families, and the conflict between lovers. The development of this theme ranges from a recognition of the killer instinct inherent in all nature, however domesticated ('Prisoners'), to a consideration of notorious historical public moments of conflict and death ('The Famine Road', 'The Greek Experience' and 'Child of Our Time', which was written after the Dublin bombings of 1974) and the archetypal deadly conflict of fathers and sons ('The Hanging Judge' and 'A Soldier's Son'). The latter poem, in which a father kills his own son, has been read as 'an image of a society at war with its own inheritance and future'. 'The War Horse', both a private and a political poem, brings a vivid personal awareness of destruction and war to leafy Dublin suburbia.

The feminine vision and view of the world is also a force in this volume. In 'The Famine Road' Boland equates the callous official lack of understanding of the famine victims with the offhand, male medical attitude meted out to a contemporary woman suffering from sterility. Racial suffering is equated with

female suffering. In 'Suburban Woman' and 'Ode to Suburbia' she deals with the
daily grind of the housewife and the conflict between a woman's traditional role
and her identity as a poet and creative artist:

> Her kitchen blind down – a white flag –
> the day's assault over, now she will shrug
>
> a hundred small surrenders off as images
> still born, unwritten metaphors, blank pages;
>
> and on this territory, blindfold, we meet
> at last, veterans of a defeat
>
> no truce will heal, no formula prevent
> breaking out fresh again. Again the print
>
> of twigs stalking her pillow will begin
> a new day and all her victims then –
> hopes unreprieved, hours taken hostage
> will newly wake, while I, on a new page
>
> will watch, like town and country, word, thought
> look for ascendancy, poise, retreat,
>
> leaving each line maimed, my forces used.
> Defeated we survive, we two, housed
>
> together in my compromise, my craft –
> who are of one another the first draft.

Boland had by this time married and moved from her city flat and literary
lifestyle to the Dublin suburb of Dundrum, where she was rearing her two
daughters. These poems and others such as 'The Other Woman' and 'Child of
Our Time' reflect an attempt to find and bring together her identity as wife,
Irishwoman, poet and mother with her life in the suburbs.

In this volume also there are some beautiful and honest personal poems on
family, love and friendship: 'Sisters', 'The Laws of Love', and 'The Botanic
Gardens' – all demonstrating peaceful alternatives to conflict.

'In Her Own Image'

In 1976 she began to work simultaneously on her next two volumes of poetry,
In Her Own Image, published in 1980, and *Night Feed,* published in 1982. *In*

Her Own Image deals with individual private female identity, 'woman's secret history'. The poems explore taboo issues: anorexia, infanticide, mastectomy, menstruation, masturbation and domestic violence. Here is a cry to look at the reality of woman, her sexuality, desires, feelings of degradation, and failure to be understood.

'Anorexia' explores female suffering; 'Mastectomy' and 'In His Own Image' explore feelings of degradation and see the female body as the object of man's desire and of his need to control and shape:

> He splits my lip with his fist,
> shadows my eye with a blow,
> knuckles my neck to its proper angle.
> What a perfectionist!
> His are a sculptor's hands:
> they summon
> form from the void,
> they bring
> me to myself again.
> I am a new woman.

'Solitary' suggests that only a woman knows the real sensual rhythms of her own body. 'Tirade for the Mimic Muse' and 'Witching' undermine the accepted conventional image of woman. 'Tirade' in particular deflates the traditional male-created image of the muse as a beautiful girl, choosing instead to deal with the less picturesque reality:

> I've caught you out. You slut. You fat trout.
> So here you are fumed in candle-stink
> Its yellow balm exhumes you for the glass.
> How you arch and pout in it!
> How you poach your face in it!
> Anyone would think you were a whore –
> An ageing out-of-work kind-hearted tart.
> I know you for the ruthless bitch you are:
> Our criminal, our tricoteuse, our Muse –
> Our Muse of Mimic Art.

These are angry poems, featuring degraded states of women, in a sort of anti-lyric verse, yet they goad the reader into considering the reality of woman, not the image.

'Night Feed'

If *In Her Own Image* featured the dark side of 'woman's secret history', *Night*

Feed features the suburban, domestic and maternal: the ordinary, traditional, everyday aspects of woman's identity. The main sequence of poems, 'Domestic Interior, 1–11', focuses on the close bond between mother and child and explores the intensity of that maternal experience. It includes the now familiar 'Night Feed'.

Night Feed

This is dawn.
Believe me
This is your season, little daughter.
The moment daisies open,
The hour mercurial rainwater
Makes a mirror for sparrows.
It's time we drowned our sorrows.

I tiptoe in.
I lift you up
Wriggling
In your rosy, zipped sleeper.
Yes, this is the hour
For the early bird and me
When finder is keeper.

I crook the bottle.
How you suckle!
This is the best I can be,
Housewife
To this nursery
Where you hold on,
Dear life.

A silt of milk.
The last suck.
And now your eyes are open,
Birth-coloured and offended.
Earth wakes.
You go back to sleep.
The feed is ended.

Worms turn.
Stars go in.
Even the moon is losing face.

Poplars stilt for dawn
And we begin
The long fall from grace.
I tuck you in.

Also in this volume is a group of poems examining artistic images of women: 'Degas Laundresses', 'Woman Posing', 'On Renoir's *The Grape Pickers*' and 'Domestic Interior'. These women are either defined in relation to their work in field or kitchen or else are putting on a false, decorative pose, fulfilling the stereotyped image man created for them. Woman's perceived need to comply with this idealised image of timeless beauty is satirised in such pieces as 'The Woman Turns Herself into a Bush', 'The Woman Changes Her Skin' and 'A Ballad of Beauty and Time'. In this last poem plastic surgery is under the poet's satirical knife:

A chin he had re-worked,
a face he had re-made.
He slit and tucked and cut.
Then straightened from his blade.

'A tuck, a hem, he said –
'I only seam the line,
I only mend the dress.
It wouldn't do for you:
your quarrel's with the weave.
The best I achieve
is just a stitch in time.'

These fake images of woman, romanticised stereotypes, are set against the real defining moments in a woman's history in the 'Domestic Interiors' sequence. On the one hand Boland is saying that it is these family relationships that are real and important, that identity can be found among the washing-machines and children's toys in suburbia. But she is also protesting that, traditionally, a woman has not had a choice about this. She has been imprisoned at hearth and home and so kept to the margins of society, removed from the centre of history-making and power. Boland seeks a more equitable balance between 'hearth and history'.

It's a Woman's World

Our way of life
has hardly changed
since a wheel first
whetted a knife.

Maybe flame
burns more greedily,
and wheels are steadier
but we're the same

who milestone
our lives
with oversights –
living by the lights

of the loaf left
by the cash register,
the washing powder
paid for and wrapped,

the wash left wet:
like most historic peoples
we are defined
by what we forget,

by what we never will be –
star-gazers,
fire-eaters,
It's our alibi

for all time:
as far as history goes
we were never
on the scene of the crime.

So when the king's head
gored its basket –
grim harvest –
we were gristing bread

or getting the recipe
for a good soup
to appetise
our gossip . . .

'The Journey'

Boland's fifth collection, *The Journey*, was published in 1982 and republished in *The Journey and Other Poems* in 1986. Prominent among its many and complex themes is the quest for identity: the poet's national identity, suburban identity, feminist identity, and identity as mother and wife. Childhood memories in England and the feeling of being different in such poems as 'I Remember', 'An Irish Childhood in England: 1951' and 'Fond Memory' provoked a consciousness of the poet's own nation and how language defines a person:

> ... the teacher in the London convent who
> when I produced 'I amn't' in the classroom
> turned and said – 'you're not in Ireland now.'
> ['An Irish Childhood in England: 1951']

This consciousness of language as part of one's identity prevails throughout the volume. Yet her relationship with her history and the women of history is not an easy one, and she resists going back to it in 'Mise Éire'. She finds the grim reality of Irish women in history, soldiers' whores or helpless immigrants, difficult to confront:

> No. I won't go back.
> My roots are brutal:
>
> I am the woman –
> a sloven's mix
> of silk at the wrists,
> a sort of dove-strut
> in the precincts of the garrison –
>
> who practises
> the quick frictions,
> the rictus of delight
> and gets cambric for it,
> rice-coloured silks.
>
> I am the woman
> in the gansy-coat
> on board the 'Mary Belle',
> in the huddling cold,
>
> holding her half-dead baby to her
> as the wind shifts East
> and North over the dirty

waters of the wharf

mingling the immigrant
guttural with the vowels
of homesickness who neither
knows nor cares that

a new language
is a kind of scar
and heals after a while
into a passable imitation
of what went before.

Yet these are the real women of the past, not those images created by many previous male poets, who idealised women and moulded them into metaphors of national sentiment and so created mythic national female figures.

'Outside History'

Outside History (1990), Boland's sixth volume, is divided into three sections: 'Object Lessons', 'Outside History: A Sequence' and 'Distances'. The object lessons, in the main, are what woman has learned about life. Some poems, such as 'The Black Lace Fan My Mother Gave Me' and 'The River', reflect on the puzzling, almost inexplicable relationship between men and women and on their different perspectives on the world ('Mountain Time'). Couples growing apart and breaking up are the focus of 'Object Lessons'. We are made to feel in this sequence how fragile and transient is all human interaction, particularly in 'We Were Neutral in the War' and 'Mountain Time'.

... darkness will be only what is left of
a mouth after kissing or a hand laced in a hand ...
['Mountain Time']

The female speaker senses that she is not regarded as significant, that she is marginalised, forced to the sidelines and excluded from the centre of happening history in 'We Were Neutral in the War'.

Your husband frowns at dinner, has no time
for the baby who has learned to crease three
fingers and wave 'day-day.' This is serious,
he says. This could be what we all feared.

You pierce a sequin with a needle.

You slide it down single-knotted thread
until it lies with all the others in
a puzzle of brightness. Then another and another one.

The female voices in these poems resemble 'The Shadow Doll', a mere replica of
a bride, a protected image, locked in a vacuum. But the speaker is a poet, with
her own recognised space, metaphorically represented as a room, and she
reaches out to other women writers, trying to imagine 'the rooms of other
women poets'. She knows that the literary and creative world has been male-
dominated, but the gift has passed into her hands.

Bright-Cut Irish Silver

I take it down
from time to time, to feel
the smooth path of silver
        meet the cicatrice of skill.

These scars, I tell myself, are learned.

This gift for wounding an artery of rock
was passed on from father to son,
        to the father
of the next son;

is an aptitude
for injuring earth
        while inferring it in curves and surfaces;

is this cold potency which has come,
by time and chance,

into my hands.

Boland's response to being marginalised as a woman poet is to explore
alternative history. 'So much that matters, so much that is powerful and frail in
human affairs seems to me, increasingly, to happen outside history: away from
the texts and symmetries of an accepted expression. And, for that very reason,
at a great risk of being edited out of the final account' (*Poetry Book Society
Bulletin*, winter 1990).

Boland feels that significance is to be found in the margins of life also, that
the unrecorded history of individuals is important too. And it is this alternative
history that is the focus of the central section of the volume *Outside History*. In

it she explores her own history, but this operates at both a personal and a universal level. Her own history can be read as a metaphor for the unrecorded female history of the nation. She explores her own personal history as a developing writer and poet. She is the young immature poet in 'The Achill Woman' who does not fully comprehend the significance of what she has experienced. She attempts to understand her developing self and to make connections between her present persona as a woman poet and her student past in 'A False Spring'. She is forging an identity as a woman poet in 'The Making of an Irish Goddess', and she is the suburban woman seeking to re-establish contact with her natural and cultural roots in 'White Hawthorn in the West of Ireland'. She finds real significance in moments of human experience, not in symbolic happening, in 'We Are Human History. We Are Not Natural History'. She feels trapped by time, and as a woman she is alienated from the male-dominated version of history in 'An Old Steel Engraving'. She feels powerless and unable to influence history in 'We Are Always Too Late'.

Many of the poems record a sense of incompleteness, such as 'A False Spring', which records the failure to find again her younger, student self and integrate that phase of her life with the embodied now. The lost cultural heritage, passed from mother to daughter but forgotten, is recorded in 'What We Lost'.

There is a keen sense of displacement in the poems. The au pair girls in 'In Exile' signify displaced woman, isolated by the barriers of language and by age and cultural differences. In the sequence we see Boland attempting to recover a sense of belonging and completeness by making connections with her personal history and her cultural history, but also by shedding the myth and the stereotyped image:

out of myth into history I move to be
part of that ordeal . . .

The third section, 'Distances', focuses mostly on the past, the distant past of her childhood memories and the more recent past of occasional moments of insight. These memories are connected to the present as if the poet is at last achieving a kind of quiet wholeness in her life. She is linked to the past, to family, to moments of love and insight, even to the future, in 'What Love Intended', where she imagines herself coming back like a ghost to a radically altered suburb.

'In a Time of Violence'

In a Time of Violence, her seventh collection, was published in 1994. It is divided into three sections, the first of which is entitled 'Writing in a Time of Violence'. The poems in this section touch on specific national and historical issues and events, such as the Famine ('That the Science of Cartography is Limited' and 'March 1, 1847. By the First Post'), agrarian violence and the Peep o' Day Boys ('The Death of Reason'), the Easter Rising ('The Dolls Museum in Dublin'), nineteenth-century women emigrants ('In a Bad Light') and language and nationality ('Beautiful Speech'). But each is examined from an interesting and unusual angle, such as the unsympathetic and insensitive view of the Famine from a woman of the ascendancy class in 'March 1, 1847. By the First Post'.

Many of the meditations are inspired by a visit to a museum or an exhibition. For example, the dress in a museum in St Louis featuring the work of Irish dressmakers sparked off thoughts of women's servitude in exile in the nineteenth century ('In a Bad Light'). But each event is re-created with authentic realism and each tale narrated with sympathy and affection. The poems offer fresh insights into old history as the poet focuses on the human experience behind these historical artefacts.

The poems in the second section, 'Legends', focus on women as mothers for the most part. The fierce protectiveness and the maternal side of women is portrayed in poems such as 'This Moment' and 'The Pomegranate'. Woman as mother is playing an age-old role and has universal significance. The ageing woman features in 'Moths', 'The Water Clock', and 'Legends'. Some of the poems stretch back to the poet's own mother and grandmother through remembrance of a particular skill ('The Parcel') or a link with an heirloom ('Lava Cameo'). Some, such as 'Legends', establish continuity with the next generation:

> Our children are our legends.
> You are mine. You have my name.
> My hair was once like yours.
> And the world
> is less bitter to me
> because you will re-tell the story.

The main work of the third section is the title poem, 'Anna Liffey'. It is, in the words of the author, 'about a river and a woman, about the destiny of water and my sense of growing older'. This section concludes with four poems examining the unsatisfactory portrayal of women in myth, art and literature. The idealised images and the stereotypes are false and suffocating.

She appeals for realism and release in 'A Woman Painted on a Leaf':

> This is not death. It is the terrible
> suspension of life.
>
> I want a poem
> I can grow old in. I want a poem I can die in.

'Object Lessons'

Her prose collection, *Object Lessons: The Life of the Woman and the Poet in Our Time*, appeared in 1995. In autobiographical mode, Boland traces her own development as a woman poet, recounts her search as a woman for some kind of arrangement with the male-dominated concept of the nation, and reviews the status of women in poetry and history

MAIN VOLUMES OF POETRY

	Poems in this selection
New Territory (1967)	
The War Horse (1975)	'The War Horse'
	'The Famine Road'
	'Child of Our Time'
In Her Own Image (1980)	
Night Feed (1982)	
The Journey (1982)	
The Journey and Other Poems (1986)	
Selected Poems (1989)	
Outside History (1990)	'The Black Lace Fan My Mother Gave Me'
	'The Shadow Doll'
	'White Hawthorn in the West of Ireland'
	'Outside History'
In a Time of Violence (1994)	'This Moment'
	'Love'
	'The Pomegranate'
Collected Poems (1995)	

The War Horse

Text of poem: New Explorations Anthology page 434

THEMES AND ISSUES

The poem stems from an encounter with a roving horse and also the excerpt from *Object Lessons* (page 304), which occurred, coincidentally, during an upsurge of disruption and violence in Northern Ireland. The poet's response is a metaphor poem with political overtones. The horse became the poetic incarnation of all those statistics of violence and death that were pouring nightly from the television screens.

The poem operates on a number of levels of significance. At an immediate level it confronts the issue of violence. We notice the seeming casualness of it, the arbitrary nature of this violence: 'the clip, clop, casual | Iron of his shoes as he stamps death | Like a mint on the innocent coinage of earth.' The treatment of the violence may be metaphorical, yet there is an awareness of the reality of death and wanton injury, which is carried in the imagery. The beheaded crocus is 'one of the screamless dead', the uprooted vegetation 'like corpses, remote, crushed, mutilated', and the eaten leaf merely 'of distant interest like a maimed limb'. The ungainly and often directionless nature of violence is suggested in the motion of the animal as 'he stumbles on like a rumour of war'. The overtones of the language become more overtly political as the poem proceeds: the rose is 'expendable ... a volunteer'; and 'atavism', 'cause' and 'betrayed' are the verbal coinage of revolutionary groups.

Could we read this poem as reflecting a Southern view of the Northern conflict – a middle-class, slightly nationalist Southern view? The speaker feels threatened by the 'casual iron of his hooves', vulnerable with 'only a rose' to form 'a mere | Line of defence against him', and afterwards breathes a sigh of relief that this only partly understood phenomenon is gone:

> But we, we are safe, our unformed fear
> Of fierce commitment gone ...

Lack of interest in this intrusive violence is at first feigned by the speaker. Others pretend he isn't there, 'use the subterfuge | Of curtains.' Yet for all that danger and disruption the speaker faintly admires the beast:

> I lift the window, watch the ambling feather
> Of hock and fetlock ...

She is also slow to blame him: 'No great harm is done. | Only a leaf of our laurel hedge ...' But most significantly of all, at the end of the poem he stirs her race memory ('my blood is still | With atavism') of colonial injustice, English aggression, and the cycle of failed rebellions:

> Of burned countryside, illicit braid:
> A cause ruined before, a world betrayed.

The speaker's attitude to the animal is a complex one and is perhaps contradictory at times, incorporating fear, resentment and relief but also furtive admiration.

Examine what Boland has to say about political poetry in the extract from *Object Lessons* below (page 298).

So, on another level the poem demonstrates how history impinges on the domestic and the artistic, which are frail in comparison. We are made aware, forcefully, of how fragile the domestic is. Boland herself has described the tension in the poem as that of 'force against formality'. The race memory of fighting against imposed order is conjured up by the modern parallel of conflict in a suburban garden, where wild nature reasserts itself over humankind's attempts to tame it. And the speaker can empathise. The rebel is not far beneath the surface of the psyche, despite the suburban veneer.

'The War Horse' is among the first of Boland's poems of the suburbs. The irony is that suburbia was really designed as slumberland, but even in safe, leafy, middle-class dormer territory the 'rumour of war ... stumbles down our short street,' awakening age-old conflicts. Boland is legitimising suburbia as a place of real experience and insight, a fit location and subject matter for poetry.

'The War Horse' is a private 'coming to awareness' of public violence, an intimate 'thoughts inside the head' reflection on the theme. In this aspect it differs from the more public scrutiny of violence in 'The Famine Road' and 'Child of Our Time'.

These notions concerning the influence of history, the relationship between art and society and the search for meaning in suburbia become important and frequently examined issues in Boland's poetry.

FEATURES AND STYLE

Versification

The poem is composed in open rhyming couplets. Unlike closed couplets, the sense here often runs from one couplet to the next. This gives a flowing rhythm, a fluid energy to the verse, which might be said to reflect the unpredictable energy and purpose of the horse. For example, the sequence of lines from 'I lift the window' to 'his snuffling head | Down', ending two couplets further on, must be read in one breath and might suggest the animal's forward momentum. Following that, the speaker's short gasp of relief ('He is gone') makes an effective contrast and also points up Boland's use of rhythm for effect.

The rhyming is very casual, composed of half-rhymes and off-rhymes for the most part: death – earth, fear – care, limb – climb, huge – subterfuge, street – wait, etc. This offhand casualness accords well with the beast's casual destruction.

Sound effects

This poet is not deaf to the music of language. Everywhere there are echoes and internal rhymes: 'hock – fetlock', 'Blown from growth', 'fear | Of fierce', etc. The alliteration of 'stumbles down our short street' emphasises the ungainly movement in the confined space. The unobtrusive musical assonance of 'Then to breathe relief lean', with its long *e* sounds, effectively conveys the speaker's sense of release, of escape.

Sound effects are an integral part of the animal portraiture here. The onomatopoeia of 'breath hissing' and 'snuffling head' conveys the threatening unfamiliarity of this beast that has invaded the suburban garden.

Imagery

The poet employs vivid graphic visual imagery, whether to convey fearsome destructive power ('Iron of his shoes ... stamps death') or beauty ('ambling feather | Of hock and fetlock'). Similes and metaphors are often striking and unusual: the torn leaf is 'Of distant interest like a maimed limb'; the broken crocus is 'one of the screamless dead'. These comparisons are very disturbing and have a nightmarish quality, which brings to consciousness the suppressed terrors that have been unleashed in the speaker by this violent visitation. Altogether the imagery and the language are vigorous and muscular, as befits the scene: 'stamps death | Like a mint'. Notice also the violence of the verbs: stamps, smashed, uprooted, stumble, etc.

Boland's recollections on the origins and significance of the poem

This extract is taken from her prose collection *Object Lessons* (1995) (chapter 8):

> It was the early seventies, a time of violence in Northern Ireland. Our front room was a rectangle with white walls, hardly any furniture and a small television chanting deaths and statistics at teatime.
>
> It was also our first winter in the suburb. The weather was cold; the road was half finished. Each morning the fields on the Dublin hills appeared as slates of frost. At night the street lamps were too few. And the road itself ran out in a gloom of icy mud and builders' huts.
>
> One evening, at the time of the news, I came into the front room with a cup of coffee in my hand. I heard something at the front door. I set down the coffee, switched on the light and went to open the door.
>
> A large, dappled head – a surreal dismemberment in the dusk – swayed low on the doorstep, then attached itself back to a clumsy horse and clattered away. I went out and stood under the street lamp. I saw its hindquarters retreating, smudged by mist and darkness. I watched it disappear around a corner. The lamp above me hissed and flickered and finally came on fully.
>
> There was an explanation. It was almost certainly a travellers' horse with some memory of our road as a travelling site and our gardens as fields where it had grazed only recently. The memory withstood the surprises of its return, but not for long. It came back four or five times. Each time, as it was startled into retreat, its huge hooves did damage. Crocus bulbs were uprooted. Hedge seedlings were dragged up. Grass seeds were churned out of their place.

Some months later I began to write a poem. I called it 'The War Horse'. Its argument was gathered around the oppositions of force and formality. Of an intrusion of nature – the horse – menacing the decorous reductions of nature which were the gardens. And of the failure of language to describe such violence and resist it.

I wrote the poem slowly, adding each couplet with care. I was twenty-six years of age. At first, when it was finished, I looked at it with pleasure and wonder. It encompassed a real event. It entered a place in my life and moved beyond it. I was young enough to craft and want nothing more.

Gradually I changed my mind, although I never disowned the poem. In fact, my doubts were less about it than about my own first sense of its completeness. The poem had drawn me easily into the charm and strength of an apparently public stance. It had dramatised for me what I already suspected: that one part of the poem in every generation is ready to be communally written. To put it another way, there is a poem in each time that waits to be set down and is therefore instantly recognisable once it has been. It may contain sentiments of outrage or details of an occasion. It may invite a general reaction to some particular circumstance. It may appeal to anger or invite a common purpose.

It hardly matters. The point is that to write in that cursive and approved script can seem, for the unwary poet, a blessed lifting of the solitude and scepticism of the poet's life. Images are easily set down; a music of argument is suddenly revealed. Then a difficult pursuit becomes a swift movement. And finally the poem takes on a glamour of meaning against a background of public interest.

Historically – in the epic, in the elegy – this has been an enrichment. But in a country like Ireland, with a nationalist tradition, there are real dangers. In my poem the horse, the hills behind it – these were private emblems which almost immediately took on a communal reference against a background of communal suffering. In a time of violence it would be all too easy to write another poem, and another. To make a construct where the difficult 'I' of perception became the easier 'we' of subtle claim. Where an unearned power would be allowed by a public engagement.

In such a poem the poet would be the subject. The object might be a horse, a distance, a human suffering. It hardly mattered. The public authorisation would give such sanction to the poet and the object would not just be silent. It would be silenced. The subject would be all-powerful.

At that point I saw [that] in Ireland, with its national traditions, its bardic past, the confusion between the political poem and the public poem was a dangerous and inviting motif. It encouraged the subject of the poem to be a representative and the object to be ornamental. In such a relation, the dangerous and private registers of feeling of the true political poem would be truly lost. At the very moment when they were most needed.

And yet I had come out of the Irish tradition as a poet. I had opened the books, read the poems, believed the rhetoric when I was young. Writing the political poem seemed to me almost a franchise of the Irish poet, an inherited privilege. I would come to see that it was more and less than that, that like other parts of the poet's life, it would involve more of solitary scruple than communal eloquence. And yet one thing remained steady: I continued to believe that a reading of the energy and virtue of any tradition can be made by looking at the political poem in its time. At who writes it and why. At who can speak in the half-light between event and perception without their voices becoming shadows as Aeneas's rivals did in the underworld of the Sixth Book.

In that winter twilight, seeing the large, unruly horse scrape the crocus bulbs up in his hooves, making my own connections between power and order, I had ventured on my first political poem. I had seen my first political image. I had even understood the difficulties of writing it. What I had not realised was that I myself was a politic within the Irish poem: a young woman who had left the assured identity of a city and its poetic customs and who had started on a life which had no place in them. I had seen and weighed and struggled with the meaning of the horse, the dark night, the sounds of death from the television. I had been far less able to evaluate my own hand on a light switch, my own form backlit under a spluttering street light against the raw neighbourhood of a suburb. And yet without one evaluation the other was incomplete.

I would learn that it was far more difficult to make myself the political subject of my own poems than to see the metaphoric possibilities in front of me in a suburban dusk. The difficulty was a disguised blessing. It warned me away from facile definitions. The more I looked at the political poem, the more I saw how easy it was to make the claim and miss the connections. And I wanted to find them.

The Famine Road

Text of poem: New Explorations Anthology page 436

A READING OF THE POEM

Boland is drawing parallels between certain aspects of the famine experience and the experience of woman today. The famine road, symbol of purposeless, thwarted lives, is equated with female sterility. The supercilious treatment of the suffering people she sees as akin to the unfeeling arrogance meted out to the childless woman.

> You never will, never you know
> but take it well woman, grow
> your garden, keep house, goodbye.

Boland feels that being a woman gives her a unique perspective on Irish history, as she elaborated in response to the question, 'What does being Irish mean to you?'

> Apart from the fact that it connects me with a past, I find it a perspective on my womanhood as well. Womanhood and Irishness are metaphors for one another. There are resonances of humiliation, oppression and silence in both of them and I think you can understand one better by experiencing the other. [From the interview in *Sleeping with Monsters*]

If we explore the poem's comparison in detail we find that both the Irish in history and women in society are generalised about and so misunderstood: 'Idle as trout in light Colonel Jones | these Irish ...' The woman in the monologue is a mere faceless statistic ('one out of every ten ...'). Neither are treated rationally ('could they not ... suck | April hailstones for water and for food'). The cruel indifference of these people's treatment is linked to the nonchalant lack of medical explanation ('Anything may have caused it, spores ... one sees | day after day these mysteries'). Both groups are different, physically or mentally segregated, condemned to an isolated life or death.

> They know it and walk clear. He has become
> a typhoid pariah, his blood tainted, although
> he shares it with some there ...

> Barren, never to know the load
> of his child in you, what is your body
> now if not a famine road?

Boland links this oppression and humiliation of the sterile woman with that of the famine people. Their blood too is wasted ('could I they not blood their knuckles on rock'). This image is an impotent echo of that authoritative gesture of Trevelyan's ('Trevelyan's I seal blooded the table') as they too put their seal on their work.

The following bleak humorous image conveys their humiliations, shows the primitive state to which they were reduced: 'cunning as housewives, each eyed – I as if at a corner butcher – the other's buttock.' Both woman and famine people are silent sufferers. Disenfranchised, they are allowed to make no contribution. The superior discussion is carried on above their heads and is quite dismissive: 'Might it be safe I Colonel, to give them roads,' and 'grow I your garden, keep house, goodbye.'

The lack of understanding, the unfeeling treatment, the callous oppression, the silent suffering, the feelings of humiliation, of uselessness, the pointlessness of it all, the sense of failure – these are the links between womanhood and Irishness in this poem.

Child of Our Time

Text of poem: New Explorations Anthology page 440

[*Note: This poem is also prescribed for Ordinary Level 2010 exam*]

BACKGROUND NOTE

The poem was inspired by a press photograph showing a firefighter carrying a dead child out of the wreckage of the Dublin bombings in May 1974.

A READING OF THE POEM

First and foremost this is an elegy for the untimely death of a child. It bemoans the senselessness and irrationality of the child's slaughter in an act of public violence.

> This song, which takes from your final cry
> Its tune, from you unreasoned end its reason;
> Its rhythm from the discord of your murder ...

In the second stanza the keen sense of loss is encouraged by the mournful litany of the literary rituals of childhood, naming again the associations of intimate moments, the rituals around sleeping and waking:

> rhymes for your waking, rhythms for your sleep,
> Names for the animals you took to bed,
> Tales to distract, legends to protect ...

This sense of loss is compounded by guilt, in that it is the adults who should have been the guardians and guides of the child:

> We who should have known how to instruct
> With rhymes for your waking ...

The elegy finishes in a prayer that adult society will learn from this horror, expressed in the paradox 'And living, learn, must learn from you dead,' and so construct a better method of social interaction so that the death will not have been in vain ('find, for your sake whose life our idle | Talk has cost, a new language.') The poem is also a searing condemnation of violence. Society stands accused ('our times have robbed your cradle'), accused also of this barbarous irrationality ('your unreasoned end' ... 'the discord of your murder'). The only hope is that society would awaken to the reality of its actions and that the child might 'Sleep in a world your final sleep has woken.'

The poem could also be read as a comment on the failure of communication. The entire poem is couched in language terminology. It is a 'lullaby', a 'song', inspired by a 'final cry', a 'tune' with 'rhythms'. In the second stanza, loss is expressed in terms of language deprivation and child rearing seen in terms of language fostering: 'rhymes for your waking', etc. The only way forward from this conflict and violence is described as 'a new language'.

So the failure of language is associated with death and destruction. But language is the only bulwark against chaos, and this is the positive message of this bleak poem. Poetry, the most artistic expression of language, can be created out of this pain – this 'tune' from 'your final cry'. It signals a victory of order over chaos, reason 'from your unreasoned end', rhythm from 'discord'. It offers a chance to rebuild broken images and visualise a better society.

FEELINGS

A delicate balance of emotions is achieved in this poem. The brutal reality of the killing is never denied, and the fact of death is faced squarely, as in 'And living, learn, must learn from you dead,' where the placing of the last word in the line gives it finality and emphasis. But the references to death are sometimes veiled in poetic terms: 'your final cry' and 'your final sleep'. Or they are intellectualised, as in 'the discord of your murder'. Here the aspect of death dwelt on is its discordance, its out-of-tuneness, the disharmony of death. Or the child's broken body is rendered as 'your broken image'. The inversion of the natural order of life and death, in the killing of a child, is expressed in the paradoxes 'from your final cry | Its tune,' 'from your unreasoned end its reason;' and 'Its rhythm from the discord of your murder'. Consideration of this death is poeticised or intellectualised to some degree.

But this is no anodyne reaction. Feelings of grief, loss, guilt and resolution to learn a better way are all conveyed. Yet there is a delicacy and gentleness to the mourning, made all the more poignant by the fact that the poem is a sort of final lullaby. So the slightly euphemistic treatment is appropriate. Death is a kind of sleep. 'Sleep in a world your final sleep has woken.' Altogether the poem seems to be an interesting combination of dirge and lullaby.

The Black Lace Fan My Mother Gave Me
Text of poem: New Explorations Anthology page 442

A READING OF THE POEM

The poem focuses on courtship and deals with the messy and sometimes enigmatic relationship between the sexes. Just as the blackbird engages in its courtship ritual, human lovers too participate in a sort of courting dance.

> She was always early.
> He was late. That evening he was later.
>
> She ordered more coffee. She stood up.

The staccato rhythms of the verse here, created by the short sentences, draw attention to a choreographed sequence of movements, as a ritual to be played out. There is evidence too of disharmony, never the perfect entry together but rather of fretting and bad timing. If the weather is a barometer of the emotions, then the indications are of a stormy relationship, oppressive and explosive: 'stifling'; 'A starless drought made the nights stormy'; 'the distance smelled of rain and lightning'; 'An airless dusk before thunder.'

The fan is seen as a symbol of courtship, both with humans and in nature. It is a thing of beauty, associated with sensual allure, a romantic symbol. And so it functions here, but it also has darker associations of plunder and violation. The tortoiseshell has been pillaged from its natural habitat, killed off, and 'keeps … an inference of its violation.' As Boland herself saw it, 'as a sign not for triumph and acquisition but for suffering itself' (*Object Lessons*). It becomes a symbol of pain rather than an erotic sign. Still, in nature it retains its sensual overtone, 'the whole, full, flirtatious span of it.' So it carries these contradictory associations, reflecting the real-life complexity of the love relationship, not some stereotyped romantic image.

In other ways too it is an unusual love poem. There is no clear perception of the lovers, no clear recollection of the emotions, no detail of the moment:

> And no way to know what happened then –
> none at all – unless, of course, you improvise.

It is an oblique love poem that focuses on the love token that has lost much of its particular significance, yet is somehow still linked (by means of the blackbird) to their perennial courtship in nature. Its most positive statement is to assert the eternity of courtship, of love gestures. It makes no claims about eternal memories or the triumph of love against time. Rather the opposite, as the particulars of the emotional encounter are lost, eroded by time. Time erodes significance, and even cherished keepsakes lose their importance. There is emphasis also on the darker undertones of love, the tempests and the suffering.

IMAGERY AND SYMBOLISM

The style of communication in this poem is somewhat oblique. Nothing is actually said: rather, we come gradually to apprehend the nuances and feelings. The core of meaning is communicated through the connotations of the images and symbols. And these images manage to transmit something of the complexity of the emotions and relations.

The fan itself, as the poet has mentioned, is not just an erotic object but also carries some notion of the violations of love, through the pain and plunder of its past. So the symbol deepens the understanding of love in the poem. The parallel image of the blackbird's wing restores some of the sensuality to the love symbol.

The tempestuous nature of the relationship is suggested in the weather imagery, as the atmosphere parallels the emotion: 'An airless dusk before thunder.' It is interesting too that all the references are to dusk or night, not the romantic kind but 'a stormless drought'. The poem explores more the darkness of the emotions than the starry insights of love.

SOME IDEAS IN THE POEM

• The love relationship is mysterious, inaccessible to outsiders and to history.
• The sensual courtship gestures in a love affair are universal, common to humans and nature.
• But here the symbol of courtship is not just an erotic object, but also a sign of pain.
• What remains are the gestures; the particular emotions are forgotten, eroded by time.
• History and memory fail us in the search for truth: we are forced to invent.
• Yet nature remains flirtatious always.

The Shadow Doll

Text of poem: New Explorations Anthology page 445

A READING OF THE POEM

This poem has similarities with 'The Black Lace Fan My Mother Gave Me', in that it too uses a symbol to tease out some truths about the image of woman and the nature of the male–female relationship. We are offered the bride's perspective, a female insight on the wedding, which is portrayed in all its turmoil, an occasion 'to be survived'.

Boland uses the symbol of the doll to point up the discrepancy between the image of woman, particularly nineteenth-century woman, and the less glamorous reality. The manufactured image is elegant, in virginal white ('blooms from the ivory tulle'; 'oyster gleam', etc.), a model of discretion and sensitivity, devoid of sexual appetites ('discreet about I visits, fevers, quickenings and lust'), certainly too polite to talk about these taboo subjects. The reality is that of real-life emotional woman ('feeling satin rise and fall with the vows') and nervous repetition of vows amid the chaotic clutter of wedding preparations.

There may even be a slight envy of the doll's calmness; yet somehow the fevered reality is more appealing than the 'airless glamour' that is 'less than real', like the stephanotis. However, speaker and doll share a sense of confinement: the doll 'Under glass, under wraps,' the speaker restrained by vows and, like the suitcase, pressed down and locked.

VIEWS OF WOMAN

- The false image versus the reality: the pure, asexual creature of 'airless glamour' is set against the emotional and physical turmoil of the reality.
- Oppressed woman is emphasised: woman confined, repressed, under glass, under vows, locked in.

IMAGERY

The imagery mediates the theme very effectively. The delicacy of 'blooms from the ivory tulle' and the 'shell-tone spray of seed pearls' helps create the notion of frail beauty, elegant if bloodless. The unreality is reinforced by the flowers ('less than real I stephanotis'). The colours, too, help to create this lifeless perfection: ivory and oyster. And of course the symbolism of the doll, which is a mere replica, underlines the falsity of this image of woman. Both the glass dome and the locked case carry, in their different ways, suggestions of oppression, secrets to be locked away, lack of true freedom.

White Hawthorn in the West of Ireland

Text of poem: New Explorations Anthology page 448

A READING OF THE POEM

This is one of a group of poems from the volume *Outside History,* in which the poet is attempting to 'make connections' with her world – to establish continuity in her personal life, family traditions and lore, to find a working relationship with her cultural history and, here, to re-establish the age-old connection with the natural world.

In this poem she is going back to nature, fleeing 'suburban gardens. | Lawnmowers. Small talk.' This toy-house neatness and inconsequential chatter of suburbia is contrasted with the wild, uncultivated beauty, the primitiveness and the naturalness of life in the west:

> Under low skies, past splashes of coltsfoot,
> I assumed
> the hard shyness of Atlantic light
> and the superstitious aura of hawthorn.

She identifies immediately with the naturalness, is at home with the earth. Her enthusiasm is communicated in the energetic rhythms of the language, the flowing, run-on lines:

> All I wanted then was to fill my arms with
> sharp flowers,
> to seem, from a distance, to be part of
> that ivory, downhill rush. But I knew . . .

Contrast this enthusiasm with the minimalist staccato phrases of lines 3 and 4: 'I left behind suburban gardens. | Lawnmowers. Small talk.'

The hawthorn is associated with supernatural forces, primitive beliefs, the strange sub-rational powers of the earth. The power underneath the ordinary benign face of nature fascinates the poet here. Like hawthorn, water has a gentle fluency combined with enormous power ('able | to re-define land'), a power that is usually veiled under the river's more usual appearance of a recreational amenity or a landscape bearing for lost travellers. Nature dominates all human exchange – 'the only language spoken in those parts.'

THEMES

- The poem contrasts two ways of life, the 'cultivated' suburban versus the natural primitiveness of life in the country.
- The superiority of the natural is proclaimed, with its excitement and energy.
- This is an 'earth poem', exploring the power beneath the ordinary face of nature, the hidden sub-rational depths.
- It might also be read as a symbolic journey, of the deracinated poet, the suburban dweller, searching for her real roots – her roots understood in both a geographical and a metaphysical sense. She is searching for a place and also for a philosophy. The undefined time of year, the 'season between seasons', seems to point up the poet's sense of 'out-of-placeness,' her unsettled state of mind.

Outside History

Text of poem: New Explorations Anthology page 450

A READING OF THE POEM

Boland rebelled against the mythicisation of Irish history: the songs, the ballads, the female icons of the nation, the romantic images. Myth obscures the reality, manipulates history. It is outside real lived history, a remote, unchanging image, a false construct.

Here Boland, as a poet, rejects myth in favour of real history as the proper authority for her poetry and her idea of nation.

The stars are symbolic of outsiders, remote and unreal, 'whose light happened | thousands of years | before our pain did'. Paradoxically, though they appear unchanging and are symbols of eternity, their illumination is thousands of years out of date when it reaches us. Ironically, it is the light that is an illusion: the darkness is real. The stars' unrelenting, cold, hard wintry light is shown in direct contrast to human vulnerability ('our pain'). The alternative to this remote, unchanging mythical framework for viewing life is the vantage point of human history, with its real suffering and mortality:

> Under them remains
> a place where you found
> you were human, and
> a landscape in which you know you are mortal.

It is necessary to choose between the two outlooks. Boland has chosen to move 'out of myth into history', to be part of the real pain and suffering of life. Only now does she begin to experience the real torment of lives endured by countless people throughout the years. In a nightmarish, Armageddon-type image suggestive of famine disaster ('roads clotted as | firmaments with the dead') she invites us in to comfort all the dying in history, real history:

> How slowly they die,
> as we kneel beside them, whisper in their ear.

The critic Jody Allen-Randolph has described it as follows: 'In a moment of power and dignity, the dead are finally allowed to die, however slowly and painfully, as both poet and audience move in to whisper the rite of contrition. Their deaths are not manipulated to serve any cause beyond their suffering which survives in the poem as a moment of collective grief.' It is a final laying to rest of the nationalist dead. But it is too late ('And we are too late. We are always too late'). This melancholic ending echoes an awareness of the suffering caused by this mythical view of history and realises that it cannot be undone fully.

This Moment

Text of poem: New Explorations Anthology page 452

[*Note: This poem is also prescribed for Ordinary Level 2010 exam*]

A READING OF THE POEM

At one level this is a simple nature lyric celebrating the moment of dusk in the suburbs. The scene is filled with the usual furniture of a suburban evening: darkening trees, lighted windows, stars, moths, rinds, children, and mothers calling them in. It is a romantic evocation of suburban twilight, creating an atmosphere of calm, of continuing growth, ripeness and natural abundance: 'One window is yellow as butter ... Moths flutter | Apples sweeten in the dark.' Boland is celebrating the ordinary, having discovered that even banal suburban routines can stimulate the poetic in her.

Yet for all its outward ordinariness there is a hint of the mysterious:

> Things are getting ready
> to happen
> out of sight.

This might refer simply to nature's continuing growth in the secrecy of night ('Apples sweeten in the dark') or to some deeper significance of this scene.

Notice that the really significant part of the moment is the reuniting of mother and child. There is a subtle dramatic build-up to this, with intimations that something is being held back slightly: 'Things are getting ready | to happen ... But not yet.' The intervening images serve to heighten the wait for the finally revealed moment:

> A woman leans down to catch a child
> who has run into her arms
> this moment.

This stanza is emphasised by having the only significant activity in the poem: 'leans', 'to catch', 'runs'. With that activity 'this moment' has arrived. So the moment celebrated is maternal, a physical demonstration of the bond between mother and child, with all its connotation of love, security and protection.

The fact that this is happening everywhere, in suburbs all over the world, gives it a universal significance, lends a mythic quality to the gesture. The woman in the poem is connected to all women in history who must have performed a similar action.

So the poem is about dusk, a moment of transition in nature; but it is also about a universal moment in woman's experience: the confirmation of maternal love.

IDEAS IN THE POEM

- The ordinary beauty and richness of nature at the mysterious hour of dusk
- That the suburbs can be poetic
- That significant moments are moments of human encounter
- A woman sharing in the universal experience of motherhood.

Love

Text of poem: New Explorations Anthology page 454

BACKGROUND NOTE

'Love' is one of a sequence of poems entitled 'Legends' that explores parallels between ancient myths and modern life. In some of the poems, such as 'Love' and 'The Pomegranate', the exploration of myth is used to deepen an understanding of woman as mother. Other poems explore themes of faithfulness, the creation of images of love, the fragility of all life, etc. In general, the point being made is that legends, myths and such stories point up the similarity of human experience throughout the ages and show a line of continuity from present days to ancient past.

Towards the end of the sequence Boland examines the end of this continuum line, her own family history, when she is prompted by personal memories or significant objects, such as an heirloom brooch or other keepsake.

In classical Greek and Roman mythology a number of the stories feature visits by the living to the underworld, Hades, the kingdom of the dead. So 'the hero' who 'crossed on his way to hell' might be the hero Odysseus, who conjured up the spirits of his dead companions by offering sacrifice on the banks of the river Ocean. But it is even more likely that the speaker refers to the story of Orpheus and Eurydice, a tale of the anguished separation of ardent lovers found in Virgil's fourth 'Georgic'. Orpheus went down into Hades to rescue his beloved Eurydice, who had been killed by a snake bite. His songs to her on his lyre had held all spellbound, and he was allowed to leave with her on condition that he did not look back. But

> He halts. Eurydice, his own is now on the lip of
> Daylight. Alas! he forgot. His purpose broke. He looked back.
> His labour was lost, the pact that he had made with the merciless king
> Annulled. Three times did thunder peal over the pool of Avernus
> 'Who', she cried, 'has doomed me to misery, who has doomed us?'
>
> Thus she spoke: and at once from his sight, like a wisp of smoke
> Thinned into air, was gone.

Wildly he grasped at shadows, waiting to say much more,
But she did not see him; nor would the ferryman of the Inferno
Let him again cross the fen that lay between them.

The story goes on to chart the months of weeping and mourning suffered by Orpheus, wandering through caves and forests, where his sorrow touched even the wild animals and the trees. Boland uses the myth as a framework for exploring ideas of love and loss and the impossibility of recovering the passionate intensity of first love.

LAYERS OF MEANING

As with many a Boland poem, this has a number of layers of significance. At one level it is a love poem, in which the speaker reflects on her present loving relationship with her husband but still yearns for the intensity of their early love, when they first lived in this American town with their young family many years before. But the speaker's thoughts are drawn continually to classical myths and legends, in which she finds experiences parallel to her own. She uses these mythical allusions to explore the infant's brush with death, the nature of her relationship with her husband, and her female consciousness and role. She identifies with the female voice in the myth, thereby establishing the continuity and importance of the female experience throughout the ages.

So this is a poem about love, about family, about female experience, and about the centrality of myth to our lives.

The poem has a number of overlapping time frames: present, recent past, and ancient time.

THEMES AND ISSUES

Love

Different facets of love are touched on in this poem. The passion and delicacy of first physical love is most keenly registered.

> And we discovered there
> love had the feather and muscle of wings
> and had come to live with us,
> a brother of fire and air.

The bird metaphor conveys the elemental nature, the naturalness, the strength and grace of love. Indeed there is an almost nostalgic yearning for the intensity of this early love: 'Will we ever live so intensely again?' etc. With great honesty she admits her need to cast her lover in a heroic mould, to see the beloved as hero. Here she is creating myths, manufacturing an image of love and lover, a classical hero in suburban America: 'I see you as a hero in a text . . . with snow on the shoulders of your coat | and a car passing with its headlights on . . . the image blazing and the edges gilded . . .' The love she speaks of in the present tense is described in terms of language – love seen as communication:

> We love each other still . . .
> we speak plainly. We hear each other clearly.

Yet a problem is hinted at here. We have less than perfect communication:

> But the words are shadows and you cannot hear me.
> You walk away and I cannot follow.

The underlying mythical allusions augment this sense of failure, as they all deal with separation and loss and the creation of insufferable barriers between lovers. So the love between speaker and husband here carries connotations of failure, of unheard words.

She also deals with love in a family context, amid kitchen tables and threatened tragedy:

> We had two infant children one of whom
> was touched by death in this town
> and spared;

This is the quiet familial love of the suffering mother who can only watch and wait.

The significance of myth and legend

Human affairs are seen in the long tradition of history, even prehistory and mythology. Love, death, pain and separation are the universal human experience. The poet uses mythical allusions to create an awareness of the continuity of human experiences and to deepen an understanding of some of them. For example, the threatened loss of her child is explored through a parallel myth. The sense of loss, the separation of death, the awful failure of communication and the waste of life's opportunities are all evoked by reference to myth.

> When the hero
> was hailed by his comrades in hell
> their mouths opened and their voices failed and
> there is no knowing what they would have asked
> about a life they had shared and lost.

Is the effect of this to distance and lessen the mother's anguish?

The experience of love is seen in the heroic terms of myth and legend, as we have seen: 'I see you as a hero in a text', etc. It is as if the ordinary, everyday reality of love is insufficient and there is a need for the heroic, the superhuman, the extraordinary quality of myth in human lives. She imagines the hero-husband edged with an aura like a god of mythology, though it is merely the effect of car headlights behind him – 'the image blazing and the edges gilded'.

But perhaps the most significant aspect of myth is that it allows the speaker to tap into female experience and the universal female voice.

THE FEMALE VOICE

The secondary role of woman is much in evidence here, yielding precedence and importance to the male hero, viewing her partner as a 'hero in a text', etc. She is silent, voiceless, but longing 'to cry out the epic question | my dear companion'. She is the unheard voice of woman, throughout myth and history: 'But the words are shadows and you cannot hear me.'

Even her role as mother here is essentially powerless in the face of the threatened death of her infant. She adopts a passive, stoical attitude, as if life and death are completely in the hands of fate. The child 'was touched by death . . . and spared . . . Our child is healed.' Perhaps this episode could be seen as referring back to an earlier theme of Boland's in 'The Journey': the fears of women with sick children.

Overall, the poet is asserting the universality of female experience, whether it be in Ancient Greece and Rome or modern America, on the banks of the mythical river Styx or a bridge over the Iowa river. By identifying with female voices of myth, and particularly with that of the abandoned Eurydice in the last lines ('You walk away and I cannot follow'), she again registers the powerlessness of women.

Imagery

The poem opens and closes with images of darkness and shadow. The prevailing darkness and Stygian gloom of the first stanza ('Dark falls . . . Dusk has hidden the bridge . . . hell') recurs in the final lines ('words are shadows'). So the poem is bracketed by gloom, which qualifies and balances the enthusiasm of the love theme. In contrast to this darkness, the hero is silhouetted in light ('the image blazing and the edges gilded'). So we get a very primal contrast of colours, reflecting love and death, good and evil. Family love and life are mediated in images of ordinary domesticity: an old apartment, a kitchen, an Amish table, a view. References to speech and dumbness abound. Death is pictured as voicelessness, love as plain speaking, and the failure of love as a failure of speech.

Perhaps the most exciting metaphor is that of love as a bird, communicating the natural energy and beauty of the emotion ('love had the feather and muscle of wings').

Form

The poem is written in loose, non-rhyming stanzas, in which the natural rhythms of speech are employed to carry the reminiscences and the personal narrative. Might it be significant that the stanzas gradually diminish in size? The first three are of five or six lines, then one of five lines, three stanzas of four lines, and finally a two-line stanza to finish. Might this mirror the diminishing scope of love as treated in the poem?

The Pomegranate

Text of poem: New Explorations Anthology page 456

A READING OF THE POEM

This poem deals with the value of myth to life, with the universal truth of legend. The poet explores this theme by recalling the interlinking of life and legend in her own experience.

She first encountered this particular legend when she was a child in exile in London, 'a city of fogs and strange consonants'. The story of separation and confinement in an alien world must have resonated powerfully with her own experience then. Another facet of the legend's theme, the mother's anguish for her lost child, struck a chord with the poet at a later stage in her life, when she 'walked out in a summer twilight | searching for my daughter at bed-time.' She also takes to heart one of the myth's bitter truths: the ravages of time and the seasons on nature and humankind.

> But I was Ceres then and I knew
> winter was in store for every leaf
> on every tree on that road.
> Was inescapable for each one we passed.
> And for me.

The legend assists the poet in understanding her daughter. Insights so gained vary from the startlingly banal fact that 'a child can be | hungry' to the deeper understanding that she must allow her daughter space, the freedom to grow up: 'I will say nothing.' The stories of legend are archetypal and run parallel to human experience in all ages, and it is a worthwhile experience, an enrichment, to move in and out of the different worlds and time zones through 'such beautiful rifts in time'.

The poem also explores the relationship between mother and daughter. It paints a picture of intimate moments, as the mother views the teenage clutter with eyes of love:

My child asleep beside her teen magazines
her can of Coke, her plate of uncut fruit.

The poet shares with Ceres that fierce maternal protectiveness. And moving through the beautiful rift in time, the images of Persephone and her own daughter fuse, and the poet's maternal instinct is to warn and protect the child then and the child now:

I could warn her. There is still a chance
The rain is cold. The road is flint coloured.
The suburb has cars and cable television.
The veiled stars are above ground.
It is another world.

Yet she realises that the girl must experience the truth of the legend for herself, must be free to experience the temptation ('the papery flushed skin in her hand'), to make mistakes, to suffer pain. If the mother protects her too much the wisdom of the legend (the gift) will mean little: 'If I defer the grief I will diminish the gift.' And what better inheritance can a mother bequeath than the eternal wisdom of myth and legend?

But what else
can a mother give her daughter but such
beautiful rifts in time?

Issues raised in the poem

- The value of myth to life: how legend embodies universal truth, conveys vital understanding, and illuminates the present.
- The relationship between mother and daughter: the intensity of the bond, the fierce protectiveness, but also an awareness of the independence of the child and her need to experience life, truth, love and passion for herself.

Imagery

Some images are used in a symbolic way. The pomegranate, for instance, has mythological significance, a fruit sacred to the underworld, drawing those who eat it down into darkness. Here it fulfils a similar function, with overtones, perhaps, of sexual temptation.

She will hold
the papery flushed skin in her hand
And to her lips.

Has the uncut fruit connotations also of the temptation and loss in the Garden of Eden? Is the mother attempting to protect her daughter from the griefs associated with sexuality?

Much of the imagery is of darkness, twilight, the underworld, etc.: 'hell', 'the cracking dusk of the underworld', 'a city of fogs', 'twilight', 'it is winter I and the stars are hidden', and 'The road is flint-coloured.' This motif of darkness is associated with both the legend and the poet's present experience and creates a somewhat bleak atmosphere. But it is a fitting setting for the poet's anxiety and the pain she suffers in conferring freedom on her daughter. The modern bedroom, if not 'a place of death' as in the legend, is still 'full of unshed tears'.

Overview of the issues in this selection of Boland's poetry

Boland's view of Irish history and the idea of nation

- Boland deals with the reality of Irish history, the familiar story of oppression, defeat and death ('The Famine Road'). The sense of national identity that comes across from 'The Famine Road' speaks of victimisation, being downtrodden and living out pointless lives: see also the suffering in 'Outside History'.
- Opposed to that view is the male-created myth, involving heroic struggle, battle and glorious defeat: see the image of the dying patriot immortalised by art in 'An Old Steel Engraving'. The woman poet feels excluded from that cultural tradition – 'One of us who turns away.'
- Boland resists this mythicisation of history, insists on the necessity of confronting the reality, facing the unburied dead of history and laying them to rest ('Outside History').
- She shows concern for the unrecorded history, for the significance of lives lived on the margins of history, away from the centre of power, far from the limelight of action. She mourns the forgotten lives in 'That the Science of Cartography is Limited'.
- In her prose writings Boland explores the idea of nation and the difficulties it produces for her as a woman poet.

> So it was with me. For this very reason, early on as a poet, certainly in my twenties, I realised that the Irish nation as an existing construct in Irish poetry was not available to me. I would not have been able to articulate it at that point, but at some preliminary level I already knew that the anguish and power of that woman's gesture on Achill, with its suggestive hinterland of pain, were not something I could predict or rely on in Irish poetry. There were glimpses here and there; sometimes more than that. But all too often, when I was searching for such an inclusion, what I found was a rhetoric of imagery which alienated me: a fusion of the national and the feminine which seemed to simplify both.
>
> It was not a comfortable realisation. There was nothing clear-cut

about my feelings. I had tribal ambivalences and doubts, and even then I had an uneasy sense of the conflict which awaited me. On the one hand, I knew that as a poet I could not easily do without the idea of a nation. Poetry in every time draws on that reserve. On the other, I could not as a woman accept the nation formulated for me by Irish poetry and its traditions. At one point it even looked to me as if the whole thing might be made up of irreconcilable differences. At the very least it seemed to me that I was likely to remain an outsider in my own national literature, cut off from its archive, at a distance from its energy. Unless, that is, I could repossess it. This proposal is about that conflict and that repossession and about the fact that repossession itself is not a static or single act. Indeed, the argument which describes it may itself be no more than a part of it.

VIOLENCE IN SOCIETY

- 'The War Horse' explores suburban, middle-class attitudes to political violence. It is really a psychological exploration of the theme 'how we respond to violence'.
- Race memory and the old antagonisms to English colonial rule still exist just beneath the surface ('The War Horse').
- The real human consequences of political violence are portrayed in 'Child of Our Time'. The poet acts as conscience of our society here.
- Violence is seen as the result of a failure of language, an inability to communicate ('Child of Our Time').

THE SIGNIFICANCE OF MYTH

- In one sense myth is seen to play a positive and enabling role, even in modern life. It gives the poet a framework for exploring human truths such as themes of love and death ('Love'). The wisdom of myths enables her to deal sensitively with her growing daughter ('The Pomegranate'). Mythical stories demonstrate the universality of human experience. The poet sometimes feels part of this tradition by doing the ordinary things and so shares in the long history of woman's experience and becomes a part of myth or universal truth ('This Moment').
- But created images can be false, limiting and confining. Idealised or mythicised images of woman are fixed in time, unable to love, breed, sweat or grow old (see 'Time and Violence').
- Boland often challenges the image of woman in mythology (also in art and literature), particularly when it shows woman as marginalised, silenced, subservient to her husband the hero, as in 'Love'.

- History is laced with myths. The unreality, the coldness and the distance of myth from real lives is symbolised in the stars of 'Outside History'.

THE EXPERIENCE OF BEING A WOMAN

Boland's strong feminine perspective lends an extra dimension of insight to all her themes. But she also considers specific issues relating to the portrayal and the treatment of women.

- The image versus the reality: 'The Shadow Doll' explores that false image of woman, specifically nineteenth-century woman, but it has universal relevance. The image is one of elegance, dignified control of emotions ('an airless glamour'), and suppressed sexuality ('discreet about | visits, fevers, quickenings and lust'). Women are forced to conform to a false image, repressed, metaphorically enclosed in glass, locked away ('The Shadow Doll').
- The image of woman in art, literature and mythology is often idealised or stereotyped. The mythological allusions in 'Love' conjure up an image of woman as powerless and silent, yearning in vain for a heroic love.
- The sufferings of woman are equated with the oppression of the nation ('The Famine Road').
- The traditional role of woman is validated in such poems as 'This Moment', which show woman as mother. That maternal gesture of catching the child in her arms is the key to the poem. The protectiveness of mothers features in 'The Pomegranate'. Also her wisdom is displayed in allowing the daughter freedom to learn for herself.
- Woman as lover features in 'The Black Lace Fan My Mother Gave Me' and 'Love'.
- Suburban woman features in many of the poems: e.g. 'The War Horse' and 'This Moment'.
- The puzzling relationship between men and women features in 'The Black Lace Fan My Mother Gave Me': the mistimings, the tempests of love, the sensual allure. Love diminishes in time, like the importance of the fan. This makes an interesting alternative view to the blinkered one of idyllic romance.
- Boland challenges the patriarchal tradition of Irish poetry. In *Object Lessons* she elaborated on her objections to the images of woman in literature.

> The majority of Irish male poets depended on women as motifs in their poetry. They moved easily, deftly, as if by right among images of women in which I did not believe and of which I could not approve. The women in their poems were often passive, decorative, raised to emblematic status. This was especially true where the woman and the idea of the nation were mixed: where the nation became a woman and the woman took on a national posture.
>
> The trouble was [that] these images did good service as

ornaments. In fact, they had a wide acceptance as ornaments by readers of Irish poetry. Women in such poems were frequently referred to approvingly as mythic, emblematic. But to me these passive and simplified women seemed a corruption. For they were not decorations, they were not ornaments. However distorted these images, they had their roots in a suffered truth.

What had happened? How had the women of our past – the women of a long struggle and a terrible survival – undergone such a transformation? How had they suffered Irish history and rooted themselves in the speech and memory of the Achill woman, only to re-emerge in Irish poetry as fictive queens and national sibyls?

The more I thought about it, the more uneasy I became. The wrath and grief of Irish history seemed to me, as it did to many, one of our true possessions. Women were part of that wrath, had endured that grief. It seemed to me a species of human insult that at the end of all, in certain Irish poems, they should become elements of style rather than aspects of truth.

AGEING

• In the later poems, such as 'The Pomegranate', Boland is conscious, in a personal sense, of the ageing process.

REPRESENTATION IN ART

• In other poems Boland is particularly concerned with the representation of women in painting.

STRIVING FOR TRUTH

• In all these areas explored – history, art and love – Boland is striving for truth and searching out the reality rather than the glittering image.

POETRY IN THE SUBURBS

• A good deal of her poetry is set in the suburbs, a setting not associated traditionally with poetic aspiration.
• The fragile nature of the beauty and order created in the suburbs is brought out in 'The War Horse'.
• The toy-house neatness of suburbia is no match for the wild, elemental attractions of nature in 'White Hawthorn in the West of Ireland'.
• In the later poems we encounter a romantic evocation of a suburban twilight ('This Moment'). Nature has colonised the suburbs ('Stars rise. I Moths flutter.' and 'One window is yellow as butter').

- But the real bleakness of the suburban street is not hidden: 'The rain is cold. The road is flint-coloured' ('The Pomegranate').

Forging a personal understanding of Boland's poetry

Think about the following points and make notes for yourself or discuss them in groups.
1. On reading Boland, which poems do you particularly like?
2. On reading Boland, what were the main issues the poems raised for you?
3. What settings, colours and moods do you associate with Boland's poetry?
4. What general understanding of the poet did you form?
   - What is important in her life?
   - How does she see herself?
   - Is she a happy or a sad person? etc.
5. Did reading her poetry add anything to your understanding of Irish history? What, and in which poems?
6. Consider her thoughts on the treatment of women in society and in history. Do you consider that she makes an important contribution to feminist thinking?
7. What insights did she give you into suburban life?
8. Would you consider her a radical poet? Explain your views.
9. Why do you think we should read her poetry?
10. What aspects of Boland's poetry strike a chord with you: particular themes; settings; point of view on the world; the images she creates; the feeling and tones in the poems? What appeals to you?

Questions

1. Outline three significant issues dealt with in the poetry of Eavan Boland. Explore, in detail, the poet's treatment of any one of these issues.
2. Do you find the poet's view of Irish history particularly bleak? Comment.
3. 'The attempt to shed the constricting husk of myth and enter the nightmare of history is an important theme in Boland's poetry' (R. Smith). Discuss.
4. 'Boland's poetry shows a consciousness of the sustaining power of cultural heritage, whether through primitive Irish superstition or classical mythology.' Discuss this statement in the light of the poems you have read.
5. 'Boland's poetry shows how idealised images of women need to be set beside the reality.' Discuss.
6. 'While she takes a feminist line, maternity and suburbia feature prominently in Boland's poetry.' Consider this statement in the light of at least two poems you have read.

7. 'The relationship between mother and daughter is an important preoccupation in Boland's' poetry.' Discuss, with reference to at least two of the poems you have read.
8. 'Boland is always conscious of the natural context in which human events occur.' Consider Boland as a nature poet.
9. 'Boland's imagination thrives in the shadows.' Would you agree?
10. 'Finding significant moments of human experience is the goal of much of Boland's poetry.' Discuss this statement, with reference to at least three poems.

Bibliography

Allen-Randolph, Jody, '*Écriture féminine* and the authorship of self in Eavan Boland's *In Her Own Image*', *Colby Quarterly*, vol. 27 (1991), 48–59.

Allen-Randolph, Jody, 'Private worlds, public realities: Eavan Boland's poetry, 1967–1990', *Irish University Review*, vol. 23 (1993), no. 1, 5–22.

Boyle Haberstroh, Patricia, *Women Creating Women: Contemporary Irish Women Poets*, Syracuse (NY): Syracuse University Press 1996, 59–92.

Dawe, Gerald, 'The suburban night: Eavan Boland, Paul Durcan and Thomas McCarthy' in *Against Piety: Essays in Irish Poetry*, Belfast: Lagan Press 1995, 169–93.

Denman, Peter, 'Ways of saying: Boland, Carson, McGuckian' in *Poetry in Contemporary Irish Literature* (Irish Literary Studies, 43), edited by Michael Kenneally, Gerrards Cross (Bucks): Colin Smythe 1995, 158–173.

Kiberd, Declan, *Inventing Ireland*, London: Jonathan Cape 1995.

Longley, Edna, 'From Cathleen to anorexia: the breakdown of Irelands' in *A Dozen Lips*, Dublin: Attic Press 1994, 162, 187.

McGuinness, Arthur, 'Hearth and history: poetry by contemporary Irish women poets' in *Cultural Contexts and Literary Idioms in Contemporary Irish Literature* (Irish Literary Studies, 31), edited by Michael Kenneally, Gerrards Cross (Bucks): Colin Smythe 1988, 197–220.

Mahoney, Rosemary, *Whoredom in Kimmage: Irish Women Coming of Age*, New York: Houghton Mifflin 1993.

Matthews, Steven, *Irish Poetry: Politics, History, Negotiation: The Evolving Debate, 1969 to the Present*, Basingstoke: Macmillan 1997.

Meaney, Geraldine, 'Sex and nation: women in Irish culture and politics' in *A Dozen Lips*, Dublin: Attic Press 1994, 188–204.

Ní Chuilleanáin, Eiléan (editor), *Irish Women: Image and Achievement*, Dublin: Arlen House 1985.

Roche, Anthony, and Allen-Randolph, Jody (editors), *Irish University Review Special Issue: Eavan Boland*, vol. 23, no. 1 (spring–summer 1993).

Ward, Margaret, 'The missing sex: putting women into Irish history' in *A Dozen Lips*, Dublin: Attic Press 1994, 205–24.

Ordinary Level, 2010 Examination

Explanatory note

Candidates taking the Ordinary (Pass) level exam in 2010 have a choice of questions when dealing with the prescribed poems. They can answer either (*a*) a question on one of the poems by a poet prescribed for Higher Level for the 2010 exam, or (*b*) a question from a list of other prescribed poems (i.e. the alternative poems discussed on pages 323–44).

(a) The poems by Higher level poets that may also be answered by Ordinary level candidates in the 2010 exam are as follows:

Keats	On First Looking into Chapman's Homer (p. 7) La Belle Dame Sans Merci (p. 10)		On Raglan Road (p. 152)
		Rich	Aunt Jennifer's Tigers (p. 171) Storm Warnings (p. 178)
Yeats	The Lake Isle of Innisfree (p. 50) The Wild Swans at Coole (p. 55) An Irish Airman Foresees his Death (p. 58)	**Walcott**	To Norline (p. 224) Summer Elegies 1 (p. 226) The Young Wife (p. 231) Wounds (p. 252)
Eliot	Preludes (p. 98) Aunt Helen (p. 104)	**Longley**	Last Requests (p. 261) An Amish Rug (p. 264)
Kavanagh	Shancoduff (p. 143) A Christmas Childhood (p. 148)	**Boland**	Child of Our Time (p. 302) This Moment (p. 309)

(*b*) The alternative poems that Ordinary level candidates sitting the exam in 2010 may choose to study instead are discussed on pages 323–44.

CONTRIBUTORS
Carole Scully
John McCarthy
John G. Fahy
David Keogh
Bernard Connolly

John Milton
When I Consider
Text of poem: New Explorations Anthology page 465

A READING OF THE POEM

In the octet of this sonnet Milton reflects on his blindness, and how his disability affects his performance of what God expects of him. Milton opens by describing his blindness in terms of light and money: 'When I consider how my light is spent'. He uses 'Talent' in the dual sense of a unit of money (referring to the 'Parable of the Talents') and as a faculty or sense. In essence the octet asks, 'Doth God exact day-labour, light deny'd'; does God expect the same productivity from him as would be expected from a fully sighted person?

In the sextet 'patience' answers 'that murmur' of complaint. 'God doth not need | Either man's work or his own gifts'. Acceptance of God's will is seen as the path to salvation: 'who best | Bear his milde yoak, they serve him best'. The majestic creator – 'his State | Is Kingly' – has a multitude of servants who are constantly in motion to do his bidding: 'Thousands at his bidding speed ... without rest'. Milton's consolation is stated in the final line: 'They also serve who only stand and waite.' Christian resignation in the face of the will of God helps Milton to deal with his scrupulous conscience.

IMAGERY

'Light' is used in the poem to represent the faculty of sight, 'day-labour' means the work potential of a sighted person, and 'light deny'd' refers to the condition of blindness.

Financial terminology is used to illustrate the 'Parable of the Talents'. Milton speaks of his light being 'spent' and a 'Talent ... Lodg'd with me ... and present | My true account'. The power and majesty of God is suggested by 'his State | Is Kingly'. This omnipotent figure does not require 'man's work'; acceptance of his will is described as 'his milde yoak'.

Henry Vaughan
Peace
Text of the poem: New Explorations Anthology page 467

A READING OF THE POEM
The poet addresses his soul and describes heaven as 'a Countrie | Far beyond the stars', guarded by a sentry 'All skilfull in the wars'. Peace sits 'crown'd with smiles' above the clamour and danger that characterise life on Earth. Christ is portrayed as a military commander commanding the angelic troops. He is the soul's friend, who for motives of 'pure love' descended to the earth to die 'for thy sake'. If the soul could 'get but thither' to Christ, in heaven 'there growes the flowre of peace'. Peace is symbolised by the 'Rose that cannot wither' and as a fortress offering security. The soul is exhorted to cease its wanderings: 'Leave then thy foolish ranges' and to embrace Christ, who 'never changes' and is 'Thy God, thy life, thy Cure.' This poem is perhaps best understood as a dramatic sermon in which Christ offers mankind peace. Peace is defined in terms of military security with Christ as the warrior prince, and offering an end to aimless wandering. In his poem 'Man' Vaughan refers to the human condition: 'Man is the shuttle . . . God ordered motion but ordained no rest'. In 'Peace', rest – 'ease' – replaces restlessness – 'foolish ranges' – in the poet's view of heaven, protected by 'one who never changes'.

IMAGERY
Vaughan's use of imagery in the poem is striking, as heaven is 'a Countrie | Far beyond the stars'. Christ is presented as a warrior; he 'Commands the Beauteous files', offering protection; he is 'skilfull in the wars'. Associated with this warlike image is 'the flowre of peace', which is 'The Rose that cannot wither'.

Christ/peace is a 'fortresse', offering an end to aimless wandering: 'thy foolish ranges'. Vaughan weaves the various strands of imagery together to dramatic effect, to convey a moral lesson, as the soul is exhorted – 'O my soul awake!' – to embrace Christ's peace.

MUSCULAR LANGUAGE
Vaughan writes with vigour, as the brisk rhythm of the short lines, with their forceful beat, builds up to the pause at the semicolon in line 16. The following line is in the imperative, as the soul is instructed to act on the knowledge gained: 'Leave then thy foolish ranges;'. Triplication in the final line enhances the rhetorical effect of the punctuation, with pauses after the key words 'Thy God, thy life, thy Cure.' The poem possesses a hymn-like quality, with its alternate lines rhyming and its simplicity of language.

William Carlos Williams
The Red Wheelbarrow

Text of poem: New Explorations Anthology page 478

A READING OF THE POEM

Williams opens his poem with four words describing his emotional reaction to the image that is at the centre of this piece: 'so much depends | upon'. He deliberately tries to convey to the reader a sense that this is an object of importance and significance in the world.

It comes as something of a surprise, then, that the image turns out to be that of a red wheelbarrow. There does not seem to be anything particularly important or significant about such an ordinary object.

However, it is this very surprise that Williams wants his readers to feel. The contrast between the expectations he created with the first four words and the reality of the image in the subsequent twelve words encourages us to go back and reassess our view of the red wheelbarrow. Williams expresses his appreciation of it in almost loving terms. He is grateful that the wheelbarrow exists as an object.

THEME

Williams deliberately challenges the idea that everyday objects are unimportant. He believed that the reality of an object gave it importance, an importance that could touch the human heart. He wanted to capture this reality in his work: 'I was interested in discovering about life, I put down daily impressions. Certain poems are very real because I was touched by real things.' For Williams, familiarity should never breed contempt!

STRUCTURE

Williams was determined to develop a style of poetry that was uniquely American. He sometimes called it 'a United Stateser way' of writing. Rather than use a poetic type of language, he decided to use the everyday speech of the American people to provide the rhythm in his poetry: 'The rhythmic pace was the pace of speech, an excited pace because I was excited when I wrote ...' In order to strengthen this sense of excitement Williams wrote in short lines.

He rejected other poetic devices such as rhyme and the use of capital letters at the beginning of each line of poetry, deciding that they were part of 'the old order which, to me, amounted to restriction.'

IMAGERY

Above all, Williams wanted to achieve simplicity in his poetry: 'I try to say it straight, whatever is to be said.' For this reason, he avoided complicated imagery. In this poem the image of the wheelbarrow is conveyed vividly by his use of the words 'red' and 'glazed'. These two words make it easy for us to imagine the brightness of the wheelbarrow, a brightness that suggests the special importance of this everyday object. The vividness is further heightened by the contrast between the shining red wheelbarrow and the feathery whiteness of the chickens. Although he uses only twelve simple words to describe two uncomplicated images, Williams achieves an overall effect of depth and detail. It is as if we are there with him, looking out at the scene and suddenly appreciating the unique and special importance of that familiar red wheelbarrow.

Dylan Thomas
The Hunchback in the Park
Text of poem: New Explorations Anthology page 485

A READING OF THE POEM
Thomas skilfully interweaves three viewpoints into this poem: his own as the poet; the boys'; and the hunchback's.

In the first stanza Thomas portrays the hunchback's life as a 'solitary' one, and this image is sustained throughout the poem. The hunchback spends his days in the park, 'Propped between trees and water'; 'Eating bread from a newspaper' and 'Drinking water from the chained cup'. At night he retreats to a 'dog kennel'. The cycle of his life is directly connected to the cycle of the world of nature that fills the park. So he comes with the 'park birds' and he settles quietly like the water that has just gushed into the lake from the opened lock. This is his world, just as it is for the grass and the trees.

Indeed, the only sense of 'belonging' that Thomas shows in the hunchback's life comes with the natural world of the park. Most of the other people who enter the park are shown in groups, 'the children', the 'truant boys' and the 'nurses'. But the hunchback's fellow human beings seem either to ignore him or to treat him with contempt because of his disability. Thomas describes him as being 'Alone between nurses', conveying a wonderful image of the poor hunchback rejected even by those who are expected to be caring, children's nannies, who are out walking with their charges in the park. Even more disturbing is the treatment that he receives at the hands of the 'truant boys'.

Because of his 'crooked bones', the boys view the hunchback as being less than human and therefore not deserving of any respect or consideration. They call him 'Mister' but only to make fun of him and they cruelly imitate him 'Hunchbacked in mockery'. Their young, healthy bodies, that can run 'On out of sound' and move quickly, 'Dodging the park keeper', give them a tremendous sense of confidence and freedom. In all their youthful exuberance they have no understanding that the hunchback with his twisted body is still a person deserving of respect.

This personhood is revealed to us by the thoughts that the hunchback has as he is in the park. He does not really notice the ways in which he is mistreated as he is more concerned with an imaginary 'woman figure without fault'. There is something wonderfully maternal and protective about this woman as she stays with him by day and night. It is this image that changes Thomas' perception of the hunchback's life. Up until now, the hunchback has seemed to Thomas to be living a poor, sad life. However, Thomas realises that the park is a place of refuge offering protection and a sense of belonging to the hunchback. Like the 'woman figure' the park is his caring companion.

Significantly, the other people who come into the park from the outside world use it for their own ends and in so doing disrupt it. The children put 'gravel' in the drinking cup and the boys climb all over the rockery shouting and screaming. Even the park keeper, by picking up the leaves, disrupts the natural cycle of the park. It is only the hunchback who blends into it and, in response, finds emotional warmth and a sense of dignity there that is sadly unavailable to him anywhere else.

THOMAS'S USE OF SOUND

Dylan Thomas wrote in the everyday, lilting, conversational words of his native Wales. He effectively conveys the wonderful musicality of language in such lines as 'And Mister they called Hey mister'. Here, he uses repetition of the word 'Mister' and the rhythm of his words to capture the sounds of the boys' voices echoing in the park. Similarly, in the line 'With his **stick** that **pick**ed up leaves', he uses assonance with the letter **i** (assonance: where two or more words close together have the same vowel sound) and the repeated **ick** sound to recreate the sound and rhythm of the park keeper's stick piercing the leaves.

Judith Wright
Request to a Year
Text of poem: New Explorations Anthology page 488

SOME APPROACHES TO THE POEM

Could this poem be read as a sneer at the colonial past, at the slightly dotty Europeans with a logic all of their own? Is it another version of the typical Australian send-up of the 'Poms'? Is this unusual moment deliberately chosen to illustrate how different the colonial ancestors were: tough, logical, and difficult to understand?

It is certainly a cool, calculated, unsentimental look at family ancestry. It is a tongue-in-cheek treatment of ancestral eccentricity, in the woman who, 'having had eight children | and little opportunity for painting pictures . . . hastily sketched the scene'. But there is also a certain tone of admiration here for her toughness: 'bring me the firmness of her hand'.

As a portrait of a woman it is unusual in that it subverts the conventional image of the caring mother. Instead we find the almost incredible detachment of the woman painting as her son is in danger of drowning.

Some of the satire is directed at the world of art and artists. We notice the unreality of the scene: art carried to extremes is more important than life. The 'legendary devotee of the arts' is taking this opportunity to paint. The distressing scene is viewed from an artistic viewpoint ('from a difficult distance') rather than a human one. It is with 'the artist's isolating eye' rather than the tearful eyes of a mother that the impending disaster is watched. Perhaps it is the cold tyranny and compulsion of the artistic temperament that is being pointed up. Perhaps it is best read as a humorous poem.

HUMOUR

The humour is created chiefly by the incongruities of the scene: the women sketches while her son drowns. The sense of fun is helped by the minute detailing: she sketched 'hastily'; it was a small 'ice-floe'; and the repeated numbering of the children – 'second son' or 'second daughter' – as if she could readily spare one! The use of the clichéd phrase 'struck rock-bottom' to describe the waterfall rings like an embarrassing gaffe. There is a deliberate underplaying of the seriousness of the situation, which adds to the incongruity and creates humour, as in the alpenstock (a long staff) 'which luckily later caught him on his way'. The relaxed feeling is conveyed through the language: 'Nothing, it was evident, could be done' and 'from a difficult distance viewed'. This deliberate emotional distance creates a sense of disbelief, and hence the humour.

STYLE OF LANGUAGE

As befits a narrative poem, the style is conversational. Yet it is slightly formal, a little stuffy. There is a formality about the style of the opening: 'If the year is meditating a suitable gift, | I should like it to be . . .' At times the structure of the sentences, the parentheses in the syntax, gives it a certain long-winded formality. We see this, for example, in 'impeded, no doubt, by the petticoats of the day' and 'Nothing, it was evident, could be done.' The contrast between the dramatic and frightful scene and the rather stylised formal telling of it is a big element in the creation of the humour of the piece.

Howard Nemerov
Wolves in the Zoo
Text of the poem: New Explorations Anthology page 492

A READING OF THE POEM

The first line of this poem is a surprising one: Nemerov describes the wolves as being like 'big dogs badly drawn'. This comparison makes the wolves appear much less frightening. It is hard to be afraid of a pack of oddly shaped dogs. After all, dogs were one of the first animals that man domesticated and we know them as 'man's best friend'.

Nemerov continues to challenge the accepted view of wolves as savage beasts. The sign on the wolves' cage states that there is 'No evidence' that wolves killed humans. Similarly, he tells us that the story of babies being thrown out of sleds in Siberia to slow down attacking packs of wolves is untrue. Most importantly of all, he questions the truth of the wolf's portrayal in the popular children's story 'Little Red Riding Hood'.

Nemerov presents us with a different side to wolves. It seems that rather than humans being the victims of wolves, it is the wolves that are the victims at the hands of humans. He states that all the untrue tales told about wolves gradually became accepted as true facts, just like the facts that are contained in 'history'. Because of this bad press humans came to see wolves as a threat, a threat that had to be destroyed or controlled. As a result, two breeds of wolf are nearing extinction.

In the final stanza of the poem, Nemerov leaves us with a sad scene. Those wolves that have not been killed by man have been forced to surrender to him. Along with the proud peacock and the majestic tiger, the wolves live a life in captivity, held in cages simply to amuse or entertain human beings. We have been shown the terrible damage that can be caused by man's unquestioning acceptance of attitudes and behaviour.

LANGUAGE

Nemerov uses conversational language to express his thoughts on the wolves. It is as if we are having a chat with him. This makes his writing come alive. We do not have to struggle with complicated poetic language or rhymes that make the meaning hard to understand. Instead, Nemerov uses simple but very effective words to encourage us to look again at the wolves' situation.

Elizabeth Jennings
One Flesh

Text of poem: New Explorations Anthology p.506

This poem is a meditation by the poet on her parents and their relationship. She examines her parents in old age and wonders whether or not they were always like this. To do so, she ponders on them in bed.

The poet goes straight into the poem; immediately the parents are presented as being in two beds in the same room, the father reading to himself and the mother tossing and turning. They are both trying to get to sleep. They have come to a pragmatic arrangement to facilitate this. Their sleeping apart should mean that they will sleep more easily, but it doesn't work. Instead they both lie in silence and 'it is as if they wait | Some new event:'.

The poet does not comprehend how her parents can have drifted so far apart, 'like flotsam from a former passion'. She is fascinated by the way 'They hardly ever touch' and finds that if they do, it is done with hesitancy and fear. The parents' lives seem to have come full circle. They have returned to the chaste lives that they may have had before they were married.

In the last verse the poet points out the contradiction in the parents' relationship, and sees that they are:

> Strangely apart, yet strangely close together,

She sees that the silence is their way of communicating now that they are ageing slowly but surely, like 'a feather touching them gently'. Finally the poet comes to the conclusion that they may not even be conscious of the differences that are coming into their relationship; they may not be fully aware that:

> These two who are my father and my mother
> Whose fire from which I came, has now grown cold?

This may seem at first like a rhetorical question, but perhaps it is not. The poet may genuinely not know how her parents, who were once in love, can seemingly have fallen out of love – especially since they are still together.

Fleur Adcock
For Heidi with Blue Hair

Text of Poem: New Explorations Anthology page 514

ISSUES

This poem deals with adolescent assertiveness and the right to choose one's own dress code, hairstyle, and so on. These issues often become symbolic of individual freedoms and rights in the conflict between the teenager and authority, whether at school or at home. This conflict between youth culture and school culture has been elevated to the status of a 'battle' in this poem.

On a broader scale we might view the poem as demonstrating the conflict between different outlooks, attitudes, or philosophies – liberalism versus the need to conform. The more relaxed tolerance of the father is pitted against the rather snooty conformism of the school. But the school is not really very authoritarian, as the teachers give in, probably taking the home background into account.

TONE

For the most part, the poem is written in humorous or mock-serious tone. The humour is brought about through the contrast between the formality of the language and the relative insignificance of the event. Examine, for instance, the formal expression and complex structure of the language in the headmistress's telephone call (stanza 2). There is also a sense of the ridiculous in the witty, repartee-style comment 'you wiped your eyes, I also not in a school colour.' The rebellious, trend-setting ending adds to the sense of mischief and lets us see where the poet's sympathies lie: with the teenager and in support of the subversive. The exuberant colours add to the lightness of atmosphere here.

The one bleak note sounded concerns the reference to the mother's death, 'that shimmered behind the arguments.' 'Shimmered' suggests a vague, ill-defined, ghost-like presence and captures well the background thoughts on the mother's death, which nobody has had the courage to formulate into words. Would this be happening if her mother was alive? Should we indulge this child a bit because of her loss?

CAPTURING CHARACTER

Adcock is particularly good at evoking the essence of characters in a spare yet effective way. The kind, liberal father is supportive of his daughter, however ridiculous her looks. He believes in 'dialogue' – talking things out: 'She discussed it with me first.' And we have the image of rebellious, defiant Heidi, reduced to tears – not so tough really! And we recognise her desperation as she tries a range of separate excuses: the cost, and the indelible nature of the dye. The teachers are well captured, however briefly: 'the teachers twittered.' We get an image of nice old dears, genteel, ladylike disapproval and all the connotations about the type of school that this conjures up.

The success of the portraiture depends to a good degree on Adcock's sharp ear for dialogue. She had a real feel for the style of conversation. She captures the father's defensive terse tones: 'She discussed . . . we checked . . .' and the headmistress's long-winded, slightly grand style, conveyed in the complex syntax of the second stanza. We can hear her careful, measured statement: '. . . not specifically forbidden.' And she captures the casual, pushy, argumentative style of the teenager Heidi: 'And anyway, Dad . . .'

Brendan Kennelly
Night Drive
Text of poem: New Explorations Anthology page 517

This poem describes a journey. The journey is obviously a painful one. The poet and Alan, possibly his brother, are going to see their father, who is on his deathbed. The poem is in three parts. The first deals with the journey to the father. The second, shortest piece is spent with the father. The final part is the journey home. The poem is a mixture of narrative and dialogue. Kennelly deals with the drama of the situation expertly. While the poem deals with his father's imminent death, it spends little time with the father physically present, yet the father is a spectral presence all the way through. He is the reason for the journey.

The first section describes the frustration felt by the brothers as they make their journey 'Along the road to Limerick'. The conditions are obviously awful and while Alan tries to make conversation, the poet is rendered speechless by the thoughts of what is to face him when he reaches his destination. Kennelly animates the horrendous weather conditions. The rain 'hammered' and it is 'Lashing the glass'. The wind's swirling motion is detailed by showing it to have a fist that 'seemed to lift the car | And pitch it hard against the ditch.'

The sense of doom is continued with the description of the violence of the river that is 'A boiling madhouse roaring for its life'. It is ripping the countryside to shreds and is described as 'insane' and 'murderous'.

'Nature gone mad' as a theme repeats in this poem. It is seen at its most vivid in the scene with the frogs. The frogs have left their haven in the swamps and fields that have become too wild and flooded for them to cope with. They are forced onto the road, where they are being squashed beneath the tyres of cars. Like the poet and his brother they have become 'Bewildered refugees, gorged with terror.' The people have no choice but to go on their journey, which means that they have to contribute to the slaughter of the frogs. They are forced to focus on the task of going to see their dying father and do not have time to comment on the 'Carnage of broken frogs.' Their focus is made obvious by the line where Alan asks himself: '"How is he now?"'

Where there was a fierce unflappable energy in the first section, there is calm in the second. The serenity is heightened by the image of the pillow and the 'white hospital bed'. The contrast is striking. In both cases there is a determination not to let the ravages of nature get in the way. Where the brothers in the car were not going to let nature get in their way and fought against it and succeeded, their father also tries to fight back the inevitable and succeeds temporarily. However, it seems clear that whatever small battle he may win, the war is beyond him. This is seen when it has reduced his ability to 'rail against the weather'.

The third section allows time for reflection. Darkness returns in the last section. The brothers have been made sombre by their experience and death is the first thing to greet them as they make their journey home. Alan is distracted by having to focus on his driving and does not have as much room to contemplate as his brother does. Alan shows optimism when he suggests; '"I think he might pull through now."'

On the other hand, Nature has left the poet in more pessimistic mode as he is haunted: 'In the suffocating darkness | I heard the heavy breathing | Of my father's pain.'

Nature has become too much for him.

Roger McGough
Bearhugs

Text of poem: New Explorations Anthology page 519

A READING OF THE POEM

McGough opens the poem with a warm and affectionate image of him and his two sons hugging each other. There is something charming about the way that the two big, strong sons are expressing their love for their father in such an open way. Although they are his sons, McGough conveys an image of their being physically much larger than he is, when he describes how they lift him off his feet and crush him with their hugs. The title of the poem, 'Bearhugs', seems very appropriate for this very 'male' demonstration of affection.

McGough is immediately struck by the adult smells that cling to his two sons: aftershave, beer, tobacco and women. Although the three seem to genuinely care for each other, they evidently do not share intimate stories about their relationships. McGough does not know who these women are and whether his sons really care about them, and neither does he ask them. Perhaps this indicates some feeling of reserve between the men, but, again, it could just be indicative of a 'male' approach to love and affection.

The intensity of their hugging is explained in the third stanza, where we learn that McGough did not live with his sons as they grew up. The implication is that because of this he did not see the continuity of their daily development, nor could they express their love for each other on an ongoing basis. Their meetings were special, intensely emotional occasions, not the casual encounters that occur when a father lives with his children.

Clearly, McGough is anxious about the ways in which his separation from the boys affected his relationship with them and the influence that he had on them. As they do not seem to look like him physically, he tries to find some resemblance between them and his side of the family. By discovering 'something' of his father and uncles in them he is reassured that he did pass some inheritance on to them.

The resemblance of his sons to his father and uncles has another effect on McGough. He recalls a childhood memory of being hugged by these men while they were on leave from the war. Again we have the suggestion of father and son being separated, meeting only on special, intensely emotional occasions.

As his sons leave, McGough's confidence in their shared love is restored. He did not live with his father and uncles for a part of his youth, but the 'Bearhugs' that were shared between the child McGough and his adult relatives left him in no doubt that he was loved. Similarly, the 'Bearhugs' that he shares with his sons have a positive effect on him because they let him know that his two boys also love him deeply, and that his connection to them is safe.

THEME

McGough explores the nature of the connection that exists in families, particularly among the male members. He realises that this connection is not really based on living together, or on discussing intimate details, or on looking like each other. Rather, the male members of McGough's family are connected by the deep and enduring love that they share for each other, expressed in the 'Bearhugs'.

Eamonn Grennan
Taking My Son to School
Text of poem: New Explorations Anthology page 525

A READING OF THE POEM

The first three words of this poem, 'His first day', have a tone of serious simplicity. They suggest a feeling of anticipation for an important day, a life-changing day when a familiar way of life will be altered forever. They find their echo in the first three words of the final stanza of the poem, 'It is done.' Here, their serious simplicity conveys a sense of completion, that a significant task has been finished.

Between these two phrases Grennan presents us with a series of images of himself and his young son that convey the emotional changes that both of them experience as they go through the little boy's 'first day' at school. Much of the impact of these emotional undercurrents lies in the contrast that Grennan establishes between the pre-school world that he and his son shared, and the post-school world where they are separated.

So before they go to the school, his son plays in the garden; trick-acts while Grennan is taking his photograph and chats away in the car confidently telling his father which way to go. The image of the child being 'in flight', suggests his happy, confident and energetic approach to life along with a wonderful sense of freedom. However, his son's attitude contrasts with Grennan's feelings of anxiety suggested by his comment 'There are no maps for this journey' and his use of the word 'wilderness'. Unlike his son, he is aware that they are embarking on a new phase of their lives that has unpredictable consequences.

Once in school his son becomes 'silent' and shy. His energetic confident movements become a tentative offering of a bunch of flowers. His ability to fly is clipped to a 'drooping' head.

Grennan conveys the moment of parting with heart-breaking honesty. The father and son, who had laughed easily together over the son's clowning, now find that they are stiff and uneasy with each other. The kiss is a cold one and the child refuses to respond.

As Grennan drives away from the school he fights the urge to return to 'rescue' his son. His last backward glimpse of the boy leaves him with an image of the child's spontaneous individuality and energetic uniqueness represented by the way his 'red hair blazes' in the midst of the other 'blondes, brunettes'. It is clear that Grennan fears that these qualities will be altered forever by his son's attendance at school.

In the final stanza, Grennan's feelings of guilt and regret break through. He has 'handed' his son over and in so doing, he has changed their worlds forever. There will be no more 'dancing | Naked and shining' in the garden.

STRUCTURE

It is the contrast that Grennan establishes between the pre-school and post-school worlds that gives this poem a strong coherent structure. This contrast is conveyed by his careful use of opposing images and verbs and by references that contrast Grennan's anxiety with his son's excitement.

For example, in the pre-school world we see the image of his son playing out in the garden; while in the post-school world the garden is 'empty'.

In the pre-school world we have the image of Grennan being physically close enough to his son to take a photograph of his whole body; while in the post-school world there is the image of a 'bleeding' distance forced between them so that he can only see the top of his son's head.

The verbs that Grennan uses about his son also highlight the differences between the pre-school and post-school world. In the pre-school world the child spontaneously and confidently 'plays', 'clowns', 'chatters', 'sings' and gives directions. In the post-school world he is cautious and uncertain as he 'stands', 'offers' and 'teeters'.

Finally, Grennan undercuts his son's excited anticipation of his first day at school by contrasting it with his own behaviour that reveals his increasing anxiety. As the child clowns around, Grennan takes his photograph in a vain attempt to freeze the moment. The child's willingness to give 'directions' during the car journey contrasts with Grennan's awareness that 'There are no maps for this journey'.

Bernard O'Donoghue
Gunpowder
Text of poem: New Explorations Anthology page 533

A READING OF THE POEM

This poem opens with a phrase, 'In the weeks afterwards'. O'Donoghue never specifies what has happened to his father but as the poem progresses it becomes clear that his father has died. O'Donoghue's reluctance to say that his father has died suggests that he is still very upset.

The six-line description of his late father's study is not a factual one, rather O'Donoghue chooses certain key features that reveal a great deal not only about the room itself but also about his family. So we see his father's jacket left hanging on the back of the door for 'weeks afterwards'. This reluctance of the family to change anything that reminds them of the father tells us that he was dearly loved by them. Although the room is called a study, which is usually an office-style room, this study is much more homely and family-centred with 'bikes and wellingtons' stored in it. Up until O'Donoghue enters the study we learn that 'No-one went near it'. Again this indicates how loved his father was. The family were unable to enter 'his' room as the memories would be too painful. However, it is not the room itself that really stirs O'Donoghue's memories of his father but the smell of gunpowder from his jacket.

Initially, it seems surprising that a man who was so deeply loved and who accepted the storing of bikes and boots in his study would have any contact with gunpowder. After all, gunpowder is an explosive substance capable of causing destruction and death. Yet, in a line that captures most effectively the way memories can be triggered O'Donoghue finds the smell reminding him of incidents in his father's life, 'The sleeves smelled of gunpowder, evoking . . .'

Significantly, the poet sums up these incidents with the words 'Celebration —— excitement – things like that, | Not destruction.'

In a series of charmingly affectionate and warm images, O'Donoghue relates some of these remembered incidents. We see his father frequently shooting at creatures and missing them because he hesitated. We see him releasing a wounded crow that had been tied to a stake and returning a wounded rabbit to its warren. O'Donoghue admits that when he was younger he found his father's behaviour puzzling. As a child reared in the countryside O'Donoghue was used to a practical, pragmatic attitude towards the life and death of creatures: the tying of the half-dead crow to a stake as a deterrent to other crows was accepted because it did work, and it would have been quite acceptable to kill one of the rabbits living in the warren that was disturbing the foundations of one of their walls. But as he grew up, O'Donoghue came to realise that just because his father smelled of gunpowder and fired a gun, he was not a pragmatic killer of creatures. Instead, his actions revealed that he valued all life.

The final lines of the poem evoke a wonderful image of O'Donoghue's father. The empty gun cartridges, that had missed all that they were aimed at, were not simply thrown away. Instead, they were used to hold his precious fountain pen 'so that | The ink wouldn't seep into his pocket.' It seems that O'Donoghue's father was a pragmatist after all, not in matters of life and death, but in matters of laundry!

MOOD

O'Donoghue creates a marvellously affectionate and emotionally warm mood in this poem. At first, the affection that he feels for his late father is linked with a great deal of sadness and a reluctance to accept the fact that his father had died: 'In the weeks afterwards'.

Then, the smell of the gunpowder triggers some of his memories of the man, all of them positive. The memory of his father continually shooting at and missing creatures is tinged with humour. His father's kindness is revealed in his treatment of the crow and rabbit, as is his determination to do what he thought was right regardless of what was considered to be acceptable. Finally, his father's use of the empty cartridges to hold his pen reveals the gentle and endearing direction that his practicality took.

By the end of the poem, O'Donoghue's sadness has faded, and moving towards an acceptance of his father's death, he can once more celebrate his deep affection for his father.

TITLE AND THEMES

Initially, the title of this poem 'Gunpowder' may seem a little puzzling. Yet, as we read the poem the part played by the gunpowder is revealed. It is the smell that triggers the poet's memories of his father and that enables him to begin to come to terms with his father's death.

In this way the title 'Gunpowder' links to two themes that are in the poem. First, there is the theme of not judging people by their appearances. Just because the jacket 'smelled of gunpowder' this did not mean that O'Donoghue's father was a pragmatic killer of the creatures of the countryside. The second theme is related to the first in that gunpowder is generally used to bring destruction and death. But for O'Donoghue it is a creative substance, enabling him to repair the emotional wound that his father's death had caused in him. The implication is that substances should also not be judged by how they are most commonly used. It is the character of the humans who use them that decides whether they are destructive or constructive.

Liz Lochhead
Kidspoem/Bairnsang
Text of poem: New Explorations Anthology page 536

A READING OF THE POEM

At first, this poem appears to be written in a completely different language to English with lines such as 'pu'ed oan ma pixie an' my pawkies'. However, there are other lines where we can recognise some of the words as being in English, 'And sent me aff across the playground'. Most of the words in this line are easily understood except for the word 'aff'. But it is clear from the meaning of the rest of the words that we would write and say it as 'off'. So it seems that Lochhead is writing in English, but she is trying to spell it in such a way that it reflects the way in which English was spoken by the people who were around her as she was growing up in Scotland.

As Irish people we can really relate to this, as we too speak English but with a particularly Irish slant to it. For instance, we use the word 'bold' to mean naughty or mischievous whereas people who live in England use 'bold' to mean brave. We have also introduced Irish words and phrases into our English and the way that we put English words together in a sentence is often based on Irish structures. Such Irish writers as James Joyce and, more recently, Roddy Doyle have tried to write English in a way that captures the Irish way of speaking it, just as Liz Lochhead does with Scottish English here.

So the first twelve lines of this poem may seem strange to us because we did not grow up in Scotland, but they would make sense to those who did.

It comes as something of a surprise when, after twelve lines, Lochhead begins to write in a way that we have no problems understanding, 'it was January | and a really dismal day'. It is even more surprising to discover that, in lines 13–24, she describes exactly the same incident, her Mum sending her to school for the first time, as she did in the previous twelve Scottish English lines. We have to go to the poem and look for the clues that will explain why Lochhead decided to do this.

The first clue is in lines 24–25, where she tells us that her Mum sent her 'to the place I'd learn to forget to say | it wis January'. Clearly this 'place' was school. The next clue is in the final five lines of the poem where she explains that, once she started school, she quickly learned that she could still speak English in a Scottish way, but when it came to writing English her schooling taught her that the only 'correct' way was to write it 'as if you were posh, grown-up, male, English and dead'.

In this one phrase, Lochhead scathingly sums up the type of English literature and language that has been studied in schools. It is true that until recently, the vast majority of the writers and poets who were on the curriculum were indeed 'posh', that is upper class, since they were usually the only ones who could afford the money and the time for education and writing. They were 'grown-up', as children's writing was considered to be of little educational value by the adults who designed the school curriculum. They were 'male' because for centuries the view was taken that women did not need any education other than in 'wifely' or 'mothering' matters and therefore they did not do much writing. They were 'English', born and bred in England, the centre of the British Empire that, at one stage, swept over not only Scotland and Ireland but also large parts of Africa, America and India. Finally, they were mostly 'dead'. For, in spite of the ways in which the English language developed and changed in the 'real' world, the education authorities persisted in using works of literature by men who were long dead because they were reluctant to move away from what was traditionally accepted as 'correct' English .

Lochhead's tone of indignation in these final lines expresses the level of her resentment that as a working-class, young, female, Scottish and living individual she should have been forced to write in such a way.

THEMES

Liz Lochhead cleverly addresses some very thought-provoking themes in this poem. Firstly, she highlights the way that education, what we learn in school, often has no connection to the world in which we live our lives outside school. Secondly, arising out of this disconnection between education and 'real' life, within schools there can often be the suggestion that what is learned in school is somehow more valuable and of better quality than the learning that we experience in our daily lives. Thirdly, she draws attention to the fact that education could be seen as a means of 'programming' people to conform to 'accepted' and 'correct' ways of thinking and behaving. After all, we write to express our thoughts on the world. If the way we write is controlled by rigid rules, might not our thinking also be controlled by such rules?

Julie O'Callaghan
The Great Blasket Island
Text of poem: New Explorations Anthology page 546

A READING OF THE POEM

O'Callaghan opens her poem with a statement of fact that sounds like a sentence from a television news bulletin: 'Six men born on this island | have come back after twenty-one years.' It surprises because of its stark, unemotional tone, not usually the stuff of which poems are made. Like a news reporter she continues in this factual way, commenting in the present tense on what the men are doing, how they climb up 'overgrown roads | to their family houses'. Because of her use of the present tense there is a great immediacy about her description: we are there watching the men as they make their journey. But then, in line 5, the tone shifts as the men 'come out shaking their heads'. At this point, emotions begin to seep into the words of the poem.

In the following two lines, 6–7, it seems that we have once more returned to the unemotional, factual tone as O'Callaghan describes how the roofs have collapsed and birds 'have nested in the rafters', but there is a kind of tremble in them stemming from the image of the men 'shaking their heads'.

As the poem moves on, this tremble increases as memories connected to the 'family houses' begin to surface. Thoughts of 'all the nagging and praying | and scolding and giggling' wash over the men and, indeed, over us, the readers. And then we hear the voice of one of these men as he recounts what happened: 'Ten of us, blown to the winds'. The emotion intensifies as we realise that out of ten only six have been able to return. We feel his heartbreak as he says 'Our whole way of life – extinct.' His tears do not appear foolish or sentimental, but an expression of a sense of loss that we are gradually coming to understand and empathise with. We stand with him as he blinks back those tears, gazing out to the horizon, silenced by his distress.

Then, O'Callaghan's voice is heard, 'Listen, mister, most of us cry sooner or later | over a Great Blasket Island of our own.' Suddenly, there are tears in our eyes as we, too, gaze 'out to the horizon', weeping for the losses that we have suffered in our own lives.

O'Callaghan considers the way in which there is a sense of loss connected to the act of living. As we live we constantly experience change, and although some changes may be good, inevitably there will be changes that involve the loss of someone or something that we hold dear.

O'Callaghan has succeeded in creating a poem that does more than simply describe this sense of loss. By her beautiful control of the tone of her writing she evokes the sense of loss that lies deep within each one of us, so that we each 'feel' the theme of this poem in an intensely personal way.

Paula Meehan
My Father Perceived as a Vision of St Francis
Text of poem: New Explorations Anthology page 552

A READING OF THE POEM

Meehan creates a wonderful sense of a dreamlike world where visions can appear in this poem. She does this by mixing commonplace details with incidents that have a surreal (bizarre, strange) quality.

The wonderful opening image of the 'dawn whinny' of 'the piebald horse in next door's garden' awakening her may seem to be one of the surreal incidents. But there are parts of Dublin where horses are kept in gardens. By using this image, Meehan, immediately injects an element of confusion into the poem. However, the sounds that she hears of the milkman delivering milk, 'Bottles chinked on the doorstep' and 'the first bus pulled up to the stop' are ordinary and everyday. So too are the sounds that her father makes as he potters around the kitchen and then moves out into the garden. Nevertheless, there is something dreamlike about this world arising from the uncertainty about her being awakened from a dream. It is unclear whether Meehan has been fully wakened from the dream by the whinny and is recalling what the dream was about, or whether the incident with 'the piebald horse' is part of her dream.

The second section opens with Meehan gazing at the 'first frost | whitened' roofs, an indication that 'Autumn was nearly done'. There is a subtle dreamlike quality in these lines. We are not told where Meehan is standing or how she got there. Her gaze moves onto her father and she is shocked that 'He was older than I had reckoned'. His 'hair completely silver' echoes the colour of the 'first frost'. He has a 'stoop | of his shoulder' and 'his leg was stiff'. The questions that Meehan asks in the final lines of this section suggest her bewilderment at her father's trip to the garden at such an early and cold hour.

The third section provides the answers to her questions. In a wonderfully evocative passage Meehan describes how birds begin flying into the garden. The birds, somewhat surreally described as being 'of every size, shape, colour', initially come from nearby, 'the hedges and shrubs'. Meehan then shifts the focus of her description a little further away as more birds come from 'eaves and garden sheds'. The focus moves further still, out to 'the industrial estate, outlying fields' and on again to 'the ditches of the North Road'. Again, there is something dreamlike about the way that Meehan is able to fly over her local area watching the birds fly towards the garden. In the final three lines of the section, she returns to the garden filled with 'pandemonium' as her father, with all the panache of a magician, 'threw up his hands | and tossed the crumbs to the air.'

The final section of the poem lifts the dreamlike quality of the poem into the world of visions. As her father throws the crumbs, 'The sun | cleared O'Reilly's chimney'. Just as the late autumn frost in the second section had found echoes in her description of her aging father's hair, Meehan now introduces the sunlight at the moment of her father's alteration as he becomes 'suddenly radiant'. In his feeding of the birds he is 'a perfect vision of St Francis'. This image captures the wonderful kindness and childlike innocence that were evident in her father's act of feeding the birds. But it is also suggestive of a figure in a mosaic or a Renaissance painting. It is as if Meehan's father has been transformed into a different form of existence. This transformation takes on miraculous qualities as the poet watches her father become 'whole' and 'young again'. The final line of the poem once again allows the commonplace to return as Meehan marvels at such a vision 'in a Finglas garden.'

TONE

Meehan controls the tone of this poem with great skill so that it effectively communicates the love that she feels for her father. The image of her lying in bed listening to the sounds of him pottering about the kitchen is described with a tone of warm affection. There is the suggestion of Meehan feeling a childlike sense of being safe and protected as she hears these sounds.

The tone in the second section expresses Meehan's shock at her father's aged appearance. The 'first frost' not only echoes the fact that her father is coming towards the 'winter' of his life, but it also suggests the chill that she feels following this realisation. The irritated tone of the questions, at the end of this section, arises out of her bewilderment at his behaviour.

The third section gradually fills with a tone of wonder as the birds 'of every size, shape, colour' invade the garden. This wonder turns to utter amazement as the sun, that ancient god of life, illuminates her 'suddenly radiant' father so that he is transformed into 'a perfect vision of St Francis | made whole, made young again'.

Rosita Boland
Naming My Daughter
Text of poem: New Explorations Anthology page 557

A READING OF THE POEM

The appearance of this poem on the page is suggestive of delicacy, rather like a spider's web of words that has been rested gently on the surface of the paper. This delicacy permeates the poem itself both in the words that Boland uses and in the expression of her emotions. But, as with the spider's web, this delicacy should not be mistaken for fragility. Boland's words speak of tragedy with a determined honesty and her emotions are expressed with an intense poignancy.

She begins the poem with an image of a list of 'possible names' for her unborn baby, pinned beside her desk. She constantly adds other names to this list and as she does so her unborn baby develops within her. Here, Boland's delicacy of selection has enabled her to create four lines that are rich in suggestion. By simply telling us that she had put up a list by her desk and kept adding to it she conveys the excitement and anticipation that she felt about this baby. The ongoing care that she takes in choosing the baby's name implies the importance that she attached to the arrival of this little person and is indicative of the ongoing care that she intended to give to her baby. Boland's use of the word 'swelled' to describe her growing tummy gives a wonderful image of her developing pregnancy and carries us forward into the second cluster of lines.

In lines 5–8, Boland recounts her daughter's birth. The baby 'was born without colour'. The unnatural quality of this paleness is highlighted by Boland's introduction of the image of bright yellow daffodils and 'greening trees' flourishing in the rain 'of a wet March.' Again, the delicacy of expression is uncompromisingly and poignantly honest. The line 'She was born without colour' is stunning in its tragedy. Even more tragic is the image of this tiny death in the midst of the lush 'swelling' growth of early spring. Her use of the two words 'wet March' is suggestive not only of the important role played by rain in triggering the arrival of new life in March, but also of the wet tears that were shed in response to the death of this little baby.

The final six lines of the poem vibrate with an emotional intensity. Boland tells us that she rejected all the names on her precious list and chose instead 'The Caribbean name of Rain'. The fact that this name comes from the Caribbean with its suggestions of warm, bright sunshine, vivid blue seas and multicoloured blossoms, seems to give the little baby something of the colour of life that she had been, so tragically, born without. Most poignantly of all, Boland explains that the reason for her choice of the name 'Rain' was so that 'something soft, familiar and constant' would 'touch and touch again | Her thin coverlet of earth.' This final image is almost overwhelming. The image of the baby lying in her grave poignantly echoes that of a baby lying in her cot. The qualities that Boland attributes to the rain, 'soft, familiar and constant', are those qualities she had hoped to bring to the care and nurturing of her baby. Boland's repetition of the word 'touch' in the line 'To touch and touch again' cries out her unbearable desolation and emptiness as her baby lies beneath 'Her thin coverlet of earth'.

A LYRIC POEM

A lyric poem is a poem in which the poet seeks to communicate an emotional or psychological state, and in this respect 'Naming My Daughter' is very much a lyric poem. As we have seen, it is filled with an immensely moving depth of emotion.

This state can be communicated by the poet or by an imaginary figure that the poet uses to give expression to his feelings and thoughts. There is no doubt that Rosita Boland speaks to us, her readers, in a very personal way about her emotions in this poem.

Finally, the lyric poem often has a 'musicality' in its language, the sounds of the words playing an important part in the poem. Boland does indeed create lines where sound makes a contribution. Her use of assonance with the letter o (assonance: where two or more words close together have the same vowel sound) in line 4, 'As the months swelled slowly on', suggests the way her tummy expanded as her pregnancy advanced. Similarly, her use of alliteration with the letter t (alliteration: where two or more words close together begin with the same letter) in line 12, 'To touch and touch again' conveys a gentle whisper of physical contact that is filled with care and love.